Arizona Court Rules

Rules of Criminal Procedure 2019

By: Jason Lee

Table of Contents

REFS & ANNOS 12

PREFATORY COMMENT TO THE 2018 AMENDMENTS 12

    R. 1, REFS & ANNOS 14

I. GENERAL PROVISIONS 14

    RULE 1.1. SCOPE 14
    RULE 1.2. PURPOSE AND CONSTRUCTION 14
    RULE 1.3. COMPUTATION OF TIME 15
    RULE 1.4. DEFINITIONS 16
    RULE 1.5. INTERACTIVE AUDIOVISUAL SYSTEMS 17
    RULE 1.6. FORM OF DOCUMENTS 19
    RULE 1.7. FILING AND SERVICE OF DOCUMENTS 22
    RULE 1.8. CLERK'S DISTRIBUTION OF MINUTE ENTRIES AND OTHER DOCUMENTS 24
    RULE 1.9. MOTIONS, ORAL ARGUMENT, AND PROPOSED ORDERS 24
    R. 2, REFS & ANNOS 25

II. PRELIMINARY PROCEEDINGS 25

    RULE 2.1. MISDEMEANORS 26
    RULE 2.2. FELONIES 26
    RULE 2.3. CONTENT OF COMPLAINT 27
    RULE 2.4. DUTY OF MAGISTRATE UPON PRESENTATION OF COMPLAINT....................28
    RULE 2.5. REFUSAL TO PROVIDE A DNA SAMPLE 28
    RULE 2.6. ABROGATED AUG. 31, 2017, EFFECTIVE JAN. 1, 2018 29
    R. 3, REFS & ANNOS 29
    RULE 3.1. ISSUANCE OF SUMMONS OR WARRANT 30
    RULE 3.2. CONTENT OF A WARRANT OR SUMMONS 31
    RULE 3.3. EXECUTION AND RETURN OF WARRANT; DEFECTIVE WARRANTS 32
    RULE 3.4. SERVICE OF SUMMONS 33
    RULE 3.5. ABROGATED AUG. 31, 2017, EFFECTIVE JAN. 1, 2018 35
    R. 4, REFS & ANNOS 35
    RULE 4.1. PROCEDURE UPON ARREST 35
    RULE 4.2. INITIAL APPEARANCE 37
    RULE 4.3. INITIAL APPEARANCE MASTERS 38
    R. 5, REFS & ANNOS 39
    RULE 5.1. RIGHT TO A PRELIMINARY HEARING; WAIVER; CONTINUANCE 40
    RULE 5.2. SUMMONING WITNESSES; RECORD OF PROCEEDINGS 41
    RULE 5.3. NATURE OF THE PRELIMINARY HEARING 42
    RULE 5.4. DETERMINING PROBABLE CAUSE 42
    RULE 5.5. REVIEW OF A MAGISTRATE'S PROBABLE CAUSE DETERMINATION 43
    RULE 5.6. TRANSMITTAL AND TRANSCRIPTION OF THE RECORD 44
    RULE 5.7. PRESERVATION OF RECORDING 45

RULE 5.8. NOTICE IF AN ARRAIGNMENT IS NOT HELD 45

R. 6, REFS & ANNOS 46

III. RIGHTS OF PARTIES 46

RULE 6.1. RIGHT TO COUNSEL; RIGHT TO A COURT-APPOINTED ATTORNEY; WAIVER OF THE RIGHT TO COUNSEL 47

RULE 6.2. APPOINTMENT OF COUNSEL FOR INDIGENT DEFENDANTS 48

RULE 6.3. DUTIES OF COUNSEL; WITHDRAWAL 49

RULE 6.4. DETERMINING WHETHER A PERSON IS INDIGENT 50

RULE 6.5. MANNER OF APPOINTMENT 51

RULE 6.6. COMPENSATION OF APPOINTED COUNSEL 52

RULE 6.7. APPOINTMENT OF INVESTIGATORS AND EXPERT WITNESSES FOR INDIGENT DEFENDANTS 53

RULE 6.8. STANDARDS FOR APPOINTMENT AND PERFORMANCE OF COUNSEL IN CAPITAL CASES 53

R. 7, REFS & ANNOS 56

RULE 7.1. DEFINITIONS 56

RULE 7.2. RIGHT TO RELEASE 57

RULE 7.3. CONDITIONS OF RELEASE 61

Rule 7.5. Review of Conditions; Revocation of Release. 65

RULE 7.6. TRANSFER AND DISPOSITION OF BOND 66

R. 8, REFS & ANNOS 68

RULE 8.1. PRIORITIES IN SCHEDULING CRIMINAL CASES 69

RULE 8.2. TIME LIMITS 70

RULE 8.3. PRISONER'S RIGHT TO A SPEEDY TRIAL 71

RULE 8.4. EXCLUDED PERIODS 72

RULE 8.5. CONTINUING A TRIAL DATE 73

RULE 8.6. DENIAL OF SPEEDY TRIAL 73

RULE 8.7. ACCELERATING TRIAL 74

RULE 9.1. THE DEFENDANT'S WAIVER OF THE RIGHT TO BE PRESENT 74

RULE 9.2. DEFENDANT'S FORFEITURE OF THE RIGHT TO BE PRESENT DUE TO DISRUPTIVE CONDUCT 75

RULE 9.3. EXCLUSION OF WITNESSES AND SPECTATORS 76

RULE 10.1. CHANGE OF JUDGE FOR CAUSE 77

RULE 10.2. CHANGE OF JUDGE AS A MATTER OF RIGHT 78

RULE 10.3. CHANGING THE PLACE OF TRIAL 80

RULE 10.4. TRANSFER TO ANOTHER COUNTY 81

RULE 10.5. ABROGATED AUG. 31, 2017, EFFECTIVE JAN. 1, 2018 82

RULE 10.6. ABROGATED AUG. 31, 2017, EFFECTIVE JAN. 1, 2018 82

R. 11, REFS & ANNOS 83

RULE 11.1. DEFINITIONS, EFFECT OF INCOMPETENCE, AND RIGHT TO COUNSEL 83

RULE 11.2. MOTION FOR AN EXAMINATION OF A DEFENDANT'S COMPETENCE TO STAND TRIAL 84

RULE 11.3. APPOINTMENT OF EXPERTS 85

RULE 11.4. DISCLOSURE OF EXPERTS' REPORTS 87

RULE 11.5. HEARING AND ORDERS 88

RULE 11.6. LATER HEARINGS 91

RULE 11.7. PRIVILEGE AND CONFIDENTIALITY 92

RULE 11.8. EXAMINATION OF A DEFENDANT'S MENTAL STATUS AT THE TIME OF THE OFFENSE 93

RULE 11.9. CAPITAL CASES 94

R. 12, REFS & ANNOS 94

IV. PRETRIAL PROCEDURES **95**

RULE 12.1. SELECTING AND PREPARING GRAND JURORS 95

RULE 12.2. GROUNDS TO DISQUALIFY A GRAND JUROR 96

RULE 12.3. GRAND JURY FOREPERSON 96

RULE 12.4. WHO MAY BE PRESENT DURING GRAND JURY SESSIONS 97

RULE 12.5. APPEARANCE OF A PERSON UNDER INVESTIGATION 98

RULE 12.6. INDICTMENT 99

RULE 12.7. RECORD OF GRAND JURY PROCEEDINGS 99

RULE 12.8. CHALLENGE TO A GRAND JURY OR A GRAND JUROR 100

RULE 12.9. CHALLENGE TO GRAND JURY PROCEEDINGS 101

RULE 12.10. ABROGATED AUG. 31, 2017, EFFECTIVE JAN. 1, 2018 102

RULE 12.21. APPLICABILITY OF OTHER PROVISIONS OF RULE 12 102

RULE 12.22. SELECTION AND PREPARATION OF STATE GRAND JURORS 103

RULE 12.23. SIZE OF STATE GRAND JURY 104

RULE 12.24. LOCATION OF STATE GRAND JURY SESSIONS 105

RULE 12.25. PRESERVATION OF STATE GRAND JURY EVIDENCE 105

RULE 12.26. RETURN OF INDICTMENT 106

RULE 12.27. DISCLOSURE OF A LACK OF INDICTMENT 107

RULE 12.28. CHALLENGE TO STATE GRAND JURY, GRAND JUROR, OR GRAND JURY PROCEEDINGS 107

RULE 12.29. EXPENSES OF PROSPECTIVE AND SELECTED STATE GRAND JURORS 108

R. 13, REFS & ANNOS 109

RULE 13.1. DEFINITIONS AND CONSTRUCTION 109

RULE 13.2. TIMELINESS OF AN INFORMATION AND DISMISSAL 110

RULE 13.3. JOINDER 111

RULE 13.4. SEVERANCE 111

RULE 13.5. AMENDING CHARGES; DEFECTS IN THE CHARGING DOCUMENT 112

R. 14, REFS & ANNOS 113

RULE 14.1. GENERAL PROVISIONS 114

RULE 14.2. WHEN AN ARRAIGNMENT IS HELD 114

RULE 14.3. THE DEFENDANT'S PRESENCE 115

RULE 14.4. PROCEEDINGS AT ARRAIGNMENT 116

RULE 14.5. PROCEEDINGS IN COUNTIES WHERE NO ARRAIGNMENT IS HELD 117

R. 15, REFS & ANNOS 118

RULE 15.1. THE STATE'S DISCLOSURES 118

RULE 15.2. THE DEFENDANT'S DISCLOSURES 122

RULE 15.3. DEPOSITIONS 125

RULE 15.4. DISCLOSURE STANDARDS 127

RULE 15.5. EXCISION AND PROTECTIVE ORDERS 129

RULE 15.6. CONTINUING DUTY TO DISCLOSE; FINAL DISCLOSURE DEADLINE; EXTENSION 130

RULE 15.7. DISCLOSURE VIOLATIONS AND SANCTIONS 131

RULE 15.8. DISCLOSURE BEFORE A PLEA AGREEMENT EXPIRES OR IS WITHDRAWN; SANCTIONS 132

RULE 15.9. ABROGATED AUG. 31, 2017, EFFECTIVE JAN. 1, 2018.................................133
R. 16, REFS & ANNOS...134
RULE 16.1. GENERAL PROVISIONS 134
RULE 16.2. PROCEDURE ON PRETRIAL MOTIONS TO SUPPRESS EVIDENCE................135
RULE 16.3. PRETRIAL CONFERENCE 136
RULE 16.4. DISMISSAL OF PROSECUTION 137
RULE 16.5. ABROGATED AUG. 31, 2017, EFFECTIVE JAN. 1, 2018.............................138
RULE 16.6. ABROGATED AUG. 31, 2017, EFFECTIVE JAN. 1, 2018.............................139
RULE 16.7. DELETED, EFFECTIVE AUG. 1, 1975 139
R. 17, REFS & ANNOS...140

V. PLEAS OF GUILTY AND NO CONTEST...**140**

RULE 17.1. THE DEFENDANT'S PLEA 140
RULE 17.2. ADVISING OF RIGHTS AND CONSEQUENCES OF A GUILTY OR NO CONTEST PLEA..142
RULE 17.3. A COURT'S DUTY TO DETERMINE WHETHER A PLEA IS ENTERED VOLUNTARILY AND
INTELLIGEN...143
RULE 17.4. PLEA NEGOTIATIONS AND AGREEMENTS 144
RULE 17.5. WITHDRAWAL OF A PLEA 146
RULE 17.6. ADMITTING A PRIOR CONVICTION...146
RULE 17.7. SUBMITTING A CASE ON THE RECORD 147
R. 18, REFS & ANNOS...148

VI. TRIAL **148**

RULE 18.1. TRIAL BY JURY 148
RULE 18.2. ADDITIONAL JURORS..149
RULE 18.3. JURORS' INFORMATION 150
RULE 18.4. CHALLENGES..151
RULE 18.5. PROCEDURE FOR JURY SELECTION 153
RULE 18.6. JURORS' CONDUCT 156
R. 19, REFS & ANNOS...158
RULE 19.1. CONDUCT OF TRIAL 158
RULE 19.2. PRESENCE OF THE DEFENDANT AT TRIAL...161
RULE 19.3. ADMONITIONS 161
RULE 19.4. A JUDGE'S DEATH, ILLNESS, OR OTHER INCAPACITY 162
RULE 19.5. PRESENCE OF A REPRESENTATIVE OF A MINOR OR INCAPACITATED VICTIM.........163
RULE 19.6. SEQUESTRATION 164
RULE 20. JUDGMENT OF ACQUITTAL OR UNPROVEN AGGRAVATOR 164
RULE 21.1. APPLICABLE LAW...165
RULE 21.2. REQUESTS FOR INSTRUCTIONS AND VERDICT FORMS 166
RULE 21.3. RULINGS ON INSTRUCTIONS AND VERDICT FORMS...............................166
RULE 21.4. VERDICT FORMS FOR NECESSARILY INCLUDED OFFENSES OR ATTEMPTS............167
RULE 22.1. INSTRUCTIONS AND RETIREMENT 167
RULE 22.2. MATERIALS USED DURING DELIBERATIONS..168
RULE 22.3. REPEATING TESTIMONY AND ADDITIONAL INSTRUCTIONS......................169
RULE 22.4. ASSISTING JURORS AT IMPASSE...170
RULE 22.5. DISCHARGING A JURY 171
RULE 23.1. FORM OF VERDICT; SEALED VERDICT..172
RULE 23.2. TYPES OF VERDICTS 173

RULE 23.3. POLLING THE JURY...174
RULE 23.4. ABROGATED AUG. 31, 2017, EFFECTIVE JAN. 1, 2018.....................174
RULE 24.1. MOTION FOR NEW TRIAL...175

VII. POST-VERDICT PROCEEDINGS **175**

RULE 24.2. MOTION TO VACATE JUDGMENT..176
RULE 24.3. MODIFICATION OF SENTENCE...177
RULE 24.4. CLERICAL ERROR..178
RULE 25. PROCEDURE AFTER A VERDICT OR FINDING OF GUILTY EXCEPT INSANE 179
R. 26, REFS & ANNOS...179
RULE 26.1. DEFINITIONS; SCOPE..180
RULE 26.2. TIME TO RENDER JUDGMENT 180
RULE 26.3. SENTENCING DATE AND TIME EXTENSIONS 181
RULE 26.4. PRESENTENCE REPORT...182
RULE 26.5. DIAGNOSTIC EVALUATION AND MENTAL HEALTH EXAMINATION 183
RULE 26.6. COURT DISCLOSURE OF REPORTS BEFORE SENTENCING 184
RULE 26.7. PRESENTENCING HEARING; PREHEARING CONFERENCE 185
RULE 26.8. THE STATE'S DISCLOSURE DUTY; OBJECTIONS AND CORRECTIONS TO A PRESENTENCE REPORT 186
RULE 26.9. THE DEFENDANT'S PRESENCE..187
RULE 26.10. PRONOUNCEMENT OF JUDGMENT AND SENTENCE.............................187
RULE 26.11. A COURT'S DUTY AFTER PRONOUNCING SENTENCE..........................188
RULE 26.12. DEFENDANT'S COMPLIANCE WITH MONETARY AND NON-MONETARY TERMS OF A SENTENCE 189
RULE 26.13. CONSECUTIVE SENTENCES 191
RULE 26.14. RESENTENCING..192
RULE 26.15. SPECIAL PROCEDURES UPON IMPOSING A DEATH SENTENCE 193
RULE 26.16. ENTRY OF JUDGMENT AND SENTENCE; WARRANT OF AUTHORITY TO EXECUTE SENTENCE 193
R. 27, REFS & ANNOS...194
RULE 27.1. CONDITIONS AND REGULATIONS OF PROBATION 194
RULE 27.2. INTERCOUNTY TRANSFERS...195
RULE 27.3. MODIFICATION OF CONDITIONS OR REGULATIONS 197
RULE 27.4. EARLY TERMINATION OF PROBATION 198
RULE 27.5. ORDER AND NOTICE OF DISCHARGE 199
RULE 27.6. PETITION TO REVOKE PROBATION AND SECURING THE PROBATIONER'S PRESENCE
....199
RULE 27.7. INITIAL APPEARANCE AFTER ARREST 200
RULE 27.8. PROBATION REVOCATION 201
RULE 27.9. ADMISSIONS BY THE PROBATIONER 202
RULE 27.10. VICTIMS' RIGHTS IN PROBATION PROCEEDINGS 203
RULE 27.11. PROBATION REVIEW HEARING REGARDING SEX OFFENDER REGISTRATION........204
RULE 27.12. ABROGATED AUG. 31, 2017, EFFECTIVE JAN. 1, 2018.....................205
RULE 28.1. DUTIES OF THE CLERK...206
RULE 28.2. DISPOSITION OF EVIDENCE...207
RULE 28.3. RETROACTIVE APPLICATION 208
R. 29, REFS & ANNOS...209
RULE 29.1. GROUNDS; NOTICE 209

RULE 29.2. APPLICATION 210
RULE 29.3. STATE'S RESPONSE 211
RULE 29.4. REPLY 212
RULE 29.5 HEARING 212
RULE 29.6 DISPOSITION 213
RULE 29.7. SPECIAL PROVISIONS FOR SEX TRAFFICKING VICTIMS 214
R. 30, REFS & ANNOS 215
RULE 30.1. GROUNDS; NOTICE 215
RULE 30.2. APPLICATION 216
RULE 30.3. STATE'S RESPONSE 217
RULE 30.4. REPLY 218
RULE 30.5. HEARING 218
RULE 30.6. DISPOSITION 219
RULE 30.7. ABROGATED AUG. 31, 2017, EFFECTIVE JAN. 1, 2018 220
RULE 31.1. SCOPE; PRECEDENCE; DEFINITIONS 221
RULE 31.2. NOTICE OF APPEAL OR NOTICE OF CROSS-APPEAL 222
RULE 31.3. SUSPENSION OF THESE RULES; SUSPENSION OF AN APPEAL; COMPUTATION OF TIME; MODIFYING A... 224
RULE 31.4. CONSOLIDATION OF APPEALS 226
RULE 31.5. APPOINTMENT OF COUNSEL ON APPEAL; WAIVER OF THE RIGHT TO APPELLATE COUNSEL 226
RULE 31.6. FILING DOCUMENTS WITH AN APPELLATE COURT; DOCUMENT FORMAT; SERVICE AND PROOF OF SERV 228
RULE 31.7. STAY OF PROCEEDINGS 229
RULE 31.8. THE RECORD ON APPEAL 230
RULE 31.9. TRANSMISSION OF THE RECORD TO THE APPELLATE COURT 235
RULE 31.10. CONTENT OF BRIEFS 236
RULE 31.11. APPENDIX 238
RULE 31.12. LENGTH AND FORM OF BRIEFS 240
RULE 31.13. DUE DATES; FILING AND SERVICE OF BRIEFS 241
RULE 31.14. PROVISIONS APPLICABLE ONLY TO BRIEFS IN CAPITAL CASE APPEALS 244
RULE 31.15. AMICUS CURIAE 245
RULE 31.16. SUPPLEMENTAL CITATION OF LEGAL AUTHORITY 247
RULE 31.17. ORAL ARGUMENT IN THE COURT OF APPEALS 248
RULE 31.18. PETITION FOR TRANSFER 249
RULE 31.19. AN APPELLATE COURT'S ORDERS AND DECISIONS 250
RULE 31.20. MOTION FOR RECONSIDERATION 251
RULE 31.21. PETITION FOR REVIEW 252
RULE 31.22. APPELLATE COURT MANDATES 256
RULE 31.23. WARRANT OF EXECUTION 258
RULE 31.24. VOLUNTARY DISMISSAL 259
RULE 31.25. ABROGATED AUG. 31, 2017, EFFECTIVE JAN. 1, 2018 260
RULE 31.26. ABROGATED AUG. 31, 2017, EFFECTIVE JAN. 1, 2018 261
RULE 31.27. ABROGATED AUG. 31, 2017, EFFECTIVE JAN. 1, 2018 261
R. 32, REFS & ANNOS 261
RULE 32.1. SCOPE OF REMEDY 262
RULE 32.2. PRECLUSION OF REMEDY 264

RULE 32.3. NATURE OF A POST-CONVICTION PROCEEDING AND RELATION TO OTHER REMEDIES 265
RULE 32.4. FILING OF NOTICE AND PETITION, AND OTHER INITIAL PROCEEDINGS 265
RULE 32.5. CONTENTS OF A PETITION FOR POST-CONVICTION RELIEF.............................269
RULE 32.6. RESPONSE AND REPLY; AMENDMENTS; REVIEW...270
    Credits..*271*
    Editors' Notes..*271*
RULE 32.7. INFORMAL CONFERENCE 271
RULE 32.8. EVIDENTIARY HEARING 272
RULE 32.9. REVIEW 273
RULE 32.10. REVIEW OF AN INTELLECTUAL DISABILITY DETERMINATION IN CAPITAL CASES 276
RULE 32.11. EXTENSIONS OF TIME; VICTIM NOTICE AND SERVICE 277
RULE 32.12. POST-CONVICTION DEOXYRIBONUCLEIC ACID TESTING 278
R. 33, REFS & ANNOS 280
RULE 33.1. DEFINITION 281
RULE 33.2. SUMMARY DISPOSITION OF CONTEMPT 282
RULE 33.3. DISPOSITION OF CONTEMPT BY NOTICE AND HEARING 282
RULE 33.4. JURY TRIAL; DISQUALIFICATION OF THE CITING JUDGE 283
RULE 34. SUBPOENAS..284

IX. MISCELLANEOUS 284

RULES 35.1 TO 35.7. ABROGATED AUG. 31, 2017, EFFECTIVE JAN. 1, 2018.....................285
RULES 35.1 TO 35.7. ABROGATED AUG. 31, 2017, EFFECTIVE JAN. 1, 2018.....................286
RULES 35.1 TO 35.7. ABROGATED AUG. 31, 2017, EFFECTIVE JAN. 1, 2018.....................286
RULES 35.1 TO 35.7. ABROGATED AUG. 31, 2017, EFFECTIVE JAN. 1, 2018.....................287
RULES 35.1 TO 35.7. ABROGATED AUG. 31, 2017, EFFECTIVE JAN. 1, 2018.....................287
RULE 36. [RESERVED] 288
RULE 37.1. FINAL DISPOSITION REPORT...288
RULE 37.2. STATE'S DUTY TO FILE A DISPOSITION FORM WITH THE COURT........................289
RULE 37.3. REPORTING PROCEDURE 290
RULE 37.4. PROCEDURE ON APPEAL 291
RULE 37.5. ABROGATED AUG. 1, 2017, EFFECTIVE JAN. 1, 2018. 291
RULE 38.1. APPLICATION FOR A SUSPENSION ORDER 292
RULE 38.2. RESUMING PROSECUTION 292
RULE 38.3. DISMISSAL OF PROSECUTION 293
RULE 39. VICTIMS' RIGHTS..294
RULE 40. TRANSFER FOR JUVENILE PROSECUTION 299
RULE 41. FORMS 301
FORM 1. RESERVED...301
FORM 2. ABROGATED APRIL 11, 2016, EFFECTIVE JULY 1, 2016 302
FORM 2(A). ARREST WARRANT: SUPERIOR COURT...302
FORM 2(B). ARREST WARRANT: LIMITED JURISDICTION COURTS.....................................304
FORM 2(C). ABROGATED 307
FORM 2(D). ABROGATED 307
FORM 2(E). ABROGATED 308
FORM 2(F). ABROGATED 308
FORM 2(G). ABROGATED 309
FORM 2(H). ABROGATED 309

FORM 3(A). SUMMONS: TEN-PRINT FINGERPRINT REQUIRED 309
FORM 3(B). SUMMONS: FINGERPRINT NOT REQUIRED 311
FORM 4(A). RELEASE QUESTIONNAIRE/LAW ENFORCEMENT 313
Effective January 1, 2016   2 of 3   AOC-CR41FORM4A

....315
Effective January 1, 2016   3 of 3   AOC-CR41FORM4A

....316
FORM 4(B). RELEASE QUESTIONNAIRE/DEFENDANT 317
    Form 4(b). Release Questionnaire/Defendant..*317*

....319
Contact Telephone No. _____

....320
FORM 4(C). RELEASE QUESTIONNAIRE 320
FORM 5(A). DEFENDANT'S FINANCIAL STATEMENT 323
FORM 5(B). MOTION FOR APPOINTMENT OF COUNSEL 327
FORM 6. RELEASE ORDER...329
YOUR RIGHT TO APPEAL.

....332
FORM 7. APPEARANCE BOND..333
FORM 7. ATTACHMENT A 336
FORM 8. NOTICE OF RIGHT TO COUNSEL AND WAIVER 338
FORM 9. NOTICE OF APPEARANCE..340
EDITORS' NOTES 341
FORM 10. WAIVER OF PRELIMINARY HEARING...341
FORM 11. BIND-OVER ORDER 343
FORM 12. TRANSMITTAL CERTIFICATION 344
FORM 13(A). INDICTMENT 346
FORM 13(B). GRAND JURY MINUTES..347
FORM 14. INFORMATION 348
FORM 15(A). NOTICE OF APPOINTMENT OF MENTAL HEALTH EXPERT (PRE-SCREEN) 349
FORM 15(B). RULE 11 ORDER AND STIPULATION 351
FORM 15(C). NOTICE OF APPOINTMENT OF MENTAL HEALTH EXPERT-COMPETENCY 352
FORM 15(D). NOTICE OF APPOINTMENT OF MENTAL HEALTH EXPERT --MENTAL CONDITION AT TIME OF OFFENSE..354
FORM 16. RESERVED 356
FORM 17. WAIVER OF RIGHT TO BE PRESENT AT DEPOSITION 356
FORM 18(A). FELONY PLEA AGREEMENT--NON-CAPITAL 358
FOOTNOTES..361
FORM 18(B). MISDEMEANOR PLEA AGREEMENT 361
FORM 19. GUILTY/NO CONTEST PLEA PROCEEDING 363
FORM 20. WAIVER OF TRIAL BY JURY (NON-CAPITAL) 366
EDITORS' NOTES 367
FORM 21. APPLICATION TO VACATE CONVICTION UNDER A.R.S. § 13-907.01 367
FORM 22. TRANSMITTAL OF RECORD ON APPEAL TO SUPERIOR COURT 369
FORM 23. NOTICE OF RIGHTS OF REVIEW AFTER CONVICTION IN SUPERIOR COURT................370
FORM 24(A). NOTICE OF APPEAL FROM SUPERIOR COURT..373
FORM 24(B). NOTICE OF POST-CONVICTION RELIEF...375

FORM 25. PETITION FOR POST-CONVICTION RELIEF 378
FORM 26. REQUEST FOR PREPARATION OF POST-CONVICTION RELIEF RECORD 381
FORM 27(A). SUBPOENA 383
FORM 27(B). SUBPOENA - ALTERNATIVE, STANDBY 384
FORM 28. TELEPHONIC GUILTY PLEA/NO CONTEST PLEA PROCEEDINGS...............................386
FORM 28(A). INSTRUCTIONS FOR COMPLETING THE FORM FOR ENTERING A "GUILTY/NO
CONTEST PLEA BY MAIL... 390
this date: _____ by (Clerk's name or initials): _____.

....393
FORM 29. ENTRY OF NOT GUILTY PLEA AND ADVISEMENTS 394
FORM 30. CERTIFICATE OF COMPLIANCE 395
FORM 31(A). APPLICATION TO SET ASIDE CONVICTION...396
Date   Defendant's Signature

....400
FORM 31(B). ORDER REGARDING APPLICATION TO SET ASIDE CONVICTION AND RESTORE GUN
RIGHTS 401
FORM 32(A). APPLICATION TO RESTORE CIVIL RIGHTS AND GUN RIGHTS 403

_____

....406

_____

....407
Date   Defendant's Signature

....408
Date   Defendant's Signature

....409
FORM 32(B). ORDER REGARDING APPLICATION TO RESTORE CIVIL RIGHTS AND GUN RIGHTS410
Judicial Officer

....411

Refs & Annos

16A A.R.S. Rules Crim.Proc., Refs & Annos

Editors' Notes
GENERAL NOTES
<The Arizona Rules of Criminal Procedure, all associated comments, and Form 7 of Rule 41, were abrogated and revised versions adopted August 31, 2017, effective January 1, 2018.>
16A A. R. S. Rules Crim. Proc., Refs & Annos, AZ ST RCRP Refs & Annos
Current with amendments received through 08/15/19

Prefatory Comment to the 2018 Amendments

(Refs & Annos)

16A A.R.S. Rules Crim.Proc., Comment
Prefatory Comment to the 2018 Amendments

The 2018 amendments make extensive changes to the Arizona Rules of Criminal Procedure ("ARCrP").

These amendments "restyle" the ARCrP in a manner similar to the 2017 restyling of the Arizona Rules of Civil Procedure. The 2018 version of the ARCrP adds informative titles and subheadings, which should make particular rules and sections easier to locate. By using clearer language and, if possible, plain English, these rules should be easier to understand. The restyled rules avoid long sentences, ambiguous terminology (such as the word "shall"), and legal jargon. These rules also use consistent formatting conventions and terminology.

The amended rules also include substantive changes, _including but not limited to the following_:

(a) Rule 1 has been extensively reorganized and revised to include a variety of provisions regarding the form of documents, service, and electronic filing. The changes are generally consistent with the 2017 amendments to the Arizona Rules of Civil Procedure.

(b) Rule 7, which deals generally with release, conditions for release, and revocation of release, has been revised to conform to the recommendations of the FAIR Justice Task Force.

(c) An amendment to Rule 8.2 requires that a trial begin within 90 days after a court enters an order for a new trial under Rule 32 or in a collateral federal proceeding.

(d) A new Rule 11.8 provides a separate rule for the determination of a defendant's mental status at the time of the offense. Currently, that inquiry is in the same rule, and subject to the same requirements, as a determination of a defendant's competence to stand trial.

(e) New provisions were added to Rule 15 to augment a party's disclosure obligations if the party's intends to call a "cold" expert, i.e., a witness who will be testifying about general principles without reference to any of the facts of the case.

(f) The multiple hearing provisions in former Rule 16.3, 16.4, and 16.5--including provisions for an "omnibus" hearing--were replaced by a single Rule 16.3 governing pretrial conferences.

(g) Rule 20 was amended to permit a defendant to make a post-verdict motion for acquittal without having made such a motion before the close of the evidence.

(h) Former Rule 30 was abrogated because it is largely duplicative of the Superior Court Rules of Appellate Procedure-Criminal.

(i) Rule 31, which deals generally with appeals in criminal cases, has been extensively revised to conform the rule to changes made in 2015 and 2017 to the Arizona Rules of Civil Appellate Procedure.

(j) Rule 32.12(d) was amended to remove the requirement that before ordering a post-conviction DNA testing, a court must find that the evidence is in a condition that allows DNA testing to be conducted. Given the current state of the art, such a determination cannot be made without actually performing the testing.

The wording of an amended rule may be very different, or only slightly different, from the rule that it replaces. The intent of these differences is to make the ARCrP more functional, and easier to understand and use. Prior case law continues to be authoritative, unless it would be inappropriate because of a new requirement or provision in these amended rules.

The amended rules attempt to incorporate substantive requirements previously contained within comments to the former ARCrP. Because of that, these amendments delete most of those comments, along with comments that have long ago outlived their usefulness. Parties may continue to refer to comments to pre-2018 versions of the ARCrP to the extent those comments still apply to these amended rules.

Credits
Added Aug. 31, 2017, effective Jan. 1, 2018.

16A A. R. S. Rules Crim. Proc., Comment, AZ ST RCRP Comment

R. 1, Refs & Annos

I. General Provisions

Rule 1. Scope, Purpose and Construction, and Other General Provisions
16A A.R.S. Rules Crim.Proc., R. 1, Refs & Annos

16A A. R. S. Rules Crim. Proc., R. 1, Refs & Annos, AZ ST RCRP R. 1, Refs & Annos
Current with amendments received through 08/15/19

Rule 1.1. Scope

(Refs & Annos)
I. General Provisions
Rule 1. Scope, Purpose and Construction, and Other General Provisions (Refs & Annos)

16A A.R.S. Rules Crim.Proc., Rule 1.1

Rule 1.1. Scope

These rules govern procedures in all criminal proceedings in Arizona state courts, unless specifically stated otherwise in a particular rule.
Credits
Added Aug. 31, 2017, effective Jan. 1, 2018.
Editors' Notes
HISTORICAL AND STATUTORY NOTES
Former Rule 1.1, relating to scope of rules, was abrogated effective Jan. 1, 2018. See, now, this rule.
16A A. R. S. Rules Crim. Proc., Rule 1.1, AZ ST RCRP Rule 1.1
Current with amendments received through 08/15/19

Rule 1.2. Purpose and Construction

(Refs & Annos)
I. General Provisions

Rule 1. Scope, Purpose and Construction, and Other General Provisions (Refs & Annos)

16A A.R.S. Rules Crim.Proc., Rule 1.2

Rule 1.2. Purpose and Construction

These rules are intended to provide for the just and speedy determination of every criminal proceeding. Courts, parties, and crime victims should construe these rules to secure simplicity in procedure, fairness in administration, the elimination of unnecessary delay and expense, and to protect the fundamental rights of the individual while preserving the public welfare.
Credits
Added Aug. 31, 2017, effective Jan. 1, 2018.
Editors' Notes
HISTORICAL AND STATUTORY NOTES
Former Rule 1.2, relating to purpose and construction, was abrogated effective Jan. 1, 2018. See, now, this rule.
16A A. R. S. Rules Crim. Proc., Rule 1.2, AZ ST RCRP Rule 1.2
Current with amendments received through 08/15/19

Rule 1.3. Computation of Time

(Refs & Annos)
I. General Provisions
Rule 1. Scope, Purpose and Construction, and Other General Provisions (Refs & Annos)

16A A.R.S. Rules Crim.Proc., Rule 1.3

Rule 1.3. Computation of Time

(a) General Time Computation. When computing any time period more than 24 hours prescribed by these rules, by court order, or by an applicable statute, the following rules apply:
(1) *Day of the Event.* Exclude the day of the act or event from which the designated time period begins to run.
(2) *Last Day.* Include the last day of the period, unless it is a Saturday, Sunday or legal holiday, in which case the period ends on the next day that is not a Saturday, Sunday, or legal holiday.
(3) *Time Period Less Than 7 Days.* If the time period is less than 7 days, exclude intermediate Saturdays, Sundays and legal holidays from the computation.

(4) *Next Day.* The "next day" is determined by counting forward when the period is measured after an event, and backward when measured before an event.

(5) *Additional Time After Service.* If a party may or must act within a specified time after service and service is made under a method authorized by Rule 1.7(c)(2)(C), (D), or (E), 5 calendar days are added after the specified time period would otherwise expire under (a)(1)-(4), except as provided in Rule 31.3(d). This provision does not apply to the clerk's distribution of notices, minute entries, or other court-generated documents.

(b) If an Arraignment Is Not Held. If an arraignment is not held under Rule 14.5, the date of arraignment for the purpose of computing time is the date the defendant receives notice of the next court date under Rule 5.8.

(c) Entry. A court order is entered when the clerk files it.

Credits

Added Aug. 31, 2017, effective Jan. 1, 2018.

Editors' Notes

HISTORICAL AND STATUTORY NOTES

Former Rule 1.3, relating to computation of time, was abrogated effective Jan. 1, 2018. See, now, this rule.

16A A. R. S. Rules Crim. Proc., Rule 1.3, AZ ST RCRP Rule 1.3

Current with amendments received through 08/15/19

Rule 1.4. Definitions

(Refs & Annos)

I. General Provisions

Rule 1. Scope, Purpose and Construction, and Other General Provisions (Refs & Annos)

16A A.R.S. Rules Crim.Proc., Rule 1.4

Rule 1.4. Definitions

(a) The Defendant. "The defendant" is a person named as such in a complaint, indictment, or information. "The defendant" as used in these rules includes an arrested person who at the time of arrest is not named in a charging document. "The defendant" in the context of certain rules includes the attorney who represents the defendant.

(b) Limited Jurisdiction Court. A "limited jurisdiction court" is a justice court under A.R.S. §§ 22-101 et seq., or a municipal court under A.R.S. §§ 22-401 et seq.

(c) Magistrate. "Magistrate" means an officer having power to issue a warrant for the arrest of a person charged with a public offense and includes the Chief Justice and justices of the Supreme Court, judges of the superior court, judges of the court of appeals, justices of the peace, and judges of a municipal court.

(d) Parties. "Parties" means the State of Arizona and the defendants in a case. Use of the word "party" in these rules means either, or any, party.

(e) Person. "Person" includes an entity.

(f) Presiding Judge.

(1) *For the Superior Court.* The superior court presiding judge is the county's presiding judge. In a county that has only one superior court judge, that judge is the presiding judge. In other counties, the Chief Justice of the Supreme Court designates the presiding judge, who may appoint other judges to carry out one or more of the presiding judge's duties.

(2) *For a Limited Jurisdiction Court.* If a court consists only of one judge, that judge is the presiding judge. In courts having more than one judge, the presiding judge is designated by the appropriate authority.

(g) The State. "The State" means the State of Arizona, or any other Arizona state or local governmental entity that files a criminal charge in an Arizona court. "The State" in the context of certain rules includes the prosecutor representing the State.

(h) Victim. "Victim" means a person as defined in A.R.S. § 13-4401.

Credits

Added Aug. 31, 2017, effective Jan. 1, 2018.

Editors' Notes

HISTORICAL AND STATUTORY NOTES

Former Rule 1.4, relating to definitions, was abrogated effective Jan. 1, 2018. See, now, this rule.

16A A. R. S. Rules Crim. Proc., Rule 1.4, AZ ST RCRP Rule 1.4

Current with amendments received through 08/15/19

Rule 1.5. Interactive Audiovisual Systems

(Refs & Annos)

I. General Provisions

Rule 1. Scope, Purpose and Construction, and Other General Provisions (Refs & Annos)

16A A.R.S. Rules Crim.Proc., Rule 1.5

Formerly cited as AZ ST RCRP Rule 1.6

Rule 1.5. Interactive Audiovisual Systems

(a) Generally. If the appearance of a defendant or counsel is required in any court, the appearance may be made by using an interactive audiovisual system that complies with the provisions of this rule. Any interactive audiovisual system must meet or exceed minimum operational guidelines adopted by the Administrative Office of the Courts.

(b) Requirements. If an interactive audiovisual system is used:

(1) the system must operate so the court and all parties can view and converse with each other simultaneously;

(2) a full record of the proceedings must be made consistent with the requirements of applicable statutes and rules; and

(3) provisions must be made to:

(A) allow for confidential communications between the defendant and defendant's counsel before, during, and immediately after the proceeding;

(B) allow a victim a means to view and participate in the proceedings and ensure compliance with all victims' rights laws;

(C) allow the public a means to view the proceedings consistent with applicable law; and

(D) allow for use of interpreter services when necessary and, if an interpreter is required, the interpreter must be present with the defendant absent compelling circumstances.

(c) When a Defendant May Appear by Videoconference.

(1) *In the Court's Discretion.* A court may require a defendant's appearance by use of an interactive audiovisual system without the parties' consent at any of the following:

(A) an initial appearance;

(B) a misdemeanor arraignment;

(C) a not-guilty felony arraignment;

(D) a hearing on a motion to continue that does not include a waiver of time under Rule 8;

(E) a hearing on an uncontested motion;

(F) a pretrial or status conference;

(G) a change of plea in a misdemeanor case; or

(H) an informal conference held under Rule 32.7.

(2) *Generally Not Permitted.* A court may not require a defendant's appearance by use of an interactive audiovisual system at any trial, contested probation violation hearing, felony sentencing, or felony probation disposition hearing, unless the court finds extraordinary circumstances and the parties consent by written stipulation or on the record.

(3) *By Stipulation.* For any proceeding not included in (c)(1) and (c)(2), the parties may stipulate that the defendant may appear at the proceeding by use of an interactive audiovisual system. The parties must file a stipulation before the proceeding begins or state the stipulation on the record at the start of the

proceeding. Before accepting the stipulation, the court must find that the defendant knowingly, intelligently and voluntarily agrees to appear at the proceeding by use of an interactive audiovisual system.

(4) *Change in Hearing's Scope.* If the scope of a hearing expands beyond that specified in (c)(1) and (c)(3), the court must reschedule a videoconference and require the defendant's personal appearance.

Credits

Added Aug. 31, 2017, effective Jan. 1, 2018.

Editors' Notes

HISTORICAL AND STATUTORY NOTES

Former Rule 1.5, relating to size of paper was, abrogated effective Jan. 1, 2018. See, now, AZ ST RCRP Rule 1.6.

16A A. R. S. Rules Crim. Proc., Rule 1.5, AZ ST RCRP Rule 1.5

Current with amendments received through 08/15/19

Rule 1.6. Form of Documents

(Refs & Annos)

I. General Provisions

Rule 1. Scope, Purpose and Construction, and Other General Provisions (Refs & Annos)

16A A.R.S. Rules Crim.Proc., Rule 1.6

Formerly cited as AZ ST RCRP Rule 1.5

Rule 1.6. Form of Documents

(a) Caption. Documents filed with the court must contain the following information as single-spaced text, typed or printed, on the first page of the document:

(1) to the left of the center and at the top of the page:

(A) the filing attorney's or self-represented litigant's name, address, telephone number, and email address; and

(B) if an attorney, the attorney's State Bar of Arizona attorney identification number, any State Bar of Arizona law firm identification number, and the name of the party the attorney represents;

(2) centered on the page and immediately below the filer information, the title of the court;

(3) below the title of the court and to the left of the center of the page, the title of the action or proceeding;

(4) opposite the title, in the space to the right of the center of the page, the case number of the action or proceeding; and

(5) immediately below the case number, a brief description of the document.

(b) Document Format.

(1) *Generally.* Unless the court orders otherwise, all filed documents, other than a document submitted as an exhibit or attachment to a filing, must be prepared as follows:

(A) Text and Background. The text must be black on a plain white background. All documents filed must be single-sided.

(B) Type Size and Font. Notwithstanding any local rule, every typed document must use at least a 13-point type size. The court prefers proportionally spaced serif fonts. Footnotes must be in at least a 13-point type size and must not appear in the space required for the bottom margin.

(C) Page Size. Each page of a document must be 8 ½ by 11 inches.

(i) Exhibits, attachments to documents, or documents from jurisdictions outside Arizona that are larger than the specified size must be folded to the specified size or folded and fastened to pages of the specified size.

(ii) Exhibits or attachments to documents smaller than the specified size must be fastened to pages of the specified size.

(iii) A document that is not in compliance with these provisions may be filed only if compliance is not reasonably practicable.

(D) Margins and Page Numbers. Page margins must be at least one inch on the top and bottom of the page and between one inch and 1 ½ inches on each side. Except for the first page, the bottom margin must include a page number.

(E) Handwritten Documents. Handwritten documents are discouraged, but if a document is handwritten, the text must be legibly printed and not include cursive writing or script. The number of pages in handwritten briefs, motions, and petitions must not exceed the number of words specified in a rule, divided by 280. A handwritten submission to an appellate court must include an original and one copy.

(F) Line Spacing. Text must be double-spaced and may not exceed 28 lines per page, but headings, quotations, and footnotes may be single-spaced. A single-spaced quotation must be indented on the left and right sides.

(G) Headings and Emphasis. Headings must be underlined, in italics, or in bold type, or in any combination of the three. Underlining, italics, or bold type also may be used for emphasis.

(H) Citations. Case names and citation signals must be in italics or underlined.

(I) Originals. Unless filing electronically, only originals may be filed. If it is necessary to file more than one copy of a document, the additional copies may be photocopies or computer-generated duplicates.

(J) Court Forms. Printed court forms, court-generated form, and forms generated by a court-authorized electronic filing system or vendor may deviate from the requirements of this rule. Such court forms must be single-sided. They may be single-spaced, but any signature lines must be at least two lines below the last line of text. All hard-copy court forms must be on paper of sufficient quality and weight to assure legibility upon duplication, microfilming, or imaging.

(2) *Signatures.* Every document filed with the court must include the attorney of record's signature. If there is no attorney of record, the document must include the signature of a self-represented person.

(c) Electronically Filed Documents. If a court has an electronic filing portal, a document may be filed electronically.

(1) *Format.*

(A) File Type. A document filed electronically that contains text, other than a scanned document image that is submitted under this rule, must be in a text-searchable .pdf, .odt, or .docx format or other format permitted by Administrative Order. *A text-searchable .pdf format is preferred.* A proposed order must be in a form that permits it to be modified, such as .odt or .docx format or other format permitted by Administrative Order, and must not be password protected.

(B) File Size. A document exceeding the file size limits allowed by the court's electronic filing portal may be broken up into multiple files to accommodate such a limit.

(2) *Formats of Attachments.*

(A) Generally. An exhibit and other attachment to an electronically filed document may be filed electronically if it is attached to the same submission as either a scanned image or an electronic copy using an approved file type and format.

(B) Official Records. A scanned copy of an official record may be filed electronically if it contains an official seal of authority or its equivalent.

(C) Notarized Documents. A scanned copy of a notarized document may be filed electronically if it contains the notary's signature and stamp or seal.

(D) Certified Mail, Return Receipt Card. When establishing proof of service by a form of mail that requires a signed and returned receipt, the return receipt may be filed electronically if both sides of the return receipt card are scanned and filed.

(E) National Courier Service. When establishing proof of service by a national courier service, the receipt for such service may be filed electronically by scanning and filing the receipt.

(3) *Bookmarks and Hyperlinks.*

(A) Bookmarks. A bookmark is a linked reference to another page within the same document. An electronically filed document may include bookmarks. A document that is incapable of bookmarking may be made accessible by a hyperlink. Bookmarks are encouraged.

(B) Hyperlinks. A hyperlink is an electronic link in a document to another document or to a website. An electronically filed document may include hyperlinks. Material that is not in the official court record does not become part of the official record merely because it is made accessible by a hyperlink. Hyperlinks are encouraged.

(4) *Originals.* An electronically filed document (or a scanned copy of a document filed in hard copy) constitutes an "original" under Arizona Rule of Evidence 1002.

(5) *Signature.* All electronic filings must be signed. A person may sign an electronic document by placing the symbol "/s/" on the signature line above the person's name. An electronic signature is equivalent to an ink signature on paper.

Credits

Added Aug. 31, 2017, effective Jan. 1, 2018. Amended on an emergency basis Jan. 26, 2018, effective Feb. 14, 2018, adopted on a permanent basis Aug. 28, 2018.

Editors' Notes

HISTORICAL AND STATUTORY NOTES

Former Rule 1.6, relating to interactive audiovisual systems, was abrogated effective Jan. 1, 2018. See, now, AZ ST RCRP Rule 1.5.

16A A. R. S. Rules Crim. Proc., Rule 1.6, AZ ST RCRP Rule 1.6

Current with amendments received through 08/15/19

Rule 1.7. Filing and Service of Documents

(Refs & Annos)

I. General Provisions

Rule 1. Scope, Purpose and Construction, and Other General Provisions (Refs & Annos)

16A A.R.S. Rules Crim.Proc., Rule 1.7

Formerly cited as AZ ST RCRP Rule 35.5

Rule 1.7. Filing and Service of Documents

(a) "Filing with the Court" Defined. The filing of a document with the court is accomplished only by filing it with the clerk. If a judge permits, a document may be submitted directly to a judge, who must transmit it to the clerk for filing and notify the clerk of the date of its receipt.

(b) Effective Date of Filing.

(1) *Paper Documents.* A document is deemed filed on the date the clerk receives and accepts it. If a document is submitted to a judge and is later transmitted to the clerk for filing, the document is deemed filed on the date the judge receives it.

(2) *Electronically Filed Documents.* An electronically filed document is filed on the date and time the clerk receives it. Unless the clerk later rejects the document based on a deficiency, the date and time shown on the email notification from the court's electronic filing portal or as displayed within the portal is the effective date of filing.

If a filing is rejected, the clerk must promptly provide the filing party with an explanation for the rejection.

(3) *Late Filing Because of an Interruption in Service.* If a person fails to meet a deadline for filing a document because of a failure in the document's electronic transmission or receipt, the person may file a motion asking the court to accept the document as timely filed. On a showing of good cause, the court may enter an order permitting the document to be deemed filed on the date that the person originally attempted to transmit the document.

(4) *Incarcerated Parties.* If a party is incarcerated and another party contends that the incarcerated party did not timely file a document, the court must deem the filing date to be the date when the document was delivered to jail or prison authorities to deposit in the mail.

(c) Service of All Documents Required; Manner of Service. Every person filing a document with any court must serve a copy of the document on all other parties as follows:

(1) *Serving an Attorney.* If a party is represented by an attorney, service under this rule must be made on the attorney unless the court orders service on the party.

(2) *Service Generally.* A document is served under this rule by any of the following:

(A) handing it to the person;

(B) leaving it:

(i) at the person's office with a clerk or other person in charge or, if no one is in charge, in a conspicuous place in the office; or

(ii) if the person has no office or the office is closed, at the person's dwelling or usual place of abode with someone of suitable age and discretion who resides there;

(C) mailing it by U.S. mail to the person's last-known address--in which event service is complete upon mailing;

(D) delivering it by any other means, including electronic means other than that described in (c)(2)(E), if the recipient consents in writing to that method of service or if the court orders service in that manner--in which event service is complete upon transmission; or

(E) transmitting it through an electronic filing service provider approved by the Administrative Office of the Courts, if the recipient is an attorney of record in the action--in which event service is complete upon transmission.

(3) *Certificate of Service.* The date and manner of service must be noted on the last page of the original of the served document or in a separate certificate, in a form substantially as follows:

A copy has been or will be mailed/emailed/hand-delivered [select one] on [insert date] to:
[Name of opposing party or attorney]
[Address of opposing party or attorney]

If the precise manner in which service has actually been made is not noted, it will be presumed that the document was served by mail. This presumption will only apply if service in some form has actually been made.
Credits
Added Aug. 31, 2017, effective Jan. 1, 2018.
Editors' Notes
HISTORICAL AND STATUTORY NOTES
Former Rule 1.7, relating to initial appearance masters, was abrogated effective Jan. 1, 2018. See, now, AZ ST RCRP Rule 4.3.
16A A. R. S. Rules Crim. Proc., Rule 1.7, AZ ST RCRP Rule 1.7
Current with amendments received through 08/15/19

Rule 1.8. Clerk's Distribution of Minute Entries and Other Documents

(Refs & Annos)
I. General Provisions
Rule 1. Scope, Purpose and Construction, and Other General Provisions (Refs & Annos)

16A A.R.S. Rules Crim.Proc., Rule 1.8
Formerly cited as AZ ST RCRP Rule 35.6

Rule 1.8. Clerk's Distribution of Minute Entries and Other Documents

(a) Generally. The clerk must distribute, either by U.S. mail, electronic mail, or attorney drop box, copies of every minute entry to all parties.
(b) Electronic Distribution. The clerk may distribute minute entries, notices and other court-generated documents to a party or a party's attorney by electronic means. Electronic distribution of a document is complete when the clerk transmits it to the email address that the party or attorney has provided to the clerk.
Credits
Added Aug. 31, 2017, effective Jan. 1, 2018.
16A A. R. S. Rules Crim. Proc., Rule 1.8, AZ ST RCRP Rule 1.8
Current with amendments received through 08/15/19

Rule 1.9. Motions, Oral Argument, and Proposed Orders

(Refs & Annos)
I. General Provisions

Rule 1. Scope, Purpose and Construction, and Other General Provisions (Refs & Annos)

16A A.R.S. Rules Crim.Proc., Rule 1.9

Formerly cited as AZ ST RCRP Rule 35.1; AZ ST RCRP Rule 35.2; AZ ST RCRP Rule 35.3; AZ ST RCRP Rule 35.4; AZ ST RCRP Rule 35.7

Rule 1.9. Motions, Oral Argument, and Proposed Orders

(a) Content. A motion must include a memorandum that states facts, arguments, and authorities pertinent to the motion.

(b) Service of Motion; Response; Reply. The moving party must serve the motion on all other parties. No later than 10 days after service, another party may file and serve a response, and, no later than 3 days after service of a response, the moving party may file and serve a reply. A reply must be directed only to matters raised in a response. If no response is filed, the court may deem the motion submitted on the record.

(c) Length. Unless the court orders otherwise, a motion or response, including a supporting memorandum, may not exceed 11 pages, exclusive of attachments, and a reply may not exceed 6 pages, exclusive of attachments.

(d) Waiver of Requirements. On a party's request or on its own, the court may waive a requirement specified in this rule, or it may overlook a formal defect in a motion.

(e) Oral Argument. On a party's request or on its own, the court may set a motion for argument or hearing.

(f) Proposed Orders. A proposed order must be prepared as a separate document and may not be included as part of a motion, stipulation, or other document. There must be at least two lines of text on the signature page of a proposed order. A party must serve the proposed order on the court and all other parties. A party must not file a proposed order, and the court will not docket it, until a judge has reviewed and signed it. Absent a notice of filing, proposed orders will not be part of the record.
Credits
Added Aug. 31, 2017, effective Jan. 1, 2018.
16A A. R. S. Rules Crim. Proc., Rule 1.9, AZ ST RCRP Rule 1.9
Current with amendments received through 08/15/19

R. 2, Refs & Annos

II. Preliminary Proceedings
Rule 2. Commencement of Criminal Proceedings

16A A. R. S. Rules Crim. Proc., R. 2, Refs & Annos, AZ ST RCRP R. 2, Refs & Annos
Current with amendments received through 08/15/19

Rule 2.1. Misdemeanors

(Refs & Annos)
II. Preliminary Proceedings
Rule 2. Commencement of Criminal Proceedings (Refs & Annos)
16A A.R.S. Rules Crim.Proc., Rule 2.1

Rule 2.1. Misdemeanors

(a) Limited Jurisdiction Courts. The State may commence misdemeanor and petty offense actions triable in limited jurisdiction courts by filing with the court:

(1) an Arizona Traffic Ticket and Complaint;

(2) any complaint form approved by the Arizona Supreme Court; or

(3) a complaint under Rule 2.3.

(b) Superior Court. The State may commence a misdemeanor action by filing an indictment or information directly in the superior court. A prosecutor also may commence a misdemeanor action not otherwise triable in the superior court by filing a complaint in the Justice Court under Rule 2.2(b) and then following the procedures applicable in felony cases.

Credits

Added Aug. 31, 2017, effective Jan. 1, 2018.

Editors' Notes

HISTORICAL AND STATUTORY NOTES

Former Rule 2.1, relating to misdemeanors, was abrogated effective Jan. 1, 2018. See, now, this rule.

16A A. R. S. Rules Crim. Proc., Rule 2.1, AZ ST RCRP Rule 2.1

Current with amendments received through 08/15/19

Rule 2.2. Felonies

(Refs & Annos)
II. Preliminary Proceedings
Rule 2. Commencement of Criminal Proceedings (Refs & Annos)
16A A.R.S. Rules Crim.Proc., Rule 2.2

Rule 2.2. Felonies

The State may commence a felony action by the following:

(a) the return of an indictment under Rule 12 which may, but need not, be preceded by a complaint; or

(b) filing a complaint in a limited jurisdiction court, or in superior court with permission of a judge of such court.

Credits

Added Aug. 31, 2017, effective Jan. 1, 2018.

Editors' Notes

HISTORICAL AND STATUTORY NOTES

Former Rule 2.2, relating to felonies, was abrogated effective Jan. 1, 2018. See, now, this rule.

16A A. R. S. Rules Crim. Proc., Rule 2.2, AZ ST RCRP Rule 2.2

Current with amendments received through 08/15/19

Rule 2.3. Content of Complaint

(Refs & Annos)

II. Preliminary Proceedings

Rule 2. Commencement of Criminal Proceedings (Refs & Annos)

16A A.R.S. Rules Crim.Proc., Rule 2.3

Rule 2.3. Content of Complaint

(a) Complaint, Generally. A complaint is a written statement of the essential facts constituting a public offense. A complaint must be:

(1) signed by a prosecutor;

(2) sworn before a magistrate; or

(3) made in compliance with A.R.S. § 13-3903.

(b) Electronic Oath or Signature. The constitutional requirement that a complaint must be under oath is satisfied by an electronic oath or by an affidavit containing an electronic signature of a peace officer or a law enforcement agency representative under penalty of perjury.

(c) Notice to the Clerk. If a complaint, indictment, or information charges a defendant with any offense listed in A.R.S. §§ 13-1401 et seq., 13-3101 et seq., 13-3501 et seq., or 13-3551 et seq., or an offense in which the victim was a juvenile at the time of the offense, the prosecuting agency must advise the clerk at the time of filing the charge that the case is subject to Supreme Court Rule 123(g)(1)(D)(ii)(h).

Credits

Added Aug. 31, 2017, effective Jan. 1, 2018.
Editors' Notes
HISTORICAL AND STATUTORY NOTES
Former Rule 2.3, relating to content of complaint, was abrogated effective Jan. 1, 2018. See, now, this rule.
16A A. R. S. Rules Crim. Proc., Rule 2.3, AZ ST RCRP Rule 2.3
Current with amendments received through 08/15/19

Rule 2.4. Duty of Magistrate upon Presentation of Complaint

(Refs & Annos)
II. Preliminary Proceedings
Rule 2. Commencement of Criminal Proceedings (Refs & Annos)
16A A.R.S. Rules Crim.Proc., Rule 2.4

Rule 2.4. Duty of Magistrate upon Presentation of Complaint

(a) Complaint Under Oath. If a complaint is presented under Rule 2.3(a)(2), the magistrate must determine whether there is probable cause to believe an offense has been committed and whether the defendant committed it. If the magistrate finds probable cause, the magistrate must proceed under Rule 3.1. If the magistrate does not find probable cause, the magistrate must dismiss the complaint.
(b) Complaint Signed by a Prosecutor. If a complaint is signed by a prosecutor, the magistrate must proceed under Rule 3.1.
Credits
Added Aug. 31, 2017, effective Jan. 1, 2018.
Editors' Notes
HISTORICAL AND STATUTORY NOTES
Former Rule 2.1, relating to duty of magistrate upon filing of complaint, was abrogated effective Jan. 1, 2018. See, now, this rule.
16A A. R. S. Rules Crim. Proc., Rule 2.4, AZ ST RCRP Rule 2.4
Current with amendments received through 08/15/19

Rule 2.5. Refusal to Provide a DNA Sample

(Refs & Annos)
II. Preliminary Proceedings
Rule 2. Commencement of Criminal Proceedings (Refs & Annos)

16A A.R.S. Rules Crim.Proc., Rule 2.5
Formerly cited as AZ ST RCRP Rule 2.6

Rule 2.5. Refusal to Provide a DNA Sample

If an arresting authority or custodial agency files a petition under penalty of perjury stating that a person in custody for an offense listed in A.R.S. § 13-610(O)(3) refused to provide buccal cells or other bodily substances for DNA testing, the court must order that the person appear at a designated time and place and permit the taking of buccal cells or other bodily substances for DNA testing. The arresting authority or custodial agency must serve the person with a copy of the court order before or at the time of taking the sample.

Credits

Added Aug. 31, 2017, effective Jan. 1, 2018.

Editors' Notes

HISTORICAL AND STATUTORY NOTES

Former Rule 2.5, relating to alternative procedure for commencing misdemeanor actions triable in Superior Court, was abrogated effective Jan. 1, 2018.

16A A. R. S. Rules Crim. Proc., Rule 2.5, AZ ST RCRP Rule 2.5

Current with amendments received through 08/15/19

Rule 2.6. Abrogated Aug. 31, 2017, effective Jan. 1, 2018

(Refs & Annos)

II. Preliminary Proceedings

Rule 2. Commencement of Criminal Proceedings (Refs & Annos)

16A A.R.S. Rules Crim.Proc., Rule 2.6

Rule 2.6. Abrogated Aug. 31, 2017, effective Jan. 1, 2018

Editors' Notes

HISTORICAL AND STATUTORY NOTES

The abrogated rule related to refusal to provide DNA sample. See, now, AZ ST RCRP Rule 2.5.

16A A. R. S. Rules Crim. Proc., Rule 2.6, AZ ST RCRP Rule 2.6

Current with amendments received through 08/15/19

R. 3, Refs & Annos

II. Preliminary Proceedings
Rule 3. Arrest Warrant or Summons upon Commencement of Criminal Proceedings
16A A.R.S. Rules Crim.Proc., R. 3, Refs & Annos

16A A. R. S. Rules Crim. Proc., R. 3, Refs & Annos, AZ ST RCRP R. 3, Refs & Annos
Current with amendments received through 08/15/19

Rule 3.1. Issuance of Summons or Warrant

(Refs & Annos)
II. Preliminary Proceedings
Rule 3. Arrest Warrant or Summons upon Commencement of Criminal Proceedings
(Refs & Annos)
16A A.R.S. Rules Crim.Proc., Rule 3.1

Rule 3.1. Issuance of Summons or Warrant

(a) Issuance. A summons commands a defendant to appear before a magistrate. A warrant commands the arrest of a defendant by a peace officer for the purpose of bringing a defendant before a magistrate.

(1) *Return of Indictment.* If a grand jury returns an indictment, the court must promptly issue a warrant or summons, or a notice of supervening indictment under Rule 12.6(c).

(2) *Finding of Probable Cause.* If a magistrate makes a finding of probable cause under Rule 2.4(a), the court must promptly issue a warrant or summons.

(3) *Prosecutor's Complaint.* If a prosecutor presents a signed complaint, the court must promptly issue a summons or, if the court finds probable cause, the court may issue a warrant.

(b) Preference for Summons. Unless there is good cause to issue a warrant, a court should issue a summons if the defendant is not in custody, the offense charged is bailable as a matter of right, and there is reason to believe that the defendant will appear. If a prosecutor requests a warrant, the prosecutor must state the reasons for issuing a warrant rather than a summons.

(c) Initial Arrest Warrant. Before issuing a warrant, the magistrate must determine that probable cause exists that the defendant committed the offense or find that such a determination was previously made. The court may issue an initial arrest warrant if:

(1) a defendant failed to appear after being served with a summons;

(2) there is good cause to believe that the defendant will not appear; or

(3) a summons cannot readily be served or delivered.

(d) Pre-Disposition Warrant. After the initial appearance and before the disposition of a case, the court may issue a warrant to secure a defendant's appearance if the defendant fails to appear after receiving proper notice.

(e) Warrants in Criminal ATTC Cases. If a person served with an Arizona Traffic Ticket and Complaint provides a written promise to appear in court at a designated time and date and fails to appear, personally or by counsel, on or before that date, the court may issue a warrant. If a complaint is filed under A.R.S. § 13-3903(F), the court must issue a warrant for that proceeding.

Credits

Added Aug. 31, 2017, effective Jan. 1, 2018.

Editors' Notes

HISTORICAL AND STATUTORY NOTES

Former Rule 3.1, relating to issuance of warrant or summons, was abrogated effective Jan. 1, 2018. See, now, this rule.

16A A. R. S. Rules Crim. Proc., Rule 3.1, AZ ST RCRP Rule 3.1

Current with amendments received through 08/15/19

Rule 3.2. Content of a Warrant or Summons

(Refs & Annos)

II. Preliminary Proceedings

Rule 3. Arrest Warrant or Summons upon Commencement of Criminal Proceedings

(Refs & Annos)

16A A.R.S. Rules Crim.Proc., Rule 3.2

Rule 3.2. Content of a Warrant or Summons

(a) Warrant. A warrant must:

(1) be signed by the issuing magistrate;

(2) contain the defendant's name or, if the defendant's name is unknown, any name or description by which the defendant can be identified with reasonable certainty;

(3) state the charged offense and whether the offense is one to which victims' rights provisions apply;

(4) command that the defendant be arrested and brought before the issuing magistrate or, if the issuing magistrate is absent or unable to act, the nearest or most accessible magistrate in the same county or in the county of arrest if the defendant is arrested outside the county where the warrant was issued; and

(5) state the amount of an appearance bond, if the defendant is bailable as a matter of right.

(b) Summons.

(1) *Form.* A summons must be in the same form as a warrant except it must summon the defendant to appear at a date, time and place no more than 30 days after an indictment, information, or complaint is filed.

(2) *Photograph and Fingerprints.* At the prosecutor's request or by court order, the summons may command the defendant to report to a designated place to be photographed and fingerprinted before the defendant's appearance in response to the summons. If the defendant fails to report to be photographed and fingerprinted as directed, the defendant may be arrested when the defendant appears in response to the summons and the magistrate must order the defendant to report immediately for photographing and fingerprinting.

(3) *10-Print Fingerprints Required.* If a summons is issued for a defendant who is charged with a felony offense, a violation of A.R.S. §§ 13-1401 et seq., a violation of A.R.S. §§ 28-1301 et seq., or a domestic violence offense as defined in A.R.S. § 13-3601, the summons must direct the defendant to provide 10-print fingerprints to the applicable law enforcement agency.

Credits

Added Aug. 31, 2017, effective Jan. 1, 2018.

Editors' Notes

HISTORICAL AND STATUTORY NOTES

Former Rule 3.2, relating to content of warrant or summons, was abrogated effective Jan. 1, 2018. See, now, this rule.

16A A. R. S. Rules Crim. Proc., Rule 3.2, AZ ST RCRP Rule 3.2

Current with amendments received through 08/15/19

Rule 3.3. Execution and Return of Warrant; Defective Warrants

(Refs & Annos)

II. Preliminary Proceedings

Rule 3. Arrest Warrant or Summons upon Commencement of Criminal Proceedings

(Refs & Annos)

16A A.R.S. Rules Crim.Proc., Rule 3.3

Formerly cited as AZ ST RCRP Rule 3.5

Rule 3.3. Execution and Return of Warrant; Defective Warrants

(a) By Whom. The warrant is directed to, and may be executed by, all peace officers in Arizona.

(b) Manner of Execution. A warrant is executed by arresting the defendant named in the warrant. The officer does not need to possess the warrant when the arrest is made, but the officer must show the warrant to the defendant as soon as possible if the defendant asks to see it. If the officer does not have the warrant when the arrest is made, the officer must inform the defendant of the charged offense and the fact that a warrant has been issued.

(c) Return. The warrant must be returned either to the magistrate who issued it or to the magistrate at the initial appearance.

(d) Defective Form. A defect in form does not invalidate the warrant or require the release of a person in custody. A magistrate may amend a warrant to correct a defect in form.

Credits

Added Aug. 31, 2017, effective Jan. 1, 2018.

Editors' Notes

HISTORICAL AND STATUTORY NOTES

Former Rule 3.3, relating to execution and return of warrant, was abrogated effective Jan. 1, 2018. See, now, this rule.

16A A. R. S. Rules Crim. Proc., Rule 3.3, AZ ST RCRP Rule 3.3

Current with amendments received through 08/15/19

Rule 3.4. Service of Summons

(Refs & Annos)

II. Preliminary Proceedings

Rule 3. Arrest Warrant or Summons upon Commencement of Criminal Proceedings

(Refs & Annos)

16A A.R.S. Rules Crim.Proc., Rule 3.4

Rule 3.4. Service of Summons

(a) Territorial Limits of Effective Service. A summons may be served anywhere within Arizona.

(b) Service by Mail. A summons may be served by first-class mail or by certified mail, return receipt requested. Return of the signed receipt is presumptive evidence of service.

(c) Serving an Individual. Unless (d), (e), or (f) applies, an individual may be served by:

(1) delivering the summons to that individual personally;

(2) leaving the summons at that individual's dwelling or usual place of abode with someone of suitable age and discretion who resides there; or

(3) delivering the summons to an agent authorized by appointment or by law to receive service of process.

(d) Serving a Minor. Unless (e) applies, a minor less than 16 years old may be served by delivering the summons to the minor in the manner set forth in (c) and also delivering the summons:

(1) to the minor's parent or guardian, if any of them reside or may be found within Arizona; or

(2) if none of them resides or is found within Arizona, to any adult having the care and control of the minor, or any person of suitable age and discretion with whom the minor resides.

(e) Serving a Minor Who Has a Guardian. If a court has appointed a guardian for a minor, the minor must be served by serving the guardian in the manner set forth in (c), and separately serving the minor in that same manner.

(f) Serving a Person Adjudicated Incompetent Who Has a Guardian. If a court has declared a person to be insane, gravely disabled, incapacitated, or mentally incompetent to manage that person's property, and has appointed a guardian for the person, the person must be served by serving the guardian in the manner set forth in (c), and separately serving the person in that same manner.

(g) Serving a Corporation, Partnership, or Other Unincorporated Association. A domestic or foreign corporation, partnership, or other unincorporated association may be served by delivering the summons to a partner, an officer, a managing or general agent, or any other agent authorized by appointment or by law to receive service of process and--if the agent is one authorized by statute and the statute so requires--by also mailing the summons to the defendant.

(h) Serving a Corporation if an Authorized Officer or Agent Is Not Found Within Arizona.

(1) *Generally.* If a domestic corporation, or a foreign corporation authorized to transact business in Arizona, does not have an officer or an agent within Arizona on whom process can be served, the corporation may be served by depositing two copies of the summons with the Arizona Corporation Commission. Following this procedure constitutes personal service on that corporation.

(2) *Evidence.* If the sheriff of the county in which the action is pending states in the return that, after diligent search or inquiry, the sheriff has been unable to find an officer or agent of such corporation on whom process may be served, the statement constitutes prima facie evidence that the corporation does not have such an officer or agent in Arizona.

(3) *Commission's Responsibilities.* The Arizona Corporation Commission must retain one of the copies of the summons being served for its records and immediately mail the other copy, postage prepaid, to the corporation or any of the corporation's officers or directors, using any address obtained from the corporation's articles of incorporation, other Corporation Commission records, or any other source.

Credits

Added Aug. 31, 2017, effective Jan. 1, 2018.

HISTORICAL AND STATUTORY NOTES
Former Rule 3.4, relating to service of summons, was abrogated effective Jan. 1, 2018. See, now, this rule.
16A A. R. S. Rules Crim. Proc., Rule 3.4, AZ ST RCRP Rule 3.4
Current with amendments received through 08/15/19

Rule 3.5. Abrogated Aug. 31, 2017, effective Jan. 1, 2018

(Refs & Annos)
II. Preliminary Proceedings
Rule 3. Arrest Warrant or Summons upon Commencement of Criminal Proceedings
(Refs & Annos)

16A A.R.S. Rules Crim.Proc., Rule 3.5

Rule 3.5. Abrogated Aug. 31, 2017, effective Jan. 1, 2018

HISTORICAL AND STATUTORY NOTES
The abrogated rule related to defective warrant. See, now, AZ ST RCRP Rule 3.3.
16A A. R. S. Rules Crim. Proc., Rule 3.5, AZ ST RCRP Rule 3.5
Current with amendments received through 08/15/19

R. 4, Refs & Annos

II. Preliminary Proceedings
Rule 4. Initial Appearance

16A A.R.S. Rules Crim.Proc., R. 4, Refs & Annos

16A A. R. S. Rules Crim. Proc., R. 4, Refs & Annos, AZ ST RCRP R. 4, Refs & Annos
Current with amendments received through 08/15/19

Rule 4.1. Procedure upon Arrest

(Refs & Annos)
II. Preliminary Proceedings

Rule 4. Initial Appearance (Refs & Annos)
16A A.R.S. Rules Crim.Proc., Rule 4.1
Rule 4.1. Procedure upon Arrest

(a) Prompt Initial Appearance. An arrested person must be promptly taken before a magistrate. At the initial appearance, the magistrate will advise the arrested person of those matters set forth in Rule 4.2. If the initial appearance does not occur within 24 hours after arrest, the arrested person must be immediately released from custody.

(b) On Arrest Without a Warrant. A person arrested without a warrant must be taken before the nearest or most accessible magistrate in the county of arrest. A complaint, if not already filed, must be promptly prepared and filed. If a complaint is not filed within 48 hours after the initial appearance before the magistrate, the arrested person must be immediately released from custody and any pending preliminary hearing dates must be vacated.

(c) On Arrest with a Warrant.

(1) *Arrest in the County of Issuance.* A person arrested in the county where the warrant was issued must be taken before the magistrate who issued the warrant for an initial appearance. If the magistrate is absent or unable to act, the arrested person must be taken to the nearest or most accessible magistrate in the same county.

(2) *Arrest in Another County.* If a person is arrested in a county other than the one where the warrant was issued, the person must be taken before the nearest or most accessible magistrate in the county of arrest. If eligible for release as a matter of right, the person must then be released under Rule 7.2. If not released immediately, the arrested person must be taken to the issuing magistrate in the county where the warrant originated, or, if that magistrate is absent or unable to act, before the nearest or most accessible magistrate in the county where the warrant originated.

(d) Assurance of Availability of Magistrate and the Setting of a Time for Initial Appearance. Each presiding judge must make a magistrate available every day of the week to hold the initial appearances required under Rule 4.1(a). The presiding judge also must set at least one fixed time each day for conducting initial appearances, and notify local law enforcement agencies of the fixed time(s).

(e) Sample for DNA Testing; Proof of Compliance. If the arresting authority is required to secure a sample of buccal cells or other bodily substances for DNA testing under A.R.S. § 13-610(K), it must provide proof of compliance to the court before the initial appearance.

Credits

Added Aug. 31, 2017, effective Jan. 1, 2018.

Editors' Notes

Rule 4.2. Initial Appearance

(Refs & Annos)
II. Preliminary Proceedings
Rule 4. Initial Appearance (Refs & Annos)
16A A.R.S. Rules Crim.Proc., Rule 4.2

Rule 4.2. Initial Appearance

(a) Generally. At an initial appearance, the magistrate must:

(1) determine the defendant's true name and address and, if necessary, amend the formal charges to correct the name and instruct the person to promptly notify the court of any change of address;

(2) inform the defendant of the charges and, if available, provide the person with a copy of the complaint, information, or indictment;

(3) inform the defendant of the right to counsel and the right to remain silent;

(4) determine whether there is probable cause for purposes of release from custody, and, if no probable cause is found, immediately release the person from custody;

(5) appoint counsel if the defendant requests and is eligible for appointed counsel under Rule 6;

(6) permit and consider any victim's oral or written comments concerning the defendant's possible release and conditions of release;

(7) unless the magistrate determines under (a)(8) that release on bail is prohibited, determine the conditions of release under Rule 7.2(a);

(8) determine whether probable cause exists to believe:

(A) the defendant committed a capital offense or any felony offense committed while the person was on pretrial release for a separate felony charge; or

(B) the defendant committed a felony for which release on bail is prohibited because the defendant poses a substantial danger and no conditions of release will reasonably assure the safety of the victim, any other person, or the community based on the considerations provided in Rule 7.2(b)(3);

(9) if the court determines that the defendant is not eligible for bail based on a determination under (a)(8)(A) or (B), schedule a bail eligibility hearing in superior court as required under Rule 7.2(b)(4);

(10) order a summoned defendant to be 10-print fingerprinted no later than 20 calendar days by the appropriate law enforcement agency at a designated time and place if:

(A) the defendant is charged with a felony offense, a violation of A.R.S. §§ 13-1401 et seq. or A.R.S. §§ 28-1301 et seq., or a domestic violence offense as defined in A.R.S. § 13-3601; and

(B) the defendant does not present a completed mandatory fingerprint compliance form to the court, or if the court has not received the process control number; and

(11) order the arresting agency to secure a sample of buccal cells or other bodily substances for DNA testing if:

(A) the defendant is in-custody and was arrested for an offense listed in A.R.S. § 13-610(O)(3); and

(B) the court has not received proof of compliance with A.R.S. § 13-610(K).

(b) Felonies Charged by Complaint. If a defendant is charged in a complaint with a felony, in addition to following the procedures in (a), the magistrate must:

(1) inform the defendant of the right to a preliminary hearing and the procedures by which that right may be waived; and

(2) unless waived, set the time for a preliminary hearing under Rule 5.1.

(c) Combining an Initial Appearance with an Arraignment. If the defendant is charged with a misdemeanor or indicted for a felony and defense counsel is present or the defendant waives the presence of counsel, the magistrate may arraign a defendant under Rule 14 during an initial appearance under (a). If, however, the magistrate lacks jurisdiction to try the offense, the magistrate may not arraign the defendant and must instead transfer the case to the proper court for arraignment. If the court finds that delaying the defendant's arraignment is indispensable to the interests of justice, the court when setting a date for the continued arraignment must provide sufficient notice to victims under Rule 39(b)(2).

Credits

Added Aug. 31, 2017, effective Jan. 1, 2018. Amended Sept. 28, 2017, effective April 2, 2018. Amended on an emergency basis June 8, 2018, effective July 1, 2018, adopted on a permanent basis Dec. 13, 2018.

Editors' Notes

HISTORICAL AND STATUTORY NOTES

Former Rule 4.2, relating to initial appearance, was abrogated effective Jan. 1, 2018. See, now, this rule.

16A A. R. S. Rules Crim. Proc., Rule 4.2, AZ ST RCRP Rule 4.2

Current with amendments received through 08/15/19

Rule 4.3. Initial Appearance Masters

(Refs & Annos)
II. Preliminary Proceedings
Rule 4. Initial Appearance (Refs & Annos)

16A A.R.S. Rules Crim.Proc., Rule 4.3

Formerly cited as AZ ST RCRP Rule 1.7

Rule 4.3. Initial Appearance Masters

(a) Appointment. A county's presiding judge may appoint one or more masters to conduct initial appearances under Rule 4. Masters under this rule have a one-year term and may be reappointed for additional terms.

(b) Compensation. The presiding judge will set masters' compensation, which will be paid from any available funding source the presiding judge identifies.

(c) Qualifications and Training. The presiding judge will determine whether an individual has sufficient education and work experience to conduct initial appearances as a master under this rule. Masters do not need to be members of the State Bar of Arizona. Before assignment, a master must successfully complete relevant training regarding the law, procedures, and judicial conduct. Masters must receive annual training concerning changes in relevant statutes, rules, and case law.

(d) Authority and Assignment. The master's authority is limited to conducting initial appearances. Presiding judges may assign masters only if no justice of the peace, magistrate, or judge pro tempore is reasonably available to conduct initial appearances.

Credits
Added Aug. 31, 2017, effective Jan. 1, 2018.
16A A. R. S. Rules Crim. Proc., Rule 4.3, AZ ST RCRP Rule 4.3
Current with amendments received through 08/15/19

R. 5, Refs & Annos

II. Preliminary Proceedings
Rule 5. Preliminary Hearing

16A A.R.S. Rules Crim.Proc., R. 5, Refs & Annos

16A A. R. S. Rules Crim. Proc., R. 5, Refs & Annos, AZ ST RCRP R. 5, Refs & Annos
Current with amendments received through 08/15/19

Rule 5.1. Right to a Preliminary Hearing; Waiver; Continuance

(Refs & Annos)

II. Preliminary Proceedings

Rule 5. Preliminary Hearing (Refs & Annos)

16A A.R.S. Rules Crim.Proc., Rule 5.1

Rule 5.1. Right to a Preliminary Hearing; Waiver; Continuance

(a) Right to a Preliminary Hearing. A defendant has a right to a preliminary hearing if charged in a complaint with a felony. A preliminary hearing must commence before a magistrate no later than 10 days after the defendant's initial appearance if the defendant is in custody, or no later than 20 days after the defendant's initial appearance if the defendant is not in custody, unless:

(1) the complaint is dismissed;

(2) the hearing is waived;

(3) the defendant has been transferred from the juvenile court for criminal prosecution on specified charges;

(4) the magistrate orders the hearing continued under (c); or

(5) the court made a probable cause finding at a bail eligibility hearing under Rule 7.2(b)(4).

(b) Waiver. The parties may waive a preliminary hearing but the waiver must be in writing and the defendant, defense counsel, and the State must sign it.

(c) Continuance.

(1) *Release Absent Continuance.* If a preliminary hearing for an in-custody defendant did not commence within 10 days as required under (a) and was not continued, the defendant must be released from custody, unless the defendant is charged with a non-bailable offense, in which case the magistrate must immediately notify that county's presiding judge of the reasons for the delay.

(2) *Continuance.* On motion or on its own, a magistrate may continue a preliminary hearing beyond the 20-day deadline specified in (a). A magistrate may continue the hearing only if it finds that extraordinary circumstances exist and that delay is indispensable to the interests of justice. The magistrate also must file a written order detailing the reasons for these findings. The court must promptly notify the parties of the order.

(3) *Resetting Hearing Date.* If the magistrate orders a continuance, the order must reset the preliminary hearing for a specific date to avoid uncertainty and additional delay.

(d) Hearing Demand. A defendant who is in custody may demand that the court hold a preliminary hearing as soon as practicable. In that event, the magistrate must set a hearing date and must not delay its commencement more than necessary to secure the attendance of counsel, a court reporter, and necessary witnesses.

Credits

Added Aug. 31, 2017, effective Jan. 1, 2018. Amended Sept. 28, 2017, effective April 2, 2018.

Editors' Notes

HISTORICAL AND STATUTORY NOTES

Former Rule 5.1, relating to right to preliminary hearing, waiver, and postponement, was abrogated effective Jan. 1, 2018. See, now, this rule.

16A A. R. S. Rules Crim. Proc., Rule 5.1, AZ ST RCRP Rule 5.1

Current with amendments received through 08/15/19

Rule 5.2. Summoning Witnesses; Record of Proceedings

(Refs & Annos)

II. Preliminary Proceedings

Rule 5. Preliminary Hearing (Refs & Annos)

16A A.R.S. Rules Crim.Proc., Rule 5.2

Rule 5.2. Summoning Witnesses; Record of Proceedings

(a) Summoning Witnesses. If requested, the magistrate must issue subpoenas to secure the attendance of witnesses.

(b) Record of Proceedings. The magistrate must make a verbatim record of the preliminary hearing. Proceedings may be recorded by a certified court reporter or by electronic or other means authorized by the superior court presiding judge. But if a party requests that a certified court reporter record the proceedings, the court must record the proceedings in that manner, unless the court is located in an area where a certified court reporter is not reasonably available.

Credits

Added Aug. 31, 2017, effective Jan. 1, 2018.

Editors' Notes

HISTORICAL AND STATUTORY NOTES

Former Rule 5.2, relating to summoning of witnesses and record of proceedings, was abrogated effective Jan. 1, 2018. See, now, this rule.

16A A. R. S. Rules Crim. Proc., Rule 5.2, AZ ST RCRP Rule 5.2

Current with amendments received through 08/15/19

Rule 5.3. Nature of the Preliminary Hearing

(Refs & Annos)
II. Preliminary Proceedings
Rule 5. Preliminary Hearing (Refs & Annos)
16A A.R.S. Rules Crim.Proc., Rule 5.3

Rule 5.3. Nature of the Preliminary Hearing

(a) Procedure.

(1) *Permitted Evidence.* During a preliminary hearing, a magistrate may admit evidence only if it is material to whether there is probable cause to hold the defendant for trial.

(2) *Cross-Examination; Witness Statements.* All parties have the right to cross-examine a witness who testifies in person at the hearing, and to review any of the witness's previous written statements before conducting cross-examination.

(3) *Probable Cause Ruling.* At the close of the State's case, the magistrate must determine and state for the record whether the State's case establishes probable cause.

(4) *Offer of Proof.* If the magistrate rules that there is probable cause, the defendant may make a specific offer of proof to the contrary, including the identities of witnesses who would testify or produce the offered evidence. The magistrate must allow the defendant to present the offered evidence, unless the magistrate determines that, even if true, the evidence would be insufficient to rebut the probable cause finding.

(b) Unlawfully Obtained Evidence. A court must not exclude evidence during a preliminary hearing solely on the ground that it was obtained unlawfully.

Credits

Added Aug. 31, 2017, effective Jan. 1, 2018.

Editors' Notes

HISTORICAL AND STATUTORY NOTES

Former Rule 5.3, relating to nature of preliminary hearing, was abrogated effective Jan. 1, 2018. See, now, this rule.

16A A. R. S. Rules Crim. Proc., Rule 5.3, AZ ST RCRP Rule 5.3

Current with amendments received through 08/15/19

Rule 5.4. Determining Probable Cause

(Refs & Annos)

II. Preliminary Proceedings
Rule 5. Preliminary Hearing (Refs & Annos)

16A A.R.S. Rules Crim.Proc., Rule 5.4

Rule 5.4. Determining Probable Cause

(a) Holding a Defendant to Answer. If a magistrate finds that there is probable cause to believe that an offense has been committed and that the defendant committed it, the magistrate must file a written order holding the defendant to answer for the offense before the superior court. Upon request, the magistrate may reconsider the conditions of release. This rule's requirements are satisfied if a probable cause finding was made at a bail eligibility hearing under Rule 7.2(b)(4).

(b) Amending the Complaint. A magistrate may grant a motion to amend a complaint so that its factual allegations conform to the evidence, but the magistrate must not hold the defendant to answer for crimes different than those charged in the original complaint.

(c) Evidence. A magistrate must base a probable cause finding on substantial evidence, which may include hearsay in the following forms:

(1) a written report of an expert witness;

(2) documentary evidence, even without foundation, if there is a substantial basis for believing that foundation will be available at trial and the document is otherwise admissible; or

(3) a witness's testimony about another person's declarations if such evidence is cumulative or if there are reasonable grounds to believe that the declarant will be personally available for trial.

(d) Lack of Probable Cause. The magistrate must dismiss the complaint and discharge the defendant if a magistrate finds that there is not probable cause to believe that an offense has been committed or that the defendant committed it.

Credits

Added Aug. 31, 2017, effective Jan. 1, 2018. Amended Sept. 28, 2017, effective April 2, 2018.

Editors' Notes

HISTORICAL AND STATUTORY NOTES

Former Rule 5.4, relating to determination of probable cause, was abrogated effective Jan. 1, 2018. See, now, this rule.

16A A. R. S. Rules Crim. Proc., Rule 5.4, AZ ST RCRP Rule 5.4

Current with amendments received through 08/15/19

Rule 5.5. Review of a Magistrate's Probable Cause Determination

(Refs & Annos)

16A A.R.S. Rules Crim.Proc., Rule 5.5

Rule 5.5. Review of a Magistrate's Probable Cause Determination

(a) Grounds. The superior court may review a magistrate's determination to bind over a defendant only if the defendant files a motion for a new probable cause finding. The court may grant the motion only if the defendant was denied a substantial procedural right or the magistrate's probable cause finding was not supported by credible evidence. If the motion challenges the sufficiency of the evidence supporting the probable cause finding, it must state specifically the ways in which credible evidence was lacking.

(b) Timeliness. A motion under this rule must be filed no later than 25 days after the preliminary hearing is completed.

(c) Evidence. A superior court's review of the evidence is limited to the certified transcript and exhibits admitted at the preliminary hearing.

(d) Relief. If the court grants a motion for a new probable cause finding, the court must remand the action to the magistrate with appropriate instructions. Unless a new preliminary hearing is commenced within 15 days after the remand order is filed, the case must be dismissed.

Credits

Added Aug. 31, 2017, effective Jan. 1, 2018.

Editors' Notes

HISTORICAL AND STATUTORY NOTES

Former Rule 5.5, relating to review of preliminary hearing, was abrogated effective Jan. 1, 2018. See, now, this rule.

16A A. R. S. Rules Crim. Proc., Rule 5.5, AZ ST RCRP Rule 5.5

Current with amendments received through 08/15/19

Rule 5.6. Transmittal and Transcription of the Record

16A A.R.S. Rules Crim.Proc., Rule 5.6

Rule 5.6. Transmittal and Transcription of the Record

(a) Transmittal. The magistrate must transmit to the superior court clerk the record of any preliminary hearing no later than 3 days after the hearing is waived or completed. The transmittal must be accompanied by a transmittal certification form and include any documents or exhibits submitted at the hearing.

(b) Transcript Preparation and Filing. If a party makes a written request and avows that there is a material need for a transcript, the court must order a certified court reporter or an authorized transcriber of an electronic recording to prepare a transcript. The court reporter or transcriber must file the transcript in the superior court no later than 20 days after the order's filing.

Credits

Added Aug. 31, 2017, effective Jan. 1, 2018.

Editors' Notes

HISTORICAL AND STATUTORY NOTES

Former Rule 5.6, relating to transmittal and transcription or record, was abrogated effective Jan. 1, 2018. See, now, this rule.

16A A. R. S. Rules Crim. Proc., Rule 5.6, AZ ST RCRP Rule 5.6

Current with amendments received through 08/15/19

Rule 5.7. Preservation of Recording

(Refs & Annos)

II. Preliminary Proceedings

Rule 5. Preliminary Hearing (Refs & Annos)

16A A.R.S. Rules Crim.Proc., Rule 5.7

Rule 5.7. Preservation of Recording

The clerk must retain and preserve any electronic recording of a preliminary hearing in the same manner as required for the original notes of a certified court reporter under Rule 28.1(c).

Credits

Added Aug. 31, 2017, effective Jan. 1, 2018.

Editors' Notes

HISTORICAL AND STATUTORY NOTES

Former Rule 5.7, relating to preservation of recording, was abrogated effective Jan. 1, 2018. See, now, this rule.

16A A. R. S. Rules Crim. Proc., Rule 5.7, AZ ST RCRP Rule 5.7

Current with amendments received through 08/15/19

Rule 5.8. Notice if an Arraignment is Not Held

(Refs & Annos)

II. Preliminary Proceedings
Rule 5. Preliminary Hearing (Refs & Annos)

16A A.R.S. Rules Crim.Proc., Rule 5.8

Rule 5.8. Notice if an Arraignment is Not Held

(a) Notice. If a defendant is held to answer in a county where an arraignment is not held as provided in Rule 14.2(d), the magistrate must:
(1) enter a plea of not guilty for the defendant and provide the defendant and defense counsel with a notice specifying that a plea of not guilty has been entered;
(2) set dates for a trial or pretrial conference;
(3) advise the parties in writing of the dates set for further proceedings and other important deadlines;
(4) advise the defendant of the defendant's right to be present at all future proceedings, that any proceeding may be held in the defendant's absence, and that if the defendant fails to appear, the defendant may be charged with an offense and a warrant may be issued for the defendant's arrest; and
(5) advise the defendant of the right to a jury trial, if applicable.
(b) Notice Form. The magistrate must provide written notice to the defendant of the matters in (a). The defendant and defense counsel must sign the notice and return it to the court.
Credits
Added Aug. 31, 2017, effective Jan. 1, 2018.
Editors' Notes
HISTORICAL AND STATUTORY NOTES
Former Rule 5.8, relating to entering a not guilty plea, was abrogated effective Jan. 1, 2018.
16A A. R. S. Rules Crim. Proc., Rule 5.8, AZ ST RCRP Rule 5.8
Current with amendments received through 08/15/19

R. 6, Refs & Annos

III. Rights of Parties
Rule 6. Right to Counsel; Duties of Counsel; Court-Appointed Attorneys, Investigators, and Experts

16A A.R.S. Rules Crim.Proc., R. 6, Refs & Annos

16A A. R. S. Rules Crim. Proc., R. 6, Refs & Annos, AZ ST RCRP R. 6, Refs & Annos

Current with amendments received through 08/15/19

Rule 6.1. Right to Counsel; Right to a Court-Appointed Attorney; Waiver of the Right to Counsel

(Refs & Annos)
III. Rights of Parties
Rule 6. Right to Counsel; Duties of Counsel; Court-Appointed Attorneys, Investigators, and Experts (Refs & Annos)
16A A.R.S. Rules Crim.Proc., Rule 6.1

Rule 6.1. Right to Counsel; Right to a Court-Appointed Attorney; Waiver of the Right to Counsel

(a) Right to Be Represented by Counsel. A defendant has the right to be represented by counsel in any criminal proceeding. The right to be represented by counsel includes the right to consult privately with counsel, or the counsel's agent, as soon as feasible after a defendant has been taken into custody, at reasonable times after being taken into custody, and sufficiently in advance of a proceeding to allow counsel to adequately prepare for the proceeding.
(b) Right to a Court-Appointed Attorney.
(1) *As of Right.* An indigent defendant is entitled to a court-appointed attorney:
(A) in any criminal proceeding that may result in punishment involving a loss of liberty; or
(B) for the limited purpose of determining release conditions at or following the initial appearance, if the defendant is detained after a misdemeanor charge is filed.
(2) *Discretionary.* In any other criminal proceeding, the court may appoint an attorney for an indigent defendant if required by the interests of justice.
(3) *Definition of "Indigent."* For the purposes of this rule, "indigent" means a person who is not financially able to retain counsel.
(c) Waiver of Right to Counsel. A defendant may waive the right to counsel if the waiver is in writing and if the court finds that the defendant's waiver is knowing, intelligent, and voluntary. After a defendant waives the right to counsel, the court may appoint advisory counsel for the defendant at any stage of the proceedings. In all further matters, the court must give advisory counsel the same notice that is given to the defendant.
(d) Unreasonable Delay in Retaining Counsel. If a defendant appears at a proceeding without counsel, the court may proceed if:
(1) the defendant is indigent and has refused appointed counsel; or

(2) the defendant is not indigent and has had a reasonable opportunity to obtain counsel.

(e) Withdrawal of Waiver. A defendant may withdraw a waiver of the right to counsel at any time. But the fact that counsel is later appointed or retained does not alone establish a basis for repeating any proceeding previously held or waived.

Credits

Added Aug. 31, 2017, effective Jan. 1, 2018.

Editors' Notes

HISTORICAL AND STATUTORY NOTES

Former Rule 6.1, relating to right to counsel and waiver to right of counsel, was abrogated effective Jan. 1, 2018. See, now, this rule.

16A A. R. S. Rules Crim. Proc., Rule 6.1, AZ ST RCRP Rule 6.1

Current with amendments received through 08/15/19

Rule 6.2. Appointment of Counsel for Indigent Defendants

(Refs & Annos)

III. Rights of Parties

Rule 6. Right to Counsel; Duties of Counsel; Court-Appointed Attorneys, Investigators, and Experts (Refs & Annos)

16A A.R.S. Rules Crim.Proc., Rule 6.2

Rule 6.2. Appointment of Counsel for Indigent Defendants

(a) Procedure. The presiding judge of each county must establish a procedure for the superior court and limited jurisdiction courts to appoint counsel for indigent defendants.

(b) Capital Trial Proceedings. In all capital trial proceedings where the defendant is indigent, the presiding judge must appoint two attorneys--lead counsel and co-counsel--under Rule 6.8(b). The appointed lead counsel may designate co-counsel if co-counsel is willing to accept the appointment and meets the requirements of Rule 6.8. If lead counsel does not promptly designate co-counsel, the court must do so.

Credits

Added Aug. 31, 2017, effective Jan. 1, 2018.

Editors' Notes

HISTORICAL AND STATUTORY NOTES

Former Rule 6.2, relating to appointment of counsel, was abrogated effective Jan. 1, 2018. See, now, this rule.

16A A. R. S. Rules Crim. Proc., Rule 6.2, AZ ST RCRP Rule 6.2

Current with amendments received through 08/15/19

Rule 6.3. Duties of Counsel; Withdrawal

(Refs & Annos)
III. Rights of Parties
Rule 6. Right to Counsel; Duties of Counsel; Court-Appointed Attorneys,
Investigators, and Experts (Refs & Annos)

16A A.R.S. Rules Crim.Proc., Rule 6.3

Rule 6.3. Duties of Counsel; Withdrawal

(a) Notice of Appearance.
(1) *Generally.* Before representing the defendant in court, counsel--whether
privately retained or appointed by the court--must file a notice of appearance.
(2) *Earlier Appearance in a Limited Jurisdiction Court.* Counsel who has filed a
notice of appearance in a felony case in a limited jurisdiction court does not need to
file a new notice of appearance if the defendant is bound over to superior court.
(b) Duty of Continuing Representation. Unless the court permits counsel to
withdraw, counsel who represents a defendant at any stage of a case has a
continuing duty to represent the defendant in all further proceedings in the trial
court, including the filing of a notice of appeal.
(c) Withdrawal.
(1) *If the Defendant Is Ineligible for Appointed Counsel.* Appointed counsel may not
withdraw after arraignment on the ground that the defendant is ineligible for
appointed counsel unless counsel shows that withdrawal will not disrupt the orderly
processing of the case.
(2) *If the Case Is Set for Trial.* After a case is set for trial, the court may not permit
counsel to withdraw unless counsel files a motion that provides:
(A) the name and address of new counsel and a signed statement from the new
counsel that acknowledges the trial date and avows that the new counsel will be
prepared for trial; or
(B) ethical grounds for withdrawing.
(d) Duty of Defense Counsel to Preserve the File. Defense counsel must:
(1) maintain records of the case in a manner that will inform successor counsel of all
significant developments relevant to the case; and
(2) make available to successor counsel the client's complete records and files, as
well as all information regarding every aspect of the representation.
(e) Duty of Successor Counsel to Collect the File in a Capital Case. Immediately
upon undertaking representation of a defendant in a capital case in which the
defendant was previously represented by counsel, defense counsel must collect the

complete file from prior counsel and maintain the records and files in a manner that complies with (d).

Credits

Added Aug. 31, 2017, effective Jan. 1, 2018.

Editors' Notes

HISTORICAL AND STATUTORY NOTES

Former Rule 6.3, relating to duties of counsel and withdrawal, was abrogated effective Jan. 1, 2018. See, now, this rule.

16A A. R. S. Rules Crim. Proc., Rule 6.3, AZ ST RCRP Rule 6.3

Current with amendments received through 08/15/19

Rule 6.4. Determining Whether a Person Is Indigent

(Refs & Annos)

III. Rights of Parties

Rule 6. Right to Counsel; Duties of Counsel; Court-Appointed Attorneys, Investigators, and Experts (Refs & Annos)

16A A.R.S. Rules Crim.Proc., Rule 6.4

Rule 6.4. Determining Whether a Person Is Indigent

(a) Questionnaire. To show indigency, a defendant must complete under oath a financial resources form approved by the Supreme Court. A judicial officer responsible for determining whether a defendant is indigent may question the defendant under oath regarding the defendant's financial resources. Before questioning, the court must advise the defendant of the penalties for perjury set forth in A.R.S. §§ 13-2701 et seq.

(b) Redetermination of Indigency. If there is a material change in circumstances, the defendant, defense counsel, or the State may request that the court make a new indigency determination.

(c) Payment by the Defendant.

(1) *Generally.* If a court finds that a defendant can afford to pay part of the cost of appointed counsel without incurring substantial hardship, the court may order the defendant to pay that amount to the clerk.

(2) *Failure to Pay.* A defendant's failure to pay an amount ordered by the court is not a basis for finding the defendant in contempt, and appointed counsel may not withdraw solely on this ground. But the county or municipality may enforce an order under (c)(1) as a civil judgment.

(3) *Court Order Required.* Without court approval, an attorney, organization, or agency may not request or accept payment from the defendant for providing legal services under the court appointment.

Credits

Added Aug. 31, 2017, effective Jan. 1, 2018.

Editors' Notes

HISTORICAL AND STATUTORY NOTES

Former Rule 6.4, relating to determination of indigency, was abrogated effective Jan. 1, 2018. See, now, this rule.

16A A. R. S. Rules Crim. Proc., Rule 6.4, AZ ST RCRP Rule 6.4

Current with amendments received through 08/15/19

Rule 6.5. Manner of Appointment

(Refs & Annos)

III. Rights of Parties

Rule 6. Right to Counsel; Duties of Counsel; Court-Appointed Attorneys, Investigators, and Experts (Refs & Annos)

16A A.R.S. Rules Crim.Proc., Rule 6.5

Rule 6.5. Manner of Appointment

(a) Appointment Order. The court must appoint counsel by a written order and provide a copy of the order to the defendant, the appointed attorney, and the State.

(b) Public Defender Appointment. In counties that have a public defender, the court must appoint the public defender to represent persons entitled to appointed counsel whenever the public defender is authorized by law to undertake the representation and is able to do so.

(c) Other Appointments. If the court does not appoint a public defender, the court must appoint a private attorney. In appointing private counsel, the court must take into account the skill likely to be required in handling the case.

(d) Requests for Representation Before a Grand Jury. A request for appointment of counsel must be made and processed as if proceedings had already begun in superior court.

Credits

Added Aug. 31, 2017, effective Jan. 1, 2018.

Editors' Notes

HISTORICAL AND STATUTORY NOTES

Former Rule 6.5, relating to manner of appointment, was abrogated effective Jan. 1, 2018. See, now, this rule.

Rule 6.6. Compensation of Appointed Counsel

(Refs & Annos)
III. Rights of Parties
Rule 6. Right to Counsel; Duties of Counsel; Court-Appointed Attorneys, Investigators, and Experts (Refs & Annos)
16A A.R.S. Rules Crim.Proc., Rule 6.6
Formerly cited as AZ ST RCRP Rule 6.7

Rule 6.6. Compensation of Appointed Counsel

(a) Where to File a Compensation Claim. A private attorney appointed to represent an indigent defendant must file a claim for compensation as provided by local rule in the county in which the appointment was made or from which the appeal was taken.

(b) When to File a Compensation Claim.

(1) *Trial Court.* Trial counsel may file claims for compensation at intervals permitted by the court, and must file a final claim at the completion of all trial, sentencing, or post-conviction proceedings.

(2) *Appellate Court.* Appellate counsel may file claims for compensation at intervals permitted by the court, and must file a final claim at the completion of all appellate proceedings.

(c) Proceedings in a Limited Jurisdiction Court. An attorney is entitled to compensation for services rendered in a limited jurisdiction court.

(d) Amount of Compensation. An attorney must be reasonably compensated for the services performed, considering the hours worked, the experience of counsel, the seriousness and complexity of the case, the quality of the work performed, and any other relevant factors. The manner of determining reasonable compensation is provided by local rule and A.R.S. § 13-4013.

Credits

Added Aug. 31, 2017, effective Jan. 1, 2018.

Editors' Notes

HISTORICAL AND STATUTORY NOTES

Former Rule 6.6, relating to appointment of counsel during appeal, was abrogated effective Jan. 1, 2018.

16A A. R. S. Rules Crim. Proc., Rule 6.6, AZ ST RCRP Rule 6.6
Current with amendments received through 08/15/19

Rule 6.7. Appointment of Investigators and Expert Witnesses for Indigent Defendants

(Refs & Annos)
III. Rights of Parties
Rule 6. Right to Counsel; Duties of Counsel; Court-Appointed Attorneys, Investigators, and Experts (Refs & Annos)
16A A.R.S. Rules Crim.Proc., Rule 6.7

Rule 6.7. Appointment of Investigators and Expert Witnesses for Indigent Defendants

(a) Appointment. On application, if the court finds that such assistance is reasonably necessary to adequately present a defense at trial or at sentencing, the court may appoint an investigator, expert witnesses, and/or, in a felony matter, a mitigation specialist for an indigent defendant at county or city expense.

(b) Ex Parte Proceeding. A defendant may not make an ex parte request under this rule without showing a need for confidentiality. The court must make a verbatim record of any ex parte proceeding, communication, or request, which must be available for appellate review.

(c) Definition of a "Mitigation Specialist." As used in this rule, a "mitigation specialist" is a person qualified by knowledge, skill, experience, or other training as a mental health or sociology professional to investigate, evaluate, and present psycho-social and other mitigation evidence.

(d) Capital Case. In a capital case, a defendant should make any motion for an expert or mitigation specialist no later than 60 days after the State makes its disclosure under Rule 15.1(i)(3).

Credits

Added Aug. 31, 2017, effective Jan. 1, 2018.

Editors' Notes

HISTORICAL AND STATUTORY NOTES

Former Rule 6.7, relating to compensation of appointed counsel, was abrogated effective Jan. 1, 2018. See, now, AZ ST RCRP Rule 6.6.

16A A. R. S. Rules Crim. Proc., Rule 6.7, AZ ST RCRP Rule 6.7

Current with amendments received through 08/15/19

Rule 6.8. Standards for Appointment and Performance of Counsel in Capital Cases

(Refs & Annos)

III. Rights of Parties
Rule 6. Right to Counsel; Duties of Counsel; Court-Appointed Attorneys, Investigators, and Experts (Refs & Annos)

16A A.R.S. Rules Crim.Proc., Rule 6.8

Rule 6.8. Standards for Appointment and Performance of Counsel in Capital Cases

(a) Generally. To be eligible for appointment in a capital case, an attorney must:

(1) have been a member in good standing of the State Bar of Arizona for at least 5 years immediately before the appointment;

(2) have practiced criminal litigation in Arizona state courts for 3 years immediately before the appointment;

(3) have demonstrated the necessary proficiency and commitment that exemplifies the quality of representation appropriate to capital cases;

(4) have successfully completed, within one year before the initial appointment, at least 6 hours of relevant training or educational programs in the area of capital defense; and successfully completed within one year before any later appointment, at least 12 hours of relevant training or educational programs in the area of criminal defense;

(5) be familiar with and guided by the performance standards in the 2003 American Bar Association Guidelines for the Appointment and Performance of Defense Counsel in Death Penalty Cases, and the 2008 Supplementary Guidelines for the Mitigation Function of Defense Teams in Death Penalty Cases.

If an attorney is a member in good standing of the State Bar of Arizona, the attorney's practice in a federal jurisdiction or in another state may be considered for purposes of satisfying the requirements of (a)(1) and (a)(2).

(b) Trial Counsel.

(1) *Lead Counsel.* To be eligible for appointment as lead trial counsel, an attorney must meet the requirements of (a) and must have:

(A) practiced criminal litigation in Arizona state courts for 5 years immediately before the appointment; and

(B) been lead counsel in at least 9 felony jury trials that were tried to completion, and have been lead counsel or co-counsel in at least one capital jury trial.

(2) *Co-Counsel.* To be eligible for appointment as co-counsel, an attorney must be a member in good standing of the State Bar of Arizona and meet the requirements of (a)(4) and (a)(5).

(c) Appellate Counsel. To be eligible for appointment as appellate counsel, an attorney must meet the qualifications set forth in (a) and the attorney must:

(1) within 3 years immediately before the appointment, have been lead counsel in an appeal in a case in which a death sentence was imposed (including petitions for

review of post-conviction proceedings); and prior experience as lead counsel in the appeal of at least 3 felony convictions; or

(2) prior experience as lead counsel in merits briefing in the appeal of at least 6 felony convictions, including two appeals from first- or second-degree murder convictions.

(d) Post-Conviction Counsel. To be eligible for appointment as post-conviction counsel, an attorney must meet the qualifications set forth in (a) and the attorney must:

(1) within 3 years immediately before the appointment, have been lead counsel in a trial in which a death sentence was sought or in an appeal or post-conviction proceeding in a case in which a death sentence was imposed, and prior experience as lead counsel in the appeal of at least 3 felony convictions and a trial or post-conviction proceeding with an evidentiary hearing; or

(2) have been lead counsel in the appeal of at least 6 felony convictions, including two appeals from first- or second-degree murder convictions, and lead counsel in at least two felony trials or post-conviction proceedings with evidentiary hearings.

(e) Exceptions. In exceptional circumstances, a court may appoint an attorney who does not meet the qualifications set forth in this rule if:

(1) the Supreme Court consents;

(2) the attorney meets the requirements set forth in (a)(3)--(5);

(3) the attorney's experience, stature, and record establishes that the attorney's ability significantly exceeds the standards set forth in this rule; and

(4) the attorney associates with a lawyer who meets the qualifications set forth in this rule and the associating attorney is appointed by the court for this purpose.
Credits
Added Aug. 31, 2017, effective Jan. 1, 2018.
Editors' Notes
COMMENT
Rule 6.8(a). The American Bar Association Guidelines for the Appointment and Performance of Defense Counsel in Death Penalty Cases (2003) and the 2008 Supplementary Guidelines for the Mitigation Function of Defense Teams in Death Penalty Cases constitute a compendium of effective capital defense representation practices. Counsel should be guided by those practices in exercising independent professional judgment. The guidelines do not, however, impose independent requirements on courts. If, for example, the guidelines recommend resources or services from a court, counsel must show a need for that resource or service based on the facts of the particular case. A deviation from the guidelines is not per se ineffective assistance of counsel. The standard for evaluating counsel's performance continues to be that set forth in *Strickland v. Washington,* 466 U.S. 668 (1984).
HISTORICAL AND STATUTORY NOTES

Former Rule 6.8, relating to standards for appointment and performance of counsel in capital cases, was abrogated effective Jan. 1, 2018. See, now, this rule.
16A A. R. S. Rules Crim. Proc., Rule 6.8, AZ ST RCRP Rule 6.8
Current with amendments received through 08/15/19

R. 7, Refs & Annos

III. Rights of Parties
Rule 7. Release
16A A.R.S. Rules Crim.Proc., R. 7, Refs & Annos

16A A. R. S. Rules Crim. Proc., R. 7, Refs & Annos, AZ ST RCRP R. 7, Refs & Annos
Current with amendments received through 08/15/19

Rule 7.1. Definitions

(Refs & Annos)
III. Rights of Parties
Rule 7. Release (Refs & Annos)
16A A.R.S. Rules Crim.Proc., Rule 7.1

Rule 7.1. Definitions

(a) Own Recognizance. "Own recognizance" is a release of a defendant without requiring the posting of a bond as a condition of release.
(b) Unsecured Appearance Bond. An "unsecured appearance bond" is an undertaking, on a form approved by the Supreme Court, to pay the clerk a specified sum of money upon the defendant's failure to comply with the conditions of the bond.
(c) Cash Bond. A "cash bond" is a secured appearance bond consisting of actual cash deposited by the defendant or someone acting on the defendant's behalf.
(d) Deposit Bond. A "deposit bond" is a partially-secured appearance bond in which the defendant, or someone acting on the defendant's behalf other than a professional bondsman, deposits a percentage of the full bond amount in cash.
(e) Secured Appearance Bond. A "secured appearance bond" is an appearance bond secured by deposit with the clerk of security equal to the full amount of the bond.
(f) Security. "Security" is cash, a surety's undertaking, or any property of value, deposited with the clerk to secure an appearance bond. The value of that property is determined by the clerk or, at the clerk's or a party's request, by the court.

(g) Surety. A "surety" is a person or company, other than the defendant, who executes an appearance bond and agrees to pay the amount of the bond if the defendant fails to comply with its conditions. A surety must file an affidavit with an appearance bond stating that the surety is not an attorney or person authorized to take bail, and that the surety owns property in Arizona (or is an Arizona resident owning property) with a value equal to or more than the amount of the appearance bond. The property's value is calculated after deducting the amount exempt from execution and all liabilities, including the amount of any other outstanding appearance bonds that the surety has entered into involving the same property.

(h) Professional Bondsman. Any person who is a surety simultaneously on more than 4 appearance bonds is a "professional bondsman." A person may not be a professional bondsman unless the person annually certifies in writing under oath to the superior court clerk that the person:

(1) is an Arizona resident;

(2) is licensed with the Arizona Department of Insurance under A.R.S. § 20-340.01;

(3) has sufficient financial net worth to satisfy reasonable obligations as a surety;

(4) agrees to assume an affirmative duty to the court to remain in regular contact with any defendant released under an appearance bond on which the person is a surety;

(5) has not been convicted of a felony, except as otherwise provided in A.R.S. § 20-340.03;

(6) has no outstanding judgments arising out of surety undertakings; and

(7) has not, within a period of two years, violated any provisions of these rules or any court order.

The clerk or the court may revoke or withhold a professional bondsman's capacity to act as surety if the bondsman violates this rule's provisions.

Credits

Added Aug. 31, 2017, effective Jan. 1, 2018.

Editors' Notes

HISTORICAL AND STATUTORY NOTES

Former Rule 7.1, relating to definitions and applicability of rule, was abrogated effective Jan. 1, 2018. See, now, this rule.

16A A. R. S. Rules Crim. Proc., Rule 7.1, AZ ST RCRP Rule 7.1

Current with amendments received through 08/15/19

Rule 7.2. Right to Release

(Refs & Annos)

III. Rights of Parties

Rule 7. Release (Refs & Annos)
16A A.R.S. Rules Crim.Proc., Rule 7.2
Rule 7.2. Right to Release

(a) Before Conviction; Bailable Offenses.
(1) *Presumption of Innocence.* A defendant charged with a crime but not yet convicted is presumed to be innocent.
(2) *Right to Release.* Except as these rules otherwise provide, any defendant charged with an offense bailable as a matter of right must be released pending and during trial on the defendant's own recognizance with only the mandatory conditions of release required under Rule 7.3(a). This rule does not apply if the court determines that such a release will not reasonably assure the defendant's appearance or protect the victim, any other person, or the community from risk of harm by the defendant. If the court makes such a determination, it must impose the least onerous conditions of release set forth in Rule 7.3(c).
(3) *Determining Method of Release or Bail Amount.* In determining the method of release or the amount of bail, the court must consider the factors set forth in A.R.S. § 13-3967(B).
(b) Before Conviction: Defendants Charged with an Offense Not Eligible for Bail.
(1) *Not Eligible Based on Commission of a Specified Felony or Any Felony While on Pretrial Release.* A defendant must not be released if the court finds the proof is evident or the presumption great that the defendant committed:
(A) a capital offense;
(B) any felony offense while the defendant was on pretrial release for a separate felony charge.
(2) *Not Eligible Based on Commission of any Felony and Other Factors.* Under article 2, section 22(A)(3) of the Arizona Constitution, the court may not release any defendant charged with a felony if the court finds all of the following:
(A) the proof is evident or the presumption great that the defendant committed one or more of the charged felony offenses;
(B) clear and convincing evidence that the defendant poses a substantial danger to the victim, any other person, or the community or, on certification by motion of the state, the defendant engaged in conduct constituting a dangerous crime against children or terrorism; and
(C) no condition or combination of conditions of release will reasonably assure the safety of the victim, any other person, or the community.
(3) *Bail Eligibility Considerations.* In making the determinations required by (b)(2)(B) and (b)(2)(C), the court must consider:

(A) the nature and circumstances of the offense charged, including whether the offense is a "dangerous offense" as defined in A.R.S. § 13-105;

(B) the weight of the evidence against the defendant;

(C) the history and characteristics of the defendant, including the defendant's character, physical and mental condition, past conduct including membership in a criminal street gang, history relating to drug or alcohol abuse, and criminal history;

(D) the nature and seriousness of the danger to the victim, any other person, or the community that would be posed by releasing the defendant on bail, including any threat to a victim or other participants in the judicial process;

(E) the recommendation of the pretrial services program based on an appropriate risk assessment instrument;

(F) any victim statement about the offense and release on bail; and

(G) any other factor relevant to the determination required under (b)(2)(B) and (b)(2)(C).

(4) *Bail Eligibility Hearing.*

(A) Generally. The superior court must hold a hearing to determine whether a defendant held in custody under Rule 4.2(a)(8) is not eligible for bail as required under (b)(1) or (b)(2), unless the defendant waives this hearing.

(B) Timing. If the State makes an oral motion under A.R.S. § 13-3961(E), the court must hold this hearing within 24 hours of the initial appearance, subject to continuances as provided in A.R.S. § 13-3961. If this motion is not made, the hearing must be held as soon as practicable, but no later than 7 days after the initial appearance unless the detained defendant moves for a continuance.

(C) Determination of Probable Cause and Release Conditions. If the court does not find the proof evident or the presumption great under (b)(1) or (b)(2)(A), the court must determine whether there is probable cause to believe that an offense was committed and that the defendant committed it. If the court finds probable cause, the court must determine release conditions under (a). If the court does not find probable cause, the defendant must be released from custody. The parties may stipulate before the bail eligibility hearing that the probable cause determination at the hearing satisfies the requirements of Rule 5. If the parties so stipulate and the court does not find probable cause, the court must dismiss the complaint and discharge the defendant. If the parties have not so stipulated, the court must schedule a preliminary hearing as provided in Rule 5.1(a).

(D) Findings on the Record. The court's findings must be on the record.

(c) After Conviction.

(1) *Superior Court.*

(A) Before Sentencing. After a defendant is convicted of an offense for which the defendant will, in all reasonable probability, receive a sentence of imprisonment, the court may not release the defendant on bail or on the defendant's own recognizance unless:

(i) the court finds that reasonable grounds exist to believe that the conviction may be set aside on a motion for new trial, judgment of acquittal, or other post-trial motion; or

(ii) the parties stipulate otherwise and the court approves the stipulation.

(B) After a Sentence Involving Imprisonment. If a defendant is convicted of a felony offense and is sentenced to prison, the court may not release the defendant on bail or on the defendant's own recognizance pending appeal unless the court finds the defendant is in such a physical condition that continued confinement would endanger the defendant's life.

(C) Protecting Safety. In determining release conditions if the defendant is released under (c)(1)(A) or (B), the court must impose conditions that will protect the victim, any other person, or the community from risk of harm by the defendant.

(D) After Sentence, Pending Appeal. If a defendant is released pending appeal but fails to diligently pursue the appeal, the court must revoke the release.

(E) Release upon Sentence Completion. A defendant held in custody pending appeal must be released if the term of incarceration is completed before the appeal is decided.

(2) *Limited Jurisdiction Courts.*

(A) Conditions of Release on Appeal. If a defendant files a timely notice of appeal of a conviction for an offense for which the court has imposed a sentence of incarceration, the defendant may remain out of custody under the same conditions of release imposed at or after the defendant's initial appearance or arraignment.

(B) Lack of Diligence on Appeal. If a defendant is released pending appeal but fails to diligently pursue the appeal, the court must revoke the release.

(C) Motion to Amend Conditions of Release.

(i) Upon the filing of a timely notice of appeal, the court--on motion or on its own-- may amend the conditions of release if it finds a substantial risk exists that the defendant presents a danger to the victim, another person or the community, or the defendant is unlikely to return to court if required to do so after the appeal concludes.

(ii) The court must hear a motion under this rule no later than 3 days after filing, although it may continue the hearing for good cause. The defendant may be detained pending the hearing. The hearing must be on the record, and the defendant is entitled to representation by counsel. Any testimony by the defendant is not admissible in another proceeding except as it relates to compliance with prior conditions of release, perjury, or impeachment. The court must state its findings on the record.

(iii) The court may amend the conditions of release in accordance with the standards set forth in Rule 7.3 and Rule 7.4(b). In determining the method of release or the amount of bail, the court must consider the nature and circumstances of the offense, family or local ties, employment, financial resources, the defendant's character and mental condition, the length of residence in the community, the record of arrests or convictions, the risk of harm to the victim, other persons, or the community, and appearances at prior court proceedings.

(D) Release upon Sentence Completion. A defendant held in custody pending appeal must be released if the defendant's term of incarceration is completed before the appeal is decided.

(E) Superior Court Review. If the trial court enters an order setting a bond or requiring incarceration during the appeal, the defendant may petition the superior court to stay the execution of sentence and to allow the defendant's release either without bond or on a reduced bond.

(d) Burden of Proof. A court must determine issues under (a) and (c) by a preponderance of the evidence. The State bears the burden of establishing factual issues under (a), (b) and (c)(2). The defendant bears the burden of establishing factual issues under (c)(1).

Credits

Added Aug. 31, 2017, effective Jan. 1, 2018. Amended Sept. 28, 2017, effective April 2, 2018. Amended on an emergency basis June 8, 2018, effective July 1, 2018, adopted on a permanent basis Dec. 13, 2018.

Editors' Notes

HISTORICAL AND STATUTORY NOTES

Former Rule 7.2, relating to right to release, was abrogated effective Jan. 1, 2018. See, now, this rule.

16A A. R. S. Rules Crim. Proc., Rule 7.2, AZ ST RCRP Rule 7.2

Current with amendments received through 08/15/19

Rule 7.3. Conditions of Release

(Refs & Annos)
III. Rights of Parties
Rule 7. Release (Refs & Annos)

16A A.R.S. Rules Crim.Proc., Rule 7.3

Rule 7.3. Conditions of Release

(a) Mandatory Conditions. Every order of release must contain the following conditions:

(1) the defendant must appear at all court proceedings;

(2) the defendant must not commit any criminal offense;

(3) the defendant must not leave Arizona without the court's permission; and

(4) if a defendant is released during an appeal after judgment and sentence, the defendant will diligently pursue the appeal.

(b) Mandatory Condition if Charged with an Offense Listed in A.R.S. § 13-610(O)(3).

(1) *Generally.* If a defendant is charged with an offense listed in A.R.S. § 13-610(O)(3) and has been summoned to appear in court, the court must order the defendant to report to the arresting law enforcement agency or its designee no later than 5 days after release, and submit a sample of buccal cells or other bodily substances for DNA testing as directed. The defendant must provide proof of compliance at the next scheduled court proceeding.

(2) *Required Notice.* The court must inform the defendant that a willful failure to comply with an order under (b)(1) will result in revocation of release.

(c) Additional Conditions. The court must order the defendant not to contact a victim if such an order is reasonable and necessary to protect a victim from physical harm, harassment, intimidation, or abuse. The court also may impose as a condition of release one or more of the following conditions, if the court finds the condition is reasonable and necessary to secure the defendant's appearance or to protect another person or the community from risk of harm by the defendant. In making determinations under this rule, the court must consider, if provided, the results of a risk assessment approved by the Supreme Court and a law enforcement agency's lethality assessment.

(1) *Non-Monetary Conditions.* A court may impose the following non-monetary conditions:

(A) placing the defendant in the custody of a designated person or organization that agrees to provide supervision;

(B) restricting the defendant's travel, associations, or residence;

(C) prohibiting the defendant from possessing any dangerous weapon;

(D) engaging in certain described activities, or consuming intoxicating liquors or any controlled substance that is not properly prescribed;

(E) requiring the defendant to report regularly to and remain under the supervision of an officer of the court;

(F) returning the defendant to custody after specified hours; or

(G) imposing any other non-monetary condition that is reasonably related to securing the defendant's appearance or protecting others or the community from risk of harm by the defendant.

(2) *Monetary Conditions.*

(A) Generally. A court's imposition of a monetary condition of release must be based on an individualized determination of the defendant's risk of non-appearance, risk of harm to others or the community, and the defendant's financial circumstances. The court may not rely on a schedule of charge-based bond amounts, and it must not impose a monetary condition that results in unnecessary pretrial incarceration solely because the defendant is unable to pay the imposed monetary condition.

(B) Least Onerous Alternative. If the court determines a monetary condition is necessary, it must impose the least onerous type of condition in the lowest amount necessary to secure the defendant's appearance or protect other persons or the community from risk of harm by the defendant.

(C) Types of Conditions. The types of monetary conditions a court may impose include the following:

(i) an unsecured appearance bond;

(ii) a deposit bond;

(iii) another type of secured bond; and

(iv) a cash bond.

Credits

Added Aug. 31, 2017, effective Jan. 1, 2018.

Editors' Notes

HISTORICAL AND STATUTORY NOTES

Former Rule 7.3, relating to conditions of release, was abrogated effective Jan. 1, 2018. See, now, this rule.

16A A. R. S. Rules Crim. Proc., Rule 7.3, AZ ST RCRP Rule 7.3

Current with amendments received through 08/15/19

Rule 7.4. Procedure

(Refs & Annos)

III. Rights of Parties

Rule 7. Release (Refs & Annos)

16A A.R.S. Rules Crim.Proc., Rule 7.4

Rule 7.4. Procedure

(a) Initial Appearance. At an initial appearance, the court must determine bail eligibility and the conditions for release. If the court decides that the defendant is eligible for release, the court must issue an order containing the conditions of release. The order must inform the defendant of the conditions and possible consequences for violating a condition, and that the court may immediately issue a warrant for the defendant's arrest if there is a violation.

(b) Bail Eligibility Hearing.

(1) *Right to Secure Witnesses, Cross-Examine, and Review Witness Statements.* At a bail eligibility hearing, each party has the right to secure the attendance of witnesses, cross-examine any witness who testifies, and to review any previous written statement by the witness before cross-examination.

(2) *Victims.* Notwithstanding the time limits of Rule 39(g)(1), a victim must be afforded the rights provided in Rule 39(g).

(3) *Admissibility.* Evidence is admissible at the hearing only if it is material to whether, and under what conditions, to release the defendant on bail and, subject to the parties' stipulation under Rule 7.2(b)(4)(C), whether probable cause exists to hold the defendant for trial on each charge. Rules or objections calling for the exclusion of evidence are inapplicable at a bail eligibility hearing.

(c) Later Review of Conditions.

(1) *Generally.* On motion or on its own, a court may reexamine bail eligibility or the conditions of release if the case is transferred to a different court or a motion alleges the existence of material facts not previously presented to the court.

(2) *Motion Requirements and Hearing.* The court may modify the conditions of release only after giving the parties an opportunity to respond to the proposed modification. A motion to reexamine the conditions of release must comply with victims' rights requirements provided in Rule 39.

(3) *Eligibility for Bail.* If the motion is by the State and involves a defendant previously held eligible for bail at the initial appearance, it need not allege new material facts. The court must hold a hearing on the record as soon as practicable, but no later than 7 days after the motion's filing.

(d) Evidence. A court may base a release determination under this rule on evidence that is not admissible under the Arizona Rules of Evidence.

(e) Defendant's Bail Status. If the court makes the findings required under Rule 7.2(b)(1) or (b)(2) to deny bail, the court must order the defendant held without bail until further order. If not, the court must order the defendant released on bail under Rule 7.2(a).

(f) Review of Conditions of Release for Misdemeanors. No later than 10 days after arraignment, the court must determine whether to amend the conditions of release for any defendant held in custody on bond for a misdemeanor.

(g) Appointment of Counsel. The court must appoint counsel in any case in which the defendant is eligible for the appointment of counsel under Rule 6.1(b).

Credits

Added Aug. 31, 2017, effective Jan. 1, 2018. Amended Sept. 28, 2017, effective April 2, 2018.

Editors' Notes

COMMENT

Rule 7.4(d). The rule's intent is to assure that a defendant will not spend more time in jail based on an inability to post bond than the defendant would spend after completing a sentence imposed for the charge, and to ensure that no defendant becomes lost in the system. The court should document its review of the case file.

HISTORICAL AND STATUTORY NOTES

Former Rule 7.4, relating to procedure, was abrogated effective Jan. 1, 2018. See, now, this rule.

16A A. R. S. Rules Crim. Proc., Rule 7.4, AZ ST RCRP Rule 7.4

Current with amendments received through 08/15/19

Rule 7.5. Review of Conditions; Revocation of Release

(Refs & Annos)
III. Rights of Parties
Rule 7. Release (Refs & Annos)
16A A.R.S. Rules Crim.Proc., Rule 7.5

Rule 7.5. Review of Conditions; Revocation of Release

(a) On State's Petition. If the State files a verified petition stating facts or circumstances showing the defendant has violated a condition of release, the court may issue a summons or warrant under Rule 3.2, or a notice setting a hearing, to secure the defendant's presence in court and to consider the matters raised in the petition. A copy of the petition must be provided with the summons, warrant, or notice.

(b) On Pretrial Services' Report. If pretrial services submits a written report to the court stating facts or circumstances showing the defendant has violated a condition of release, the court may issue a summons or warrant under Rule 3.2, or a notice setting a hearing, to secure the defendant's presence in court and to consider the matters raised in the report. A copy of the report must be provided to the State and provided with the summons, warrant, or notice.

(c) On Victim's Petition. If the prosecutor decides not to file a petition under (a), the victim may petition the court to revoke the defendant's bond or own recognizance release, or otherwise modify the defendant's conditions of release. Before filing a petition, the victim must consult with the prosecutor about the requested relief. The petition must include a statement under oath by the victim asserting any harassment, threats, physical violence, or intimidation by the defendant, or on the defendant's behalf, against the victim or the victim's immediate family.

(d) Hearing; Modification of Conditions; Revocation.

(1) *Modification of Conditions of Release.* After a hearing on the matters set forth in the petition or report, the court may impose different or additional conditions of release if it finds that the defendant has willfully violated the conditions of release.

(2) *Revocation of Release on a Felony Offense.* The court may revoke release of a defendant charged with a felony if, after a hearing, the court finds that the proof is evident or presumption great as to the present charge and:

(A) probable cause exists to believe that the defendant committed another felony during the period of release; or

(B) the defendant poses a substantial danger to another person or the community, and no other conditions of release will reasonably assure the safety of the other person or the community.

(e) Revocation of Release: DNA Testing. The State may file a motion asking the court to revoke a defendant's release for failing to comply with the court's order to provide a sample of buccal cells or other bodily substances for DNA testing under A.R.S. § 13-3967(F)(4) and to provide proof of compliance. The motion must state facts establishing probable cause to believe that the defendant has not complied with the order. At the defendant's next court appearance, the court must proceed in accordance with this rule's requirements and A.R.S. § 13-3967(F)(4).

(f) Revocation of Release: 10-print Fingerprinting. If a defendant fails to timely present a completed mandatory fingerprint compliance form or if the court has not received the process control number, the court may remand the defendant into custody for 10-print fingerprinting. If otherwise eligible for release, the defendant must be released from custody after being 10-print fingerprinted.

Credits

Added Aug. 31, 2017, effective Jan. 1, 2018.

Editors' Notes

HISTORICAL AND STATUTORY NOTES

Former Rule 7.5, relating to review of conditions and revocation of release, was abrogated effective Jan. 1, 2018. See, now, this rule.

16A A. R. S. Rules Crim. Proc., Rule 7.5, AZ ST RCRP Rule 7.5

Current with amendments received through 08/15/19

Rule 7.6. Transfer and Disposition of Bond

(Refs & Annos)

III. Rights of Parties

Rule 7. Release (Refs & Annos)

16A A.R.S. Rules Crim.Proc., Rule 7.6

Rule 7.6. Transfer and Disposition of Bond

(a) Transfer upon Supervening Indictment. An appearance bond or release order issued following the filing of a felony complaint in justice court will automatically be transferred to a criminal case in superior court after an indictment is filed that alleges the same charges.

(b) Filing and Custody of Appearance Bonds and Security. A defendant must file an appearance bond and security, if ordered, with the clerk of the court in which a case is pending or the court in which the initial appearance is held. If the case is transferred to another court, the transferring court must transfer any appearance bond and security.

(c) Forfeiture Procedure.

(1) *Arrest Warrant and Notice to Surety.* If the court is informed that the defendant has violated a condition of an appearance bond, it may issue a warrant for the defendant's arrest. No later than 10 days after the warrant's issuance, the court must notify the surety, in writing or electronically, that the warrant was issued.

(2) *Hearing and Notice.* After issuing the arrest warrant, the court must set a hearing within a reasonable time, no later than 120 days after it issued the warrant, requiring the parties and any surety to show cause why the bond should not be forfeited. The court must notify the parties and any surety of the hearing in writing or electronically. The forfeiture hearing may be combined with a Rule 7.5(d) hearing.

(3) *Forfeiture.* If the court finds that the violation is not excused, it may enter an order forfeiting all or part of the bond amount, and the State may enforce that order as a civil judgment. The order must comply with Arizona Rule of Civil Procedure 58(a).

(d) Exoneration.

(1) *Generally.* If the court finds before a violation that there is no further need for an appearance bond, it must exonerate the bond and order the return of any security.

(2) *Amount Returned.* When a deposit bond or cash bond is exonerated, the court must order the return of the entire amount deposited unless forfeited under Rule 7.6(c)(3) or the bond depositor authorizes it be applied to a financial obligation.

(3) *If the Defendant Is Surrendered, In-Custody, or Transferred.* The court must exonerate the bond if:

(A) the surety surrenders the defendant to the sheriff of the county in which the prosecution is pending, and:

(i) the surrender is on or before the day and time the defendant is ordered to appear in court; and

(ii) the sheriff informs the court of the defendant's surrender;

(B) the defendant is in the custody of the sheriff of the county in which the prosecution is pending on or before the day and time the defendant is ordered to appear in court under the following conditions:

(i) the surety provides the sheriff with an affidavit of surrender of the appearance bond; and

(ii) the sheriff reports the defendant is in custody and that the surety has provided an affidavit of surrender of the appearance bond; or

(C) before the defendant was released to the custody of the surety, the defendant was released or transferred to the custody of another government agency, preventing the defendant from appearing in court on the scheduled court date and the surety establishes:

(i) the surety did not know and could not have reasonably known of the release or transfer or that a release or transfer was likely to occur; and

(ii) the defendant's failure to appear was a direct result of the release or transfer.

(4) *Conditions When Not Required to Exonerate Bond.* The court is not required to exonerate the bond under (d)(2)(C) if a detainer was placed on the defendant before the bond was posted or the release or transfer to another government agency was for 24 hours or less.

(5) *Other Circumstances.* In all other instances, the decision whether or not to exonerate a bond is within the discretion of the court.

(6) *Post-Forfeiture Notice.* After filing an order of forfeiture, the court must provide:

(A) a copy of the order to the State, the defendant, the defendant's attorney, and the surety; and

(B) a copy of a signed order to the county attorney for collection.

Credits

Added Aug. 31, 2017, effective Jan. 1, 2018.

Editors' Notes

HISTORICAL AND STATUTORY NOTES

Former Rule 7.6, relating to transfer and disposition of bond, was abrogated effective Jan. 1, 2018. See, now, this rule.

16A A. R. S. Rules Crim. Proc., Rule 7.6, AZ ST RCRP Rule 7.6

Current with amendments received through 08/15/19

R. 8, Refs & Annos

III. Rights of Parties
Rule 8. Speedy Trial

16A A.R.S. Rules Crim.Proc., R. 8, Refs & Annos

16A A. R. S. Rules Crim. Proc., R. 8, Refs & Annos, AZ ST RCRP R. 8, Refs & Annos
Current with amendments received through 08/15/19

Rule 8.1. Priorities in Scheduling Criminal Cases

(Refs & Annos)
III. Rights of Parties
Rule 8. Speedy Trial (Refs & Annos)
16A A.R.S. Rules Crim.Proc., Rule 8.1

Rule 8.1. Priorities in Scheduling Criminal Cases

(a) Priority of Criminal Trials. A trial of a criminal case has priority over a trial of a civil case.

(b) Preferences. The trial of a defendant in custody, and the trial of a defendant whose pretrial liberty may present unusual risks, have preference over other criminal cases.

(c) Duty of the Prosecutor. The prosecutor must advise the court of facts relevant to the priority of cases for trial.

(d) Duty of Defense Counsel. Defense counsel must advise the court of an impending expiration of time limits. A court may sanction counsel for failing to do so, and should consider a failure to timely notify the court of an expiring time limit in determining whether to dismiss an action with prejudice under Rule 8.6.

(e) Suspension of Rule 8. No later than 25 days after a superior court arraignment, either party may move for a hearing to establish extraordinary circumstances requiring a suspension of Rule 8. No later than 5 days after the motion is filed, the court must hold a hearing on the motion and make findings of fact about whether extraordinary circumstances exist that justify the suspension of Rule 8. If the trial court finds that Rule 8 should be suspended, the court must immediately transmit its findings to the Supreme Court Chief Justice. If the Chief Justice approves the findings, the trial court may suspend Rule 8's provisions and reset the trial for a later specified date.

Credits

Added Aug. 31, 2017, effective Jan. 1, 2018.

Editors' Notes

HISTORICAL AND STATUTORY NOTES

Former Rule 8.1, relating to priorities in scheduling criminal cases, was abrogated effective Jan. 1, 2018. See, now, this rule.

Rule 8.2. Time Limits

(Refs & Annos)
III. Rights of Parties
Rule 8. Speedy Trial (Refs & Annos)
16A A.R.S. Rules Crim.Proc., Rule 8.2
Rule 8.2. Time Limits

(a) Generally. Subject to Rule 8.4, the court must try every defendant against whom an indictment, information, or complaint is filed within the following times:
(1) *Defendants in Custody.* No later than 150 days after arraignment if the defendant is in custody, except as provided in (a)(3).
(2) *Defendants out of Custody.* No later than 180 days after arraignment if the defendant is released under Rule 7, except as provided in (a)(3).
(3) *Defendants in Complex Cases.* No later than 270 days after arraignment if the defendant is charged with any of the following:
(A) first degree murder, except as provided in (a)(4);
(B) offenses that will require the court to consider evidence obtained as the result of an order permitting the interception of wire, electronic, or oral communication; or
(C) any case the court determines by written factual findings to be complex.
(4) *Capital Cases.* No later than 24 months after the date the State files a notice of intent to seek the death penalty under Rule 15.1(i).
(b) Waiver of Appearance at Arraignment. If a defendant waives an appearance at arraignment under Rule 14.3, the date of an arraignment held in the defendant's absence is deemed to be the arraignment date.
(c) New Trial. A trial ordered after a mistrial or the granting of a new trial must begin no later than 60 days after entry of the court's order. A trial ordered upon an appellate court's reversal of a judgment must begin no later than 90 days after the appellate court issues its mandate. A new trial ordered by a state court under Rule 32 or a federal court under collateral review must begin no later than 90 days after entry of the court's order.
(d) Extension of Time Limits. The court may extend the time limits in (a) and (c) under Rule 8.5.
(e) Specific Date for Trial. The superior court must set a specific trial date either at the arraignment or a pretrial conference, unless the court has suspended Rule 8.
Credits

Added Aug. 31, 2017, effective Jan. 1, 2018.

Editors' Notes
HISTORICAL AND STATUTORY NOTES
Former Rule 8.2, relating to time limits, was abrogated effective Jan. 1, 2018. See, now, this rule.
16A A. R. S. Rules Crim. Proc., Rule 8.2, AZ ST RCRP Rule 8.2
Current with amendments received through 08/15/19

Rule 8.3. Prisoner's Right to a Speedy Trial

(Refs & Annos)
III. Rights of Parties
Rule 8. Speedy Trial (Refs & Annos)
16A A.R.S. Rules Crim.Proc., Rule 8.3

Rule 8.3. Prisoner's Right to a Speedy Trial

(a) Prisoner in Another State. Within 90 days after receiving a written request from a person charged with a crime who is incarcerated in another state, or within a reasonable time after otherwise learning of the person's incarceration, the State must take action as required by law to obtain that person's presence for trial. The defendant must be brought to trial no later than 90 days after having been delivered into the custody of the appropriate authority of the State of Arizona.

(b) Prisoner in Arizona.

(1) *Request for Final Disposition.* A defendant imprisoned in Arizona may request the final disposition of any untried indictment, information, or complaint pending in Arizona. The request must be in writing, addressed to the court in which the case is filed, and to the responsible prosecuting agency. The request must state the defendant's place of imprisonment.

(2) *Detainer.* No later than 30 days after a detainer is filed against a defendant incarcerated in Arizona, the prosecuting agency that is prosecuting the charge that resulted in the detainer must inform the defendant about the detainer and about the defendant's right to request its final disposition under (b)(1).

(3) *Deadline for Acting on a Request.* The defendant must be brought to trial on the charge no later than 90 days after sending a request for final disposition to the court and prosecutor.

(4) *Escape from Custody.* A defendant's request for final disposition is void if the defendant later escapes from custody.

Credits
Added Aug. 31, 2017, effective Jan. 1, 2018.

Rule 8.4. Excluded Periods

(Refs & Annos)
III. Rights of Parties
Rule 8. Speedy Trial (Refs & Annos)
16A A.R.S. Rules Crim.Proc., Rule 8.4

Rule 8.4. Excluded Periods

(a) Generally. Delays caused or resulting from the following time periods are excluded from the time computations set forth in Rules 8.2 and 8.3:

(1) those caused by or on behalf of the defendant, whether or not intentional or willful, including, but not limited to, delays caused by an examination and hearing to determine competency or intellectual disability, the defendant's absence or incompetence, or the defendant's inability to be arrested or taken into custody in Arizona;

(2) a remand for a new probable cause determination under Rules 5.5 or 12.9;

(3) a time extension for disclosure under Rule 15.6;

(4) trial calendar congestion, but only if the congestion is due to extraordinary circumstances, in which case the presiding judge must promptly apply to the Supreme Court Chief Justice to suspend Rule 8 or any other Rule of Criminal Procedure;

(5) continuances granted under Rule 8.5;

(6) joinder for trial with another defendant for whom the time limits have not run, if good cause exists for denying severance, but in all other cases, severance should be granted to preserve the applicable time limits; and

(7) the setting of a transfer hearing under Rule 40.

(b) Excluding Time After a Finding of Competency or Restoration. If a court finds that a defendant is competent, has been restored to competency, or is no longer absent, and if the finding is made within 30 days of when the time limits in Rules 8.2 and 8.3 will otherwise expire, the court must exclude an additional 30 days in computing the time limits under those rules.
Credits

Added Aug. 31, 2017, effective Jan. 1, 2018.

Editors' Notes

HISTORICAL AND STATUTORY NOTES

Former Rule 8.4, relating to excluded periods, was abrogated effective Jan. 1, 2018. See, now, this rule.

16A A. R. S. Rules Crim. Proc., Rule 8.4, AZ ST RCRP Rule 8.4

Current with amendments received through 08/15/19

Rule 8.5. Continuing a Trial Date

(Refs & Annos)

III. Rights of Parties

Rule 8. Speedy Trial (Refs & Annos)

16A A.R.S. Rules Crim.Proc., Rule 8.5

Rule 8.5. Continuing a Trial Date

(a) Motion. A party may ask to continue trial by filing a motion stating the specific reasons for the request.

(b) Grounds. A court may continue trial only on a showing that extraordinary circumstances exist and that delay is indispensable to the interests of justice, and only for so long as is necessary to serve the interests of justice. The court must consider the rights of the defendant and any victim to a speedy disposition of the case. The court must state specific reasons for continuing trial.

Credits

Added Aug. 31, 2017, effective Jan. 1, 2018.

Editors' Notes

HISTORICAL AND STATUTORY NOTES

Former Rule 8.5, relating to continuances, was abrogated effective Jan. 1, 2018. See, now, this rule.

16A A. R. S. Rules Crim. Proc., Rule 8.5, AZ ST RCRP Rule 8.5

Current with amendments received through 08/15/19

Rule 8.6. Denial of Speedy Trial

(Refs & Annos)

III. Rights of Parties

Rule 8. Speedy Trial (Refs & Annos)

16A A.R.S. Rules Crim.Proc., Rule 8.6

Rule 8.6. Denial of Speedy Trial

If the court determines, after excluding any applicable time periods, that a time limit established by these rules has been violated, the court must dismiss the prosecution with or without prejudice.
Credits
Added Aug. 31, 2017, effective Jan. 1, 2018.
Editors' Notes
HISTORICAL AND STATUTORY NOTES
Former Rule 8.6, relating to denial of speedy trial, was abrogated effective Jan. 1, 2018. See, now, this rule.
16A A. R. S. Rules Crim. Proc., Rule 8.6, AZ ST RCRP Rule 8.6
Current with amendments received through 08/15/19

Rule 8.7. Accelerating Trial

(Refs & Annos)
III. Rights of Parties
Rule 8. Speedy Trial (Refs & Annos)
16A A.R.S. Rules Crim.Proc., Rule 8.7

Rule 8.7. Accelerating Trial

If there are special circumstances relating to the victim or other good cause, the court may accelerate the trial to the earliest possible date consistent with the defendant's right to a fair trial. The presiding judge may assign another judge to preside at trial to ensure that the trial begins on the scheduled date.
Credits
Added Aug. 31, 2017, effective Jan. 1, 2018.
Editors' Notes
HISTORICAL AND STATUTORY NOTES
Former Rule 8.7, relating to acceleration of trial, was abrogated effective Jan. 1, 2018. See, now, this rule.
16A A. R. S. Rules Crim. Proc., Rule 8.7, AZ ST RCRP Rule 8.7
Current with amendments received through 08/15/19

Rule 9.1. The Defendant's Waiver of the Right to Be Present

(Refs & Annos)

III. Rights of Parties
Rule 9. Presence of the Defendant, Witnesses, and Spectators
16A A.R.S. Rules Crim.Proc., Rule 9.1

Rule 9.1. The Defendant's Waiver of the Right to Be Present

Except for sentencing or as these rules otherwise provide, a defendant's voluntary absence waives the right to be present at any proceeding. The court may infer that a defendant's absence is voluntary if the defendant had actual notice of the date and time of the proceeding, notice of the right to be present, and notice that the proceeding would go forward in the defendant's absence.

Credits

Added Aug. 31, 2017, effective Jan. 1, 2018.

Editors' Notes

HISTORICAL AND STATUTORY NOTES

Former Rule 9.1, relating to defendant's waiver of right to be present, was abrogated effective Jan. 1, 2018. See, now, this rule.

16A A. R. S. Rules Crim. Proc., Rule 9.1, AZ ST RCRP Rule 9.1

Current with amendments received through 08/15/19

Rule 9.2. Defendant's Forfeiture of the Right to Be Present Due to Disruptive Conduct

(Refs & Annos)

III. Rights of Parties
Rule 9. Presence of the Defendant, Witnesses, and Spectators
16A A.R.S. Rules Crim.Proc., Rule 9.2

Rule 9.2. Defendant's Forfeiture of the Right to Be Present Due to Disruptive Conduct

(a) Generally. A defendant who engages in disruptive conduct, after being warned that such conduct will result in expulsion from a proceeding, forfeits the right to be present at that proceeding. At the time of expulsion, the court must inform the defendant that he or she can return upon a promise to the court of future orderly conduct.

(b) Continuing Duty to Permit Participation. After expulsion, the court must use every feasible means to allow the defendant to watch, hear, and be informed of the proceeding's progress, and to consult with counsel at reasonable intervals. The court should inquire periodically if the defendant wishes to reacquire the right to be present.

(c) Reacquiring the Right. The court must allow the defendant to return to the proceeding if the defendant personally assures the court of future good behavior. If the defendant later engages in disruptive conduct, the court may exclude the defendant from the proceeding without additional warning.

Credits

Added Aug. 31, 2017, effective Jan. 1, 2018.

Editors' Notes

HISTORICAL AND STATUTORY NOTES

Former Rule 9.2, relating to defendant's forfeiture of right to be present, was abrogated effective Jan. 1, 2018. See, now, this rule.

16A A. R. S. Rules Crim. Proc., Rule 9.2, AZ ST RCRP Rule 9.2

Current with amendments received through 08/15/19

Rule 9.3. Exclusion of Witnesses and Spectators

(Refs & Annos)

III. Rights of Parties

Rule 9. Presence of the Defendant, Witnesses, and Spectators

16A A.R.S. Rules Crim.Proc., Rule 9.3

Rule 9.3. Exclusion of Witnesses and Spectators

(a) Witnesses.

(1) *Generally.* The court may, and at the request of either party must, exclude prospective witnesses from the courtroom during opening statements and other witnesses' testimony. If the court finds that a party's claim that a person is a prospective witness is not made in good faith, it may not exclude the person.

(2) *Exceptions.*

(A) Victim. A victim has a right to be present at all proceedings at which the defendant has that right.

(B) Investigator. If the court enters an exclusion order, both the defendant and the State are nevertheless entitled to the presence of one investigator at counsel table.

(3) *Instruction.* As part of its exclusion order, the court must instruct the witnesses not to communicate with each other about the case until all of them have testified.

(4) *After Testifying.* Once a witness has testified on direct examination and has been made available to all parties for cross-examination, the court must allow the witness to remain in the courtroom, unless a party requests continued exclusion because the

witness may be recalled or the court finds that the witness's presence would be prejudicial to a fair trial.

(b) Spectators.

(1) *Generally.* All proceedings must be open to the public, including news media representatives, unless the court finds, on motion or on its own, that an open proceeding presents a clear and present danger to the defendant's right to a fair trial by an impartial jury.

(2) *Record.* The court must keep a complete record of any closed proceedings and make it available to the public following the trial's completion or, if no trial occurs, the final disposition of the case.

(c) Protection of a Witness. The court may exclude all spectators, except news media representatives, during a witness's testimony if the court finds it is reasonably necessary to protect the witness's safety or to protect the witness from embarrassment or emotional disturbance.

Credits

Added Aug. 31, 2017, effective Jan. 1, 2018.

Editors' Notes

HISTORICAL AND STATUTORY NOTES

Former Rule 9.3, relating to exclusion of witnesses and spectators, was abrogated effective Jan. 1, 2018. See, now, this rule.

16A A. R. S. Rules Crim. Proc., Rule 9.3, AZ ST RCRP Rule 9.3

Current with amendments received through 08/15/19

Rule 10.1. Change of Judge for Cause

(Refs & Annos)

III. Rights of Parties

Rule 10. Change of Judge or Place of Trial

16A A.R.S. Rules Crim.Proc., Rule 10.1

Rule 10.1. Change of Judge for Cause

(a) Grounds. A party is entitled to a change of judge if the party shows that the assigned judge's interest or prejudice would prevent a fair and impartial hearing or trial.

(b) Procedure.

(1) *Motion, Timing, and Form.* A party seeking a change of judge for cause must file a motion no later than 10 days after discovering that grounds exist, but may not file a motion after a hearing or trial begins. The motion must state specific grounds for the change of judge and be supported by an affidavit. Allegations of interest or

prejudice that prevent a fair and impartial hearing or trial that arise after commencement of the hearing or trial may be preserved for appeal by making an appropriate motion.

(2) *Further Action by Judge.* If a party files a timely motion for change of judge, the judge should not proceed, except to enter necessary temporary orders before the action can be transferred to the presiding judge or the presiding judge's designee. If the named judge is the presiding judge, that judge must assign the motion to another judge.

(c) Hearing, Disposition, and Effect on Other Defendants.

(1) *Hearing and Ruling.* Promptly after a party files a timely motion under this rule, the presiding judge must provide for a hearing on the motion before a judge other than the challenged judge. After holding the hearing, the hearing judge must decide the issues by a preponderance of the evidence and enter an order stating findings and ruling on the motion. The hearing judge will then return the matter to the presiding judge.

(2) *Assignment or Reassignment.* The presiding judge will promptly assign the action back to the original judge if the motion is denied, or will make a new assignment if the motion is granted.

(3) *Effect on Other Defendants.* If there are multiple defendants, the grant of a motion for change of judge filed by one or more defendants does not require a change of judge as to the other defendants, even though the change of judge may result in severance for trial purposes.

Credits

Added Aug. 31, 2017, effective Jan. 1, 2018.

Editors' Notes

HISTORICAL AND STATUTORY NOTES

Former Rule 10.1, relating to change of judge for cause, was abrogated effective Jan. 1, 2018. See, now, this rule.

16A A. R. S. Rules Crim. Proc., Rule 10.1, AZ ST RCRP Rule 10.1

Current with amendments received through 08/15/19

Rule 10.2. Change of Judge as a Matter of Right

(Refs & Annos)

III. Rights of Parties

Rule 10. Change of Judge or Place of Trial

16A A.R.S. Rules Crim.Proc., Rule 10.2

Formerly cited as AZ ST RCRP Rule 10.4

Rule 10.2. Change of Judge as a Matter of Right

(a) Entitlement.

(1) *Generally.* Each side in a criminal case is entitled to one change of judge as a matter of right. If two or more parties on a side have adverse or hostile interests, the presiding judge or that judge's designee may allow additional changes of judge as a matter of right.

(2) *Meaning of "Side."* Each case, including one that is consolidated, is treated as having only two sides.

(3) *Per Party Limit.* A party exercising a change of judge as a matter of right is not entitled to another change of judge as a matter of right.

(4) *Inapplicability to Certain Proceedings.* A party is not entitled to a change of judge as a matter of right in a proceeding under Rule 32 or a remand for resentencing.

(b) Procedure.

(1) *Generally.* A party may exercise a right to change of judge by filing a "Notice of Change of Judge" signed by counsel or a self-represented defendant, and stating the name of the judge to be changed. The notice also must include an avowal that the party is making the request in good faith and not for an improper purpose. An attorney's avowal is in the attorney's capacity as an officer of the court.

(2) *"Improper Purpose."* "Improper purpose" means:

(A) for the purpose of delay;

(B) to obtain a severance;

(C) to interfere with the judge's reasonable case management practices;

(D) to remove a judge for reasons of race, gender or religious affiliation;

(E) for the purpose of using the rule against a particular judge in a blanket fashion by a prosecuting agency, defender group, or law firm;

(F) to obtain a more convenient geographical location; or

(G) to obtain an advantage or avoid a disadvantage in connection with a plea bargain or at sentencing, except as permitted under Rule 17.4(g).

(3) *Further Action by the Judge.* If a notice of change of judge is timely filed, the judge should proceed no further in the action, except to enter any necessary temporary orders before the action can be transferred to the presiding judge or the presiding judge's designee. If the named judge is the presiding judge, that judge may continue to perform the functions of the presiding judge.

(c) Timing.

(1) *Generally.* Except as provided in (c)(2), or extended by local rule, a party must file a notice of change of judge no later than 10 days after any of the following:

(A) the arraignment, if the case is assigned to a judge and the parties are given actual notice of the assignment at or before the arraignment;

(B) the superior court clerk's filing of a mandate issued by an appellate court; or

(C) in all other cases, actual notice to the requesting party of the assignment of the case to a judge.

(2) *Exception.* Despite (c)(1), if a new judge is assigned to a case less than 10 days before trial (inclusive of the date of assignment), a notice of change of judge must be filed, with appropriate actual notice to the other party or parties, no later than by 5:00 p.m. on the next business day following actual receipt of a notice of the assignment or by the start of trial, whichever occurs earlier.

(d) Assignment to a New Judge and Effect on Other Defendants.

(1) *On Stipulation.* If a notice of change of judge is timely filed, the notice may inform the court that all the parties have agreed on a judge who is available and willing to accept the assignment. Such an agreement may be honored and, if so, it bars further changes of judge as a matter of right, unless the agreed-on judge later becomes unavailable. If a judge to whom the action has been assigned by agreement later becomes unavailable because of a change of calendar assignment, death, illness, or other legal incapacity, the parties may assert any rights under this rule that existed immediately before the assignment of the action to that judge.

(2) *Absent Stipulation.* If a timely notice of judge has been filed and no judge has been agreed on, the presiding judge must immediately reassign the action to another judge.

(3) *Effect on Other Defendants.* If there are multiple defendants, a notice of change of judge filed by one or more defendants does not require a change of judge as to the other defendants, even though the notice of change of judge may result in severance for trial purposes.

(e) Waiver. A party loses the right to a change of judge under this rule if the party participates before that judge in any contested matter in the case, a proceeding under Rule 17, or the beginning of trial.

(f) Following Remand. Unless previously exercised, a party may exercise a change of judge as a matter of right following an appellate court's remand for new trial, and no event connected with the first trial constitutes a waiver. A party may not exercise a change of judge as a matter of right following a remand for resentencing.

Credits

Added Aug. 31, 2017, effective Jan. 1, 2018.

Editors' Notes

HISTORICAL AND STATUTORY NOTES

Former Rule 10.2, relating to change of judge upon request, was abrogated effective Jan. 1, 2018. See, now, this rule.

16A A. R. S. Rules Crim. Proc., Rule 10.2, AZ ST RCRP Rule 10.2

Current with amendments received through 08/15/19

Rule 10.3. Changing the Place of Trial

16A A.R.S. Rules Crim.Proc., Rule 10.3

Rule 10.3. Changing the Place of Trial

(a) Grounds. A party is entitled to change the place of trial to another county if the party shows that the party cannot have a fair and impartial trial in that place for any reason other than the trial judge's interest or prejudice.

(b) Prejudicial Pretrial Publicity. If the grounds to change the place of trial are based on pretrial publicity, the moving party must prove that the dissemination of the prejudicial material probably will result in the party being deprived of a fair trial.

(c) Procedure. A party seeking to change the place of trial must file a motion seeking that relief. The motion must be filed before trial, and, in superior court, at or before a pretrial conference.

(d) Waiver. A party loses the right to change the place of trial if the party allows a proceeding to begin or continue without raising a timely objection after learning of the cause for challenge.

(e) Renewal on Remand. If an appellate court remands an action for a new trial on one or more offenses charged in an indictment or information, all parties' rights to change the place of trial are renewed, and no event connected with the first trial constitutes a waiver.

Credits

Added Aug. 31, 2017, effective Jan. 1, 2018.

Editors' Notes

HISTORICAL AND STATUTORY NOTES

Former Rule 10.3, relating to change of the place of trial, was abrogated effective Jan. 1, 2018. See, now, this rule.

16A A. R. S. Rules Crim. Proc., Rule 10.3, AZ ST RCRP Rule 10.3

Current with amendments received through 08/15/19

Rule 10.4. Transfer to Another County

16A A.R.S. Rules Crim.Proc., Rule 10.4

Formerly cited as AZ ST RCRP Rule 10.5
Rule 10.4. Transfer to Another County

If the court transfers a case to another county, the clerk in the transferring county must transmit to the clerk in the receiving county the court file, any evidence in the clerk's custody, and any appearance bond or security. If the defendant is in custody, the sheriff in the transferring county must transport the defendant to the sheriff of the receiving county.

The action will retain the case number and geographic designation of the matter while it was in the transferring county.

Credits

Added Aug. 31, 2017, effective Jan. 1, 2018.

Editors' Notes

HISTORICAL AND STATUTORY NOTES

Former Rule 10.4, relating to waiver and renewal, was abrogated effective Jan. 1, 2018. See, now, AZ ST RCRP Rule 10.2.

16A A. R. S. Rules Crim. Proc., Rule 10.4, AZ ST RCRP Rule 10.4

Current with amendments received through 08/15/19

Rule 10.5. Abrogated Aug. 31, 2017, effective Jan. 1, 2018

(Refs & Annos)

III. Rights of Parties

Rule 10. Change of Judge or Place of Trial

16A A.R.S. Rules Crim.Proc., Rule 10.5

Rule 10.5. Abrogated Aug. 31, 2017, effective Jan. 1, 2018

Editors' Notes

HISTORICAL AND STATUTORY NOTES

The abrogated rule related to transfer to another judge or county. See, now, AZ ST RCRP Rule 10.4.

16A A. R. S. Rules Crim. Proc., Rule 10.5, AZ ST RCRP Rule 10.5

Current with amendments received through 08/15/19

Rule 10.6. Abrogated Aug. 31, 2017, effective Jan. 1, 2018

(Refs & Annos)

III. Rights of Parties

Rule 10. Change of Judge or Place of Trial
16A A.R.S. Rules Crim.Proc., Rule 10.6

Rule 10.6. Abrogated Aug. 31, 2017, effective Jan. 1, 2018

Editors' Notes
HISTORICAL AND STATUTORY NOTES
The abrogated rule related to duty of judge upon filing of motion or request under Rules 10.1 or 10.2.
16A A. R. S. Rules Crim. Proc., Rule 10.6, AZ ST RCRP Rule 10.6
Current with amendments received through 08/15/19

R. 11, Refs & Annos

III. Rights of Parties
Rule 11. Incompetence and Mental Examinations
16A A.R.S. Rules Crim.Proc., R. 11, Refs & Annos

16A A. R. S. Rules Crim. Proc., R. 11, Refs & Annos, AZ ST RCRP R. 11, Refs & Annos
Current with amendments received through 08/15/19

Rule 11.1. Definitions, Effect of Incompetence, and Right to Counsel

(Refs & Annos)
III. Rights of Parties
Rule 11. Incompetence and Mental Examinations (Refs & Annos)
16A A.R.S. Rules Crim.Proc., Rule 11.1

Rule 11.1. Definitions, Effect of Incompetence, and Right to Counsel

(a) Definitions.
(1) *Mental Illness, Defect, or Disability.* "Mental illness, defect, or disability" means a psychiatric or neurological disorder that is evidenced by behavioral or emotional symptoms, including congenital mental conditions, conditions resulting from injury or disease, and developmental disabilities as defined in A.R.S. § 36-551.
(2) *Incompetence.* "Incompetence" means a defendant is unable to understand the nature and objective of the proceedings or to assist in his or her defense because of a mental illness, defect, or disability.

(b) Effect of Incompetence. A defendant may not be tried, convicted, or sentenced while that defendant is incompetent. A defendant is not incompetent to stand trial merely because the defendant has a mental illness, defect, or disability. This rule does not bar a court from proceeding under A.R.S. § 36-3707(D).

(c) Right to Counsel. During proceedings under this rule, a defendant is entitled to representation by counsel as provided in Rule 6.

Credits

Added Aug. 31, 2017, effective Jan. 1, 2018.

Editors' Notes

HISTORICAL AND STATUTORY NOTES

Former Rule 11.1, relating to definition and effect of incompetency, was abrogated effective Jan. 1, 2018. See, now, this rule.

16A A. R. S. Rules Crim. Proc., Rule 11.1, AZ ST RCRP Rule 11.1

Current with amendments received through 08/15/19

Rule 11.2. Motion for an Examination of a Defendant's Competence to Stand Trial

(Refs & Annos)

III. Rights of Parties

Rule 11. Incompetence and Mental Examinations (Refs & Annos)

16A A.R.S. Rules Crim.Proc., Rule 11.2

Rule 11.2. Motion for an Examination of a Defendant's Competence to Stand Trial

(a) Motion and Order for Examination.

(1) *Generally.* At any time after an information is filed or an indictment is returned in superior court or a misdemeanor complaint is filed, the court may, on motion or on its own, order a defendant's examination to determine whether the defendant is competent to stand trial.

(2) *Motion to Determine Competence.* The moving party or the court must state facts for the requested mental examination.

(3) *Parties Authorized to Move for Competence Determination.* Any party, including a co-defendant, may move for a competence evaluation.

(4) *Proposed Examiners.* A party's motion may include a list of 3 mental health experts qualified under Rule 11.3 to conduct the examination. Any other party may include such a list in its response to the motion.

(b) Medical and Criminal History Records. No later than 3 days after the appointment of experts, the parties must provide the examining mental health experts with all of the defendant's available medical and criminal history records.

(c) Preliminary Examination. A court may order the defendant to undergo a preliminary examination to assist the court in determining if reasonable grounds exist to order the defendant's further examination.

(d) Jurisdiction.

(1) *Superior Court.* The superior court has exclusive jurisdiction over all competence hearings except as provided in (d)(2). If a limited jurisdiction court determines that reasonable grounds exist for further competence hearings, it must immediately transfer the matter to the superior court for the appointment of mental health experts.

(2) *Limited Jurisdiction Court.* If the matter of a defendant's competence arises in a misdemeanor case in a limited jurisdiction court, a limited jurisdiction court judge may hear the matter if the presiding superior court judge has issued an administrative order authorizing the limited jurisdiction court to do so.

(e) If Defendant Is Competent. If any court determines that a defendant is either competent or restored to competence, regular proceedings must proceed without delay.

(f) Dismissal of Misdemeanor Charges. If the court finds that a person has been previously adjudicated incompetent to stand trial under this rule, the court may hold a hearing to dismiss any misdemeanor charge against the incompetent person under A.R.S. § 13-4504.

Credits

Added Aug. 31, 2017, effective Jan. 1, 2018.

Editors' Notes

HISTORICAL AND STATUTORY NOTES

Former Rule 11.2, relating to motion to have defendant's mental condition examined, was abrogated effective Jan. 1, 2018. See, now, this rule.

16A A. R. S. Rules Crim. Proc., Rule 11.2, AZ ST RCRP Rule 11.2

Current with amendments received through 08/15/19

Rule 11.3. Appointment of Experts

(Refs & Annos)

III. Rights of Parties

Rule 11. Incompetence and Mental Examinations (Refs & Annos)

16A A.R.S. Rules Crim.Proc., Rule 11.3

Rule 11.3. Appointment of Experts

(a) Appointment of Experts.

(1) *Definition of a "Mental Health Expert."* "Mental health expert" means a physician licensed under A.R.S. §§ 32-1421 to -1437 or 32-1721 to -1730; or a psychologist licensed under A.R.S. §§ 32-2071 to--2076.

(2) *Generally.* If the court finds that reasonable grounds exist for a competence examination, it must appoint two or more qualified mental health experts to:

(A) examine the defendant;

(B) report to the court in writing no later than 10 business days after examining the defendant; and

(C) testify, if necessary, about the defendant's competence.

(3) *Psychiatry Background.* A party may request or the court may order that at least one of the mental health experts be a physician specializing in psychiatry.

(4) *Stipulation for Only One Examiner.* With the court's approval, the State and the defendant may stipulate to the appointment of only one expert.

(5) *Examiner Qualifications.* A mental health expert must be:

(A) familiar with Arizona's standards and statutes for competence and criminal and involuntary commitment statutes;

(B) familiar with the treatment, training, and restoration programs that are available in Arizona; and

(C) approved by the court as meeting court-developed guidelines, including demonstrated experience in forensics matters, required attendance at a court-approved training program of not less than 16 hours and any court-required continuing forensic education programs, and annual review criteria.

(6) *Replacement.* If the appointed expert is unable to examine the defendant within the time allotted, the expert must immediately inform the court, and the court may appoint a different expert to perform the examination.

(b) Custody Status of the Defendant During Competence Proceedings. Pending the court's determination of competence, the court must determine the defendant's custody status under A.R.S. § 13-4507.

(c) Expert Report. An expert's report must conform to A.R.S. § 13-4509.

(d) Additional Expert Assistance. If necessary for an adequate determination of the defendant's mental competence, the court may appoint additional experts and order the defendant to submit to additional physical, neurological, or psychological examinations.

Credits

Added Aug. 31, 2017, effective Jan. 1, 2018.

Editors' Notes

HISTORICAL AND STATUTORY NOTES

Former Rule 11.3, relating to appointment of experts, was abrogated effective Jan. 1, 2018. See, now, this rule.

16A A. R. S. Rules Crim. Proc., Rule 11.3, AZ ST RCRP Rule 11.3

Rule 11.4. Disclosure of Experts' Reports

(Refs & Annos)
III. Rights of Parties
Rule 11. Incompetence and Mental Examinations (Refs & Annos)
16A A.R.S. Rules Crim.Proc., Rule 11.4

Rule 11.4. Disclosure of Experts' Reports

(a) Reports of Appointed Experts Under Rule 11.3.

(1) *Deadline.* An expert appointed under Rule 11.3, or under A.R.S. § 13-4517, must submit a report to the court no later than 10 business days after the expert's examination is completed. The expert must inform the court if the report cannot be made available at least 7 days before the scheduled hearing.

(2) *Availability.* An expert's report completed under Rule 11.3 must be made available to the examined defendant and the State, except that any statement by the defendant about the charged offense or any other charged or uncharged offense (or any summary of such a statement) may be made available only to the defendant. Upon receipt, court staff will copy and provide the expert's report to the court and defense counsel. Defense counsel is responsible for editing a copy of the report for the State. Defense counsel must provide the edited report to court staff to be made available to the State no later than 3 days after receiving the unedited report.

(b) Reports of Other Experts. For any other mental health expert who has personally examined the defendant or any evidence in connection with the case to determine competence or the defendant's mental status at the time of the offense, the defendant and the State must disclose to each other at least 15 business days before any Rule 11.5 hearing:

(1) the expert's name and address;

(2) the results of any mental examinations, scientific tests, experiments, or comparisons conducted on the defendant or on any evidence in the case by or on the behalf of the mental health expert; and

(3) any written report or statement in connection with the case.

Credits

Added Aug. 31, 2017, effective Jan. 1, 2018. Amended Dec. 13, 2017, effective April 2, 2018.

Editors' Notes

HISTORICAL AND STATUTORY NOTES

Former Rule 11.4, relating to disclosure of mental health evidence, was abrogated effective Jan. 1, 2018. See, now, this rule.

16A A. R. S. Rules Crim. Proc., Rule 11.4, AZ ST RCRP Rule 11.4

Current with amendments received through 08/15/19

Rule 11.5. Hearing and Orders

(Refs & Annos)
III. Rights of Parties
Rule 11. Incompetence and Mental Examinations (Refs & Annos)
16A A.R.S. Rules Crim.Proc., Rule 11.5

Rule 11.5. Hearing and Orders

(a) Hearing. No later than 30 days after the experts appointed under Rule 11.3 submit their reports to the court, the court must hold a hearing to determine the defendant's competence. The court may grant additional time for good cause. The defendant and the State may introduce other evidence about the defendant's mental condition. If the defendant and the State stipulate in writing or on the record, the court may determine competence based solely on the experts' reports.

(b) Orders.

(1) *If Competent.* If the court finds that the defendant is competent, the court must direct that proceedings continue without delay.

(2) *If Incompetent but Restorable.*

(A) Superior Court. If a superior court determines that the defendant is incompetent, it must either dismiss the charges on the State's motion or order competency restoration treatment, unless there is clear and convincing evidence that the defendant will not regain competence within 15 months.

(B) Limited Jurisdiction Court. If a limited jurisdiction court determines that the defendant is incompetent, it must dismiss the charges on the State's motion, transfer the case to the superior court for further proceedings pursuant to A.R.S. § 13-4517, or, if authorized by the presiding judge of the superior court, order competency restoration treatment, unless there is clear and convincing evidence that the defendant will not regain competence within the time period provided for the maximum possible sentence as defined in A.R.S. § 13-4515.

(C) Extended Treatment. The court may extend treatment if it finds that the defendant is progressing toward competence. The extension may be 6 months beyond the 15-month limit so long as this period does not exceed the defendant's maximum possible sentence as defined in A.R.S. § 13-4515.

(D) Involuntary Treatment. The court must determine whether the defendant will be subject to treatment without consent.

(E) Treatment Order. A treatment order must specify:

(i) the place where treatment will occur;

(ii) whether the treatment is inpatient or outpatient under A.R.S. § 13-4512(A);

(iii) the means of transportation to the treatment site;

(iv) the length of treatment;

(v) the means of transporting the defendant after treatment; and

(vi) that the court is to be notified if the defendant regains competence before the expiration of the treatment order.

(F) Modification and Limitation. The court may modify a treatment order at any time. Treatment orders are effective for no longer than 6 months.

(3) *If Incompetent and Not Restorable.*

(A) Superior Court. If the superior court determines that the defendant is incompetent and that there is no substantial probability that the defendant will become competent within 21 months or within the defendant's maximum possible sentence as defined by A.R.S. § 13-4515, whichever is less, the court may on request of the examined defendant or the State do one or more of the following:

(i) Remand the defendant to an evaluating agency approved and licensed under Title 36 to begin civil commitment proceedings under A.R.S. §§ 36-501 et seq.;

(ii) Order appointment of a guardian under A.R.S. §§ 14-5301 et seq.;

(iii) Release the defendant from custody and dismiss the charges without prejudice; or

(iv) Retain jurisdiction and enter further orders as specified in A.R.S. §§ 13-4517 and 13-4518.

(B) Limited Jurisdiction Court. If a limited jurisdiction court determines that the defendant is incompetent and that there is no substantial probability that the defendant will become competent within the timeframes as defined in A.R.S. § 13-4515, the court must do one of the following:

(i) Dismiss the action on the State's motion; or

(ii) Transfer the case to the superior court for further proceedings pursuant to A.R.S. § 13-4517.

(4) *Additional Actions.* If the court enters an order under (b)(3)(A)(i) or (ii), it may retain jurisdiction and enter further orders as specified in A.R.S. §§ 13-4517 and 13-4518.

(c) Restoration to Competency: Reports About Treatment.

(1) *Generally.* The court must order the treatment supervisor to submit a report to the court and to provide copies to defense counsel and the clinical liaison. Defense counsel may redact the report under Rule 11.4(a)(2) before returning it to the court to be provided to the State.

(2) *When to Report.* The treatment supervisor must submit a report:

(A) for inpatient treatment, 120 days after the filing of the court's original treatment order and then every 180 days after the first report;

(B) for outpatient treatment, every 60 days following the filing of the court's original treatment order;

(C) when the treatment supervisor believes the defendant is competent to stand trial;

(D) when the treatment supervisor concludes that the defendant will not be restored to competence within 21 months of the court's finding of incompetence; and

(E) 14 days before the expiration of the court's last treatment order.

(3) *Content of Report.*

(A) Generally. The treatment supervisor's report must include at least the following:

(i) the treatment supervisor's name;

(ii) a description of the nature, content, extent, and results of the supervisor's examination of the defendant and any tests the supervisor conducted;

(iii) the facts on which the treatment supervisor's findings are based; and

(iv) the treatment supervisor's opinion regarding the defendant's competence to understand the nature of the court proceedings against the defendant and to assist in his or her defense.

(B) If Still Incompetent. If the treatment supervisor finds the defendant is still incompetent, the report also must include:

(i) the nature of the mental illness, defect, or disability that is the cause of the incompetence;

(ii) a prognosis regarding the defendant's restoration to competence and an estimate of how long it will take to restore the defendant's competence; and

(iii) any recommendations for treatment modifications.

(C) If Competent. If the treatment supervisor finds the defendant has regained competence, the report also must include any limitations on the defendant's competence caused by medications used in the defendant's treatment.

(d) Time Calculation. When calculating time limits under A.R.S. § 13-4515(A), the court must consider only the time a defendant actually spends in a program to restore competence.

Credits

Added Aug. 31, 2017, effective Jan. 1, 2018. Amended Dec. 13, 2017, effective April 2, 2018; Aug. 28, 2018, effective Jan. 1, 2019.

Editors' Notes

COMMENT

The court should hold review hearings every two to three months to monitor a defendant's treatment status and progress.

HISTORICAL AND STATUTORY NOTES

Former Rule 11.5, relating to hearing and orders, was abrogated effective Jan. 1, 2018. See, now, this rule.

16A A. R. S. Rules Crim. Proc., Rule 11.5, AZ ST RCRP Rule 11.5

Current with amendments received through 08/15/19

Rule 11.6. Later Hearings

(Refs & Annos)
III. Rights of Parties
Rule 11. Incompetence and Mental Examinations (Refs & Annos)
16A A.R.S. Rules Crim.Proc., Rule 11.6

Rule 11.6. Later Hearings

(a) Grounds. The court must hold an additional hearing to determine the defendant's competence:

(1) upon receiving a report from an authorized official of the institution in which a defendant is treated under Rule 11.5(b)(2) or (b)(3)(A) stating that, in the official's opinion, the defendant has become competent to stand trial;

(2) upon a defendant's motion supported by the certificate of a mental health expert stating that, in the expert's opinion, the defendant is competent to stand trial;

(3) at the expiration of the maximum period set by the court under Rule 11.5(b)(2); or

(4) if the court determines that it is appropriate to do so.

(b) Experts. The court may appoint new mental health experts under Rule 11.3.

(c) Finding of Competence. If the court finds that the defendant is competent, regular proceedings must begin again without delay. The defendant is entitled to repeat any proceeding if there are reasonable grounds to believe the defendant was prejudiced by previous incompetence.

(d) Finding of Continuing Incompetence. If the court finds that the defendant is still incompetent, it must proceed in accordance with Rules 11.5(b)(2) or (3). If the court determines that there is a substantial probability that the defendant will regain competence in the foreseeable future, then the court may renew and may modify the treatment order for no more than an additional 180 days or the time period provided for the defendant's maximum possible sentence by A.R.S. § 13-4515, whichever is less.

(e) Dismissal of Charges. At any time after providing notice and a hearing under A.R.S. § 13-4515(C), the court may order the dismissal of the charges against a defendant adjudged incompetent. The defendant must be released from custody

upon dismissal of the charges unless the court finds that the defendant's mental condition warrants a civil commitment hearing under A.R.S. §§ 36-501 et seq.
Credits
Added Aug. 31, 2017, effective Jan. 1, 2018. Amended Aug. 28, 2018, effective Jan. 1, 2019.
Editors' Notes
HISTORICAL AND STATUTORY NOTES
Former Rule 11.6, relating to subsequent hearings, was abrogated effective Jan. 1, 2018. See, now, this rule.
16A A. R. S. Rules Crim. Proc., Rule 11.6, AZ ST RCRP Rule 11.6
Current with amendments received through 08/15/19

Rule 11.7. Privilege and Confidentiality

(Refs & Annos)
III. Rights of Parties
Rule 11. Incompetence and Mental Examinations (Refs & Annos)
16A A.R.S. Rules Crim.Proc., Rule 11.7
Formerly cited as AZ ST RCRP Rule 11.8

Rule 11.7. Privilege and Confidentiality

(a) Generally. Evidence obtained under Rule 11 is not admissible in a proceeding to determine guilt, unless the defendant presents evidence, either directly or through cross-examination, intended to rebut the presumption of sanity.
(b) Privileged Statements of the Defendant.
(1) *Concerning the Charged Offense.* Unless the defendant consents or the exception in (a) applies, no statement of a defendant obtained under Rule 11, or evidence resulting from such a statement, concerning the factual basis for the charged offense is admissible at the defendant's trial, or at any later proceeding to determine guilt.
(2) *Concerning Other Events or Transactions.* Unless the defendant consents or the exception in (a) applies, no statement of a defendant obtained under Rule 11, or evidence resulting from such a statement, concerning any other event or transaction is admissible at any later proceeding to determine the defendant's guilt.
(3) *In Title 36 Proceedings.* Notwithstanding (b)(1) and (b)(2), a statement of the defendant obtained in a Rule 11 matter, or evidence resulting from that statement, may be used by any party in a hearing to determine whether the defendant is eligible for court-ordered treatment under A.R.S. §§ 36-501 et seq., or is a sexually violent person.
(c) Confidentiality of Reports.

(1) *Generally.* The court and counsel must treat reports of Rule 11 experts as confidential in all respects. They may, however, disclose other expert reports to mental health experts in proceedings related to A.R.S. §§ 13-4501 et seq., § 13-4518, and §§ 36-501 et seq., or as otherwise excluded in A.R.S. §§ 13-4508 and 13-4516.

(2) *Sealing.* After the defendant is found competent or unable to regain competence, the court must order the mental health experts' reports sealed. By later order, the court may grant access to a report, but only for further competence or sanity evaluations, statistical study, the examined defendant's mitigation investigation, or if necessary to assist in mental health treatment for restoration of competence or under A.R.S. § 13-502.

Credits

Added Aug. 31, 2017, effective Jan. 1, 2018. Amended Dec. 13, 2017, effective April 2, 2018.

Editors' Notes

HISTORICAL AND STATUTORY NOTES

Former Rule 11.7, relating to privilege, was abrogated effective Jan. 1, 2018. See, now, this rule.

16A A. R. S. Rules Crim. Proc., Rule 11.7, AZ ST RCRP Rule 11.7

Current with amendments received through 08/15/19

Rule 11.8. Examination of a Defendant's Mental Status at the Time of the Offense

(Refs & Annos)

III. Rights of Parties

Rule 11. Incompetence and Mental Examinations (Refs & Annos)

16A A.R.S. Rules Crim.Proc., Rule 11.8

Rule 11.8. Examination of a Defendant's Mental Status at the Time of the Offense

(a) Applicability. At any time after an information is filed or an indictment is returned in superior court or a misdemeanor complaint is filed, an examination under this rule may be requested separately from, or in addition to, an examination under Rule 11.2.

(b) Screening Report. On its own or on motion of the defendant or the State with the defendant's consent, the court may order an initial screening report to preliminarily investigate the defendant's mental status at the time of the offense.

(c) If the Guilty Except Insane Defense Is Raised. If the defendant raises a defense under A.R.S. § 13-502 and a reasonable basis exists to support the defense, the court may, on its own or on motion of the defendant or the State, order that an appointed mental health expert provide a screening report. Either the screening report under (b) or the examination under (c) must include the following:

(1) the defendant's mental status at the time of the offense; and

(2) if the expert determines that the defendant suffered from a mental disease, defect, or disability at the time of the offense, the relationship of the disease, defect, or disability to the alleged offense.

(d) Required Records. No later than 3 days after the appointment of experts, the parties must provide the examining mental health expert with all of the defendant's available medical and criminal history records. No later than 10 business days after the expert's appointment, the parties must provide the appointed expert with any additional medical or criminal history records requested by the court or the appointed expert.

Credits

Added Aug. 31, 2017, effective Jan. 1, 2018.

Editors' Notes

HISTORICAL AND STATUTORY NOTES

Former Rule 11.8, relating to records, was abrogated effective Jan. 1, 2018. See, now, AZ ST RCRP Rule 11.7.

16A A. R. S. Rules Crim. Proc., Rule 11.8, AZ ST RCRP Rule 11.8

Current with amendments received through 08/15/19

Rule 11.9. Capital Cases

(Refs & Annos)

III. Rights of Parties

Rule 11. Incompetence and Mental Examinations (Refs & Annos)

16A A.R.S. Rules Crim.Proc., Rule 11.9

Rule 11.9. Capital Cases

Unless the defendant objects, the court in a capital case must order the defendant to undergo one or more mental health examinations required under A.R.S. §§ 13-753 and 13-754.

Credits

Added Aug. 31, 2017, effective Jan. 1, 2018.

16A A. R. S. Rules Crim. Proc., Rule 11.9, AZ ST RCRP Rule 11.9

Current with amendments received through 08/15/19

R. 12, Refs & Annos

IV. Pretrial Procedures
Rule 12. The Grand Jury
16A A.R.S. Rules Crim.Proc., R. 12, Refs & Annos

16A A. R. S. Rules Crim. Proc., R. 12, Refs & Annos, AZ ST RCRP R. 12, Refs & Annos

Current with amendments received through 08/15/19

Rule 12.1. Selecting and Preparing Grand Jurors

(Refs & Annos)
IV. Pretrial Procedures
Rule 12. The Grand Jury (Refs & Annos)
Section One. Rules for Grand Juries
16A A.R.S. Rules Crim.Proc., Rule 12.1

Rule 12.1. Selecting and Preparing Grand Jurors

(a) Summons. Grand jurors are summoned and impaneled as provided by law.

(b) Voir Dire. Each prospective grand juror must be examined under oath or affirmation to confirm that the prospective juror will act impartially and without prejudice, and that the prospective juror is qualified under A.R.S. § 21-201. Inquiry also may be made about other relevant subjects.

(c) Oath. Each grand juror must take the following oath: "I swear (or affirm) that I will give careful attention to the proceedings, abide by the court's instructions, and decide matters placed before the grand jury in accordance with the law and evidence presented to me (so help me God)."

(d) Instructions. The court must inform the grand jurors of:

(1) the duty to be present at each grand jury session;

(2) the duty to inquire into every offense that is presented;

(3) the duty of a grand juror to disqualify himself or herself in a particular matter for any of the reasons listed in Rule 12.2;

(4) the duty to return an indictment only if they are convinced there is probable cause to believe an offense has been committed and the person under investigation committed it;

(5) the right to ask the State to present additional evidence; and

(6) the confidentiality of grand jury matters and materials, and the penalties for unlawful disclosure.

Credits

Added Aug. 31, 2017, effective Jan. 1, 2018.

Editors' Notes

HISTORICAL AND STATUTORY NOTES

Former Rule 12.1, relating to selection and preparation of grand jurors, was abrogated effective Jan. 1, 2018. See, now, this rule.

16A A. R. S. Rules Crim. Proc., Rule 12.1, AZ ST RCRP Rule 12.1

Current with amendments received through 08/15/19

Rule 12.2. Grounds to Disqualify a Grand Juror

(Refs & Annos)

IV. Pretrial Procedures

Rule 12. The Grand Jury (Refs & Annos)

Section One. Rules for Grand Juries

16A A.R.S. Rules Crim.Proc., Rule 12.2

Rule 12.2. Grounds to Disqualify a Grand Juror

A grand juror is disqualified from serving in any particular matter if the juror is:

(a) a witness in the matter;

(b) interested directly or indirectly in the matter under investigation;

(c) related within the fourth degree by either consanguinity or affinity to a person under investigation, a victim, or a witness; or

(d) biased or prejudiced in favor of either the State or a person under investigation.

Credits

Added Aug. 31, 2017, effective Jan. 1, 2018.

Editors' Notes

HISTORICAL AND STATUTORY NOTES

Former Rule 12.2, relating to grounds for disqualification, was abrogated effective Jan. 1, 2018. See, now, this rule.

16A A. R. S. Rules Crim. Proc., Rule 12.2, AZ ST RCRP Rule 12.2

Current with amendments received through 08/15/19

Rule 12.3. Grand Jury Foreperson

(Refs & Annos)

IV. Pretrial Procedures

Rule 12. The Grand Jury (Refs & Annos)
Section One. Rules for Grand Juries

16A A.R.S. Rules Crim.Proc., Rule 12.3

Formerly cited as AZ ST RCRP Rule 12.4

Rule 12.3. Grand Jury Foreperson

(a) Appointment and Powers. The court must appoint a foreperson and an acting foreperson to serve in the foreperson's absence. The foreperson will preside over the grand jury's proceedings and act as the court's representative in maintaining order, administering oaths, excluding unauthorized persons and persons acting in an unauthorized manner, appointing officers within the grand jury as necessary for its orderly functioning, and performing other duties as may be imposed on the foreperson by law or by court order.

(b) Request for Contempt Proceeding. The foreperson may request the court to initiate a contempt proceeding against a person whose conduct violates these rules or disrupts grand jury proceedings.

Credits

Added Aug. 31, 2017, effective Jan. 1, 2018.

Editors' Notes

HISTORICAL AND STATUTORY NOTES

Former Rule 12.3, relating to challenge to grand jury or grand juror, was abrogated effective Jan. 1, 2018. See, now, AZ ST RCRP Rule 12.8.

16A A. R. S. Rules Crim. Proc., Rule 12.3, AZ ST RCRP Rule 12.3

Current with amendments received through 08/15/19

Rule 12.4. Who May Be Present During Grand Jury Sessions

(Refs & Annos)

IV. Pretrial Procedures

Rule 12. The Grand Jury (Refs & Annos)

Section One. Rules for Grand Juries

16A A.R.S. Rules Crim.Proc., Rule 12.4

Formerly cited as AZ ST RCRP Rule 12.5

Rule 12.4. Who May Be Present During Grand Jury Sessions

(a) General. Only the following individuals may be present during grand jury sessions:

(1) the witness under examination;

(2) counsel for a witness if the witness is a person under investigation by the grand jury;

(3) a law enforcement officer or detention officer accompanying an in-custody witness;

(4) prosecutors authorized to present evidence to the grand jury;

(5) a certified court reporter; and

(6) an interpreter, if any.

(b) Deliberations. Only grand jurors may be present during their deliberation and voting.

Credits

Added Aug. 31, 2017, effective Jan. 1, 2018.

Editors' Notes

HISTORICAL AND STATUTORY NOTES

Former Rule 12.4, relating to former of the grand jury, was abrogated effective Jan. 1, 2018. See, now, AZ ST RCRP Rule 12.3.

16A A. R. S. Rules Crim. Proc., Rule 12.4, AZ ST RCRP Rule 12.4

Current with amendments received through 08/15/19

Rule 12.5. Appearance of a Person Under Investigation

(Refs & Annos)

IV. Pretrial Procedures

Rule 12. The Grand Jury (Refs & Annos)

Section One. Rules for Grand Juries

16A A.R.S. Rules Crim.Proc., Rule 12.5

Formerly cited as AZ ST RCRP Rule 12.6

Rule 12.5. Appearance of a Person Under Investigation

(a) The Person. A person under investigation by the grand jury may be compelled to appear before the grand jury, or may be permitted to appear upon the person's written request. The person must be advised of the right to remain silent and the right to have counsel present to advise the person while giving testimony.

(b) Counsel. If counsel accompanies the person under investigation, counsel may not communicate, or attempt to communicate, with anyone other than the person. The foreperson may expel counsel from the grand jury session if counsel violates this rule.

Credits

Added Aug. 31, 2017, effective Jan. 1, 2018.

Editors' Notes

HISTORICAL AND STATUTORY NOTES
Former Rule 12.5, relating to persons authorized to be present during sessions of the grand jury, was abrogated effective Jan. 1, 2018. See, now, AZ ST RCRP Rule 12.4.
16A A. R. S. Rules Crim. Proc., Rule 12.5, AZ ST RCRP Rule 12.5
Current with amendments received through 08/15/19

Rule 12.6. Indictment

(Refs & Annos)
IV. Pretrial Procedures
Rule 12. The Grand Jury (Refs & Annos)
Section One. Rules for Grand Juries
16A A.R.S. Rules Crim.Proc., Rule 12.6
Formerly cited as AZ ST RCRP Rule 12.7

Rule 12.6. Indictment

(a) Number of Grand Jurors Necessary to Indict. An indictment requires the concurrence of at least 9 grand jurors, regardless of the number of grand jurors hearing a matter.

(b) Return of Indictment. The indictment must be returned by the foreperson in open court and in the presence of the grand jury and the prosecutor.

(c) Notice of Supervening Indictment. If the defendant previously has had an initial appearance under Rule 4.2, the court must prepare and send to the defendant and defense counsel a notice of supervening indictment instead of issuing a warrant or summons.

(d) No Indictment Returned. If a person is in custody or has posted bond on a matter presented to the grand jury and no indictment is returned, the foreperson through the prosecutor must promptly inform the court in writing that the grand jury did not return an indictment.

Credits
Added Aug. 31, 2017, effective Jan. 1, 2018.
Editors' Notes

HISTORICAL AND STATUTORY NOTES
Former Rule 12.6, relating to appearance of persons under investigation, was abrogated effective Jan. 1, 2018. See, now, AZ ST RCRP Rule 12.5.
16A A. R. S. Rules Crim. Proc., Rule 12.6, AZ ST RCRP Rule 12.6
Current with amendments received through 08/15/19

Rule 12.7. Record of Grand Jury Proceedings

(Refs & Annos)

IV. Pretrial Procedures

Rule 12. The Grand Jury (Refs & Annos)

Section One. Rules for Grand Juries

16A A.R.S. Rules Crim.Proc., Rule 12.7

Formerly cited as AZ ST RCRP Rule 12.8

Rule 12.7. Record of Grand Jury Proceedings

(a) Court Reporter. The presiding or impaneling judge must assign a certified court reporter to record all grand jury proceedings, except its deliberations.

(b) Foreperson. The foreperson must keep a record of how many grand jurors voted for and against an indictment, but must not record how each grand juror voted. If the grand jury returns an indictment, the foreperson's record of the vote must be transcribed by the court reporter and filed with the court no later than 20 days after the return of the indictment, and may be made available only to the court, the State, and the defendant.

(c) Filing the Transcript and Minutes. The court reporter's record of grand jury proceedings must be transcribed and filed with the superior court clerk no later than 20 days after return of the indictment, and may be made available only to the court, the State, and the defendant.

Credits

Added Aug. 31, 2017, effective Jan. 1, 2018.

Editors' Notes

HISTORICAL AND STATUTORY NOTES

Former Rule 12.7, relating to indictment, was abrogated effective Jan. 1, 2018. See, now, AZ ST RCRP Rule 12.6.

16A A. R. S. Rules Crim. Proc., Rule 12.7, AZ ST RCRP Rule 12.7

Current with amendments received through 08/15/19

Rule 12.8. Challenge to a Grand Jury or a Grand Juror

(Refs & Annos)

IV. Pretrial Procedures

Rule 12. The Grand Jury (Refs & Annos)

Section One. Rules for Grand Juries

16A A.R.S. Rules Crim.Proc., Rule 12.8

Formerly cited as AZ ST RCRP Rule 12.3

Rule 12.8. Challenge to a Grand Jury or a Grand Juror

(a) Grounds for a Challenge.
(1) The grand jury may be challenged only on the ground that the grand jurors were not drawn or selected according to law.
(2) An individual grand juror may be challenged on the ground that the juror is not qualified to sit on the grand jury or on a particular matter.
(b) Method of Challenge.
(1) A challenge by the State to a grand jury or a grand juror must be directed to the presiding or impaneling judge.
(2) A defendant may challenge a grand jury or grand juror only after the indictment has been returned.
(3) Any challenge made after the grand jurors are sworn must be in writing.
(c) Effect of Sustaining a Challenge.
(1) If a challenge to the grand jury is sustained, the grand jury must be discharged.
(2) If a challenge to an individual juror is sustained, the juror must be discharged or excluded from deliberation on the particular matter that was the subject of the challenge.
Credits
Added Aug. 31, 2017, effective Jan. 1, 2018.
Editors' Notes
HISTORICAL AND STATUTORY NOTES
Former Rule 12.8, relating to record of proceedings before grand jury, was abrogated effective Jan. 1, 2018. See, now, AZ ST RCRP Rule 12.7.
16A A. R. S. Rules Crim. Proc., Rule 12.8, AZ ST RCRP Rule 12.8
Current with amendments received through 08/15/19

Rule 12.9. Challenge to Grand Jury Proceedings

(Refs & Annos)
IV. Pretrial Procedures
Rule 12. The Grand Jury (Refs & Annos)
Section One. Rules for Grand Juries
16A A.R.S. Rules Crim.Proc., Rule 12.9

Rule 12.9. Challenge to Grand Jury Proceedings

(a) Grounds. A defendant may challenge a grand jury proceeding only by filing a motion for a new finding of probable cause alleging that the defendant was denied a substantial procedural right or that an insufficient number of qualified grand jurors concurred in the indictment.

(b) Timing. A defendant must file a motion under (a) no later than 45 days after the certified transcript and minutes of the grand jury proceedings are filed or no later than 45 days after the defendant's arraignment, whichever is later.

(c) Relief. If the court grants a motion for a new finding of probable cause, the State may proceed with the prosecution of the case by filing a complaint under Rule 2 or by resubmitting the matter to the same or another grand jury. On motion or on its own, the court must dismiss the case without prejudice unless a complaint is filed, or a grand jury's consideration begins, no later than 15 days after entry of the order granting the motion for a new finding of probable cause.

Credits

Added Aug. 31, 2017, effective Jan. 1, 2018.

Editors' Notes

HISTORICAL AND STATUTORY NOTES

Former Rule 12.9, relating to challenge to grand jury proceedings, was abrogated effective Jan. 1, 2018. See, now, this rule.

16A A. R. S. Rules Crim. Proc., Rule 12.9, AZ ST RCRP Rule 12.9

Current with amendments received through 08/15/19

Rule 12.10. Abrogated Aug. 31, 2017, effective Jan. 1, 2018

(Refs & Annos)

IV. Pretrial Procedures

Rule 12. The Grand Jury (Refs & Annos)

Section One. Rules for Grand Juries

16A A.R.S. Rules Crim.Proc., Rule 12.10

Rule 12.10. Abrogated Aug. 31, 2017, effective Jan. 1, 2018

Editors' Notes

HISTORICAL AND STATUTORY NOTES

The abrogated rule related to entering a not guilty plea.

16A A. R. S. Rules Crim. Proc., Rule 12.10, AZ ST RCRP Rule 12.10

Current with amendments received through 08/15/19

Rule 12.21. Applicability of Other Provisions of Rule 12

(Refs & Annos)

16A A.R.S. Rules Crim.Proc., Rule 12.21

Rule 12.21. Applicability of Other Provisions of Rule 12

The provisions of Rule 12 pertaining to grand juries also apply to state grand juries, except that Rule 12.22(a) ["Summons"] applies instead of Rule 12.1(a); 12.22(d) ["Examination"] applies instead of Rule 12.1(b); and Rule 12.28 ["Challenge to State Grand Jury Proceedings"] applies instead of Rule 12.8.

Credits
Added Aug. 31, 2017, effective Jan. 1, 2018.
Editors' Notes
HISTORICAL AND STATUTORY NOTES
Former Rule 12.21, relating to applicability of , was abrogated effective Jan. 1, 2018. See, now, this rule.
16A A. R. S. Rules Crim. Proc., Rule 12.21, AZ ST RCRP Rule 12.21
Current with amendments received through 08/15/19

Rule 12.22. Selection and Preparation of State Grand Jurors

16A A.R.S. Rules Crim.Proc., Rule 12.22

Rule 12.22. Selection and Preparation of State Grand Jurors

(a) Summons. State grand jurors are summoned and impaneled as provided by statute and Rule 12.

(b) Assistance. The Supreme Court Chief Justice must designate the assignment judge for a state grand jury, as provided in A.R.S. § 21-421. The presiding judge and jury commissioner in each county must assist the assignment judge in impaneling a state grand jury. At the assignment judge's direction, the jury commissioner of each county must submit to the assignment judge, by a date set by that judge, a specified number of prospective jurors selected at random. The total number of prospective jurors must be based on reasonably proportional representation for each county according to the most recently published federal statewide census, and should include no less than 3 prospective state grand jurors from each county.

(c) Preliminary Selection. With the assistance of the jury commissioner in the county in which the assignment judge is serving, the assignment judge must send a questionnaire to each prospective state grand juror. From those prospective state grand jurors who return questionnaires and who are qualified and not excused, the jury commissioner must select at random a number of them sufficient for the final selection of state grand jurors. Each person must be summoned to appear before the assignment judge for final selection. The jury commissioner must keep a permanent record of the reason for excusing a prospective state grand juror.

(d) Examination. Each prospective state grand juror must be examined under oath or affirmation to confirm that the prospective juror is qualified to be a state grand juror; that service as a state grand juror would not impose an undue hardship; and that the prospective juror will act impartially and without prejudice. Inquiry also may be made about other relevant subjects. A verbatim record of this examination must be made, transcribed, and filed with the superior court clerk of the county in which the assignment judge is serving.

Credits

Added Aug. 31, 2017, effective Jan. 1, 2018.

Editors' Notes

HISTORICAL AND STATUTORY NOTES

Former Rule 12.22, relating to selection and preparation of state grand jurors, was abrogated effective Jan. 1, 2018. See, now, this rule.

16A A. R. S. Rules Crim. Proc., Rule 12.22, AZ ST RCRP Rule 12.22

Current with amendments received through 08/15/19

Rule 12.23. Size of State Grand Jury

(Refs & Annos)

IV. Pretrial Procedures

Rule 12. The Grand Jury (Refs & Annos)

Section Two. Rules for State Grand Juries

16A A.R.S. Rules Crim.Proc., Rule 12.23

Rule 12.23. Size of State Grand Jury

When impaneled, a state grand jury must be composed of at least 12 but not more than 16 persons.

Credits

Added Aug. 31, 2017, effective Jan. 1, 2018.

Editors' Notes

HISTORICAL AND STATUTORY NOTES

Former Rule 12.23, relating to size of state grand jury, was abrogated effective Jan. 1, 2018. See, now, this rule.

16A A. R. S. Rules Crim. Proc., Rule 12.23, AZ ST RCRP Rule 12.23

Current with amendments received through 08/15/19

Rule 12.24. Location of State Grand Jury Sessions

(Refs & Annos)

IV. Pretrial Procedures

Rule 12. The Grand Jury (Refs & Annos)

Section Two. Rules for State Grand Juries

16A A.R.S. Rules Crim.Proc., Rule 12.24

Rule 12.24. Location of State Grand Jury Sessions

Sessions of a state grand jury may be held at any county seat in the State of Arizona designated by the assignment judge.

Credits

Added Aug. 31, 2017, effective Jan. 1, 2018.

Editors' Notes

HISTORICAL AND STATUTORY NOTES

Former Rule 12.24, relating to location of state grand jury sessions, was abrogated effective Jan. 1, 2018. See, now, this rule.

16A A. R. S. Rules Crim. Proc., Rule 12.24, AZ ST RCRP Rule 12.24

Current with amendments received through 08/15/19

Rule 12.25. Preservation of State Grand Jury Evidence

(Refs & Annos)

IV. Pretrial Procedures

Rule 12. The Grand Jury (Refs & Annos)

Section Two. Rules for State Grand Juries

16A A.R.S. Rules Crim.Proc., Rule 12.25

Rule 12.25. Preservation of State Grand Jury Evidence

(a) Transmittal. The foreperson must transmit all physical evidence, including records, presented to or considered by a state grand jury to the superior court clerk of the county in which the assignment judge is serving. The clerk must preserve the evidence and make it available in the same manner as a transcript of grand jury proceedings.

(b) Release or Retention. Nothing in this rule is intended to abrogate any right of a person under applicable law to possess or regain custody of physical evidence, but the assignment judge may impose limitations on access, use, transport, care, and disposal as may be necessary to ensure that the evidence is preserved.

Credits

Added Aug. 31, 2017, effective Jan. 1, 2018.

Editors' Notes

HISTORICAL AND STATUTORY NOTES

Former Rule 12.25, relating to preservation of State Grand Jury evidence, was abrogated effective Jan. 1, 2018. See, now, this rule.

16A A. R. S. Rules Crim. Proc., Rule 12.25, AZ ST RCRP Rule 12.25

Current with amendments received through 08/15/19

Rule 12.26. Return of Indictment

(Refs & Annos)

IV. Pretrial Procedures

Rule 12. The Grand Jury (Refs & Annos)

Section Two. Rules for State Grand Juries

16A A.R.S. Rules Crim.Proc., Rule 12.26

Rule 12.26. Return of Indictment

The foreperson must return an indictment in open court in the presence of the state grand jury and the Attorney General or the Attorney General's designee. The assignment judge or court commissioner must order the indictment to be kept secret until the defendant is in custody or served with a summons. No one may disclose the indictment's contents except if necessary to issue and execute a warrant or summons.

Credits

Added Aug. 31, 2017, effective Jan. 1, 2018.

Editors' Notes

HISTORICAL AND STATUTORY NOTES

Former Rule 12.26, relating to return of indictment, was abrogated effective Jan. 1, 2018. See, now, this rule.

16A A. R. S. Rules Crim. Proc., Rule 12.26, AZ ST RCRP Rule 12.26

Current with amendments received through 08/15/19

Rule 12.27. Disclosure of a Lack of Indictment

(Refs & Annos)
IV. Pretrial Procedures
Rule 12. The Grand Jury (Refs & Annos)
Section Two. Rules for State Grand Juries
16A A.R.S. Rules Crim.Proc., Rule 12.27

Rule 12.27. Disclosure of a Lack of Indictment

If a state grand jury investigation ends or is terminated without the return of any indictments, the assignment judge may publicly disclose this fact in a minute entry if extraordinary circumstances exist and the furtherance of justice requires it.
Credits
Added Aug. 31, 2017, effective Jan. 1, 2018.
Editors' Notes
HISTORICAL AND STATUTORY NOTES
Former Rule 12.27, relating to disclosure of lack of indictment, was abrogated effective Jan. 1, 2018. See, now, this rule.
16A A. R. S. Rules Crim. Proc., Rule 12.27, AZ ST RCRP Rule 12.27
Current with amendments received through 08/15/19

Rule 12.28. Challenge to State Grand Jury, Grand Juror, or Grand Jury Proceedings

(Refs & Annos)
IV. Pretrial Procedures
Rule 12. The Grand Jury (Refs & Annos)
Section Two. Rules for State Grand Juries
16A A.R.S. Rules Crim.Proc., Rule 12.28

Rule 12.28. Challenge to State Grand Jury, Grand Juror, or Grand Jury Proceedings

(a) Grounds for Challenge.
(1) A state grand jury may be challenged only on the ground that the state grand jurors were not drawn or selected according to law or Rule 12.22.
(2) An individual state grand juror may be challenged only on the ground that the juror is not qualified to sit on the state grand jury or on a particular matter.
(3) A defendant may challenge the grand jury proceeding under Rule 12.9.
(b) Method of Challenge.

(1) A challenge by the State to a state grand jury or a state grand juror must be directed to the assignment judge.

(2) A defendant may not challenge a state grand jury or a state grand juror until after the indictment has been returned.

(3) Any challenge made after the grand jurors are sworn must be in writing.

(c) Relief. If the court grants a motion under Rule 12.9(a), the Attorney General or the Attorney General's designee may proceed with the prosecution of the case by filing a complaint under Rule 2 or by resubmitting the matter to the same state grand jury or to another grand jury. On motion or on its own, the court must dismiss the case without prejudice unless a complaint is filed, or a grand jury consideration begins, no later than 15 days after the order is entered granting the motion under Rule 12.9(a).

Credits

Added Aug. 31, 2017, effective Jan. 1, 2018.

Editors' Notes

HISTORICAL AND STATUTORY NOTES

Former Rule 12.28, relating to challenge to State Grand Jury proceedings, was abrogated effective Jan. 1, 2018. See, now, this rule.

16A A. R. S. Rules Crim. Proc., Rule 12.28, AZ ST RCRP Rule 12.28

Current with amendments received through 08/15/19

Rule 12.29. Expenses of Prospective and Selected State Grand Jurors

(Refs & Annos)

IV. Pretrial Procedures

Rule 12. The Grand Jury (Refs & Annos)

Section Two. Rules for State Grand Juries

16A A.R.S. Rules Crim.Proc., Rule 12.29

Rule 12.29. Expenses of Prospective and Selected State Grand Jurors

(a) Generally. A person called for prospective grand jury impanelment or a person serving on a state grand jury is entitled to reimbursement for lodging and meal expenses if:

(1) the session is held more than 50 miles from the person's residence; and

(2) the expense is incurred either:

(A) the night before the session; or

(B) after the session, if the assignment judge determines that the session did not end early enough to permit the person to return to his or her residence by a reasonable hour.

(b) Limitation of Expenses. The financial limitations on reimbursement of expenses are the same as those imposed by statute or regulation on employees of the State of Arizona.

(c) Exceptional Circumstances. In exceptional circumstances, the assignment judge may authorize reimbursement of an expense incurred by a prospective or serving state grand juror that is not otherwise authorized in this rule.

Credits

Added Aug. 31, 2017, effective Jan. 1, 2018.

Editors' Notes

HISTORICAL AND STATUTORY NOTES

Former Rule 12.29, relating to expensive of prospective and selected state grand jurors, was abrogated effective Jan. 1, 2018. See, now, this rule.

16A A. R. S. Rules Crim. Proc., Rule 12.29, AZ ST RCRP Rule 12.29

Current with amendments received through 08/15/19

R. 13, Refs & Annos

IV. Pretrial Procedures

Rule 13. Indictment and Information

16A A.R.S. Rules Crim.Proc., R. 13, Refs & Annos

16A A. R. S. Rules Crim. Proc., R. 13, Refs & Annos, AZ ST RCRP R. 13, Refs & Annos

Current with amendments received through 08/15/19

Rule 13.1. Definitions and Construction

(Refs & Annos)

IV. Pretrial Procedures

Rule 13. Indictment and Information (Refs & Annos)

16A A.R.S. Rules Crim.Proc., Rule 13.1

Formerly cited as AZ ST RCRP Rule 13.2

Rule 13.1. Definitions and Construction

(a) General Definition. An "indictment" or "information" is a plain, concise statement of the facts sufficiently definite to inform the defendant of a charged offense.

(b) Indictment Defined. An "indictment" is a written statement charging the defendant with the commission of a public offense, endorsed as a "true bill," signed by a grand jury foreperson, and presented to the court by a grand jury.

(c) Information Defined. An "information" is a written statement charging the defendant with the commission of a public offense, signed and presented to the court by the State.

(d) Charging the Offense. Each count of an indictment or information must state the official or customary citation of the statute, rule, regulation or other provision of law the defendant allegedly violated.

(e) Necessarily Included Offenses. An offense specified in an indictment, information, or complaint is a charge of that offense and all necessarily included offenses.

Credits

Added Aug. 31, 2017, effective Jan. 1, 2018.

Editors' Notes

HISTORICAL AND STATUTORY NOTES

Former Rule 13.1, relating to definitions and timeliness, was abrogated effective Jan. 1, 2018. See, now, this rule and AZ ST RCRP Rule 13.2.

16A A. R. S. Rules Crim. Proc., Rule 13.1, AZ ST RCRP Rule 13.1

Current with amendments received through 08/15/19

Rule 13.2. Timeliness of an Information and Dismissal

(Refs & Annos)

IV. Pretrial Procedures

Rule 13. Indictment and Information (Refs & Annos)

16A A.R.S. Rules Crim.Proc., Rule 13.2

Formerly cited as AZ ST RCRP Rule 13.1

Rule 13.2. Timeliness of an Information and Dismissal

The State must file an information in superior court no later than 10 days after a magistrate finds probable cause or the defendant waives a preliminary hearing. If the State fails to file a timely information, a court must dismiss the information if the defendant files a motion seeking that relief under Rule 16.1(b). A dismissal under this rule is without prejudice, but if the prosecution is refiled, the time limits under Rule 8.2 must be computed from the defendant's initial appearance on the original complaint.

Credits

Added Aug. 31, 2017, effective Jan. 1, 2018.

Rule 13.3. Joinder

(Refs & Annos)
IV. Pretrial Procedures
Rule 13. Indictment and Information (Refs & Annos)
16A A.R.S. Rules Crim.Proc., Rule 13.3

Rule 13.3. Joinder

(a) Of Offenses. Two or more offenses may be joined in an indictment, information, or complaint if they are each stated in a separate count and if they:
(1) are of the same or similar character;
(2) are based on the same conduct or are otherwise connected together in their commission; or
(3) are alleged to have been a part of a common scheme or plan.
(b) Of Defendants. Two or more defendants may be joined if each defendant is charged with each alleged offense, or if the alleged offenses are part of an alleged common conspiracy, scheme, or plan, or are otherwise so closely connected that it would be difficult to separate proof of one from proof of the others.
(c) Consolidation. If offenses or defendants are charged in separate proceedings, the court, on motion or on its own, may wholly or partly consolidate the proceedings in the interests of justice.
Credits
Added Aug. 31, 2017, effective Jan. 1, 2018.

Rule 13.4. Severance

16A A.R.S. Rules Crim.Proc., Rule 13.4

Rule 13.4. Severance

(a) Generally. On motion or on its own, and if necessary to promote a fair determination of any defendant's guilt or innocence of any offense, a court must order a severance of counts, defendants, or both.

(b) As of Right. A defendant is entitled to a severance of offenses joined solely under Rule 13.3(a)(1), unless evidence of the other offense or offenses would be admissible if the offenses were tried separately.

(c) Timeliness and Waiver. A defendant must move to sever at least 20 days before trial or as the court otherwise orders. If the motion is denied, the defendant must renew the motion during trial before or at the close of evidence. If a ground for severance previously unknown to a defendant arises during trial, the defendant must move for severance before or at the close of evidence. The right to severance is waived if the defendant fails to timely file and renew a proper motion for severance.

(d) Jeopardy. The court may not grant the State's motion to sever offenses after trial begins unless the defendant consents. Offenses severed during trial on the defendant's motion or with the defendant's consent will not bar a later trial of that defendant on the severed offenses.

Credits

Added Aug. 31, 2017, effective Jan. 1, 2018.

Editors' Notes

HISTORICAL AND STATUTORY NOTES

Former Rule 13.4, relating to severance, was abrogated effective Jan. 1, 2018. See, now, this rule.

16A A. R. S. Rules Crim. Proc., Rule 13.4, AZ ST RCRP Rule 13.4

Current with amendments received through 08/15/19

Rule 13.5. Amending Charges; Defects in the Charging Document

16A A.R.S. Rules Crim.Proc., Rule 13.5

Rule 13.5. Amending Charges; Defects in the Charging Document

(a) Prior Convictions and Other Noncapital Sentencing Allegations; Challenges. Within the time limits of Rule 16.1(b), the State may amend an indictment, information, or complaint to add allegations of one or more prior convictions and other noncapital sentencing allegations that must be found by a jury. A defendant may challenge the legal sufficiency of the State's allegations by filing a motion under Rule 16.

(b) Altering Charges; Amending to Conform to the Evidence. A preliminary hearing or grand jury indictment limits the trial to the specific charge or charges stated in the magistrate's order or the grand jury indictment. Unless the defendant consents, a charge may be amended only to correct mistakes of fact or remedy formal or technical defects. The charging document is deemed amended to conform to the evidence admitted during any court proceeding. Nothing in this rule precludes the defendant from consenting to the addition of a charge as part of a plea agreement.

(c) Amending to Conform to Capital Sentencing Allegation; Challenges. The filing of a notice to seek the death penalty that includes aggravating circumstances amends the charging document, and the State is not required to file any further pleading. A defendant may challenge the legal sufficiency of the State's allegation by filing a motion under Rule 16.

(d) Defects in Charging Document. A defendant may object to a defect in the charging document only by filing a motion under Rule 16.

Credits

Added Aug. 31, 2017, effective Jan. 1, 2018.

Editors' Notes

HISTORICAL AND STATUTORY NOTES

Former Rule 13.5, relating to amendment of the charges and defects in the charging document, was abrogated effective Jan. 1, 2018. See, now, this rule.

16A A. R. S. Rules Crim. Proc., Rule 13.5, AZ ST RCRP Rule 13.5

Current with amendments received through 08/15/19

R. 14, Refs & Annos

IV. Pretrial Procedures

Rule 14. Arraignment

16A A.R.S. Rules Crim.Proc., R. 14, Refs & Annos

16A A. R. S. Rules Crim. Proc., R. 14, Refs & Annos, AZ ST RCRP R. 14, Refs & Annos

Rule 14.1. General Provisions

(Refs & Annos)
IV. Pretrial Procedures
Rule 14. Arraignment (Refs & Annos)
16A A.R.S. Rules Crim.Proc., Rule 14.1

Rule 14.1. General Provisions

The purpose of an arraignment is to formally advise defendants of the charges against them and their legal rights, to assure they are provided counsel if applicable, to enter a plea, and to set a trial date or a later court date. At an arraignment, a magistrate informs defendants of the matters in Rule 14.4.
Credits
Added Aug. 31, 2017, effective Jan. 1, 2018.
Editors' Notes
HISTORICAL AND STATUTORY NOTES
Former Rule 14.1, relating to when held, was abrogated effective Jan. 1, 2018. See, now, AZ ST RCRP Rule 14.2.
16A A. R. S. Rules Crim. Proc., Rule 14.1, AZ ST RCRP Rule 14.1
Current with amendments received through 08/15/19

Rule 14.2. When an Arraignment Is Held

(Refs & Annos)
IV. Pretrial Procedures
Rule 14. Arraignment (Refs & Annos)
16A A.R.S. Rules Crim.Proc., Rule 14.2
Formerly cited as AZ ST RCRP Rule 14.1

Rule 14.2. When an Arraignment Is Held

(a) Generally. An arraignment must be held:
(1) for defendants in custody, no later than 10 days after the filing of an indictment, information, or complaint; and
(2) for defendants not in custody, no later than 30 days after the filing of an indictment, information, or complaint.

(b) Exception for Special Situations. If the court cannot hold the arraignment within the time specified in (a) because the defendant has not yet been arrested or summoned, or is in custody elsewhere, the court must hold the arraignment as soon as possible after those time periods.

(c) Exceptions for Limited Jurisdiction Courts. An arraignment is not necessary if:

(1) the defense counsel has entered a plea of not guilty; or

(2) the court permits a defendant to enter a not-guilty plea by mail and to receive notice of a court date by mail. Delivery of the notice is presumed if the notice is deposited in the U.S. mail, addressed to the defendant's last known address, and the notice is not returned to the court.

(d) Exception for Superior Court. The superior court is not required to conduct an arraignment after the filing of an indictment or information if the presiding judge issues an order that Rule 14 does not apply to superior court cases in that county.

(e) Combined Proceedings. If the defendant's first court appearance occurs after the State files a complaint and if the initial appearance is held in the trial court, the court may hold the arraignment in conjunction with the initial appearance before the magistrate. If the initial appearance is not held in the trial court, the court must order the defendant to appear for arraignment in the trial court no later than 10 days after the initial appearance, and a written notice of the arraignment date must be delivered to the defendant.

Credits

Added Aug. 31, 2017, effective Jan. 1, 2018.

Editors' Notes

HISTORICAL AND STATUTORY NOTES

Former Rule 14.2, relating to presence of the defendant, was abrogated effective Jan. 1, 2018. See, now, AZ ST RCRP Rule 14.3.

16A A. R. S. Rules Crim. Proc., Rule 14.2, AZ ST RCRP Rule 14.2

Current with amendments received through 08/15/19

Rule 14.3. The Defendant's Presence

(Refs & Annos)

IV. Pretrial Procedures

Rule 14. Arraignment (Refs & Annos)

16A A.R.S. Rules Crim.Proc., Rule 14.3

Formerly cited as AZ ST RCRP Rule 14.2

Rule 14.3. The Defendant's Presence

(a) Personal Presence Required. A defendant must be arraigned personally before the trial court or by an interactive video appearance under Rule 1.5.

(b) Personal Presence Not Required if Waived. A defendant who personally appeared at an initial appearance may waive personal presence at an arraignment by filing a written waiver at least two days before the arraignment date. The defendant and defense counsel must sign and notarize the waiver. A defendant also must file a notarized affidavit no later than 20 days after arraignment stating that the defendant is aware of all scheduled court appearances and understands that failure to appear at sentencing may result in losing the right to a direct appeal.

Credits

Added Aug. 31, 2017, effective Jan. 1, 2018.

Editors' Notes

HISTORICAL AND STATUTORY NOTES

Former Rule 14.3, relating to proceedings at arraignment, was abrogated effective Jan. 1, 2018. See, now, AZ ST RCRP Rule 14.4.

16A A. R. S. Rules Crim. Proc., Rule 14.3, AZ ST RCRP Rule 14.3

Current with amendments received through 08/15/19

Rule 14.4. Proceedings at Arraignment

(Refs & Annos)

IV. Pretrial Procedures

Rule 14. Arraignment (Refs & Annos)

16A A.R.S. Rules Crim.Proc., Rule 14.4

Formerly cited as AZ ST RCRP Rule 14.3

Rule 14.4. Proceedings at Arraignment

At an arraignment, the court must:

(a) enter the defendant's plea of not guilty, unless the defendant pleads guilty or no contest and the court accepts the plea;

(b) decide motions concerning release conditions under Rule 7 if:

(1) the arraignment is held with the defendant's initial appearance under Rule 4.2;

(2) the moving party provides 5 days' notice of a contested release motion; or

(3) all parties agree;

(c) set the date for trial or a pretrial conference;

(d) provide written notice of the dates of further proceedings and other important deadlines;

(e) inform the defendant of the following:

(1) the right to counsel and the right to court-appointed counsel if eligible;

(2) the right to jury trial, if applicable;

(3) the right to be present at all future proceedings;

(4) the failure to appear at future proceedings may result in the defendant being charged with a new offense and the court issuing an arrest warrant;

(5) all proceedings may be held in the defendant's absence, other than sentencing; and

(6) the defendant may lose the right to a direct appeal if the defendant's absence from sentencing causes sentencing to occur more than 90 days after any conviction;

(f) appoint counsel if applicable;

(g) order a summoned defendant to be 10-print fingerprinted no later than 20 calendar days by the appropriate law enforcement agency at a designated time and place if:

(1) the defendant is charged with a felony offense, a violation of A.R.S. §§ 13-1401 et seq. or A.R.S. §§ 28-1301 et seq., or a domestic violence offense as defined in A.R.S. § 13-3601; and

(2) the defendant does not present a completed mandatory fingerprint compliance form to the court, or if the court has not received the process control number.

Credits

Added Aug. 31, 2017, effective Jan. 1, 2018.

16A A. R. S. Rules Crim. Proc., Rule 14.4, AZ ST RCRP Rule 14.4

Current with amendments received through 08/15/19

Rule 14.5. Proceedings in Counties Where No Arraignment Is Held

(Refs & Annos)

IV. Pretrial Procedures

Rule 14. Arraignment (Refs & Annos)

16A A.R.S. Rules Crim.Proc., Rule 14.5

Rule 14.5. Proceedings in Counties Where No Arraignment Is Held

In a county where an arraignment is not held as provided in Rule 14.2(d), a defendant must be brought before a magistrate no later than 10 days after the indictment is returned. The defendant may waive personal presence under Rule 14.3(b). The magistrate must comply with Rule 14.4.

Credits

Added Aug. 31, 2017, effective Jan. 1, 2018.

16A A. R. S. Rules Crim. Proc., Rule 14.5, AZ ST RCRP Rule 14.5

Current with amendments received through 08/15/19

IV. Pretrial Procedures
Rule 15. Disclosure

16A A.R.S. Rules Crim.Proc., R. 15, Refs & Annos

16A A. R. S. Rules Crim. Proc., R. 15, Refs & Annos, AZ ST RCRP R. 15, Refs &
Annos
Current with amendments received through 08/15/19

Rule 15.1. The State's Disclosures

(Refs & Annos)
IV. Pretrial Procedures
Rule 15. Disclosure (Refs & Annos)

16A A.R.S. Rules Crim.Proc., Rule 15.1

Rule 15.1. The State's Disclosures

(a) Initial Disclosures in a Felony Case. Unless a local rule provides or the court
orders otherwise:
(1) the State must make available to the defendant all reports containing
information identified in (b)(3) and (b)(4) that the charging attorney possessed when
the charge was filed; and
(2) the State must make these reports available by the preliminary hearing or, if no
preliminary hearing is held, the arraignment.
(b) Supplemental Disclosure. Except as provided by Rule 39(b), the State must make
available to the defendant the following material and information within the State's
possession or control:
(1) the name and address of each person the State intends to call as a witness in the
State's case-in-chief and any relevant written or recorded statement of the witness;
(2) any statement of the defendant and any co-defendant;
(3) all existing original and supplemental reports prepared by a law enforcement
agency in connection with the charged offense;
(4) for each expert who has examined a defendant or any evidence in the case, or
who the State intends to call at trial:
(A) the expert's name, address, and qualifications;

(B) any report prepared by the expert and the results of any completed physical examination, scientific test, experiment, or comparison conducted by the expert; and

(C) if the expert will testify at trial without preparing a written report, a summary of the general subject matter and opinions on which the expert is expected to testify;

(5) a list of all documents, photographs, other tangible objects, and electronically stored information the State intends to use at trial or that were obtained from or purportedly belong to the defendant;

(6) a list of the defendant's prior felony convictions the State intends to use at trial;

(7) a list of the defendant's other acts the State intends to use at trial;

(8) all existing material or information that tends to mitigate or negate the defendant's guilt or would tend to reduce the defendant's punishment;

(9) whether there has been any electronic surveillance of any conversations to which the defendant was a party, or of the defendant's business or residence;

(10) whether a search warrant has been executed in connection with the case; and

(11) whether the case involved an informant, and, if so, the informant's identity, subject to the restrictions under Rule 15.4(b)(2).

(c) Time for Supplemental Disclosures. Unless the court orders otherwise, the State must disclose the material and information listed in (b) no later than:

(1) in the superior court, 30 days after arraignment.

(2) in a limited jurisdiction court, at the first pretrial conference.

(d) Prior Felony Convictions. The State must make available to a defendant a list of prior felony convictions of each witness the State intends to call at trial and a list of the prior felony convictions the State intends to use to impeach a disclosed defense witness at trial:

(1) in a felony case, no later than 30 days before trial or 30 days after the defendant's request, whichever occurs first; and

(2) in a misdemeanor case, no later than 10 days before trial.

(e) Disclosures upon Request.

(1) *Generally.* Unless the court orders otherwise, the State must make the following items available to the defendant for examination, testing, and reproduction no later than 30 days after receiving a defendant's written request:

(A) any of the items specified in the list submitted under (b)(5);

(B) any 911 calls existing at the time of the request that the record's custodian can reasonably ascertain are related to the case; and

(C) any completed written report, statement, and examination notes made by an expert listed in (b)(1) and (b)(4) related to the case.

(2) *Conditions.* The State may impose reasonable conditions, including an appropriate stipulation concerning chain of custody to protect physical evidence or to allow time for the examination or testing of any items.

(f) Scope of the State's Disclosure Obligation. The State's disclosure obligation extends to material and information in the possession or control of any of the following:

(1) the prosecutor, other attorneys in the prosecutor's office, and members of the prosecutor's staff;

(2) any law enforcement agency that has participated in the investigation of the case and is under the prosecutor's direction or control; and

(3) any other person who is under the prosecutor's direction or control and who participated in the investigation or evaluation of the case.

(g) Disclosure by Court Order.

(1) *Disclosure Order.* On the defendant's motion, a court may order any person to make available to the defendant material or information not included in this rule if the court finds:

(A) the defendant has a substantial need for the material or information to prepare the defendant's case; and

(B) the defendant cannot obtain the substantial equivalent by other means without undue hardship.

(2) *Modifying or Vacating Order.* On the request of any person affected by an order, the court may modify or vacate the order if the court determines that compliance would be unreasonable or oppressive.

(h) Disclosure of Rebuttal Evidence. Upon receiving the defendant's notice of defenses under Rule 15.2(b), the State must disclose the name and address of each person the State intends to call as a rebuttal witness, and any relevant written or recorded statement of the witness.

(i) Additional Disclosures in a Capital Case.

(1) *Notice of Intent to Seek the Death Penalty.*

(A) Generally. No later than 60 days after a defendant's arraignment in superior court on a charge of first-degree murder, the State must provide notice to the defendant of whether the State intends to seek the death penalty.

(B) Time Extensions. The court may extend the State's deadline for providing notice by an additional 60 days if the parties file a written stipulation agreeing to the extension. If the court approves the extension, the case is considered a capital case for all administrative purposes, including, but not limited to, scheduling, appointment of counsel under Rule 6.8, and the assignment of a mitigation specialist. The court may grant additional extensions if the parties file written stipulations agreeing to them.

(C) Victim Notification. If the victim has requested notice under A.R.S. § 13-4405, the prosecutor must confer with the victim before agreeing to extend the deadline under (i)(1)(B).

(2) *Aggravating Circumstances.* If the State files a notice of intent to seek the death penalty, the State must, at the same time, provide the defendant with a list of aggravating circumstances that the State intends to prove in the aggravation phase of the trial.

(3) *Initial Disclosures.*

(A) Generally. No later than 30 days after filing a notice of intent to seek the death penalty, the State must disclose the following to the defendant:

(i) the name and address of each person the State intends to call as a witness at the aggravation hearing to support each alleged aggravating circumstance, and any written or recorded statement of the witness;

(ii) the name and address of each expert the State intends to call at the aggravation hearing to support each alleged aggravating circumstance, and any written or recorded statement of the expert or other disclosure as required in (b)(4);

(iii) a list of all documents, photographs, other tangible objects, or electronically stored information the State intends to use to support each identified aggravating circumstance at the aggravation hearing; and

(iv) all material or information that might mitigate or negate the finding of an aggravating circumstance or mitigate the defendant's culpability.

(B) Time Extensions. The court may extend the deadline for the State's initial disclosures under (i)(3) or allow the State to amend those disclosures only if the State shows good cause or the parties stipulate to the deadline extension.

(4) *Rebuttal and Penalty Phase Disclosures.* No later than 60 days after receiving the defendant's disclosure under Rule 15.2(h)(1), the State must disclose the following to the defendant:

(A) the name and address of each person the State intends to call as a rebuttal witness on each identified aggravating circumstance, and any written or recorded statement of the witness;

(B) the name and address of each person the State intends to call as a witness at the penalty hearing, and any written or recorded statement of the witness;

(C) the name and address of each expert the State intends to call at the penalty hearing, and any report the expert has prepared or other disclosure as required in (b)(4); and

(D) a list of all documents, photographs, other tangible objects, or electronically stored information the State intends to use during the aggravation and penalty hearings.

(j) Item Prohibited by A.R.S. §§ 13-3551 et seq., or Is the Subject of a Prosecution Under A.R.S. § 13-1425.

(1) *Scope.* This rule applies to an item that cannot be produced or possessed under A.R.S. §§ 13-3551 et seq. or is an image that is the subject of a prosecution under A.R.S. § 13-1425, but is included in the list disclosed under (b)(5).

(2) *Disclosure Obligation.* The State is not required to reproduce the item or release it to the defendant for testing or examination except as provided in (j)(3) and (j)(4). The State must make the item reasonably available for inspection by the defendant, but only under such terms and conditions necessary to protect a victim's rights.

(3) *Court-Ordered Disclosure for Examination or Testing.*

(A) Generally. The court may order the item's reproduction or its release to the defendant for examination or testing if the defendant makes a substantial showing that it is necessary for the effective investigation or presentation of a defense, including an expert's analysis.

(B) Conditions. A court must issue any order necessary to protect a victim's rights, document the chain of custody, or protect physical evidence.

(4) *General Restrictions.* In addition to any court order issued, the following restrictions apply to the reproduction or release of any item to the defendant for examination or testing:

(A) the item must not be further reproduced or distributed except as the court order allows;

(B) the item may be viewed or possessed only by the persons authorized by the court order;

(C) the item must not be possessed or viewed by the defendant outside the direct supervision of defense counsel, advisory counsel, or a defense expert;

(D) the item must be delivered to defense counsel or advisory counsel, or if expressly permitted by court order, to a specified defense expert; and

(E) the item must be returned to the State by a deadline set by the court.

Credits

Added Aug. 31, 2017, effective Jan. 1, 2018. Amended Aug. 28, 2018, effective Jan. 1, 2019.

Editors' Notes

HISTORICAL AND STATUTORY NOTES

Former Rule 15.1, relating to disclosure by state, was abrogated effective Jan. 1, 2018. See, now, this rule.

16A A. R. S. Rules Crim. Proc., Rule 15.1, AZ ST RCRP Rule 15.1

Current with amendments received through 08/15/19

Rule 15.2. The Defendant's Disclosures

(Refs & Annos)

IV. Pretrial Procedures

Rule 15. Disclosure (Refs & Annos)

16A A.R.S. Rules Crim.Proc., Rule 15.2

Rule 15.2. The Defendant's Disclosures

(a) Physical Evidence.

(1) *Generally.* At any time after the filing of an indictment, information or complaint, and upon the State's written request, the defendant must, in connection with the particular offense with which the defendant is charged:

(A) appear in a line-up;

(B) speak for identification by one or more witnesses;

(C) be fingerprinted, palm-printed, foot-printed, or voice printed;

(D) pose for photographs not involving a re-enactment of an event;

(E) try on clothing;

(F) permit the taking of samples of hair, blood, saliva, urine, or other specified materials if doing so does not involve an unreasonable intrusion of the defendant's body;

(G) provide handwriting specimens; and

(H) submit to a reasonable physical or medical inspection of the defendant's body, but such an inspection must not include a psychiatric or psychological examination.

(2) *Presence of Counsel.* The defendant is entitled to have counsel present when the State takes evidence under this rule.

(3) *Other Procedures.* This rule supplements and does not limit any other procedures established by law.

(b) Notice of Defenses.

(1) *Generally.* By the deadline specified in (d), the defendant must provide written notice to the State specifying all defenses the defendant intends to assert at trial, including, but not limited to, alibi, insanity, self-defense, defense of others, entrapment, impotency, marriage, insufficiency of a prior conviction, mistaken identity, and good character.

(2) *Witnesses.* For each listed defense, the notice must specify each person, other than the defendant, that the defendant intends to call as a witness at trial in support of the defense.

(3) *Signature and Filing.* Defense counsel-or if the defendant is self-represented, the defendant-must sign the notice and file it with the court.

(c) Content of Disclosure. At the same time the defendant files a notice of defenses under (b), the defendant must provide the following information:

(1) the name and address of each person, other than the defendant, the defendant intends to call as a witness at trial, and any written or recorded statement of the witness;

(2) for each expert the defendant intends to call at trial:

(A) the expert's name, address, and qualifications;

(B) any report prepared by the expert and the results of any completed physical examination, scientific test, experiment, or comparison conducted by the expert; and

(C) if the expert will testify at trial without preparing a written report, a summary of the general subject matter and opinions on which the expert is expected to testify; and

(3) a list of all documents, photographs, other tangible objects, and electronically stored information the defendant intends to use at trial.

(d) Time for Disclosures. Unless the court orders otherwise, the defendant must disclose the material and information listed in (b) and (c) no later than:

(1) in superior court, 40 days after arraignment, or 10 days after the State's disclosure under Rule 15.1(b), whichever occurs first;

(2) in a limited jurisdiction court, 20 days after the State's disclosure under Rule 15.1(b).

(e) Additional Disclosures upon Request.

(1) *Generally.* Unless the court orders otherwise, the defendant must make the following items available to the State for examination, testing, and reproduction no later than 30 days after receiving the State's written request:

(A) any of the items specified in the list submitted under (c)(3); and

(B) any completed written report, statement, and examination notes made by an expert listed in (c)(2) in connection with the particular case.

(2) *Conditions.* The defendant may impose reasonable conditions, including an appropriate stipulation concerning chain of custody for physical evidence or to allow time for the examination or testing of any items.

(f) Scope of Disclosure. A defendant's disclosure obligation extends to material and information within the possession or control of the defendant, defense counsel, staff, agents, investigators, or any other persons who have participated in the investigation or evaluation of the case and who are under the defendant's direction or control.

(g) Disclosure by Court Order.

(1) *Disclosure Order.* On the State's motion, a court may order any person to make available to the State material or information not included in this rule if the court finds:

(A) the State has a substantial need for the material or information for the preparation of the State's case;

(B) the State cannot obtain the substantial equivalent by other means without undue hardship; and

(C) the disclosure of the material or information would not violate the defendant's constitutional rights.

(2) *Modifying or Vacating Order.* The court may modify or vacate an order if the court determines that compliance would be unreasonable or oppressive.

(h) Additional Disclosures in a Capital Case.

(1) *Initial Disclosures.*

(A) Generally. No later than 180 days after receiving the State's initial disclosure under Rule 15.1(i)(3), the defendant must disclose the following to the State:

(i) a list of all mitigating circumstances the defendant intends to prove;

(ii) the name and address of each person, other than the defendant, the defendant intends to call as a witness during the aggravation and penalty hearings, and any written or recorded statement of the witness;

(iii) the name and address of each expert the defendant intends to call during the aggravation and penalty hearings, and any written or recorded statements of the expert or other disclosure as required in (c)(2), excluding any portions containing statements by the defendant; and

(iv) a list of all documents, photographs, other tangible objects, or electronically stored information the defendant intends to use during the aggravation and penalty hearings.

(B) Time Extensions. The court may extend the deadline for the defendant's initial disclosures under (h)(i) or allow the defendant to amend those disclosures only if the defendant shows good cause or the parties stipulate to the deadline extension.

(2) *Later Disclosures.* No later than 60 days after receiving the State's supplemental disclosure under Rule 15.1(i)(4), the defendant must disclose the following to the State:

(A) the name and address of each person the defendant intends to call as a rebuttal witness, and any written or recorded statement of the witness; and

(B) the name and address of each expert the defendant intends to call as a witness at the penalty hearing, and any report the expert has prepared.

Credits

Added Aug. 31, 2017, effective Jan. 1, 2018. Amended Aug. 28, 2018, effective Jan. 1, 2019.

Editors' Notes

HISTORICAL AND STATUTORY NOTES

Former Rule 15.2, relating to disclosure by defendant, was abrogated effective Jan. 1, 2018. See, now, this rule.

16A A. R. S. Rules Crim. Proc., Rule 15.2, AZ ST RCRP Rule 15.2

Current with amendments received through 08/15/19

Rule 15.3. Depositions

(Refs & Annos)

IV. Pretrial Procedures

Rule 15. Disclosure (Refs & Annos)

16A A.R.S. Rules Crim.Proc., Rule 15.3

Rule 15.3. Depositions

(a) Availability. A party or a witness may file a motion requesting the court to order the examination of any person, except the defendant and a victim, by oral deposition under the following circumstances:

(1) a party shows that the person's testimony is material to the case and that there is a substantial likelihood that the person will not be available at trial; or

(2) a party shows that the person's testimony is material to the case or necessary to adequately prepare a defense or investigate the offense, that the person was not a witness at the preliminary hearing or at the probable cause phase of the juvenile transfer hearing, and that the person will not cooperate in granting a personal interview; or

(3) a witness is incarcerated for failing to give satisfactory security that the witness will appear and testify at a trial or hearing.

(b) Follow-up Examination. If a witness testifies at a preliminary hearing or probable cause phase of a juvenile transfer hearing, the court may order the person to attend and give testimony at a follow-up deposition if:

(1) the magistrate limited the person's previous testimony under Rule 5.3; and

(2) the person will not cooperate in granting a personal interview.

(c) Motion for Taking Deposition; Notice; Service.

(1) *Requirements.* A motion to take a deposition must:

(A) state the name and address of the person to be deposed;

(B) show that a deposition may be ordered under (a) or (b);

(C) specify the time and place for taking the deposition; and

(D) designate any nonprivileged documents, photographs, other tangible objects, or electronically stored information that the person must produce at the deposition.

(2) *Order.* If the court grants the motion, it may modify any of the moving party's proposed terms and specify additional conditions governing how the deposition will be conducted.

(3) *Notice and Subpoena.* If the court grants the motion, the moving party must notice the deposition in the manner provided in Arizona Rule of Civil Procedure 30(b). The notice must specify the terms and conditions in the court's order granting the deposition. The moving party also must serve a subpoena on the deponent in the manner provided in A.R.S. § 13-4072(A)-(E) or as otherwise ordered by the court.

(d) Manner of Taking.

(1) *Generally.* Unless this rule provides or the court orders otherwise, the parties must conduct depositions in the manner provided in Rules 28(a) and 30 of the Arizona Rules of Civil Procedure.

(2) *Deposition by Written Questions.* If the parties consent, the court may order that a deposition be taken on written questions in the manner provided in Rule 31 of the Arizona Rules of Civil Procedure.

(3) *Deponent Statement.* Before the deposition, a party who possesses a statement of a deponent must make it available to any other party who would be entitled to the statement at trial.

(4) *Recording.* A deposition may be recorded by someone other than a certified court reporter. If someone other than a certified court reporter records the deposition, the party taking the deposition must provide every other party with a copy of the recording no later than 14 days after the deposition, or no later than 10 days before trial, whichever is earlier.

(5) *Remote Means.* The parties may agree or the court may order that the parties conduct the deposition by telephone or other remote means.

(e) The Defendant's Right to Be Present. A defendant has the right to be present at any deposition ordered under (a)(1) or (a)(3). If a defendant is in custody, the moving party must notify the custodial officer of the deposition's time and place. Unless the defendant waives the right to be present, the officer must produce the defendant for the deposition and remain with the defendant until it is completed.

(f) Use. A party may use a deposition in the same manner as former testimony.

Credits

Added Aug. 31, 2017, effective Jan. 1, 2018. Amended Aug. 28, 2018, effective Jan. 1, 2019.

Editors' Notes

HISTORICAL AND STATUTORY NOTES

Former Rule 15.3, relating to depositions, was abrogated effective Jan. 1, 2018. See, now, this rule.

16A A. R. S. Rules Crim. Proc., Rule 15.3, AZ ST RCRP Rule 15.3

Current with amendments received through 08/15/19

Rule 15.4. Disclosure Standards

(Refs & Annos)

IV. Pretrial Procedures

Rule 15. Disclosure (Refs & Annos)

16A A.R.S. Rules Crim.Proc., Rule 15.4

Rule 15.4. Disclosure Standards

(a) Statements.

(1) *Definition of a "Statement."* In Rule 15, the term "statement" includes:

(A) a writing prepared, signed or otherwise adopted or approved by a person;

(B) a recording of a person's oral communications or a transcript of the communication; or

(C) a written record or summary of a person's oral communications.

(2) *Definition of a "Writing."* A "writing" consists of words or their equivalent, recorded in physical, electronic, or other form.

(3) *Exclusion of Superseded Notes.* Handwritten notes are not a statement if they were substantially incorporated into a document or report no later than 30 calendar days of their creation, or were preserved electronically, mechanically, or by verbatim dictation.

(b) Materials Not Subject to Disclosure.

(1) *Work Product.* A party is not required to disclose legal research or records, correspondence, reports, or memoranda to the extent they contain the opinions, theories, or conclusions of the prosecutor or defense counsel, members of their respective legal or investigative staff, or law enforcement officers.

(2) *Informants.* A party is not required to disclose the existence or identity of an informant who will not be called to testify if:

(A) disclosure would result in substantial risk to the informant or to the informant's operational effectiveness; and

(B) a failure to disclose will not infringe on the defendant's constitutional rights.

(c) Failure to Call a Witness or Raise a Defense. At trial, a party may not comment on the fact that a witness's name or a defense is on a list furnished under Rule 15, yet not called or raised, unless the court allows the comment after finding that inclusion of the witness's name or the defense constituted an abuse of the applicable disclosure rule.

(d) Use of Materials. Any materials furnished to a party or counsel under Rule 15 must not be disclosed to the public, and may be disclosed only to the extent necessary for the proper conduct of the case.

(e) Requests for Disclosure. All requests for disclosure must be made to the opposing party.

(f) Filing of Papers; Exception for Misdemeanors and Petty Offenses Filed in Limited Jurisdiction Courts. For misdemeanor and petty offenses triable in limited jurisdiction courts, parties must not file materials disclosed under Rules 15.1 and 15.2, or notices of their service, unless the court orders otherwise or they are filed as attachments or exhibits to other documents relevant to the determination of an issue before the court.

Credits

Added Aug. 31, 2017, effective Jan. 1, 2018.
Editors' Notes
HISTORICAL AND STATUTORY NOTES
Former Rule 15.4, relating to general standards, was abrogated effective Jan. 1, 2018. See, now, this rule.
COMMENT
Rule 15.4(a). It is intended that an attorney's actual trial notes, such as his outline of questions to ask a witness, will be encompassed within the work product exception of Rule 15.4(b)(1), even though they fall within the definition of statement.
16A A. R. S. Rules Crim. Proc., Rule 15.4, AZ ST RCRP Rule 15.4
Current with amendments received through 08/15/19

Rule 15.5. Excision and Protective Orders

(Refs & Annos)
IV. Pretrial Procedures
Rule 15. Disclosure (Refs & Annos)

16A A.R.S. Rules Crim.Proc., Rule 15.5

Rule 15.5. Excision and Protective Orders

(a) A Court's Discretion to Deny, Defer or Regulate Disclosure.
(1) *Witness Identity.* For good cause, a court may grant a request to defer disclosing a witness's identity for a reasonable period of time, but no later than 5 days before trial.
(2) *Other Matters.* A court may order that other disclosures required by Rule 15 be denied, deferred, or regulated if it finds that:
(A) disclosure would result in a risk or harm outweighing any usefulness of the disclosure to any party; and
(B) the risk cannot be eliminated by a less substantial restriction of discovery rights.
(b) A Court's Discretion to Authorize Excision. If the court finds that only a portion of material or other information is subject to disclosure under Rule 15, it may enter an order authorizing the disclosing party to excise the portion that is not subject to disclosure.
(c) Protective and Excision Order Proceedings. If a party files a motion seeking a protective or excision order or requesting the court to determine whether any material or other information is subject to disclosure, the court may conduct an in camera inspection of the material. Counsel for all parties have the right to be heard on the matter before any in camera inspection is conducted.

(d) Preserving the Record. If the court orders that any portion of any material or information is not subject to disclosure under Rule 15, the entire text of the material or information must be sealed and preserved in the record for appeal.

(e) Claims of Privilege or Protection. A party who redacts a portion of a disclosed document must clearly identify the redaction and state the legal basis, if it is not clear from the context.

Credits

Added Aug. 31, 2017, effective Jan. 1, 2018.

Editors' Notes

HISTORICAL AND STATUTORY NOTES

Former Rule 15.5, relating to excision and protective orders, was abrogated effective Jan. 1, 2018. See, now, this rule.

16A A. R. S. Rules Crim. Proc., Rule 15.5, AZ ST RCRP Rule 15.5

Current with amendments received through 08/15/19

Rule 15.6. Continuing Duty to Disclose; Final Disclosure Deadline; Extension

(Refs & Annos)
IV. Pretrial Procedures
Rule 15. Disclosure (Refs & Annos)

16A A.R.S. Rules Crim.Proc., Rule 15.6

Rule 15.6. Continuing Duty to Disclose; Final Disclosure Deadline; Extension

(a) Continuing Duties. The parties' duties under Rule 15 are continuing duties without awaiting a specific request from any other party.

(b) Additional Disclosures. Any party who anticipates a need to provide additional disclosure no later than 30 days before trial must immediately notify both the court and all other parties of the circumstances and when the party will make the additional disclosure.

(c) Final Deadline for Disclosure. Unless otherwise permitted, all disclosure required by Rule 15 must be completed at least 7 days before trial.

(d) Disclosure After the Final Deadline.

(1) *Motion to Extend Disclosure.* If a party seeks to use material or information that was disclosed less than 7 days before trial, the party must file a motion to extend the disclosure deadline and to use the material or information. The moving party also must file a supporting affidavit setting forth facts justifying an extension.

(2) *Order Granting Motion.* The court must extend the disclosure deadline and allow the use of the material or information if it finds the material or information:

(A) could not have been discovered or disclosed earlier with due diligence; and

(B) was disclosed immediately upon its discovery.

(3) *Order Denying Motion or Granting Continuance; Sanctions.* If the court finds that the moving party has failed to establish facts sufficient to justify an extension under (d)(2), it may:

(A) deny the motion to extend the disclosure deadline and deny the use of the material or information; or

(B) extend the disclosure deadline and allow the use of the material or information and, if it extends the deadline, the court may impose any sanction listed in Rule 15.7 except preclusion or dismissal.

(e) Extension of Time for Completion of Testing.

(1) *Motion.* Before the final disclosure deadline in (c), a party may move to extend the deadline to permit the completion of scientific or other testing. The motion must be supported by an affidavit from a crime laboratory representative or other scientific expert stating that additional time is needed to complete the testing or a report based on the testing. The affidavit must specify how much additional time is needed.

(2) *Order.* If a motion is filed under (e)(1), the court must grant reasonable time to complete disclosure unless the court finds that the need for the extension resulted from dilatory conduct or neglect, or that the request is being made for an improper reason by the moving party or a person listed in Rule 15.1(f) or 15.2(f).

(3) *Extending Time.* If the court grants a motion under (e)(2), the court may extend other disclosure deadlines as necessary.

Credits

Added Aug. 31, 2017, effective Jan. 1, 2018.

Editors' Notes

HISTORICAL AND STATUTORY NOTES

Former Rule 15.6, relating to continuing duty to disclose, final disclosure deadline, and extension, was abrogated effective Jan. 1, 2018. See, now, this rule.

16A A. R. S. Rules Crim. Proc., Rule 15.6, AZ ST RCRP Rule 15.6

Current with amendments received through 08/15/19

Rule 15.7. Disclosure Violations and Sanctions

(Refs & Annos)

IV. Pretrial Procedures

Rule 15. Disclosure (Refs & Annos)

16A A.R.S. Rules Crim.Proc., Rule 15.7

Rule 15.7. Disclosure Violations and Sanctions

(a) Motion. Any party may move to compel disclosure or request an appropriate sanction for a disclosure violation of Rule 15 or both. Any motion to compel disclosure or for sanctions must include a separate statement that the moving party has personally consulted with opposing counsel and has made good faith efforts to resolve the matter. Any motion filed without the separate statement will not be heard or scheduled for a hearing.

(b) Order. If the court finds that a party violated a disclosure obligation under Rule 15, it must order disclosure as necessary and impose an appropriate sanction, unless the court finds that:

(1) the failure to comply was harmless; or

(2) the party could not have disclosed the information earlier with due diligence and the party disclosed the information immediately upon its discovery.

(c) Sanctions. In considering an appropriate sanction for nondisclosure or untimely disclosure, a court must determine the significance of the information not timely disclosed, the violation's impact on the overall administration of the case, the sanction's impact on the party and the victim, and the stage of the proceedings when the party ultimately made the disclosure. Available sanctions include, but are not limited to:

(1) precluding or limiting a witness, the use of evidence, or an argument supporting or opposing a charge or defense;

(2) dismissing the case with or without prejudice;

(3) granting a continuance or declaring a mistrial if necessary in the interests of justice;

(4) holding in contempt a witness, a party, or a person acting under the direction or control of a party;

(5) imposing costs of continuing the proceeding; or

(6) any other appropriate sanction.

Credits

Added Aug. 31, 2017, effective Jan. 1, 2018.

Editors' Notes

HISTORICAL AND STATUTORY NOTES

Former Rule 15.7, relating to sanctions, was abrogated effective Jan. 1, 2018. See, now, this rule.

16A A. R. S. Rules Crim. Proc., Rule 15.7, AZ ST RCRP Rule 15.7

Current with amendments received through 08/15/19

Rule 15.8. Disclosure Before a Plea Agreement Expires or Is Withdrawn; Sanctions

(Refs & Annos)

Rule 15. Disclosure (Refs & Annos)

16A A.R.S. Rules Crim.Proc., Rule 15.8

Rule 15.8. Disclosure Before a Plea Agreement Expires or Is Withdrawn; Sanctions

(a) Disclosure Obligation. If the State has filed an indictment or information in superior court and extends a plea offer to a defendant, the State must disclose to the defendant when it makes the offer the items listed in Rule 15.1(b) to the extent that it possesses the required information and has not previously made such a disclosure.

(b) Violation. If the State makes the disclosure less than 30 days before the offer expires or is withdrawn, a court may sanction the State under (d) unless the State shows that the prosecutor reasonably believed, based on newly discovered information, that an offer should be withdrawn because it was contrary to the interests of justice.

(c) Effect on Other Required Disclosures. This rule does not affect any disclosure obligation otherwise imposed by law. While a plea offer is pending, the prosecutor must continue to comply with Rule 15.6, but additional disclosures under that rule do not extend the 30-day period specified in (b). Disclosure of evidence after the offer expires or is withdrawn, including the results of any scientific testing, does not violate this rule if the evidence did not exist, or the State was not aware of it, when the State extended the offer.

(d) Sanctions. On a defendant's motion alleging a violation of this rule, the court must consider the impact of any violation of (a) on the defendant's decision to accept or reject a plea offer. If the court finds that the State's failure to provide a required disclosure materially affected the defendant's decision and if the State declines to reinstate the lapsed or withdrawn plea offer, the court--as a presumptive minimum sanction--must preclude the admission at trial of any evidence not disclosed as required by (a).

Credits

Added Aug. 31, 2017, effective Jan. 1, 2018.

Editors' Notes

HISTORICAL AND STATUTORY NOTES

Former Rule 15.8, relating to disclosure prior to expiration or withdrawal of a plea offer and sanctions, was abrogated effective Jan. 1, 2018. See, now, this rule.

Former Rule 15.8, relating to non-severability, was repealed as obsolete.

16A A. R. S. Rules Crim. Proc., Rule 15.8, AZ ST RCRP Rule 15.8

Current with amendments received through 08/15/19

Rule 15.9. Abrogated Aug. 31, 2017, effective Jan. 1, 2018

(Refs & Annos)
IV. Pretrial Procedures
Rule 15. Disclosure (Refs & Annos)
16A A.R.S. Rules Crim.Proc., Rule 15.9

Rule 15.9. Abrogated Aug. 31, 2017, effective Jan. 1, 2018

Editors' Notes
HISTORICAL AND STATUTORY NOTES
The abrogated rule related to appointment of investigators and expert witnesses for
indigent defendants.
16A A. R. S. Rules Crim. Proc., Rule 15.9, AZ ST RCRP Rule 15.9
Current with amendments received through 08/15/19

R. 16, Refs & Annos

IV. Pretrial Procedures
Rule 16. Pretrial Motions and Hearings
16A A.R.S. Rules Crim.Proc., R. 16, Refs & Annos

16A A. R. S. Rules Crim. Proc., R. 16, Refs & Annos, AZ ST RCRP R. 16, Refs &
Annos
Current with amendments received through 08/15/19

Rule 16.1. General Provisions

(Refs & Annos)
IV. Pretrial Procedures
Rule 16. Pretrial Motions and Hearings (Refs & Annos)
16A A.R.S. Rules Crim.Proc., Rule 16.1
Rule 16.1. General Provisions

(a) Scope. Rule 16 governs court procedures between arraignment and trial, unless
another rule provides a more specific procedure.
(b) Pretrial Motions. All motions must meet the requirements of Rules 1.6 and 1.9
and be served as provided in Rule 1.7. Parties must make all motions no later than
20 days before trial, except that lack of jurisdiction may be raised at any time.

Responsive pleadings are allowed as provided in Rule 1.9. The court may modify motion deadlines.

(c) Effect of a Failure to File or Make a Timely Motion. The court may preclude any motion, defense, objection, or request not timely raised by motion under (b), unless the basis was not then known and could not have been known through reasonable diligence, and the party raises it promptly after the basis is known.

(d) Finality of Pretrial Determinations. A court may not reconsider an issue previously decided in the case except for good cause or as these rules provide otherwise.

Credits

Added Aug. 31, 2017, effective Jan. 1, 2018.

Editors' Notes

COMMENT

Rule 16.1(d). This rule does not preclude the defendant from presenting relevant issues and properly disclosed defenses to the jury, such as voluntariness, reliability of expert testimony, or identification. *See Manson v. Brathwaite,* 432 U.S. 98, 114 (1977) (identification); *Neil v. Biggers*, 409 U.S. 188, 200-01 (1972) (identification); *Jackson v. Denno*, 378 U.S. 368, 379 (1964) (voluntariness); *State v. Romero*, 239 Ariz. 6, 12 ¶ 28, 365 P.3d 358, 364 (2016) (expert reliability); *State v. Lehr*, 201 Ariz. 509, 517 ¶ 24, 38 P.3d 1172, 1180 (2002) (expert reliability); *State v. Amaya-Ruiz*, 166 Ariz. 152, 168, 800 P.2d 1260, 1276 (1990) (expert reliability); *State v. Dessureault*, 104 Ariz. 380, 381-85, 453 P.2d 951, 952-56 (1969) (identification); A.R.S. § 13-3988 (voluntariness).

HISTORICAL AND STATUTORY NOTES

Former Rule 16.1, relating to general provisions, was abrogated effective Jan. 1, 2018. See, now, this rule.

16A A. R. S. Rules Crim. Proc., Rule 16.1, AZ ST RCRP Rule 16.1

Current with amendments received through 08/15/19

Rule 16.2. Procedure on Pretrial Motions to Suppress Evidence

(Refs & Annos)

IV. Pretrial Procedures

Rule 16. Pretrial Motions and Hearings (Refs & Annos)

16A A.R.S. Rules Crim.Proc., Rule 16.2

Rule 16.2. Procedure on Pretrial Motions to Suppress Evidence

(a) Definition. For purposes of this rule, "suppress" refers to the exclusion of evidence that was unlawfully obtained due to a constitutional violation.

(b) Burden of Proof on Pretrial Motions to Suppress Evidence.

(1) *Generally.* Subject to (b)(2), the State has the burden of proving by a preponderance of the evidence the lawfulness in all respects of the acquisition of all evidence that the State will use at trial.

(2) *Defendant's Burden.* If any of the conditions listed below are present, the State's burden of proof under (b)(1) arises only after the defendant alleges specific circumstances and establishes a prima facie case supporting the suppression of the evidence at issue:

(A) the evidence involves a confession, identification, search, or seizure, and the defendant is entitled under Rule 15 to discover how the evidence was obtained;

(B) defense counsel was present when the evidence was taken; or

(C) the evidence was obtained under a warrant.

(c) Duty of Court to Inform the Defendant. If an issue arises before trial concerning the constitutionality of using specific evidence against the defendant and the defendant is not represented by counsel, the court must inform the defendant that:

(1) the defendant may, but is not required to, testify at a pretrial hearing about the circumstances surrounding the acquisition of the evidence;

(2) if the defendant testifies at the hearing, the defendant will be subject to cross-examination;

(3) by testifying at the hearing, the defendant does not waive the right to remain silent at trial; and

(4) the defendant's testimony at the hearing, including the fact that such testimony occurred, will not be disclosed to the jury unless the defendant testifies at trial concerning the same matters.

Credits

Added Aug. 31, 2017, effective Jan. 1, 2018.

Editors' Notes

HISTORICAL AND STATUTORY NOTES

Former Rule 16.2, relating to procedure on pretrial motions to suppress evidence, was abrogated effective Jan. 1, 2018. See, now, this rule.

16A A. R. S. Rules Crim. Proc., Rule 16.2, AZ ST RCRP Rule 16.2

Current with amendments received through 08/15/19

Rule 16.3. Pretrial Conference

(Refs & Annos)

IV. Pretrial Procedures

Rule 16. Pretrial Motions and Hearings (Refs & Annos)

16A A.R.S. Rules Crim.Proc., Rule 16.3

Rule 16.3. Pretrial Conference

(a) Generally. A court may conduct one or more pretrial conferences. The court may establish procedures and requirements that are necessary to accomplish a conference's objectives, including identifying appropriate cases for pretrial conferences, identifying who must attend, and determining sanctions for failing to attend. A superior court must conduct at least one pretrial conference.

(b) Objectives. The objectives of a pretrial conference may include:

(1) providing a forum and a process for the fair, orderly, and just disposition of cases without trial;

(2) permitting the parties, without prejudice to their rights to trial, to engage in disclosure and to conduct negotiations for dispositions without trial;

(3) discussing compliance with discovery requirements set forth in these rules and constitutional law; and

(4) enabling the court to set a trial date.

(c) Duty to Confer. The court may require the parties to confer and submit memoranda before the conference.

(d) Scope of Proceeding. At the conference, the court may:

(1) hear motions made at or filed before the conference;

(2) set additional pretrial conferences and evidentiary hearings as appropriate;

(3) obtain stipulations to relevant facts; and

(4) discuss and determine any other matters that will promote a fair and expeditious trial, including imposing time limits on trial proceedings, using juror notebooks, giving brief pre-voir dire opening statements and preliminary instructions, and managing documents and exhibits effectively during trial.

(e) Stipulated Evidence. At a pretrial conference or any time before the start of an evidentiary hearing, the parties may submit any issue to the court for decision based on stipulated evidence.

(f) Record of Proceedings. Proceedings at a pretrial conference must be on the record.

Credits

Added Aug. 31, 2017, effective Jan. 1, 2018.

Editors' Notes

HISTORICAL AND STATUTORY NOTES

Former Rule 16.3, relating to procedure on omnibus hearings, was abrogated effective Jan. 1, 2018. See, now, AZ ST RCRP Rule 16.5.

16A A. R. S. Rules Crim. Proc., Rule 16.3, AZ ST RCRP Rule 16.3

Current with amendments received through 08/15/19

Rule 16.4. Dismissal of Prosecution

16A A.R.S. Rules Crim.Proc., Rule 16.4
Formerly cited as AZ ST RCRP Rule 16.6

Rule 16.4. Dismissal of Prosecution

(a) On the State's Motion. On the State's motion and for good cause, the court may order a prosecution dismissed without prejudice if it finds that the dismissal is not to avoid Rule 8 time limits.

(b) On a Defendant's Motion. On a defendant's motion, the court must order a prosecution's dismissal if it finds that the indictment, information, or complaint is insufficient as a matter of law.

(c) Record. If the court grants a motion to dismiss a prosecution, it must state on the record its reasons for ordering dismissal.

(d) Effect of Dismissal. Dismissal of a prosecution is without prejudice to commencing another prosecution, unless the court finds that the interests of justice require that the dismissal to be with prejudice.

(e) Release of Defendant; Exoneration of Bond. If a court dismisses a prosecution, the court must order the release of the defendant from custody, unless the defendant also is being held on another charge. It also must exonerate any appearance bond.

Credits

Added Aug. 31, 2017, effective Jan. 1, 2018.

Editors' Notes

HISTORICAL AND STATUTORY NOTES

Former Rule 16.4, relating to mandatory prehearing conference, was abrogated effective Jan. 1, 2018.

16A A. R. S. Rules Crim. Proc., Rule 16.4, AZ ST RCRP Rule 16.4

Current with amendments received through 08/15/19

Rule 16.5. Abrogated Aug. 31, 2017, effective Jan. 1, 2018

16A A.R.S. Rules Crim.Proc., Rule 16.5

Rule 16.5. Abrogated Aug. 31, 2017, effective Jan. 1, 2018

HISTORICAL AND STATUTORY NOTES
The abrogated rule related to procedure on pretrial conference. See, now, AZ ST RCRP Rule 16.3.
16A A. R. S. Rules Crim. Proc., Rule 16.5, AZ ST RCRP Rule 16.5
Current with amendments received through 08/15/19

Rule 16.6. Abrogated Aug. 31, 2017, effective Jan. 1, 2018

(Refs & Annos)
IV. Pretrial Procedures
Rule 16. Pretrial Motions and Hearings (Refs & Annos)
16A A.R.S. Rules Crim.Proc., Rule 16.6

Rule 16.6. Abrogated Aug. 31, 2017, effective Jan. 1, 2018

HISTORICAL AND STATUTORY NOTES   ˙
The abrogated rule related to dismissal of prosecution. See, now, AZ ST RCRP Rule 16.4.
16A A. R. S. Rules Crim. Proc., Rule 16.6, AZ ST RCRP Rule 16.6
Current with amendments received through 08/15/19

Rule 16.7. Deleted, effective Aug. 1, 1975

(Refs & Annos)
IV. Pretrial Procedures
Rule 16. Pretrial Motions and Hearings (Refs & Annos)
16A A.R.S. Rules Crim.Proc., Rule 16.7

Rule 16.7. Deleted, effective Aug. 1, 1975

HISTORICAL NOTES
Deleted Rule 16.7 related to the dismissal of prosecutions.
See, now, Rule 16.6.
16A A. R. S. Rules Crim. Proc., Rule 16.7, AZ ST RCRP Rule 16.7
Current with amendments received through 08/15/19

V. Pleas of Guilty and NO Contest
Rule 17. Pleas of Guilty and NO Contest; Submitting a Case on the Record
16A A.R.S. Rules Crim.Proc., R. 17, Refs & Annos

16A A. R. S. Rules Crim. Proc., R. 17, Refs & Annos, AZ ST RCRP R. 17, Refs & Annos
Current with amendments received through 08/15/19

Rule 17.1. The Defendant's Plea

(Refs & Annos)
V. Pleas of Guilty and NO Contest
Rule 17. Pleas of Guilty and NO Contest; Submitting a Case on the Record (Refs & Annos)
16A A.R.S. Rules Crim.Proc., Rule 17.1
Rule 17.1. The Defendant's Plea

(a) Jurisdiction; Personal Appearance.
(1) *Jurisdiction.* Only a court having jurisdiction to try the offense may accept a plea of guilty or no contest.
(2) *Personal Appearance.* Except as provided in these rules, a court may accept a plea only if the defendant makes it personally in open court. If the defendant is a corporation, defense counsel or a corporate officer may enter a plea for the corporation. For purposes of this rule, a defendant who makes an appearance under Rule 1.5 is deemed to personally appear.
(b) Voluntary and Intelligent Plea. A court may accept a plea of guilty or no contest only if the defendant enters the plea voluntarily and intelligently. Courts must use the procedures in Rules 17.2, 17.3, and 17.4 to assure compliance with this rule.
(c) No Contest Plea. A plea of no contest may be accepted only after the court gives due consideration to the parties' views and to the interest of the public in the effective administration of justice.
(d) Record of a Plea. The court must make a complete record of all plea proceedings.
(e) Waiver of Appeal. By pleading guilty or no contest in a noncapital case, a defendant waives the right to have the appellate courts review the proceedings on a

direct appeal. A defendant who pleads guilty or no contest may seek review only by filing a petition for post-conviction relief under Rule 32 and, if it is denied, a petition for review.

(f) Limited Jurisdiction Court Alternatives for Entering a Plea.

(1) *Telephonic Pleas.*

(A) Eligibility. A limited jurisdiction court has discretion to accept a telephonic plea of guilty or no contest to an offense if the defendant provides written certification and the court finds the defendant:

(i) resides out-of-state or more than 100 miles from the court in which the plea is taken; or

(ii) has a serious medical condition so that appearing in person would be an undue hardship, regardless of distance to the court.

(B) Procedure. The defendant must submit the plea in writing substantially in the form set forth in Rule 41, Form 28. It must include the following:

(i) a statement by the defendant that the defendant has read and understands the information in the form, waives applicable constitutional rights for a plea, and enters a plea of guilty or no contest to each of offenses in the complaint; and

(ii) a certification from a peace officer in the state in which the defendant resides--or, if the defendant is an Arizona resident, a peace officer in the county in which the defendant resides--that the defendant personally appeared before the officer and signed the certification described in (f)(1)(B)(i), and the officer affixes the defendant's fingerprint to the form.

(C) Judicial Findings. Before accepting a plea, the court must hold a telephonic hearing with the parties, inform the defendant that the offense may be used as a prior conviction, and find:

(i) it has personally advised the defendant of the items set forth in the form;

(ii) a factual basis exists for believing the defendant is guilty of the charged offenses; and

(iii) the defendant's plea is knowingly, voluntarily, and intelligently entered.

(2) *Plea by Mail.*

(A) Eligibility. A limited jurisdiction court has discretion to accept by mail a written plea of guilty or no contest to a misdemeanor or petty offense if the court finds that a personal appearance by the defendant would constitute an undue hardship such as illness, physical incapacity, substantial travel distance, or incarceration. The presiding judge of each court must establish a policy for the State's participation in pleas submitted by mail.

(B) When a Plea May Not Be Accepted by Mail. A court may not accept a plea by mail in a case:

(i) involving a victim;

(ii) in which the court may impose a jail term, unless the defendant is sentenced to time served or the defendant is currently incarcerated and the proposed term of incarceration would be served concurrently and not extend the period of incarceration;

(iii) in which the court may sentence the defendant to a term of probation;

(iv) involving an offense for which A.R.S. § 13-607 requires the taking of a fingerprint upon sentencing; or

(v) in which this method of entering a plea would not be in the interests of justice.

(C) Procedure. The defendant must submit the plea in writing substantially in the form set forth in Rule 41, Form 28(a). The defendant must sign the plea form, which must include the following:

(i) a statement that the defendant has read and understands the information on the form, waives applicable constitutional rights for a plea, and enters a plea of guilty or no contest to each of the offenses in the complaint and consents to the entry of judgment; and

(ii) a statement for the court to consider when determining the sentence.

(D) Mailing. The court must mail a copy of the judgment to the defendant.

Credits

Added Aug. 31, 2017, effective Jan. 1, 2018.

Editors' Notes

HISTORICAL AND STATUTORY NOTES

Former Rule 17.1, relating to pleading by defendant, was abrogated effective Jan. 1, 2018. See, now, this rule.

16A A. R. S. Rules Crim. Proc., Rule 17.1, AZ ST RCRP Rule 17.1

Current with amendments received through 08/15/19

Rule 17.2. Advising of Rights and Consequences of a Guilty or No Contest Plea

(Refs & Annos)

V. Pleas of Guilty and NO Contest

Rule 17. Pleas of Guilty and NO Contest; Submitting a Case on the Record (Refs & Annos)

16A A.R.S. Rules Crim.Proc., Rule 17.2

Rule 17.2. Advising of Rights and Consequences of a Guilty or No Contest Plea

(a) Generally. Except as provided in Rule 17.1(f)(2), before accepting a plea of guilty or no contest, the court must address the defendant personally, inform the defendant of the following, and determine that the defendant understands:

(1) the nature of the charges to which the defendant will plead;

(2) the range of possible sentences for the offenses to which the defendant is pleading, any special conditions regarding sentencing, parole, or commutation imposed by statute;

(3) the constitutional rights that the defendant foregoes by pleading guilty or no contest, including the right to counsel if defendant is not represented by counsel;

(4) the right to plead not guilty; and

(5) in a noncapital case, the defendant's plea of guilty or no contest will waive the right to appellate court review of the proceedings on a direct appeal; and that the defendant may seek review only by filing a petition for post-conviction relief under Rule 32 and, if it is denied, a petition for review.

(b) Immigration Advisement.

(1) *Advisement.* The court must advise that a plea may have immigration consequences and specifically state:

"If you are not a citizen of the United States, pleading guilty or no contest to a crime may affect your immigration status. Admitting guilt may result in deportation even if the charge is later dismissed. Your plea or admission of guilt could result in your deportation or removal, could prevent you from ever being able to get legal status in the United States, or could prevent you from becoming a United States citizen."

(2) *Advisement Before Admission of Facts.* A court also must give the advisement in (b)(1) before any admission of facts sufficient to warrant a finding of guilt, or before any submission on the record.

(3) *Disclosure of Immigration Status.* A court may not require a defendant to disclose his or her legal status in the United States.

Credits

Added Aug. 31, 2017, effective Jan. 1, 2018.

Editors' Notes

HISTORICAL AND STATUTORY NOTES

Former Rule 17.2, relating to duty of court to advise of defendant's rights and of the consequences of pleading guilty or no contest, or of admitting guilt, or of submitting on the record, was abrogated effective Jan. 1, 2018. See, now, this rule.

16A A. R. S. Rules Crim. Proc., Rule 17.2, AZ ST RCRP Rule 17.2

Current with amendments received through 08/15/19

Rule 17.3. A Court's Duty to Determine Whether a Plea Is Entered Voluntarily and Intelligen...

(Refs & Annos)

V. Pleas of Guilty and NO Contest

Rule 17. Pleas of Guilty and NO Contest; Submitting a Case on the Record (Refs & Annos)

16A A.R.S. Rules Crim.Proc., Rule 17.3

Rule 17.3. A Court's Duty to Determine Whether a Plea Is Entered Voluntarily and Intelligently

(a) Required Judicial Determination. Except as provided in Rule 17.1(f)(2), a court may not accept a plea of guilty or no contest unless it determines, after addressing the defendant personally in open court, that:

(1) the defendant wishes to forego the constitutional rights of which the defendant has been advised; and

(2) the defendant's plea is voluntary and not the result of force, threats or promises (other than that which is included in the plea agreement).

(b) Determining a Factual Basis. The court must find a factual basis for all guilty or no contest pleas. When making this finding, the court may consider the defendant's statements, police reports, certified transcripts of grand jury proceedings, or other satisfactory information. The court may make this finding at the time of the plea, or it may defer that determination until judgment is entered.

Credits

Added Aug. 31, 2017, effective Jan. 1, 2018.

Editors' Notes

HISTORICAL AND STATUTORY NOTES

Former Rule 17.3, relating to duty of court to determine voluntariness and intelligence of the plea, was abrogated effective Jan. 1, 2018. See, now, this rule.

16A A. R. S. Rules Crim. Proc., Rule 17.3, AZ ST RCRP Rule 17.3

Current with amendments received through 08/15/19

Rule 17.4. Plea Negotiations and Agreements

(Refs & Annos)

V. Pleas of Guilty and NO Contest

Rule 17. Pleas of Guilty and NO Contest; Submitting a Case on the Record (Refs & Annos)

16A A.R.S. Rules Crim.Proc., Rule 17.4

Rule 17.4. Plea Negotiations and Agreements

(a) Plea Negotiations.

(1) *Generally.* The parties may negotiate and reach agreement on any aspect of a case.

(2) *Judicial Participation.* At either party's request or on its own, a court may order counsel with settlement authority to participate in good faith discussions to resolve the case in a manner that serves the interests of justice. The assigned trial judge may participate in this discussion only if the parties consent. In all other cases, the discussion must be before another judge. If settlement discussions do not result in an agreement, the case must be returned to the trial judge.

(3) *Victim Participation.* The victim must have an opportunity to confer with the prosecutor, if they have not already conferred, before any case resolution. The prosecutor or the victim's representative must inform the court and defense counsel of the victim's position. If the defendant is present during settlement discussions, the victim also must have the opportunity to be present and to be heard regarding settlement.

(b) Plea Agreement. The terms of a plea agreement must be in writing and be signed by the defendant, defense counsel (if any), and the prosecutor. The parties must file the agreement with the court. Any party may withdraw from an agreement before the court accepts it.

(c) Determining Accuracy, Voluntariness, and Intelligent Acceptance of the Agreement. Before accepting the plea agreement, the court must address the defendant and confirm that the written plea agreement contains all the agreement's terms and that the defendant understands and agrees to the terms.

(d) Accepting the Plea. After making the determinations required by this rule and after considering any comments expressed by the victim, the court must either accept or reject the submitted plea. The court is not bound by any provision in the plea agreement regarding the sentence or probation terms and conditions if, after accepting the agreement and reviewing a presentence report, the court rejects the provision as inappropriate.

(e) Rejecting the Plea. If the court rejects a plea agreement or any provision in the agreement, it must give the defendant an opportunity to withdraw the plea. The court must inform the defendant that if the plea is not withdrawn, the disposition of the case may be less favorable to the defendant than what the agreement provided.

(f) Admissibility or Inadmissibility of a Plea, Plea Discussions, and Related Statements. Arizona Rule of Evidence 410 governs the admissibility of a plea, a plea discussion, and any related statement.

(g) Change of Judge if Plea Withdrawn. A defendant who withdraws a plea after a presentence report is submitted may exercise a change of judge as a matter of right under Rule 10.2 if the defendant has not previously exercised that right.

Credits

Added Aug. 31, 2017, effective Jan. 1, 2018.

HISTORICAL AND STATUTORY NOTES
Former Rule 17.4, relating to plea negotiations and agreements, was abrogated effective Jan. 1, 2018. See, now, this rule.
16A A. R. S. Rules Crim. Proc., Rule 17.4, AZ ST RCRP Rule 17.4
Current with amendments received through 08/15/19

Rule 17.5. Withdrawal of a Plea

(Refs & Annos)
V. Pleas of Guilty and NO Contest
Rule 17. Pleas of Guilty and NO Contest; Submitting a Case on the Record (Refs & Annos)

16A A.R.S. Rules Crim.Proc., Rule 17.5

Rule 17.5. Withdrawal of a Plea

The court may allow a defendant to withdraw a plea of guilty or no contest if it is necessary to correct a manifest injustice. Upon withdrawal of a plea, the charges against the defendant will be reinstated automatically as they existed before the plea agreement.
Credits
Added Aug. 31, 2017, effective Jan. 1, 2018.
HISTORICAL AND STATUTORY NOTES
Former Rule 17.5, relating to withdrawal of plea, was abrogated effective Jan. 1, 2018. See, now, this rule.
16A A. R. S. Rules Crim. Proc., Rule 17.5, AZ ST RCRP Rule 17.5
Current with amendments received through 08/15/19

Rule 17.6. Admitting a Prior Conviction

(Refs & Annos)
V. Pleas of Guilty and NO Contest
Rule 17. Pleas of Guilty and NO Contest; Submitting a Case on the Record (Refs & Annos)

16A A.R.S. Rules Crim.Proc., Rule 17.6

Rule 17.6. Admitting a Prior Conviction

The court may accept the defendant's admission to an allegation of a prior conviction only under the procedures of this rule, unless the defendant admits the allegation while testifying in court.

Credits

Added Aug. 31, 2017, effective Jan. 1, 2018.

Editors' Notes

HISTORICAL AND STATUTORY NOTES

Former Rule 17.6, relating to admission of prior conviction, was abrogated effective Jan. 1, 2018. See, now, this rule.

16A A. R. S. Rules Crim. Proc., Rule 17.6, AZ ST RCRP Rule 17.6

Current with amendments received through 08/15/19

Rule 17.7. Submitting a Case on the Record

(Refs & Annos)

V. Pleas of Guilty and NO Contest

Rule 17. Pleas of Guilty and NO Contest; Submitting a Case on the Record (Refs & Annos)

16A A.R.S. Rules Crim.Proc., Rule 17.7

Rule 17.7. Submitting a Case on the Record

(a) Submission; Advising of Rights and Consequences of a Submission on the Record. If a defendant and the State agree, the parties may submit a case to the court on a stipulated record. The court must address the defendant personally and inform the defendant:

(1) the judge will determine guilt or innocence based solely on the submitted record;

(2) of the range of sentence and any special conditions of sentencing;

(3) of all Rule 17.2 disclosures under Rule 17.2(a)(1)-(4) and (b) about plea rights and consequences;

(4) of the defendant's waiver of the right to a jury trial (if the offense is eligible);

(5) the defendant's waiver of the right to be represented by counsel at such a trial; and

(6) if the defendant is found guilty, the defendant has the right to appeal.

(b) Accepting the Submission. A court may accept an agreement to submit the case on a stipulated record only if it determines that the defendant has entered the agreement voluntarily and intelligently.

Credits

Added Aug. 31, 2017, effective Jan. 1, 2018.

16A A. R. S. Rules Crim. Proc., Rule 17.7, AZ ST RCRP Rule 17.7

VI. Trial

Rule 18. Trial by Jury; Waiver; Selection and Preparation of Jurors

16A A.R.S. Rules Crim.Proc., R. 18, Refs & Annos

Editors' Notes

CONSTITUTIONAL PROVISIONS

Article 2, § 23, provides: "The right of trial by jury shall remain inviolate. Juries in criminal cases in which a sentence of death or imprisonment for thirty years or more is authorized by law shall consist of twelve persons. In all criminal cases the unanimous consent of the jurors shall be necessary to render a verdict. In all other cases, the number of jurors, not less than six, and the number required to render a verdict, shall be specified by law."

16A A. R. S. Rules Crim. Proc., R. 18, Refs & Annos, AZ ST RCRP R. 18, Refs & Annos

Current with amendments received through 08/15/19

Rule 18.1. Trial by Jury

(Refs & Annos)

VI. Trial

Rule 18. Trial by Jury; Waiver; Selection and Preparation of Jurors (Refs & Annos)

16A A.R.S. Rules Crim.Proc., Rule 18.1

Rule 18.1. Trial by Jury

(a) By Jury. The number of jurors required to try a case and render a verdict is provided by law.

(b) Waiver.

(1) *Generally.* The defendant may waive the right to a trial by jury if the State and the court consent. If the State and the court agree, a defendant also may waive the right to have a jury determine aggravation or the penalty in a capital case.

(2) *Voluntariness.* Before accepting a defendant's waiver of a jury trial, the court must address the defendant personally, inform the defendant of the defendant's

right to a jury trial, and determine that the defendant's waiver is knowing, voluntary, and intelligent.

(3) *Form of Waiver.* A defendant's waiver of a jury trial must be in writing or on the record in open court.

(4) *Withdrawal of Waiver.* With the court's permission, a defendant may withdraw a waiver of jury trial, but a defendant may not withdraw a waiver after the court begins taking evidence.

Credits

Added Aug. 31, 2017, effective Jan. 1, 2018.

Editors' Notes

COMMENT

Rule 18.1(a). The right of trial by jury is inviolate. A jury must consist of 12 persons in a criminal case in which a sentence of death or imprisonment for 30 years or more is authorized by law. In all such cases, the verdict must be unanimous. In all other cases, a jury must consist of at least 6 jurors, with the number required to render a verdict as specified by law. *See generally* Ariz. Const. art. 2, § 23 (restating comment); A.R.S. § 21-102 (jury size, degree of unanimity required; waiver); *Williams v. Florida*, 399 U.S. 78, 103 (1970) (Sixth Amendment does not require 12-person jury in a criminal matter; Sixth Amendment rights not violated by Florida statute providing for a 6-person jury).

The right to a jury trial for misdemeanor offenses extends to charges where the statutory offense has a common law antecedent that guaranteed the right to jury trial at the time of statehood, or where the offense qualifies as a "serious" offense with "additional severe, direct and uniformly applied statutory consequences." *Derendal v. Griffith*, 209 Ariz. 416, 423 ¶ 26, 104 P.3d 147, 154 (2005). Statutory offenses with 6 months or less of possible incarceration are presumptively not "serious offenses" unless the "additional grave consequences" of the misdemeanor conviction indicate the legislative determination that the offense is "serious" and mandates a jury. *Id.* at 422 ¶ 21, 104 P.3d at 153.

Rule 18.1(b). Rule 18.1(b)(1) reflects the constitutional provision that a defendant may waive a jury trial only with the consent of the court and the State. Ariz. Const. art. 6, § 17 (a jury may be waived by the parties in a criminal case with the court's consent); *see also* Ariz. R. Crim. P. 41, Form 20 (form for waiving jury trial).

HISTORICAL AND STATUTORY NOTES

Former Rule 18.1, relating to trial by jury, was abrogated effective Jan. 1, 2018. See, now, this rule.

16A A. R. S. Rules Crim. Proc., Rule 18.1, AZ ST RCRP Rule 18.1

Current with amendments received through 08/15/19

Rule 18.2. Additional Jurors

(Refs & Annos)

VI. Trial

Rule 18. Trial by Jury; Waiver; Selection and Preparation of Jurors (Refs & Annos)

16A A.R.S. Rules Crim.Proc., Rule 18.2

Rule 18.2. Additional Jurors

As deemed necessary, the court may empanel jurors in excess of the number required to render a verdict as it deems necessary. All jurors are deemed trial jurors until alternate jurors are designated under Rule 18.5(h).

Credits

Added Aug. 31, 2017, effective Jan. 1, 2018.

Editors' Notes

HISTORICAL AND STATUTORY NOTES

Former Rule 18.2, relating to additional jurors, was abrogated effective Jan. 1, 2018. See, now, this rule.

16A A. R. S. Rules Crim. Proc., Rule 18.2, AZ ST RCRP Rule 18.2

Current with amendments received through 08/15/19

Rule 18.3. Jurors' Information

(Refs & Annos)

VI. Trial

Rule 18. Trial by Jury; Waiver; Selection and Preparation of Jurors (Refs & Annos)

16A A.R.S. Rules Crim.Proc., Rule 18.3

Rule 18.3. Jurors' Information

(a) Information Provided to the Parties. Before conducting voir dire examination, the court must furnish each party with a list of the names of the prospective jurors on the panel called for the case. The list must include each prospective juror's zip code, employment status, occupation, employer, residency status, education level, prior jury duty experience, and any prior felony conviction within a specified time established by the jury commissioner or the court.

(b) Confidentiality. The court must obtain and maintain juror information in a manner and form approved by the Supreme Court, and this information may be used only for the purpose of jury selection. The court must keep all jurors' home and business telephone numbers and addresses confidential, and may not disclose them unless good cause is shown.

Credits
Added Aug. 31, 2017, effective Jan. 1, 2018.
Editors' Notes
HISTORICAL AND STATUTORY NOTES
Former Rule 18.3, relating to jury information, was abrogated effective Jan. 1, 2018.
See, now, this rule.
16A A. R. S. Rules Crim. Proc., Rule 18.3, AZ ST RCRP Rule 18.3
Current with amendments received through 08/15/19

Rule 18.4. Challenges

(Refs & Annos)
VI. Trial
Rule 18. Trial by Jury; Waiver; Selection and Preparation of Jurors (Refs & Annos)
16A A.R.S. Rules Crim.Proc., Rule 18.4

Rule 18.4. Challenges

(a) **Challenge to the Panel.** Any party may challenge the panel on the ground that its selection involved a material departure from the requirements of law. Challenges to the panel on this ground must be in writing, specify the factual basis for the challenge, and make a showing of prejudice to the party. A party must make, and the court must decide, a challenge to a panel before the examination of any individual prospective juror.

(b) **Challenge for Cause.** On motion or on its own, the court must excuse a prospective juror or jurors from service in the case if there is a reasonable ground to believe that the juror or jurors cannot render a fair and impartial verdict. A challenge for cause may be made at any time, but the court may deny a challenge if the party was not diligent in making it.

(c) **Peremptory Challenges.**

(1) *Generally.* The court must allow both parties the following number of peremptory challenges:

(A) 10, if the offense charged is punishable by death;

(B) 6, in all other cases tried in superior court; and

(C) two, in all cases tried in limited jurisdiction courts.

(2) *If Several Defendants Are Tried Jointly.* If there is more than one defendant, each defendant is allowed one-half the number of peremptory challenges allowed to one defendant. The State is not entitled to any additional peremptory challenges.

(3) *Agreement Between the Parties.* The parties may agree to exercise fewer than the allowable number of peremptory challenges.

Credits

Added Aug. 31, 2017, effective Jan. 1, 2018.

Editors' Notes

COMMENT

Rule 18.4(b). When the predecessor to this section was adopted in 1973, it replaced the catalog of 15 grounds set forth in the 1956 Arizona , Rule 219. The omission of the list is carried over to this amended rule and is intended to direct the attention of attorneys and judges to the essential question--whether a juror can try a case fairly. A challenge for cause can be based on a showing of facts from which an ordinary person would imply a likelihood of predisposition in favor of one of the parties.

In addition, a juror may be challenged who:

(1) has been convicted of a felony;

(2) lacks any of the qualifications prescribed by law to render a person a competent juror;

(3) is of such unsound mind or body as to render him incapable of performing the duties of a juror;

(4) is related by consanguinity or affinity within the fourth degree to the person alleged to be injured by the offense charged, or on whose complaint the prosecution was instituted, or to the defendant;

(5) stands in the relationship of guardian and ward, attorney and client, master and servant, or landlord and tenant, or is an employee of or member of the family of the defendant, or of the person alleged to be injured by the offense charged or on whose complaint the prosecution was instituted;

(6) has been a party adverse to the defendant in a civil action, or has complained against or been accused by him in a criminal prosecution;

(7) has served on the grand jury which found the indictment, or on a coroner's jury which inquired into the death of a person whose death is the subject of the indictment or information;

(8) has served on the trial jury which has tried another person for the offense charged in the indictment or information;

(9) has been a member of the jury formerly sworn to try the same charge and whose verdict was set aside, or which was discharged without a verdict after the case was submitted to it;

(10) has served as a juror in a civil action brought against the defendant for the act charged as an offense;

(11) is on the bond of the defendant or engaged in business with the defendant or with the person alleged to be injured by the offense charged or on whose complaint the prosecution was instituted;

(12) is a witness on the part of the prosecution or defendant or has been served with a subpoena or bound by an undertaking as such;

(13) has a state of mind in reference to the action or to the defendant or to the person alleged to have been injured by the offense charged or on whose complaint the prosecution was instituted, which will prevent him from acting with entire impartiality and without prejudice to the substantial rights of either party;

(14) if the offense charged is punishable by death, entertains conscientious opinions which would preclude his finding the defendant guilty, in which case he must neither be permitted nor compelled to serve as a juror; or

(15) does not understand the English language sufficiently well to comprehend the testimony offered at the trial.

This section also permits a challenge for cause to be made whenever the cause appears. Under Rule 18.4(b), the trial court may deny the challenge if not seasonably made, but there is no absolute time limitation imposed by rule. Once the trial has begun, the prosecutor may be unable, because of double jeopardy, to invoke the right to challenge, unless there are sufficient alternate jurors to enable the trial to continue with one less juror.

HISTORICAL AND STATUTORY NOTES

Former Rule 18.3, relating to challenges, was abrogated effective Jan. 1, 2018. See, now, this rule.

16A A. R. S. Rules Crim. Proc., Rule 18.4, AZ ST RCRP Rule 18.4

Current with amendments received through 08/15/19

Rule 18.5. Procedure for Jury Selection

(Refs & Annos)

VI. Trial

Rule 18. Trial by Jury; Waiver; Selection and Preparation of Jurors (Refs & Annos)
16A A.R.S. Rules Crim.Proc., Rule 18.5

Rule 18.5. Procedure for Jury Selection

(a) Swearing the Jury Panel. All members of the jury panel must swear or affirm that they will truthfully answer all questions concerning their qualifications.

(b) Calling Jurors for Examination. The court may call to the jury box a number of prospective jurors equal to the number to serve plus the number of alternates plus the number of peremptory challenges that the parties are permitted. Alternatively, and at the court's discretion, all members of the panel may be examined.

(c) Inquiry by the Court; Brief Opening Statements. Before examining the prospective jurors, the court must identify the parties and their counsel, briefly outline the nature of the case, and explain the purpose of the examination. The court must then ask any necessary questions about the prospective jurors' qualifications to serve in the case. With the court's permission and before voir dire examination, the parties may present brief opening statements to the entire jury panel.

(d) Voir Dire Examination. In courts of record, voir dire examination must be conducted on the record. The court must conduct a thorough oral examination of the prospective jurors and control the voir dire examination. Upon request, the court must allow the parties a reasonable time, with other reasonable limitations, to conduct a further oral examination of the prospective jurors. However, the court may limit or terminate the parties' voir dire on grounds of abuse. Nothing in this rule precludes submitting written questionnaires to the prospective jurors or examining individual prospective jurors outside the presence of other prospective jurors.

(e) Scope of Examination. The court must ensure the reasonable protection of the prospective jurors' privacy. Questioning must be limited to inquiries designed to elicit information relevant to asserting a possible challenge for cause or enabling a party to intelligently exercise the party's peremptory challenges.

(f) Challenge for Cause. Challenges for cause must be on the record and made out of the hearing of the prospective jurors. If the court grants a challenge for cause, it must excuse the affected prospective juror. If insufficient prospective jurors remain on the list, the court must add a prospective juror from a new panel. All challenges for cause must be made and decided before the court may call on the parties to exercise their peremptory challenges.

(g) Exercise of Peremptory Challenges. After examining the prospective jurors and completing all challenges for cause, the parties must exercise their peremptory challenges on the list of prospective jurors by alternating strikes, beginning with the State, until the peremptory challenges are exhausted or a party elects not to exercise further challenges. Failure of a party to exercise a challenge in turn operates as a waiver of the party's remaining challenges, but it does not deprive the other party of that party's full number of challenges. If the parties fail to exercise the full number of allowed challenges, the court will strike the jurors on the bottom of the list of prospective jurors until only the number to serve, plus alternates, remain.

(h) Selection of Jury; Alternate Jurors.

(1) *Trial Jurors.* After the completion of the procedures in (g), the prospective jurors remaining in the jury box or on the list of prospective jurors constitute the trial jurors.

(2) *Selection of Alternates and Instruction.* Just before the jury retires to begin deliberations, the clerk or court official must determine the alternate juror or jurors by lot or stipulation. When the jury retires to deliberate, the alternate or alternates may not participate, but the court must instruct the alternate juror or jurors to continue to observe the admonitions to jurors until the court informs them that a verdict has been returned or the jury has been discharged.

(3) *Replacing a Deliberating Juror.* If the court excuses a deliberating juror due to the juror's inability or disqualification to perform the required duties, the court may substitute an alternate juror to join the deliberations, choosing the alternate from among the qualified alternates in the order previously designated. If an alternate joins the deliberations, the court must instruct the jury to begin its deliberations anew.

(i) Deliberations in a Capital Case.

(1) *Retaining Alternates.* In a capital case, alternate jurors not selected to participate in the guilt phase deliberations must not be excused if the jury returns a guilty verdict of first-degree murder. This rule governs their continued participation in the case.

(A) Aggravation Phase. During the aggravation phase, the alternate jurors must listen to the evidence and argument presented to the jury. When the jury retires to deliberate on aggravation, the alternate or alternates may not participate, but the court must instruct the alternates to continue to observe the admonitions to jurors until the court informs the alternates that they are discharged.

(B) Penalty Phase. If the jury returns a verdict finding one or more aggravating factors, the alternate jurors must listen to the evidence and argument presented at the penalty phase. When the jury retires to deliberate on the penalty, the alternate or alternates may not participate, but the court must instruct the alternates to continue to observe the admonitions to jurors until the court informs the alternates that they are discharged.

(2) *Replacing a Deliberating Juror.*

(A) Generally. If a deliberating juror is excused during either the aggravation or penalty phases due to the juror's inability or disqualification to perform required duties, the court may substitute an alternate juror to join the deliberations, choosing from among the qualified alternates in the order previously designated.

(B) Scope of Deliberations. If an alternate or alternates are substituted during the aggravation or penalty deliberations, the jurors must begin their deliberations anew only for the phase that they are currently deliberating. The jurors may not deliberate anew a verdict already reached and entered.

Credits

Added Aug. 31, 2017, effective Jan. 1, 2018.

Editors' Notes

COMMENT

Rule 18.5(b). Before a 1995 amendment, Rule 18.5(b) was interpreted to require trial judges to use the traditional "strike and replace" method of jury selection, where only a portion of the jury panel is examined, the remaining jurors being called upon to participate in jury selection only upon excusing for cause a juror in the initial group. A juror excused for cause leaves the courtroom, after which the excused juror's position is filled by a panel member who responds to all previous and future questions of the potential jurors.

As currently drafted, the trial judge is allowed to use the "struck" method of selection if the judge chooses. This procedure is thought by some to offer more advantages than the "strike and replace" method. *See* T. Munsterman, R. Strand and J. Hart, *The Best Method of Selecting Jurors*, THE JUDGES' JOURNAL 9 (Summer 1990); A.B.A. Standards Relating to Juror Use and Management, Standard 7, at 68-74 (1983); and "The Jury Project," Report to the Chief Judge of the State of New York 58-60 (1994).

The "struck" method calls for all of the jury panel members to participate in voir dire examination by the judge and counsel. Following disposition of the for cause challenges, the juror list is given to counsel for the exercise of their peremptory strikes. When all the peremptory strikes have been taken and the court has resolved all related issues under *Batson v. Kentucky*, 476 U.S. 79 (1986), the clerk calls the first 8 or 12 names, as the law may require, remaining on the list, plus the number of alternate jurors thought necessary by the judge, who become the trial jury.

Rule 18.5(d). The court should instruct counsel that voir dire is permitted to enable counsel to ask questions seeking relevant information from jurors, but not to ask questions intended to raise arguments to the jurors. The court should be particularly sensitive to the prejudice that can arise from voir dire by an unrepresented defendant.

HISTORICAL AND STATUTORY NOTES

Former Rule 18.5, relating to procedure for selecting a jury, was abrogated effective Jan. 1, 2018. See, now, this rule.

16A A. R. S. Rules Crim. Proc., Rule 18.5, AZ ST RCRP Rule 18.5

Current with amendments received through 08/15/19

Rule 18.6. Jurors' Conduct

(Refs & Annos)
VI. Trial
Rule 18. Trial by Jury; Waiver; Selection and Preparation of Jurors (Refs & Annos)
16A A.R.S. Rules Crim.Proc., Rule 18.6

Rule 18.6. Jurors' Conduct

(a) Information. The court may provide prospective jurors with orientation information about jury service.

(b) Oath. Each juror must take the following oath:

"Do you swear (or affirm) that you will give careful attention to the proceedings, follow the court's instructions, including the admonition, and render a verdict in accordance with the law and evidence presented to you, (so help you God)?"

If a juror affirms, the clause "so help you God" must be omitted. In justice court cases, the court should give jurors the oath prescribed by A.R.S. § 22-322.

(c) Preliminary Instructions. After the jury is sworn, the court must instruct the jury concerning its duties, its conduct, the order of proceedings, the procedure for submitting written questions to witnesses or the court as set forth in (e), and legal principles that will govern the proceeding. Instructions should be as readily understandable as possible by individuals unfamiliar with the legal system.

(d) Juror Note Taking and Notebooks.

(1) *Juror Note Taking.* The court must instruct the jurors that they may take notes. The court must provide materials suitable for this purpose.

(2) *Juror Notebooks.* To aid the jurors in performing their duties, the court may authorize the parties to provide the jurors with notebooks containing documents and exhibits.

(3) *Juror Access.* Jurors must have access to their notes and notebooks during recesses and deliberations. In a capital case, the jurors must have access to their notes from the trial and all phases of the proceeding until the jury renders a penalty verdict or is dismissed.

(4) *Disposal of Juror Notes.* When the jury is discharged, all juror notes, including deliberation notes, must be promptly collected and destroyed.

(e) Juror Questions. Jurors must be instructed that they are permitted to submit to the court written questions directed to witnesses or to the court and that the court will give the parties an opportunity to object to those questions outside the jury's presence. Despite this general rule, the court may prohibit or limit the submission of questions to witnesses for good cause.

(f) Additional Communications. During the course of the trial, the court must provide additional instructions to the jury as necessary. All communications between the judge and members of the jury panel must be in writing or on the record.

Credits

Added Aug. 31, 2017, effective Jan. 1, 2018.

Editors' Notes

COMMENT

Rule 18.6(d). In trials of unusual duration or involving complex issues, juror notebooks are a significant aid to juror comprehension and recall of evidence. Notebooks may contain: (1) a copy of the preliminary jury instructions; (2) jurors' notes; (3) witnesses' names, photographs and/or biographies; (4) copies of key documents and an index of all exhibits; (5) a glossary of technical terms; and (6) a copy of the court's final instructions.

Rule 18.6(e). The court should instruct that any questions directed to witnesses or the court must be in writing, unsigned and given to a designated court officer. The court should further instruct that, if a juror has a question for a witness or the court, the juror should hand it to the bailiff during a recess, or if the witness is about to leave the witness stand, the juror should signal to the bailiff. The court also should instruct the jury that they are not to discuss the questions among themselves but rather each juror must decide independently any question the juror may have for a witness. If the court determines that the juror's question calls for admissible evidence, the court--or, in the court's discretion, counsel--should ask the question. The question may be answered by stipulation or other appropriate means, including, but not limited to, additional testimony on such terms and limitations as the court prescribes. If the court determines that the juror's question calls for inadmissible evidence, the question must not be read or answered. If a juror's question is rejected, the jury should be told that trial rules do not permit some questions to be asked and that the jurors should not attach any significance to the failure of having their question asked.

HISTORICAL AND STATUTORY NOTES

Former Rule 18.6, relating to preparation of jurors, was abrogated effective Jan. 1, 2018. See, now, this rule.

16A A. R. S. Rules Crim. Proc., Rule 18.6, AZ ST RCRP Rule 18.6
Current with amendments received through 08/15/19

R. 19, Refs & Annos

VI. Trial
Rule 19. Trial

16A A.R.S. Rules Crim.Proc., R. 19, Refs & Annos

16A A. R. S. Rules Crim. Proc., R. 19, Refs & Annos, AZ ST RCRP R. 19, Refs & Annos
Current with amendments received through 08/15/19

Rule 19.1. Conduct of Trial

(Refs & Annos)

VI. Trial
Rule 19. Trial (Refs & Annos)
16A A.R.S. Rules Crim.Proc., Rule 19.1
Rule 19.1. Conduct of Trial

(a) Generally.

(1) *Application.* This rule generally applies to all trials, but portions of this rule may not apply to non-jury trials.

(2) *Modification.* With permission of the court, the parties may agree to a different method of proceeding than described in this rule.

(b) Order of Proceedings. A trial proceeds in the following order unless the court directs otherwise:

(1) the court reads the indictment, information, or complaint to the jury and states the defendant's plea;

(2) the State may make an opening statement;

(3) the defendant may make or defer an opening statement;

(4) the State must offer evidence in support of the charge;

(5) the defendant may make an opening statement if it was deferred, and offer evidence in his or her defense;

(6) the parties may offer evidence in rebuttal unless the court, for good cause, allows a party's case-in-chief to be reopened;

(7) the parties may present arguments, with the State having an opening and a closing argument; and

(8) the court must instruct the jury.

(c) Proceedings if the Defendant Is Charged with Prior Convictions or Noncapital Sentencing Allegations.

(1) *During Determination of Guilt or Innocence.* If a prior conviction or noncapital sentencing allegation must be found following a guilty verdict, the trial must proceed initially as though there were no prior conviction or sentencing allegations, unless the conviction or sentencing allegation is an element of the charged crime.

(A) When the court reads the indictment, information or complaint, it must omit all references to prior conviction or sentencing allegations.

(B) During trial, the court must not instruct, refer to, or admit evidence concerning a prior conviction or noncapital sentencing allegation, except as permitted by the Arizona Rules of Evidence.

(2) *After a Guilty Verdict.* If the jury renders a guilty verdict:

(A) the defendant may admit any noncapital sentencing allegation;

(B) the State must prove to the jury any noncapital sentencing allegation not admitted by the defendant, but it need not do so for any aggravator that is already an element of the offense; and

(C) the court decides the existence of any prior conviction allegation.

(d) Aggravation Phase in a Capital Case. If a defendant is convicted of first-degree murder and the State has filed a notice of intent to seek the death penalty, the aggravation phase proceeds as follows:

(1) the court must read the alleged aggravators to the jury;

(2) the State may make an opening statement;

(3) the defendant may make or defer an opening statement;

(4) the State must offer evidence in support of the alleged aggravating circumstances;

(5) the defendant may make an opening statement if it was deferred, and offer evidence in defense of the alleged aggravating circumstances;

(6) the parties may offer evidence in rebuttal unless the court, for good cause, allows a party's case-in-chief to be reopened;

(7) the parties may present arguments, with the State having an opening and a closing argument; and

(8) the court must instruct the jury.

(e) Penalty Phase in a Capital Case. If a jury finds one or more aggravating circumstances, the penalty phase proceeds as follows:

(1) the defendant may make an opening statement;

(2) the State may make or defer an opening statement;

(3) the victim's survivors may make a statement relating to the victim's characteristics and the crime's impact on the victim's family, but they may not offer any opinion or recommendation about an appropriate sentence;

(4) the defendant may offer evidence in support of mitigation;

(5) the State may make an opening statement if it was deferred, and offer any evidence relevant to mitigation;

(6) the defendant may offer evidence in rebuttal, unless the court, for good cause, allows a party's case-in-chief to be reopened;

(7) the defendant may present statements of allocution to the jury;

(8) the parties may present argument, with the defendant having the opening and closing arguments; and

(9) the court must instruct the jury.

Credits

Added Aug. 31, 2017, effective Jan. 1, 2018.

Editors' Notes

COMMENT

Rule 19.1. The court has discretion to give final instructions to the jury before closing arguments of counsel instead of after, to enhance jurors' ability to apply the applicable law to the facts. In that event, the court may wish to withhold giving the necessary procedural and housekeeping instructions until after closing arguments, to offset the impact of the last counsel's argument.

HISTORICAL AND STATUTORY NOTES

Former Rule 19.1, relating to conduct of trial, was abrogated effective Jan. 1, 2018. See, now, this rule.

16A A. R. S. Rules Crim. Proc., Rule 19.1, AZ ST RCRP Rule 19.1

Current with amendments received through 08/15/19

Rule 19.2. Presence of the Defendant at Trial

(Refs & Annos)

VI. Trial

Rule 19. Trial (Refs & Annos)

16A A.R.S. Rules Crim.Proc., Rule 19.2

Rule 19.2. Presence of the Defendant at Trial

A defendant in a felony or misdemeanor trial has the right to be present at every stage of the trial, including, if applicable, the impaneling of the jury, the giving of additional instructions under Rule 22, and the return of the verdict. This right may be waived under Rule 9.

Credits

Added Aug. 31, 2017, effective Jan. 1, 2018.

Editors' Notes

HISTORICAL AND STATUTORY NOTES

Former Rule 19.2, relating to presence of defendant at trial, was abrogated effective Jan. 1, 2018. See, now, this rule.

16A A. R. S. Rules Crim. Proc., Rule 19.2, AZ ST RCRP Rule 19.2

Current with amendments received through 08/15/19

Rule 19.3. Admonitions

(Refs & Annos)

VI. Trial

Rule 19. Trial (Refs & Annos)

16A A.R.S. Rules Crim.Proc., Rule 19.3

Rule 19.3. Admonitions

The court must admonish jurors not to:

(a) converse among themselves or with anyone else on any subject connected with the trial until instructed to deliberate;

(b) permit themselves to be exposed to news accounts about the proceeding;

(c) form or express any opinion about the case until it is finally submitted to them;

(d) view in person or through technological means the place where the offense allegedly was committed; or

(e) conduct any independent research, investigation, or experiments, or otherwise consult any outside source about any issue in the case.

Credits

Added Aug. 31, 2017, effective Jan. 1, 2018.

Editors' Notes

COMMENT

Former Arizona Rule of Criminal Procedure 19.3, which set forth the rules of evidence applicable in criminal proceedings, was abrogated as unnecessary in light of the adoption of the Arizona Rules of Evidence, including Arizona Rules of Evidence 801(d)(1)(A) and 804(b)(1).

HISTORICAL AND STATUTORY NOTES

Former Rule 19.3, relating to evidence, was abrogated effective Jan. 1, 2018.

16A A. R. S. Rules Crim. Proc., Rule 19.3, AZ ST RCRP Rule 19.3

Current with amendments received through 08/15/19

Rule 19.4. A Judge's Death, Illness, or Other Incapacity

(Refs & Annos)

VI. Trial

Rule 19. Trial (Refs & Annos)

16A A.R.S. Rules Crim.Proc., Rule 19.4

Formerly cited as AZ ST RCRP Rule 19.5

Rule 19.4. A Judge's Death, Illness, or Other Incapacity

If the judge who is hearing or trying a criminal proceeding becomes ill or is otherwise incapacitated, that judge may be replaced by another judge of the same court. If no other judge is available, the clerk or bailiff must recess the court and notify the presiding judge or, if unavailable, the Supreme Court Chief Justice, who will enter an order continuing the trial until selection of another judge to resume the proceeding. A court of appeals judge or a judge pro tempore may be appointed as a substitute. If the new judge believes after reviewing the record that continuing the proceeding would be unduly prejudicial, the judge must order a new trial or proceeding. The judge should consider the manifest necessity of declaring a mistrial over the objection of the defendant before ordering it.

Credits

Added Aug. 31, 2017, effective Jan. 1, 2018.

Editors' Notes

COMMENT

The substitute judge need not be another trial judge; and may be a judge in the court of appeals or a judge *pro tempore*. The court reporter need not transcribe notes if the new judge prefers an alternative method of reviewing the record. *Arizona v. Washington*, 434 U.S. 497, 503 (1978) ("Because jeopardy attaches before the judgment becomes final, the constitutional protection [against double jeopardy] also embraces the defendant's 'valued right to have his trial completed by a particular tribunal.'" (citation omitted)).

HISTORICAL AND STATUTORY NOTES

Former Rule 19.4, relating to separation and detention of jurors, was abrogated effective Jan. 1, 2018. See, now, AZ ST RCRP Rule 19.6.

16A A. R. S. Rules Crim. Proc., Rule 19.4, AZ ST RCRP Rule 19.4

Current with amendments received through 08/15/19

Rule 19.5. Presence of a Representative of a Minor or Incapacitated Victim

(Refs & Annos)

VI. Trial

Rule 19. Trial (Refs & Annos)

16A A.R.S. Rules Crim.Proc., Rule 19.5

Formerly cited as AZ ST RCRP Rule 19.6

Rule 19.5. Presence of a Representative of a Minor or Incapacitated Victim

If a representative of a minor victim or an incapacitated victim wishes to be recognized during trial, the representative must notify the prosecutor, who must then inform the court out of the presence of the jury. Any communications between the representative and the court during trial must be conducted in the presence of the parties or their counsel, and outside the jury's presence. Any substantive communications must be on the record.

Credits

Added Aug. 31, 2017, effective Jan. 1, 2018.

Editors' Notes

HISTORICAL AND STATUTORY NOTES
Former Rule 19.5, relating to death, illness or other incapacity of judge, was abrogated effective Jan. 1, 2018. See, now, AZ ST RCRP Rule 19.4.
16A A. R. S. Rules Crim. Proc., Rule 19.5, AZ ST RCRP Rule 19.5
Current with amendments received through 08/15/19

Rule 19.6. Sequestration

(Refs & Annos)
VI. Trial
Rule 19. Trial (Refs & Annos)
16A A.R.S. Rules Crim.Proc., Rule 19.6
Formerly cited as AZ ST RCRP Rule 19.4

Rule 19.6. Sequestration

The court may permit jurors to separate or, on motion or on its own, may sequester jurors under the charge of a proper officer whenever they leave the jury box.
Credits
Added Aug. 31, 2017, effective Jan. 1, 2018.
Editors' Notes
HISTORICAL AND STATUTORY NOTES
Former Rule 19.6, relating to presence of minor victim or incapacitated victim representative, was abrogated effective Jan. 1, 2018. See, now, AZ ST RCRP Rule 19.5.
16A A. R. S. Rules Crim. Proc., Rule 19.6, AZ ST RCRP Rule 19.6
Current with amendments received through 08/15/19

Rule 20. Judgment of Acquittal or Unproven Aggravator

(Refs & Annos)
VI. Trial
Rule 20. Judgment of Acquittal or Unproven Aggravator
16A A.R.S. Rules Crim.Proc., Rule 20

Rule 20. Judgment of Acquittal or Unproven Aggravator

(a) Before Verdict.
(1) *Acquittal.* After the close of evidence on either side, and on motion or on its own, the court must enter a judgment of acquittal on any offense charged in an

indictment, information, or complaint if there is no substantial evidence to support a conviction.

(2) *Aggravation.* After the close of evidence on either side in an aggravation phase, and on motion or on its own, the court must enter a judgment that an aggravating circumstance or other sentence enhancement was not proven if there is no substantial evidence to support the allegation.

(3) *Timing.* The court must rule on a defendant's motion with all possible speed. Until the motion is decided, the defendant is not required to proceed.

(b) After Verdict.

(1) *On Motion.* A defendant may make or renew a motion for judgment of acquittal or unproven aggravator or other sentence enhancement on any conviction or allegation no later than 10 days after any verdict is returned.

(2) *On Court's Own Initiative.* After the verdict, if the court determines that there is no substantial evidence to support the verdict, the court on its own must order a judgment of acquittal or find an aggravator or other sentence enhancement not proven.

Credits

Added Aug. 31, 2017, effective Jan. 1, 2018.

Editors' Notes

HISTORICAL AND STATUTORY NOTES

Former Rule 20, relating to judgment of acquittal, was abrogated effective Jan. 1, 2018. See, now, this rule.

16A A. R. S. Rules Crim. Proc., Rule 20, AZ ST RCRP Rule 20

Current with amendments received through 08/15/19

Rule 21.1. Applicable Law

(Refs & Annos)

VI. Trial

Rule 21. Jury Instructions and Verdict Forms

16A A.R.S. Rules Crim.Proc., Rule 21.1

Rule 21.1. Applicable Law

Except as otherwise provided, the procedures in Arizona Rule of Civil Procedure 51 apply in criminal proceedings.

Credits

Added Aug. 31, 2017, effective Jan. 1, 2018.

Editors' Notes

HISTORICAL AND STATUTORY NOTES

Former Rule 21.1, relating to applicable law, was abrogated effective Jan. 1, 2018. See, now, this rule.

16A A. R. S. Rules Crim. Proc., Rule 21.1, AZ ST RCRP Rule 21.1

Current with amendments received through 08/15/19

Rule 21.2. Requests for Instructions and Verdict Forms

(Refs & Annos)

VI. Trial

Rule 21. Jury Instructions and Verdict Forms

16A A.R.S. Rules Crim.Proc., Rule 21.2

Rule 21.2. Requests for Instructions and Verdict Forms

At a time the court directs, but no later than the close of the evidence, the parties must submit to the court written requests for instructions and may submit to the court proposed verdict forms. Requested instructions and proposed verdict forms must be provided to the other parties, including co-defendants.

Credits

Added Aug. 31, 2017, effective Jan. 1, 2018.

Editors' Notes

HISTORICAL AND STATUTORY NOTES

Former Rule 21.2, relating to requests for instructions and forms of verdict, was abrogated effective Jan. 1, 2018. See, now, this rule.

16A A. R. S. Rules Crim. Proc., Rule 21.2, AZ ST RCRP Rule 21.2

Current with amendments received through 08/15/19

Rule 21.3. Rulings on Instructions and Verdict Forms

(Refs & Annos)

VI. Trial

Rule 21. Jury Instructions and Verdict Forms

16A A.R.S. Rules Crim.Proc., Rule 21.3

Rule 21.3. Rulings on Instructions and Verdict Forms

(a) Conference. The court must confer with the parties before closing argument and inform them of its proposed jury instructions and verdict forms.

(b) Record of Objections. Any objection to the court's giving or failing to give any instruction or a portion of an instruction or a form of verdict must be made before the jury retires to consider its verdict. The objection must be on the record and distinctly state the matter to which the party objects and the grounds for the objection. If a party does not make a proper objection, appellate review may be limited.

(c) Source of the Instructions. The court must not inform the jury which instructions were requested by a particular party.

(d) Jurors' Copies. The court's preliminary and final instructions must be in writing, and the court must furnish a copy of the instructions to each juror before the court reads them.

Credits

Added Aug. 31, 2017, effective Jan. 1, 2018.

Editors' Notes

HISTORICAL AND STATUTORY NOTES

Former Rule 21.3, relating to rulings on instructions and forms of verdict, was abrogated effective Jan. 1, 2018. See, now, this rule.

16A A. R. S. Rules Crim. Proc., Rule 21.3, AZ ST RCRP Rule 21.3

Current with amendments received through 08/15/19

Rule 21.4. Verdict Forms for Necessarily Included Offenses or Attempts

(Refs & Annos)

VI. Trial

Rule 21. Jury Instructions and Verdict Forms

16A A.R.S. Rules Crim.Proc., Rule 21.4

Rule 21.4. Verdict Forms for Necessarily Included Offenses or Attempts

(a) Generally. On request by any party and if supported by the evidence, the court must submit forms of verdicts to the jury for:

(1) all offenses necessarily included in the offense charged;

(2) an attempt to commit the offense charged if such an attempt is a crime; and

(3) all offenses necessarily included in an attempt.

(b) If No Form is Provided. If the court did not submit to the jury a form of verdict for an offense, the jury may not find the defendant guilty of that offense.

Credits

Added Aug. 31, 2017, effective Jan. 1, 2018.

16A A. R. S. Rules Crim. Proc., Rule 21.4, AZ ST RCRP Rule 21.4

Current with amendments received through 08/15/19

Rule 22.1. Instructions and Retirement

16A A.R.S. Rules Crim.Proc., Rule 22.1

Rule 22.1. Instructions and Retirement

(a) Retirement.

(1) *Instructions.* Before the jury begins its deliberations, the court must instruct the jury on the applicable law, the procedures it must follow during deliberations, and the appropriate method to report the results of its deliberations. The instructions must be recorded or in writing, and be available to the jurors during deliberations.

(2) *Foreperson.* The court must appoint, or instruct the jurors to elect, a foreperson.

(3) *Retirement.* After instructing the jury, the court must direct the jury to retire under the charge of a court official to begin its deliberations.

(b) Permitting the Jury to Disperse. The court may permit the jurors to disperse after they begin their deliberations. The court must instruct the jurors when to reassemble and admonish the jury under Rule 19.3.

(c) Length of Jury Deliberations. The court must not require a jury to deliberate after normal working hours unless the court, after consulting with the jury and the parties, determines that evening or weekend deliberations are necessary in the interest of justice and will not impose an undue hardship on the jurors.

Credits

Added Aug. 31, 2017, effective Jan. 1, 2018.

Editors' Notes

HISTORICAL AND STATUTORY NOTES

Former Rule 22.1, relating to retirement of jurors, was abrogated effective Jan. 1, 2018. See, now, this rule.

16A A. R. S. Rules Crim. Proc., Rule 22.1, AZ ST RCRP Rule 22.1

Current with amendments received through 08/15/19

Rule 22.2. Materials Used During Deliberations

16A A.R.S. Rules Crim.Proc., Rule 22.2

Rule 22.2. Materials Used During Deliberations

(a) Generally. Upon retiring for deliberations, jurors must take into the jury room:

(1) forms of verdict approved by the court;

(2) jurors' copies of the court's instructions;

(3) jurors' notes; and

(4) tangible evidence as the court directs.

(b) Verdict Form Limitation. The form of verdict must not indicate whether the described offense is a felony or a misdemeanor.

Credits

Added Aug. 31, 2017, effective Jan. 1, 2018.

Editors' Notes

HISTORICAL AND STATUTORY NOTES

Former Rule 22.2, relating to materials used during deliberation, was abrogated effective Jan. 1, 2018. See, now, this rule.

16A A. R. S. Rules Crim. Proc., Rule 22.2, AZ ST RCRP Rule 22.2

Current with amendments received through 08/15/19

Rule 22.3. Repeating Testimony and Additional Instructions

(Refs & Annos)

VI. Trial

Rule 22. Deliberations

16A A.R.S. Rules Crim.Proc., Rule 22.3

Rule 22.3. Repeating Testimony and Additional Instructions

(a) Repeating Testimony. If, after the jury retires, jurors request that any testimony be repeated, the court may recall the jury to the courtroom and order the testimony read or replayed. The court also may order other testimony repeated so as not to give undue emphasis to particular testimony.

(b) Additional Instructions. If, after the jury retires, the jury or a party requests additional instructions, the court may recall the jury to the courtroom and further instruct the jury as appropriate.

(c) Notice. The court must give the parties notice before testimony is repeated or before giving additional instructions.

Credits

Added Aug. 31, 2017, effective Jan. 1, 2018.

Editors' Notes

HISTORICAL AND STATUTORY NOTES

Former Rule 22.3, relating to further review of evidence and additional instructions, was abrogated effective Jan. 1, 2018. See, now, this rule.
16A A. R. S. Rules Crim. Proc., Rule 22.3, AZ ST RCRP Rule 22.3
Current with amendments received through 08/15/19

Rule 22.4. Assisting Jurors at Impasse

(Refs & Annos)
VI. Trial
Rule 22. Deliberations

16A A.R.S. Rules Crim.Proc., Rule 22.4

Rule 22.4. Assisting Jurors at Impasse

If the jury advises the court that it has reached an impasse in its deliberations, the court may, in the parties' presence, ask the jury to determine whether and how the court and counsel can assist the jury's deliberations. After receiving the jurors' response, if any, the court may direct further proceedings as appropriate.
Credits
Added Aug. 31, 2017, effective Jan. 1, 2018.
Editors' Notes
COMMENT
Rule 22.4. Many juries, after reporting to the judge that they have reached an impasse in their deliberations, are needlessly discharged and a mistrial declared even though it might be appropriate and helpful for the judge to offer some assistance in hopes of improving the chances of a verdict. The judge's offer would be designed and intended to address the issues that divide the jurors, if it is legally and practically possible to do so. The invitation to dialogue should not be coercive, suggestive, or unduly intrusive.
The judge's response to the jurors' report of impasse could take the following form: This is offered to help you, not to force you to reach a verdict.
As jurors, you have a duty to discuss the case with one another and to deliberate in an effort to reach a just verdict. Each of you must decide the case for yourself, but only after you consider the evidence impartially with your fellow jurors. During your deliberations, you should not hesitate to re-examine your own views and change your opinion if you become convinced that it is wrong. However, you should not change your belief concerning the weight or effect of the evidence solely because of the opinions of your fellow jurors, or for the mere purpose of returning a verdict. You may wish to identify areas of agreement and disagreement and then discuss the law and the evidence as they relate to the areas of disagreement.

If you still disagree, you may wish to tell the attorneys and me which issues, questions, law or facts you would like us to assist you with. If you decide to follow these steps, please write down the issues where further assistance might help bring about a verdict and give the note to the bailiff. The attorneys and I will then discuss your note and try to help you.

I do not wish to or intend to force a verdict. We are merely trying to be responsive to your apparent need for help. If it is possible that you could reach a verdict as a result of this procedure, you should consider doing so.

Please take a few minutes and discuss the instruction among yourselves. Then advise me in writing of whether we can attempt to assist you in the manner indicated above or whether you do not believe that such assistance and additional deliberation would assist you in reaching a verdict.

RAJI (CRIMINAL) 3D, Standard Criminal 42 (Supp. 2010).

If the jury identifies one or more issues that divide them, the court, with the help of the attorneys, can decide whether and how the issues can be addressed. Among the obvious options are the following: giving additional instructions; clarifying earlier instructions; directing the attorneys to make additional closing argument; reopening the evidence for limited purposes; or a combination of these measures. Of course, the court might decide that it is not legally or practically possible to respond to the jury's concerns.

HISTORICAL AND STATUTORY NOTES

Former Rule 22.4, relating to assisting jurors at impasse, was abrogated effective Jan. 1, 2018. See, now, this rule.

16A A. R. S. Rules Crim. Proc., Rule 22.4, AZ ST RCRP Rule 22.4

Current with amendments received through 08/15/19

Rule 22.5. Discharging a Jury

(Refs & Annos)
VI. Trial
Rule 22. Deliberations

16A A.R.S. Rules Crim.Proc., Rule 22.5

Rule 22.5. Discharging a Jury

(a) Generally. The court must discharge the jury:

(1) when its verdict has been recorded under Rule 23;

(2) if the court determines there is no reasonable probability that the jurors can agree upon a verdict; or

(3) when the court determines a necessity exists for its discharge.

(b) Disclosures and Release from Confidentiality. When discharging a jury at the conclusion of the case, the court must advise the jurors that they are released from service. If appropriate, the court must release them from their duty of confidentiality and explain their rights regarding inquiries from counsel, the media, or any person.
Credits
Added Aug. 31, 2017, effective Jan. 1, 2018.
Editors' Notes
HISTORICAL AND STATUTORY NOTES
Former Rule 22.5, relating to discharge, was abrogated effective Jan. 1, 2018. See, now, this rule.
16A A. R. S. Rules Crim. Proc., Rule 22.5, AZ ST RCRP Rule 22.5
Current with amendments received through 08/15/19

Rule 23.1. Form of Verdict; Sealed Verdict

(Refs & Annos)
VI. Trial
Rule 23. Verdict

16A A.R.S. Rules Crim.Proc., Rule 23.1

Rule 23.1. Form of Verdict; Sealed Verdict

(a) Form of Verdict. The jury's verdict must be in writing, signed by the foreperson, and returned to the judge in open court. The foreperson may sign the verdict, either by affixing his or her signature on the verdict or by writing his or her juror number and initials on the verdict.
(b) Sealed Verdicts.
(1) *Procedure.* The court may instruct the jurors that if they agree on a verdict during a temporary adjournment of the court, the foreperson may sign the verdict as provided in (a), seal it in an envelope, and deliver it to the officer in charge. The jurors then may disperse and reassemble at a specified time and place. The officer must deliver the sealed verdict to the clerk as soon as practical. When the jurors have reassembled in the courtroom, the clerk must return the envelope to the judge in open court.
(2) *Admonition.* If the court authorizes a sealed verdict, it must admonish the jurors not to make any disclosure concerning their verdict, or speak with others concerning the case, until the verdict has been returned and the jury has been discharged.
Credits
Added Aug. 31, 2017, effective Jan. 1, 2018.
Editors' Notes

Former Rule 23.1, relating to time and form of verdict, was abrogated effective Jan. 1, 2018. See, now, this rule.

16A A. R. S. Rules Crim. Proc., Rule 23.1, AZ ST RCRP Rule 23.1

Current with amendments received through 08/15/19

Rule 23.2. Types of Verdicts

(Refs & Annos)
VI. Trial
Rule 23. Verdict

16A A.R.S. Rules Crim.Proc., Rule 23.2

Rule 23.2. Types of Verdicts

(a) General Verdicts. Except as this rule specifies otherwise, in every case the jury must render a verdict finding the defendant either guilty or not guilty.

(b) Insanity Verdicts. If a jury that determines a defendant is guilty except insane, it must state this determination in its verdict.

(c) Different Offenses. If an indictment or information charges different counts or offenses, the verdict must specify each count or offense for which the jury has found the defendant guilty or not guilty.

(d) Different Degrees. If the verdict of guilty is to an offense that is divided into degrees, the verdict must specify the degree of the offense for which the jury has found the defendant guilty.

(e) Aggravation Verdict. After a guilty verdict and an aggravation phase, the jury must render a verdict determining whether the State proved each of the alleged aggravating circumstances submitted to the jury.

(f) Penalty Verdict in a Capital Case. At the conclusion of the penalty phase in a capital case, the jury must render a verdict stating whether to impose a sentence of death or life.

Credits

Added Aug. 31, 2017, effective Jan. 1, 2018.

Editors' Notes

HISTORICAL AND STATUTORY NOTES

Former Rule 23.2, relating to types of verdict, was abrogated effective Jan. 1, 2018. See, now, this rule.

16A A. R. S. Rules Crim. Proc., Rule 23.2, AZ ST RCRP Rule 23.2

Current with amendments received through 08/15/19

Rule 23.3. Polling the Jury

16A A.R.S. Rules Crim.Proc., Rule 23.3
Formerly cited as AZ ST RCRP Rule 23.4

Rule 23.3. Polling the Jury

(a) Generally. After the jury returns a verdict and before the court dismisses the jury, the court must poll the jury at the request of any party or on the court's own initiative. If the jurors' responses to the poll do not support the verdict, the court may direct them to deliberate further or the court may dismiss the jury.

(b) Juror Confidentiality. When polling a jury, the court must not identify individual jurors by name, but must use such other methods or form of identification that are appropriate to ensure the jurors' privacy and an accurate record of the poll.

Credits

Added Aug. 31, 2017, effective Jan. 1, 2018.

Editors' Notes

HISTORICAL AND STATUTORY NOTES

Former Rule 23.3, relating to conviction of necessarily included offenses, was abrogated effective Jan. 1, 2018.

16A A. R. S. Rules Crim. Proc., Rule 23.3, AZ ST RCRP Rule 23.3

Current with amendments received through 08/15/19

Rule 23.4. Abrogated Aug. 31, 2017, effective Jan. 1, 2018

16A A.R.S. Rules Crim.Proc., Rule 23.4

Rule 23.4. Abrogated Aug. 31, 2017, effective Jan. 1, 2018

Editors' Notes

HISTORICAL AND STATUTORY NOTES

The abrogated rule related to polling the jury. See, now, AZ ST RCRP Rule 23.3.

16A A. R. S. Rules Crim. Proc., Rule 23.4, AZ ST RCRP Rule 23.4

Current with amendments received through 08/15/19

Rule 24.1. Motion for New Trial

(Refs & Annos)

VII. Post-Verdict Proceedings
Rule 24. Post-Trial Motions

16A A.R.S. Rules Crim.Proc., Rule 24.1

Rule 24.1. Motion for New Trial

(a) The Court's Authority. After a verdict in any phase of trial, capital or noncapital, the court may order a new trial or phase of trial on the defendant's motion or on its own, with the defendant's consent.

(b) Timeliness. A party must file a motion for a new trial no later than 10 days after return of the verdict being challenged. This deadline is jurisdictional and the court may not extend it.

(c) Grounds. The court may grant a new trial or phase of trial if:

(1) the verdict is contrary to law or the weight of the evidence;

(2) the State is guilty of misconduct;

(3) one or more jurors committed misconduct by:

(A) receiving evidence not admitted during the trial or phase of trial;

(B) deciding the verdict by lot;

(C) perjuring himself or herself, or willfully failing to respond fully to a direct question posed during the voir dire examination;

(D) receiving a bribe or pledging his or her vote in any other way;

(E) being intoxicated during trial proceedings or deliberations; or

(F) conversing before the verdict with any interested party about the outcome of the case;

(4) the court erred in deciding a matter of law or in instructing the jury on a matter of law; or

(5) for any other reason, not due to the defendant's own fault, the defendant did not receive a fair and impartial trial or phase of trial.

(d) Admissibility of Juror Evidence to Impeach the Verdict. If a verdict's validity is challenged under (c)(3), the court may receive the testimony or affidavit of any witness, including members of the jury, that relates to the conduct of a juror, a court official, or a third person. But the court may not receive testimony or an affidavit that relates to the subjective motives or mental processes leading a juror to agree or disagree with the verdict.

Credits

Added Aug. 31, 2017, effective Jan. 1, 2018.

Editors' Notes

HISTORICAL AND STATUTORY NOTES

Former Rule 24.1, relating to motion for new trial, was abrogated effective Jan. 1, 2018. See, now, this rule.

16A A. R. S. Rules Crim. Proc., Rule 24.1, AZ ST RCRP Rule 24.1

Current with amendments received through 08/15/19

Rule 24.2. Motion to Vacate Judgment

(Refs & Annos)

VII. Post-Verdict Proceedings

Rule 24. Post-Trial Motions

16A A.R.S. Rules Crim.Proc., Rule 24.2

Rule 24.2. Motion to Vacate Judgment

(a) Grounds. The court must vacate a judgment if it finds that:

(1) the court did not have jurisdiction;

(2) newly discovered material facts exist satisfying the standards in Rule 32.1(e); or

(3) the conviction was obtained in violation of the United States or Arizona constitutions.

(b) Time for Filing. A party must file a motion under this rule no later than 60 days after the entry of judgment and sentence, or, if a notice of appeal has already been filed under Rule 31, no later than 15 days after the appellate clerk distributes a notice under Rule 31.9(e) that the record on appeal has been filed.

(c) Motion Filed After Notice of Appeal. If a party files a motion to vacate judgment after a notice of appeal is filed, the superior court clerk must immediately send copies of the motion to the Attorney General and to the clerk of the appellate court in which the appeal was filed.

(d) Appeal from a Decision on the Motion. In noncapital cases, the party appealing a final decision on the motion must file a notice of appeal with the trial court clerk no later than 20 days after entry of the decision for a superior court case, or no later than 14 days after entry of the decision for a limited jurisdiction court case. In a capital case, if the court denies the motion, it must order the clerk to file a notice of appeal from that denial.

(e) State's Motion to Vacate Judgment. Notwithstanding (b), the State may move the court to vacate the judgment at any time after the entry of judgment and sentence if:

(1) clear and convincing evidence exists establishing that the defendant was convicted of an offense that the defendant did not commit; or

(2) the conviction was based on an erroneous application of the law.

Credits

Added Aug. 31, 2017, effective Jan. 1, 2018.

Editors' Notes

COMMENT

Rules 24.2 and 24.3 replace the criminal rules' pre-1974 reliance on Rule 60(c) of the Arizona Rules of Civil Procedure with specifically criminal post-trial remedies of similarly broad scope. Rule 60(c) does not have any further application to criminal cases.

Rule 24.2(a). If a motion under Rule 24.2 has been filed but not decided within 15 days after the appellate court distributes a notice under Rule 31.9(e) that the record on appeal has been filed, both trial and appellate courts will have jurisdiction. If the trial court grants the Rule 24.2 motion, the appeal may be mooted after the record for the appeal has been completed. The rules include the following mechanism to alleviate most confusion--notice to the appellate court of the Rule 24.2 motion (Rules 31.2(e)(4) and 24.2(c)); the appellate court's power to stay the appeal pending determination of the Rule 24.2 motion (Rule 31.3(b)); and the direction in Rule 31.3(c) that, more than 15 days after the clerk distributes a notice under Rule 31.9(e) that the record on appeal has been filed, all new matters be addressed to the appellate court.

Rule 24.2(c). Rule 24.2(c) is intended to minimize problems caused by concurrent jurisdiction in the trial and appellate courts. The rule requires that notice be given only of Rule 24.2 motions brought after a notice of appeal has been filed.

Although A.R.S. § 13-121 states as a jurisdictional requirement that notice of all proceedings brought in the trial court after judgment and sentence be sent to the attorney general, the requirement does not apply to motions filed within the ambit of the trial court's original trial jurisdiction.

Rule 24.2(d). Rule 31.2(h) requires that a party seeking appellate review of a Rule 24 order that was issued after a notice of appeal or cross-appeal has been filed under Rule 31.2 must file an amended notice of appeal.

HISTORICAL AND STATUTORY NOTES

Former Rule 24.2, relating to motion to vacate judgment, was abrogated effective Jan. 1, 2018. See, now, this rule.

16A A. R. S. Rules Crim. Proc., Rule 24.2, AZ ST RCRP Rule 24.2

Current with amendments received through 08/15/19

Rule 24.3. Modification of Sentence

(Refs & Annos)

VII. Post-Verdict Proceedings
Rule 24. Post-Trial Motions

16A A.R.S. Rules Crim.Proc., Rule 24.3

Rule 24.3. Modification of Sentence

(a) Generally. No later than 60 days of the entry of judgment and sentence or, if a notice of appeal has already been filed under Rule 31, no later than 15 days after the appellate clerk distributes a notice under Rule 31.9(e) that the record on appeal has been filed, the court may correct any unlawful sentence or one imposed in an unlawful manner.

(b) Mitigation. Unless otherwise provided by law, the court may mitigate a monetary obligation imposed at sentencing. The provisions of Rule 39 apply to any criminal proceeding concerning mitigation of a monetary obligation.

(c) Appeal.

(1) *Noncapital Cases.* In noncapital cases, the party appealing a final decision under Rule 24.3 must file a notice of appeal with the trial court clerk no later than 20 days after entry of the decision in superior court cases, or no later than 14 days after entry of the decision in limited jurisdiction court cases.

(2) *Capital Cases.* In capital cases, after denying modification of a sentence of death, the court must order the clerk to file a notice of appeal from the denial.

Credits

Added Aug. 31, 2017, effective Jan. 1, 2018. Amended Dec. 13, 2018, effective Jan. 1, 2019.

Editors' Notes

HISTORICAL AND STATUTORY NOTES

Former Rule 24.3, relating to modification of sentence, was abrogated effective Jan. 1, 2018. See, now, this rule.

16A A. R. S. Rules Crim. Proc., Rule 24.3, AZ ST RCRP Rule 24.3

Current with amendments received through 08/15/19

Rule 24.4. Clerical Error

(Refs & Annos)
VII. Post-Verdict Proceedings
Rule 24. Post-Trial Motions

16A A.R.S. Rules Crim.Proc., Rule 24.4

Rule 24.4. Clerical Error

The court on its own or on a party's motion may, at any time, correct clerical errors, omissions, and oversights in the record. The court must notify the parties of any correction.
Credits
Added Aug. 31, 2017, effective Jan. 1, 2018.
Editors' Notes
HISTORICAL AND STATUTORY NOTES
Former Rule 24.4, relating to clerical mistakes, was abrogated effective Jan. 1, 2018. See, now, this rule.
16A A. R. S. Rules Crim. Proc., Rule 24.4, AZ ST RCRP Rule 24.4
Current with amendments received through 08/15/19

Rule 25. Procedure After a Verdict or Finding of Guilty Except Insane

(Refs & Annos)
VII. Post-Verdict Proceedings
Rule 25. Procedure After a Verdict or Finding of Guilty Except Insane
16A A.R.S. Rules Crim.Proc., Rule 25

Rule 25. Procedure After a Verdict or Finding of Guilty Except Insane

After a verdict or finding under A.R.S. § 13-502 of guilty except insane, the court must commit the defendant to a secure mental health facility under the procedures provided in A.R.S. § 13-3994.
Credits
Added Aug. 31, 2017, effective Jan. 1, 2018.
Editors' Notes
HISTORICAL AND STATUTORY NOTES
Former Rule 25, relating to procedure after verdict or finding of not guilty by reason of insanity, was abrogated effective Jan. 1, 2018. See, now, this rule.
16A A. R. S. Rules Crim. Proc., Rule 25, AZ ST RCRP Rule 25
Current with amendments received through 08/15/19

R. 26, Refs & Annos

VII. Post-Verdict Proceedings
Rule 26. Judgment, Presentence Report, Presentencing Hearing, Sentence
16A A.R.S. Rules Crim.Proc., R. 26, Refs & Annos

16A A. R. S. Rules Crim. Proc., R. 26, Refs & Annos, AZ ST RCRP R. 26, Refs & Annos

Current with amendments received through 08/15/19

Rule 26.1. Definitions; Scope

(Refs & Annos)
VII. Post-Verdict Proceedings
Rule 26. Judgment, Presentence Report, Presentencing Hearing, Sentence (Refs & Annos)

16A A.R.S. Rules Crim.Proc., Rule 26.1

Rule 26.1. Definitions; Scope

(a) Determination of Guilt. "Determination of guilt" means the court's acceptance of a guilty or no contest plea or a guilty verdict by a jury or the court.

(b) Judgment. "Judgment" means the court's adjudication that the defendant is guilty or not guilty based on the jury's or the court's verdict, or the defendant's plea.

(c) Sentence. "Sentence" means the court's pronouncement of the penalty imposed on the defendant after a judgment of guilty.

(d) Scope. Rule 26 does not apply to minor traffic offenses. Rules 26.4, 26.5, 26.6, 26.7, 26.8, and 26.15 apply only to the superior court.

Credits

Added Aug. 31, 2017, effective Jan. 1, 2018.

Editors' Notes

HISTORICAL AND STATUTORY NOTES

Former Rule 26.1, relating to definitions and scope, was abrogated effective Jan. 1, 2018. See, now, this rule.

16A A. R. S. Rules Crim. Proc., Rule 26.1, AZ ST RCRP Rule 26.1

Current with amendments received through 08/15/19

Rule 26.2. Time to Render Judgment

(Refs & Annos)
VII. Post-Verdict Proceedings
Rule 26. Judgment, Presentence Report, Presentencing Hearing, Sentence (Refs & Annos)

16A A.R.S. Rules Crim.Proc., Rule 26.2

Rule 26.2. Time to Render Judgment

(a) Upon Acquittal. If a defendant is found not guilty of any charge or any count of any charge, the court must immediately enter judgment pertaining to that count or charge.

(b) Upon Conviction. Upon a determination of guilt on any charge or on any count of any charge, the court must enter judgment and either pronounce sentence or set a date for sentencing under Rule 26.3.

(c) Upon a Death Verdict. Upon a death verdict, the court must immediately enter the judgment and sentence. The court must send, or direct the clerk to send, to the Department of Corrections the sentencing order and copies of all medical and mental health reports prepared for, or relating to, the defendant.

Credits

Added Aug. 31, 2017, effective Jan. 1, 2018.

Editors' Notes

HISTORICAL AND STATUTORY NOTES

Former Rule 26.2, relating to time of rendering judgment, was abrogated effective Jan. 1, 2018. See, now, this rule.

16A A. R. S. Rules Crim. Proc., Rule 26.2, AZ ST RCRP Rule 26.2

Current with amendments received through 08/15/19

Rule 26.3. Sentencing Date and Time Extensions

(Refs & Annos)

VII. Post-Verdict Proceedings

Rule 26. Judgment, Presentence Report, Presentencing Hearing, Sentence (Refs & Annos)

16A A.R.S. Rules Crim.Proc., Rule 26.3

Rule 26.3. Sentencing Date and Time Extensions

(a) Sentencing Date.

(1) *Superior Court.*

(A) Generally. Upon a determination of guilt, the court must set a date for sentencing.

(B) Deadline for Sentencing. The court must pronounce sentence no less than 15 nor more than 30 days after the determination of guilt unless the court, after informing the defendant of the right to a presentence report, grants the defendant's request that the court pronounce sentence earlier.

(C) The Defendant's Presence or Absence. When setting a sentencing date, the court must order the defendant to be present for sentencing and, if the defendant fails to appear, issue a warrant for the defendant's arrest. Additionally, following a conviction based on a trial, the court must notify the defendant that if the defendant's absence prevents the court from sentencing the defendant no later than 90 days after the determination of guilt, the defendant will lose the right to have an appellate court review the trial proceedings by direct appeal.

(2) *Limited Jurisdiction Courts.* A limited jurisdiction court may pronounce sentence immediately upon determining guilt unless the court orders, on its own or on a party's or a victim's request, that the court will pronounce sentence at a later date that is not more than 30 days after the determination of guilt.

(b) Time Extension. If a presentencing hearing is requested under Rule 26.7 or for good cause, the court may reset the sentencing date, but the new date should be no later than 60 days after the determination of guilt.

Credits

Added Aug. 31, 2017, effective Jan. 1, 2018.

Editors' Notes

HISTORICAL AND STATUTORY NOTES

Former Rule 26.3, relating to date of sentencing and extension, was abrogated effective Jan. 1, 2018. See, now, this rule.

16A A. R. S. Rules Crim. Proc., Rule 26.3, AZ ST RCRP Rule 26.3

Current with amendments received through 08/15/19

Rule 26.4. Presentence Report

(Refs & Annos)

VII. Post-Verdict Proceedings

Rule 26. Judgment, Presentence Report, Presentencing Hearing, Sentence (Refs & Annos)

16A A.R.S. Rules Crim.Proc., Rule 26.4

Rule 26.4. Presentence Report

(a) When Required. The court must order a presentence report in every case in which it has discretion over the penalty. However, a presentence report is optional if:

(1) the defendant may only be sentenced to imprisonment for less than one year;

(2) the court granted a request under Rule 26.3(a)(1)(B); or

(3) a presentence report concerning the defendant is already available.

(b) When Prepared. A presentence report may not be prepared until after the court makes a determination of guilt or the defendant enters a plea of guilty or no contest.

(c) When Due. Unless the court grants a request under Rule 26.3(a)(1)(B) for an earlier sentencing, the presentence report must be delivered to the sentencing judge and to all counsel at least two days before the date set for sentencing.

(d) Inadmissibility. Neither a presentence report nor any statement made in connection with its preparation is admissible as evidence in any proceeding bearing on the issue of guilt.

Credits

Added Aug. 31, 2017, effective Jan. 1, 2018.

Editors' Notes

HISTORICAL AND STATUTORY NOTES

Former Rule 26.4, relating to pre-sentence report, was abrogated effective Jan. 1, 2018. See, now, this rule.

16A A. R. S. Rules Crim. Proc., Rule 26.4, AZ ST RCRP Rule 26.4

Current with amendments received through 08/15/19

Rule 26.5. Diagnostic Evaluation and Mental Health Examination

(Refs & Annos)

VII. Post-Verdict Proceedings

Rule 26. Judgment, Presentence Report, Presentencing Hearing, Sentence (Refs & Annos)

16A A.R.S. Rules Crim.Proc., Rule 26.5

Rule 26.5. Diagnostic Evaluation and Mental Health Examination

At any time before the court pronounces sentence, it may order the defendant to undergo a mental health examination or diagnostic evaluation. Unless the court orders otherwise, any report concerning such an examination or evaluation is due at the same time as the presentence report.

Credits

Added Aug. 31, 2017, effective Jan. 1, 2018.

Editors' Notes

HISTORICAL AND STATUTORY NOTES

Former Rule 26.5, relating to diagnostic evaluation and mental health examination, was abrogated effective Jan. 1, 2018. See, now, this rule.

16A A. R. S. Rules Crim. Proc., Rule 26.5, AZ ST RCRP Rule 26.5

Current with amendments received through 08/15/19

Rule 26.6. Court Disclosure of Reports Before Sentencing

(Refs & Annos)
VII. Post-Verdict Proceedings
Rule 26. Judgment, Presentence Report, Presentencing Hearing, Sentence (Refs & Annos)
16A A.R.S. Rules Crim.Proc., Rule 26.6

Rule 26.6. Court Disclosure of Reports Before Sentencing

(a) Disclosure to the Parties. The court must permit the State, defense counsel, and a self-represented defendant to review all presentence, diagnostic, and mental health reports concerning the defendant. If the court makes a portion of any report unavailable to one party, it must not make that portion available to any other party.

(b) Disclosure to a Victim. The court must permit the victim to review the presentence report after it makes the report available to the defendant, excluding any portions the court excises or that are confidential by law.

(c) Date of Disclosure. A report prepared under Rule 26.7(c) must be available to the parties no later than two days after it is delivered to the court and no less than two days before a presentencing hearing, unless the parties agree otherwise.

(d) Excision.

(1) *Generally.* The court may excise from copies of presentence, diagnostic and mental health reports disclosed to the parties:

(A) diagnostic opinions that might seriously disrupt a program of rehabilitation;

(B) sources of information obtained on a promise of confidentiality; and

(C) information that would disrupt an ongoing law enforcement investigation.

(2) *Disclosure.* The court must inform the parties if a portion of a report is not disclosed, and must state on the record its reasons for not disclosing it.

(e) Court Disclosure of Reports After Sentencing.

(1) *Disclosure to Personnel Responsible for the Defendant.* After sentencing, the court must furnish to persons having direct responsibility for the defendant's custody, rehabilitation, treatment, or release all diagnostic, mental health, and presentence reports, except for portions excised under (d)(1)(B) and (C).

(2) *Disclosure to Courts.* The court must make an unexcised version of any report listed in (e)(1) available to:

(A) a reviewing court when a relevant issue has been raised; and

(B) a court sentencing the defendant after a later conviction.

(f) Public Disclosure of Reports. A report prepared under Rules 26.4, 26.5, or 26.7(c) is a public record unless the court orders otherwise or it is confidential by law.
Credits

Added Aug. 31, 2017, effective Jan. 1, 2018.

Editors' Notes

HISTORICAL AND STATUTORY NOTES

Former Rule 26.6, relating to disclosure of the pre-sentence, diagnostic, and mental health reports, was abrogated effective Jan. 1, 2018. See, now, this rule.

16A A. R. S. Rules Crim. Proc., Rule 26.6, AZ ST RCRP Rule 26.6

Current with amendments received through 08/15/19

Rule 26.7. Presentencing Hearing; Prehearing Conference

(Refs & Annos)

VII. Post-Verdict Proceedings

Rule 26. Judgment, Presentence Report, Presentencing Hearing, Sentence (Refs & Annos)

16A A.R.S. Rules Crim.Proc., Rule 26.7

Rule 26.7. Presentencing Hearing; Prehearing Conference

(a) Request for a Presentencing Hearing. If the court has discretion concerning the imposition of a penalty, it may--and, on any party's request, must--hold a presentencing hearing before sentencing.

(b) Timing and Conduct of a Presentencing Hearing.

(1) *Timing.* The court may not hold a presentencing hearing until the parties have had an opportunity to review all reports concerning the defendant prepared under Rules 26.4 and 26.5.

(2) *Presenting Evidence.* At the hearing, any party may introduce any reliable, relevant evidence, including hearsay, to show aggravating or mitigating circumstances, to show why the court should not impose a particular sentence, or to correct or amplify the presentence, diagnostic, or mental health reports.

(3) *Record.* A presentencing hearing must be held in open court, and the court must make a complete record of the proceedings.

(c) Prehearing Conference.

(1) *Generally.* On motion or on its own, the court may hold a prehearing conference to determine what matters are in dispute, and to limit or otherwise expedite a presentencing hearing.

(2) *Attendance of Probation Officer.* The court may order the probation officer who prepared the presentence report to attend a prehearing conference.

(3) *Postponing Sentencing and Presentencing Hearing.* At the conference, the court may postpone the date of sentencing for no more than 10 days beyond the maximum extension permitted by Rule 26.3(b), and may delay the presentencing hearing

accordingly, to allow the probation officer to investigate any matter the court specifies, or to refer the defendant for mental health examinations or diagnostic tests.

Credits

Added Aug. 31, 2017, effective Jan. 1, 2018.

Editors' Notes

HISTORICAL AND STATUTORY NOTES

Former Rule 26.7, relating to pre-sentencing hearing, and request, purpose, and pre-hearing conference, was abrogated effective Jan. 1, 2018. See, now, this rule.

16A A. R. S. Rules Crim. Proc., Rule 26.7, AZ ST RCRP Rule 26.7

Current with amendments received through 08/15/19

Rule 26.8. The State's Disclosure Duty; Objections and Corrections to a Presentence Report

(Refs & Annos)

VII. Post-Verdict Proceedings

Rule 26. Judgment, Presentence Report, Presentencing Hearing, Sentence (Refs & Annos)

16A A.R.S. Rules Crim.Proc., Rule 26.8

Rule 26.8. The State's Disclosure Duty; Objections and Corrections to a Presentence Report

(a) The State's Disclosure Duty. The State must disclose any information in its possession or control it has not already disclosed that would tend to reduce the defendant's punishment.

(b) Notice of Objections. At least one day before the presentencing hearing, each party must notify the court and other parties of the party's objections, if any, to the contents of any report prepared under Rules 26.4, 26.5 or 26.7(c).

(c) Corrections to a Presentence Report. If the court sustains any objection to a presentence report's contents, it may take appropriate action, including but not limited to:

(1) excising portions of the report, including any objectionable language;

(2) ordering a new presentence report to be prepared with specific instructions and directions;

(3) directing that a different probation officer prepare a new presentence report; or

(4) ordering the presentence report sealed.

Credits

Added Aug. 31, 2017, effective Jan. 1, 2018.

HISTORICAL AND STATUTORY NOTES

Former Rule 26.8, relating to notice of objections, special duty of the prosecutor, and corrections to pre-sentence report, was abrogated effective Jan. 1, 2018. See, now, this rule.

16A A. R. S. Rules Crim. Proc., Rule 26.8, AZ ST RCRP Rule 26.8

Current with amendments received through 08/15/19

Rule 26.9. The Defendant's Presence

(Refs & Annos)

VII. Post-Verdict Proceedings

Rule 26. Judgment, Presentence Report, Presentencing Hearing, Sentence (Refs & Annos)

16A A.R.S. Rules Crim.Proc., Rule 26.9

Rule 26.9. The Defendant's Presence

The defendant has a right to be present at a presentencing hearing and must be present at sentencing.

Credits

Added Aug. 31, 2017, effective Jan. 1, 2018.

HISTORICAL AND STATUTORY NOTES

Former Rule 26.9, relating to presence of the defendant, was abrogated effective Jan. 1, 2018. See, now, this rule.

16A A. R. S. Rules Crim. Proc., Rule 26.9, AZ ST RCRP Rule 26.9

Current with amendments received through 08/15/19

Rule 26.10. Pronouncement of Judgment and Sentence

(Refs & Annos)

VII. Post-Verdict Proceedings

Rule 26. Judgment, Presentence Report, Presentencing Hearing, Sentence (Refs & Annos)

16A A.R.S. Rules Crim.Proc., Rule 26.10

Rule 26.10. Pronouncement of Judgment and Sentence

(a) Judgment. In pronouncing judgment on any noncapital count, the court must indicate whether the defendant's conviction is pursuant to a plea or trial, the offense for which the defendant was convicted, and whether the offense falls in the categories of dangerous, non-dangerous, repetitive, or non-repetitive offenses.

(b) Sentence. When the court pronounces sentence, it must:

(1) give the defendant an opportunity to address the court;

(2) state that it has considered the time the defendant has spent in custody on the present charge;

(3) explain to the defendant the terms of the sentence or probation;

(4) specify the beginning date for the term of imprisonment and the amount of time to be credited against the sentence as required by law;

(5) for any felony offense or a violation of §§ 13-1802, 13-1805, 28-1381, or 28-1382, permanently affix the defendant's right index fingerprint to the sentencing document or order; and

(6) if the court sentences the defendant to a prison term, the court must send, or direct the clerk to send, to the Department of Corrections the sentencing order and copies of all presentence reports, probation violation reports, and medical and mental health reports prepared for, or relating to, the defendant.

Credits

Added Aug. 31, 2017, effective Jan. 1, 2018. Amended and effective on an emergency basis August 9, 2017, adopted on a permanent basis Dec. 13, 2017.

Editors' Notes

HISTORICAL AND STATUTORY NOTES

Former Rule 26.10, relating to pronouncement of judgment and sentence, was abrogated effective Jan. 1, 2018. See, now, this rule.

16A A. R. S. Rules Crim. Proc., Rule 26.10, AZ ST RCRP Rule 26.10

Current with amendments received through 08/15/19

Rule 26.11. A Court's Duty After Pronouncing Sentence

(Refs & Annos)

VII. Post-Verdict Proceedings

Rule 26. Judgment, Presentence Report, Presentencing Hearing, Sentence (Refs & Annos)

16A A.R.S. Rules Crim.Proc., Rule 26.11

Rule 26.11. A Court's Duty After Pronouncing Sentence

(a) Disclosures. After pronouncing judgment and sentence, the court must:

(1) inform the defendant:

(A) of the right to appeal the judgment, sentence, or both;

(B) of the right to seek post-conviction relief;

(C) that the failure to file a timely notice of appeal or timely notice of post-conviction relief will result in the loss of those rights; and

(D) of the right to apply to have the judgment of conviction set aside, except as provided in A.R.S. § 13-907(K).

(2) advise that:

(A) if the defendant is indigent, as defined in Rule 6.1(b), the court will appoint counsel to represent the defendant on appeal;

(B) if the defendant is unable to pay for certified copies of the record on appeal and a certified transcript, the county will provide them; and

(3) advise that the defendant may waive the right to appellate counsel by filing a written notice no later than 30 days after filing the notice of appeal.

(b) Written Notice. The court must provide the defendant with a written notice of the rights set forth in (a) and the procedures the defendant must follow to exercise them. The record must show affirmatively the defendant's receipt of the notice.

Credits

Added Aug. 31, 2017, effective Jan. 1, 2018. Amended on an emergency basis June 15, 2018, effective Aug. 3, 2018, adopted on a permanent basis Dec. 13, 2018.

Editors' Notes

COMMENT

The defendant's trial counsel has a duty under Rule 6.3(b) to advise the client whether or not an appeal would be beneficial and to continue representing the defendant if an appeal is taken, unless counsel shows good cause why counsel should be allowed to withdraw. Rule 41, Form 23 should be used to notify the defendant of the rights to appeal and to counsel on appeal.

The Superior Court Rules of Appellate Procedure-Criminal govern appeals from justice courts and municipal courts.

HISTORICAL AND STATUTORY NOTES

Former Rule 26.11, relating to duty of the court after pronouncing sentence, was abrogated effective Jan. 1, 2018. See, now, this rule.

16A A. R. S. Rules Crim. Proc., Rule 26.11, AZ ST RCRP Rule 26.11

Current with amendments received through 08/15/19

Rule 26.12. Defendant's Compliance with Monetary and Non-Monetary Terms of a Sentence

(Refs & Annos)

VII. Post-Verdict Proceedings

Rule 26. Judgment, Presentence Report, Presentencing Hearing, Sentence (Refs & Annos)

16A A.R.S. Rules Crim.Proc., Rule 26.12

Rule 26.12. Defendant's Compliance with Monetary and Non-Monetary Terms of a Sentence

(a) Method of Payment--Installments. The court may permit the defendant to pay any fine, restitution, or other monetary obligation within a specified period of time or in specified installments. The defendant must pay restitution as promptly as possible, given the defendant's ability to pay.

(b) Method of Payment--to Whom. The defendant must pay a fine, restitution, or other monetary obligations to the court, unless the court orders otherwise. The court must apply the defendant's payments first to satisfy the restitution order and the payment of any restitution in arrears. The court must forward restitution payments to the victim as promptly as practicable.

(c) Failure to Pay a Monetary Obligation or to Comply with Court Orders.

(1) *Defendants Not on Supervised Probation.* If a defendant who is not on supervised probation fails to pay a fine, restitution, or other monetary obligation, or fails to comply with any other term or condition of sentence within the prescribed time, the court must promptly notify the State.

(2) *Defendants on Supervised Probation.* If a defendant who is on supervised probation fails to pay a fine, restitution, or other monetary obligation, or fails to comply with any other term or condition of probation within the prescribed time, the court must promptly notify the defendant's probation officer.

(3) *Court Action upon Failure of a Defendant to Pay a Fine, Restitution, or Other Monetary Obligation or to Comply with Court Orders.* If the defendant fails to timely pay a fine, restitution, or other monetary obligation, or otherwise fails to comply with a court order, and fails to respond to a court notice informing the defendant of the consequences and resolution options, the court may issue an arrest warrant or a summons and require the defendant to show cause why he or she should not be held in contempt. The court must issue a summons unless there is reason to believe a warrant is required to secure the defendant's appearance. A prosecutor who requests a warrant, or a judge who orders a warrant, must state the reasons for the issuance of a warrant rather than a summons.

(4) *Authority to Modify Monetary Obligation.* If the court finds the defendant's default is not willful and the defendant is unable to pay all or part of the monetary obligation, unless otherwise provided by law, the court may mitigate the monetary obligation. In determining whether the defendant is unable to pay all or part of a

financial sanction, the court may consider any relevant evidence including the factors listed in A.R.S. § 13-825.

(5) *Exclusion of Certain Income.* Under federal and state law, in determining whether to find the defendant in contempt, the court must exclude income derived from the following sources:

(A) The Temporary Assistance for Needy Families Program established by § 403 of Title IV of the Social Security Act (A.R.S. 46-207.01);

(B) The Supplemental Security Income Program (42 U.S.C. §§ 1381 through 1383f);

(C) The Social Security Disability Insurance Program (42 U.S.C. §§ 401-433); and

(D) Veterans Disability Compensation.

(6) *Incarceration for Contempt.* If the court finds the defendant in contempt for failure to pay a monetary obligation or failure to comply with a court order, before ordering the defendant incarcerated for contempt, the court must determine that no reasonable measures other than incarceration are adequate to meet the State's interests and permit the defendant a reasonable period of time to pay the obligation in full or make other payment arrangements.

Credits

Added Aug. 31, 2017, effective Jan. 1, 2018. Amended Dec. 13, 2017, effective Jan. 1, 2018; Dec. 13, 2018, effective Jan. 1, 2019.

Editors' Notes

HISTORICAL AND STATUTORY NOTES

Former Rule 26.12, relating to compliance with sentence, was abrogated effective Jan. 1, 2018. See, now, this rule.

16A A. R. S. Rules Crim. Proc., Rule 26.12, AZ ST RCRP Rule 26.12

Current with amendments received through 08/15/19

Rule 26.13. Consecutive Sentences

(Refs & Annos)

VII. Post-Verdict Proceedings

Rule 26. Judgment, Presentence Report, Presentencing Hearing, Sentence (Refs & Annos)

16A A.R.S. Rules Crim.Proc., Rule 26.13

Rule 26.13. Consecutive Sentences

If the court imposes separate sentences of imprisonment on a defendant for two or more offenses, the sentences run consecutively unless the judge expressly directs otherwise. This rule applies even if the offenses are not charged in the same

indictment or information. There is no presumption favoring consecutive sentences rather than concurrent sentences.
Credits
Added Aug. 31, 2017, effective Jan. 1, 2018.
Editors' Notes
HISTORICAL AND STATUTORY NOTES
Former Rule 26.13, relating to concurrent or consecutive sentences, was abrogated effective Jan. 1, 2018. See, now, this rule.
16A A. R. S. Rules Crim. Proc., Rule 26.13, AZ ST RCRP Rule 26.13
Current with amendments received through 08/15/19

Rule 26.14. Resentencing

(Refs & Annos)
VII. Post-Verdict Proceedings
Rule 26. Judgment, Presentence Report, Presentencing Hearing, Sentence (Refs & Annos)
16A A.R.S. Rules Crim.Proc., Rule 26.14

Rule 26.14. Resentencing

If a judgment or sentence, or both, have been set aside--either on appeal, by collateral attack, or on a post-trial motion--the court may not impose a sentence for the same offense, or a different offense based on the same conduct, which is more severe than the earlier sentence unless the court determines:
(a) the earlier sentence is no longer appropriate based on evidence about the defendant's conduct occurring after the court pronounced the earlier sentence;
(b) the earlier sentence was unlawful and it is corrected so the court may impose a lawful sentence; or
(c) other circumstances exist and there is no reasonable likelihood that an increase in the sentence is the product of actual vindictiveness by the sentencing judge.
Credits
Added Aug. 31, 2017, effective Jan. 1, 2018.
Editors' Notes
HISTORICAL AND STATUTORY NOTES
Former Rule 26.14, relating to re-sentencing, was abrogated effective Jan. 1, 2018. See, now, this rule.
16A A. R. S. Rules Crim. Proc., Rule 26.14, AZ ST RCRP Rule 26.14
Current with amendments received through 08/15/19

Rule 26.15. Special Procedures upon Imposing a Death Sentence

(Refs & Annos)
VII. Post-Verdict Proceedings
Rule 26. Judgment, Presentence Report, Presentencing Hearing, Sentence (Refs & Annos)

16A A.R.S. Rules Crim.Proc., Rule 26.15

Rule 26.15. Special Procedures upon Imposing a Death Sentence

After imposing a sentence of death, the court must order the clerk to file a notice of appeal from the judgment and sentence.
Credits
Added Aug. 31, 2017, effective Jan. 1, 2018.
Editors' Notes
HISTORICAL AND STATUTORY NOTES
Former Rule 26.15, relating to special procedures upon imposition of a sentence of death, was abrogated effective Jan. 1, 2018. See, now, this rule.
16A A. R. S. Rules Crim. Proc., Rule 26.15, AZ ST RCRP Rule 26.15
Current with amendments received through 08/15/19

Rule 26.16. Entry of Judgment and Sentence; Warrant of Authority to Execute Sentence

(Refs & Annos)
VII. Post-Verdict Proceedings
Rule 26. Judgment, Presentence Report, Presentencing Hearing, Sentence (Refs & Annos)

16A A.R.S. Rules Crim.Proc., Rule 26.16

Rule 26.16. Entry of Judgment and Sentence; Warrant of Authority to Execute Sentence

(a) Entry of Judgment and Sentence. The judgment of conviction and sentencing on the judgment are complete and valid at the time the court orally pronounces them in open court.
(b) Warrant of Authority.
(1) *Entry of Judgment and Sentence.* The court must enter the exact terms of the judgment and sentence in the court's orders.

(2) *Notice to Appropriate Officer.* The court must furnish a certified copy of the sentencing order, signed by the sentencing judge, to the appropriate officer. No other authority is necessary to execute any sentence the court imposes. If the sentence is for death or imprisonment, the appropriate officer must receive the defendant for execution of the sentence upon delivery to him or her of a signed, certified copy of the sentencing order.

Credits

Added Aug. 31, 2017, effective Jan. 1, 2018.

Editors' Notes

HISTORICAL AND STATUTORY NOTES

Former Rule 26.16, relating to entry of judgment and sentence, and warrant of authority to execute sentence, was abrogated effective Jan. 1, 2018. See, now, this rule.

16A A. R. S. Rules Crim. Proc., Rule 26.16, AZ ST RCRP Rule 26.16

Current with amendments received through 08/15/19

R. 27, Refs & Annos

VII. Post-Verdict Proceedings

Rule 27. Probation and Probation Revocation

16A A.R.S. Rules Crim.Proc., R. 27, Refs & Annos

16A A. R. S. Rules Crim. Proc., R. 27, Refs & Annos, AZ ST RCRP R. 27, Refs & Annos

Current with amendments received through 08/15/19

Rule 27.1. Conditions and Regulations of Probation

(Refs & Annos)

VII. Post-Verdict Proceedings

Rule 27. Probation and Probation Revocation (Refs & Annos)

16A A.R.S. Rules Crim.Proc., Rule 27.1

Rule 27.1. Conditions and Regulations of Probation

The sentencing court may impose conditions on a probationer that promote rehabilitation and protect any victim. The probation officer or any other person the court designates also may impose regulations that are necessary to implement the

court's conditions and that are consistent with them. The court and probation officer must give the probationer a written copy of the conditions and regulations. Unless there is an intergovernmental agreement to the contrary, references to and notice requirements for probation officers do not apply in limited jurisdiction courts.
Credits
Added Aug. 31, 2017, effective Jan. 1, 2018.
Editors' Notes
HISTORICAL AND STATUTORY NOTES
Former Rule 27.1, relating to manner of imposing probation, was abrogated effective Jan. 1, 2018. See, now, this rule.
16A A. R. S. Rules Crim. Proc., Rule 27.1, AZ ST RCRP Rule 27.1
Current with amendments received through 08/15/19

Rule 27.2. Intercounty Transfers

(Refs & Annos)
VII. Post-Verdict Proceedings
Rule 27. Probation and Probation Revocation (Refs & Annos)
16A A.R.S. Rules Crim.Proc., Rule 27.2

Rule 27.2. Intercounty Transfers

(a) Definitions.
(1) *Courtesy Transfer of Probation Supervision.* "Courtesy transfer of probation" means the transfer of the probationer's supervision to another jurisdiction. The sending court retains jurisdiction over the probationer.
(2) *Transfer of Probation Jurisdiction.* "Transfer of probation jurisdiction" means the transfer of jurisdiction over a case to another jurisdiction, including the transfer of the probationer's supervision.
(b) Courtesy Transfer of Probation Supervision.
(1) *Generally.* The superior court or its adult probation department in the sending county may authorize a courtesy transfer of probation supervision to allow a probationer to reside in the receiving county if it verifies that the receiving county:
(A) accepts the probationer; and
(B) can supervise the probationer in accordance with the conditions of the individual's probation.
(2) *Amending Conditions.* If the receiving county is unable to supervise the probationer in accordance with the conditions of probation, the court in the sending county, after a hearing, may amend the conditions to enable the transfer.

(3) *Retention of Jurisdiction.* The court in the sending county retains jurisdiction over the probationer and any probation violation proceeding, and remains responsible for the collection of the probationer's monetary obligations.

(c) Transfer of Probation Jurisdiction.

(1) *Authorizing Transfer.*

(A) Generally. The superior court in the sending county may order the transfer of probation jurisdiction to another Arizona county upon agreement of the original prosecuting agency, the probationer, the sending and receiving county probation departments, and the superior court in the receiving county.

(B) Victim's Rights. A victim of the offense may request an opportunity to be heard concerning a transfer. The court in the sending county must give the victim notice of a proposed transfer and any hearing.

(2) *Transmitting Court Records.* No later than 20 days after the transfer order is filed, the clerk in the sending county must certify the probationer's financial obligations in the case and forward the court's file and entire record, together with a transmittal letter, to the clerk in the receiving county. The clerk may transmit these records in either electronic or paper format. The entire record must include all exhibits, unless they were discarded under Rule 28. Upon receipt, the clerk in the receiving county must sign the transmittal letter and return it to the clerk in the sending county.

(3) *Transmitting Probation Records and Transferring Probationary Jurisdiction.* The county probation department transferring jurisdiction over a probationer must send copies of the file and any other pertinent information to the chief probation officer in the receiving county. The transfer is deemed complete when the chief probation officer in the receiving county receives the file and the probationer checks in with the new probation officer. Until the transfer is complete, the sending county probation department retains jurisdiction over the probationer.

(4) *Assuming Jurisdiction in the Receiving County.* Upon filing an order approving the transfer, the superior court in the receiving county assumes jurisdiction over the probationer's case and has all powers of the sentencing court, including the power to restore civil rights. The chief probation officer may request the court in the receiving county to conduct a hearing to affirm or modify the conditions of supervision, including the payment of fees and restitution.

(5) *Monetary Obligations.* The court in the receiving county is responsible for collecting the probationer's monetary obligations. The receiving county must disperse to the sending county any money it collects for fees, costs or expenses that the probationer owes to the sending county.

(6) *Remand of the Case.* If a probationer's case is remanded for a new trial, the receiving court must transfer the case back to the sending county. In all other remands, the receiving county may do one of the following:

(A) retain jurisdiction;

(B) transfer the case in its entirety back to the sending county; or

(C) transfer the case back to the sending county and retain jurisdiction only over probation supervision and revocation.

(7) *Transmitting Court Records After a Remand for New Trial.* No later than 20 days after an order is filed remanding a transferred case for a new trial, the clerk in the receiving county must return the court file and entire record, including exhibits, and send a transmittal letter to the clerk of the sending county. The clerk may transmit the file and record in either electronic or paper format. Upon receipt, the clerk in the sending county must sign the transmittal letter and return it to the clerk of the receiving county.

(8) *Transmitting Probation Records After a Remand for New Trial.* Upon entry of an order remanding a case for a new trial, the receiving county's probation department must send a copy of its file and any other pertinent information to the chief probation officer in the sending county.

Credits

Added Aug. 31, 2017, effective Jan. 1, 2018.

Editors' Notes

HISTORICAL AND STATUTORY NOTES

Former Rule 27.2, relating to intercounty transfers, was abrogated effective Jan. 1, 2018. See, now, this rule.

16A A. R. S. Rules Crim. Proc., Rule 27.2, AZ ST RCRP Rule 27.2

Current with amendments received through 08/15/19

Rule 27.3. Modification of Conditions or Regulations

(Refs & Annos)

VII. Post-Verdict Proceedings

Rule 27. Probation and Probation Revocation (Refs & Annos)

16A A.R.S. Rules Crim.Proc., Rule 27.3

Rule 27.3. Modification of Conditions or Regulations

(a) Definitions.

(1) *Condition.* "Condition" means any court-ordered term of probation.

(2) *Regulation.* "Regulation" means any term imposed by the probation department, or by any other person the court designates to implement a court-imposed condition of probation.

(b) By a Probation Officer. A probation officer or any other person the court designates may modify or clarify any regulation imposed.

(c) By the Court.

(1) *Generally.* After giving notice to the State, the probationer, and a victim who has the right to notice under Rule 27.10, the court may modify or clarify any term, condition, or regulation of probation. The court's authority to modify probation must comply with due process, statutory limitations, and party agreement.

(2) *Who May Request Modification or Clarification.* At any time before the probationer's absolute discharge, a probationer, probation officer, the State, or any other person the court designates, may ask the court to modify or clarify any condition or regulation.

(3) *Restitution.* At any time before the probationer's absolute discharge, persons entitled to restitution under a court order may ask the court, based on changed circumstances, to modify or clarify the manner in which restitution is paid.

(4) *Hearing.* The court may hold a hearing on any request for modification or clarification under (c)(2) or (c)(3).

(d) Written Copy and Effect. The probationer must be given a written copy of any modification or clarification of a condition or regulation of probation. A modification of a regulation may go into effect immediately. An oral modification may not be the sole basis for revoking probation unless the condition or regulation is in writing and the probationer received a copy before the violation.

Credits

Added Aug. 31, 2017, effective Jan. 1, 2018.

Editors' Notes

HISTORICAL AND STATUTORY NOTES

Former Rule 27.3, relating to modification and clarification of conditions and regulations, was abrogated effective Jan. 1, 2018. See, now, this rule.

16A A. R. S. Rules Crim. Proc., Rule 27.3, AZ ST RCRP Rule 27.3

Current with amendments received through 08/15/19

Rule 27.4. Early Termination of Probation

(Refs & Annos)

VII. Post-Verdict Proceedings

Rule 27. Probation and Probation Revocation (Refs & Annos)

16A A.R.S. Rules Crim.Proc., Rule 27.4

Rule 27.4. Early Termination of Probation

(a) Discretionary Probation Termination. At any time during the term of probation, the court may terminate probation and discharge the probationer as provided by law. The court may take such action on the probationer's motion, the probation officer's motion, or on its own, but only after any required notice to the victim and the State.

(b) Earned Time Credit Probation Termination. The court may reduce the term of supervised probation for earned time credit as provided by law.

Credits

Added Aug. 31, 2017, effective Jan. 1, 2018.

Editors' Notes

HISTORICAL AND STATUTORY NOTES

Former Rule 27.4, relating to early termination of probation, was abrogated effective Jan. 1, 2018. See, now, this rule.

16A A. R. S. Rules Crim. Proc., Rule 27.4, AZ ST RCRP Rule 27.4

Current with amendments received through 08/15/19

Rule 27.5. Order and Notice of Discharge

(Refs & Annos)

VII. Post-Verdict Proceedings

Rule 27. Probation and Probation Revocation (Refs & Annos)

16A A.R.S. Rules Crim.Proc., Rule 27.5

Rule 27.5. Order and Notice of Discharge

Upon expiration or early termination of probation, the superior court must order the probationer's discharge from probation. Upon expiration or early termination of probation imposed by a limited jurisdiction court, the probationer is discharged from probation. Upon the probationer's request, the court must furnish the probationer with a certified copy of the discharge order in superior court or of the early termination order in a limited jurisdiction court.

Credits

Added Aug. 31, 2017, effective Jan. 1, 2018.

Editors' Notes

HISTORICAL AND STATUTORY NOTES

Former Rule 27.5, relating to order and notice of discharge, was abrogated effective Jan. 1, 2018. See, now, this rule.

16A A. R. S. Rules Crim. Proc., Rule 27.5, AZ ST RCRP Rule 27.5

Current with amendments received through 08/15/19

Rule 27.6. Petition to Revoke Probation and Securing the Probationer's Presence

(Refs & Annos)

VII. Post-Verdict Proceedings
Rule 27. Probation and Probation Revocation (Refs & Annos)
16A A.R.S. Rules Crim.Proc., Rule 27.6

Rule 27.6. Petition to Revoke Probation and Securing the Probationer's Presence

The probation officer or the State may petition the court to revoke probation if there is reasonable cause to believe that a probationer has violated a written condition or regulation of probation. After a petition to revoke is filed, the court may issue a summons directing the probationer to appear on a specified date for a revocation hearing, or it may issue a warrant for the probationer's arrest.
Credits
Added Aug. 31, 2017, effective Jan. 1, 2018.
Editors' Notes
HISTORICAL AND STATUTORY NOTES
Former Rule 27.6, relating to initiation of revocation proceedings, securing the probationer's presence, and notice, was abrogated effective Jan. 1, 2018. See, now, this rule.
16A A. R. S. Rules Crim. Proc., Rule 27.6, AZ ST RCRP Rule 27.6
Current with amendments received through 08/15/19

Rule 27.7. Initial Appearance After Arrest

(Refs & Annos)
VII. Post-Verdict Proceedings
Rule 27. Probation and Probation Revocation (Refs & Annos)
16A A.R.S. Rules Crim.Proc., Rule 27.7

Rule 27.7. Initial Appearance After Arrest

(a) Probationer Arrested. If a probationer is arrested on a warrant issued under Rule 27.6 or is arrested by the probationer's probation officer under A.R.S. § 13-901(D), the probationer must be taken without unreasonable delay to the court with jurisdiction over the probationer.
(b) Notice. If a probationer is arrested on a warrant issued under Rule 27.6, the court must immediately notify the probationer's probation officer of the initial appearance.
(c) Procedure. At the initial appearance, the court must advise the probationer of the probationer's right to counsel under Rule 6, inform the probationer that any statement the probationer makes before the hearing may be used against the

probationer, set the date of the revocation arraignment, and make a release determination.

Credits

Added Aug. 31, 2017, effective Jan. 1, 2018.

Editors' Notes

HISTORICAL AND STATUTORY NOTES

Former Rule 27.7, relating to initial appearance after arrest, was abrogated effective Jan. 1, 2018. See, now, this rule.

16A A. R. S. Rules Crim. Proc., Rule 27.7, AZ ST RCRP Rule 27.7

Current with amendments received through 08/15/19

Rule 27.8. Probation Revocation

(Refs & Annos)

VII. Post-Verdict Proceedings

Rule 27. Probation and Probation Revocation (Refs & Annos)

16A A.R.S. Rules Crim.Proc., Rule 27.8

Rule 27.8. Probation Revocation

(a) Revocation Arraignment.

(1) *Timing.* The court must hold a revocation arraignment no later than 7 days after the summons is served or after the probationer's initial appearance under Rule 27.7.

(2) *Conduct of the Proceeding.* The court must inform the probationer of each alleged probation violation, and the probationer must admit or deny each allegation.

(3) *Setting a Violation Hearing.* If the probationer does not admit to a violation or if the court does not accept an admission, the court must set a violation hearing, unless both parties agree that a violation hearing may proceed immediately after the arraignment.

(b) Violation Hearing.

(1) *Timing.* The court must hold a hearing to determine whether a probationer has violated a written condition or regulation of probation no less than 7 and no more than 20 days after the revocation arraignment, unless the probationer in writing or on the record requests, and the court agrees, to set the hearing for another date.

(2) *Probationer's Right to Be Present.* The probationer has a right to be present at the violation hearing. If the probationer was previously arraigned under Rule 27.8, the hearing may proceed in the probationer's absence under Rule 9.1.

(3) *Conduct of the Hearing.* A violation must be established by a preponderance of the evidence. Each party may present evidence and has the right to cross-examine

any witness who testifies. The court may receive any reliable evidence, including hearsay, that is not legally privileged.

(4) *Admissions.* An admission by the probationer at any hearing in the same case relating to the probationer's failure to pay a monetary obligation imposed in the case is inadmissible in the probation violation hearing, unless the probationer was represented by counsel at the hearing in which the admission was made.

(5) *Findings and Setting a Disposition Hearing.* If the court finds that the probationer committed a violation of a condition or regulation of probation, it must make specific findings of the facts that establish the violation and then set a disposition hearing.

(c) Disposition Hearing.

(1) *Timing.* The court must hold a disposition hearing no less than 7 nor more than 20 days after making a determination that the probationer has violated a condition or regulation of probation.

(2) *Disposition.* Upon finding that the probationer violated a condition or regulation of probation, the court may revoke, modify, or continue probation. If the court revokes probation, the court must pronounce sentence in accordance with Rule 26. The court may not find a violation of a condition or regulation that the probationer did not receive in writing.

(d) Waiver of Disposition Hearing. If a probationer admits, or the court finds, a violation of a condition or regulation of probation, the probationer may waive a disposition hearing. If the court accepts the waiver, it may proceed immediately to a disposition under (c)(2).

(e) Disposition upon Determination of Guilt for a Later Offense. If a court makes a determination of guilt under Rule 26.1(a) that the probationer committed a later criminal offense, the court need not hold a violation hearing and may set the matter for a disposition hearing at the time set for entry of judgment on the criminal offense.

(f) Record. The court must make a record of the revocation arraignment, violation hearing, and disposition hearing.

Credits

Added Aug. 31, 2017, effective Jan. 1, 2018.

Editors' Notes

HISTORICAL AND STATUTORY NOTES

Former Rule 27.8, relating to revocation of probation, was abrogated effective Jan. 1, 2018. See, now, this rule.

16A A. R. S. Rules Crim. Proc., Rule 27.8, AZ ST RCRP Rule 27.8

Current with amendments received through 08/15/19

Rule 27.9. Admissions by the Probationer

(Refs & Annos)

VII. Post-Verdict Proceedings

Rule 27. Probation and Probation Revocation (Refs & Annos)

16A A.R.S. Rules Crim.Proc., Rule 27.9

Rule 27.9. Admissions by the Probationer

(a) Required Inquiries. Before accepting an admission that the probationer violated a condition or regulation of probation, the court must address the probationer personally and determine that the probationer understands:

(1) the nature of the probation violation that the probationer will be admitting;

(2) the right to counsel, if the probationer is not already represented by counsel;

(3) the right to cross-examine witnesses who may testify against the probationer;

(4) the right to present witnesses on the probationer's behalf;

(5) that by admitting a violation of a condition or regulation of probation, the probationer waives the right to appellate court review by direct appeal, and may seek review only by filing a petition for post-conviction relief under Rule 32 and, if denied, by filing a petition for review; and

(6) regardless of the outcome of the probation violation proceeding, if the alleged violation involves a criminal offense for which the probationer has not yet been tried, the probationer may still be tried for that offense, and any statement made by the probationer at the probation violation proceeding may be used to impeach the probationer's testimony at the trial of that other offense.

(b) Required Determinations. The court may accept the probationer's admission only if it determines that:

(1) the probationer wishes to forego the rights in (a);

(2) the admission is voluntary and not the result of force, threats, or promises; and

(3) the admission has a factual basis.

Credits

Added Aug. 31, 2017, effective Jan. 1, 2018.

Editors' Notes

HISTORICAL AND STATUTORY NOTES

Former Rule 27.9, relating to admissions by the probationer, was abrogated effective Jan. 1, 2018. See, now, this rule.

16A A. R. S. Rules Crim. Proc., Rule 27.9, AZ ST RCRP Rule 27.9

Current with amendments received through 08/15/19

Rule 27.10. Victims' Rights in Probation Proceedings

16A A.R.S. Rules Crim.Proc., Rule 27.10
Formerly cited as AZ ST RCRP Rule 27.11

Rule 27.10. Victims' Rights in Probation Proceedings

The court must afford a victim who has requested notice under Rule 39 the opportunity to be present and to be heard at any proceeding involving:

(a) the termination of any type of probation;

(b) probation revocation dispositions;

(c) a modification of probation or intensive probation conditions or regulations that would substantially affect the probationer's contact with, or safety of, the victim or that would affect restitution or incarceration status; or

(d) transfers of probation jurisdiction.

Credits

Added Aug. 31, 2017, effective Jan. 1, 2018.

Editors' Notes

HISTORICAL AND STATUTORY NOTES

Former Rule 27.10, relating to revocation of probation in absentia, was abrogated effective Jan. 1, 2018. See, now, AZ ST RCRP Rule 27.11.

16A A. R. S. Rules Crim. Proc., Rule 27.10, AZ ST RCRP Rule 27.10

Current with amendments received through 08/15/19

Rule 27.11. Probation Review Hearing Regarding Sex Offender Registration

16A A.R.S. Rules Crim.Proc., Rule 27.11
Formerly cited as AZ ST RCRP Rule 27.12

Rule 27.11. Probation Review Hearing Regarding Sex Offender Registration

(a) Right to Hearing. The court must conduct a probation review hearing at least once a year if requested by a probationer who is:

(1) under 22 years of age; and

(2) serving a term of probation for an offense that:

(A) requires registration under A.R.S. § 13-3821; and

(B) was committed when the probationer was under 18 years of age.

(b) Notice of Right to Hearing. The court must inform a probationer of the right to a hearing under (a) when it imposes probation.

(c) Request for Hearing and Timing. To obtain a hearing, the probationer must file a request with the court and provide a copy of the request to the State. A probationer must file a request for a hearing no later than 30 days before the probationer's twenty-second birthday.

(d) Setting a Hearing and Providing Notice.

(1) *Timing.* The court must hold a hearing no later than 30 days after a timely request is filed.

(2) *Notice.*

(A) Generally. The court must notify the following of the hearing date:

(i) the State, which in turn must notify any victim or victim's attorney entitled to be present and heard under the Arizona Constitution, statute, or court rule;

(ii) the probationer's attorney, if any; and

(iii) the probation officer.

(B) Notice to the State. In any case involving a victim, the court must give the State at least 7 calendar days' notice of the hearing date.

(e) Prehearing Conference. The court may hold a prehearing conference. The people who may be present and the conference's scope are specified by A.R.S. § 13-923.

(f) Probation Review Report. The court must require the preparation of a probation review report before a probation review hearing. The probation office must deliver the report to the judge conducting the hearing at least 7 calendar days before the scheduled hearing date.

(g) Scope of Hearing. At the hearing, the court must consider and decide whether to:

(1) continue, modify, or terminate probation;

(2) continue to require, suspend, or terminate the probationer's registration under A.R.S. § 13-3821; and

(3) continue, defer, or terminate community notification under A.R.S. § 13-3825.

Credits

Added Aug. 31, 2017, effective Jan. 1, 2018.

Editors' Notes

HISTORICAL AND STATUTORY NOTES

Former Rule 27.11, relating to victim's rights in probation proceedings, was abrogated effective Jan. 1, 2018. See, now, AZ ST RCRP Rule 27.10.

16A A. R. S. Rules Crim. Proc., Rule 27.11, AZ ST RCRP Rule 27.11

Current with amendments received through 08/15/19

Rule 27.12. Abrogated Aug. 31, 2017, effective Jan. 1, 2018

(Refs & Annos)
VII. Post-Verdict Proceedings
Rule 27. Probation and Probation Revocation (Refs & Annos)
16A A.R.S. Rules Crim.Proc., Rule 27.12

Rule 27.12. Abrogated Aug. 31, 2017, effective Jan. 1, 2018

Editors' Notes
HISTORICAL AND STATUTORY NOTES
The abrogated rule related to probation review hearings. See, now, AZ ST RCRP Rule 27.11.
16A A. R. S. Rules Crim. Proc., Rule 27.12, AZ ST RCRP Rule 27.12
Current with amendments received through 08/15/19

Rule 28.1. Duties of the Clerk

(Refs & Annos)
VII. Post-Verdict Proceedings
Rule 28. Retention and Destruction of Records and Evidence
16A A.R.S. Rules Crim.Proc., Rule 28.1

Rule 28.1. Duties of the Clerk

(a) Retention of Records and Evidence. The clerk receives and maintains all court filings and evidence admitted in criminal cases.
(b) Destruction of Certain Records.
(1) *Generally.* When a case is no longer subject to modification, the clerk must destroy certain records under retention and destruction schedules established by the Supreme Court.
(2) *Definition of "Subject to Modification."* A case is no longer "subject to modification:"
(A) after the defendant is acquitted or the court dismisses with prejudice the charges against the defendant;
(B) 60 days after the entry of judgment and sentence, unless a party files a notice of appeal or a post-trial motion;
(C) 90 days after either a court denies a post-trial motion or receives an appellate court mandate affirming the defendant's conviction, unless a petition for writ of certiorari is filed with the United States Supreme Court;

(D) 25 days after the United States Supreme Court denies certiorari or issues a mandate affirming a conviction, unless a petition for rehearing is filed;

(E) after the United States Supreme Court denies a petition for rehearing; or

(F) one year after exhausting all state remedies if the defendant did not file a petition for habeas corpus, or after exhausting all federal remedies if the defendant filed a petition for a writ of habeas corpus.

(c) Court Reporter Notes. Court reporters' notes must be retained under retention and destruction schedules established by the Supreme Court.

Credits

Added Aug. 31, 2017, effective Jan. 1, 2018.

Editors' Notes

HISTORICAL AND STATUTORY NOTES

Former Rule 28.1, relating to duties of the clerk, was abrogated effective Jan. 1, 2018. See, now, this rule.

16A A. R. S. Rules Crim. Proc., Rule 28.1, AZ ST RCRP Rule 28.1

Current with amendments received through 08/15/19

Rule 28.2. Disposition of Evidence

(Refs & Annos)

VII. Post-Verdict Proceedings

Rule 28. Retention and Destruction of Records and Evidence

16A A.R.S. Rules Crim.Proc., Rule 28.2

Rule 28.2. Disposition of Evidence

(a) Manner of Disposition. Unless the court orders otherwise, after the case is no longer subject to modification under Rule 28.1, the clerk must return evidence to the party who submitted it.

(b) Disposal of Evidence; Right to Examine and Record of Disposal.

(1) *Disposal of Evidence.* Before disposing of any evidence seized or otherwise obtained for a filed criminal prosecution, a law enforcement agency must notify the responsible prosecuting agency and the Attorney General, who may:

(A) photograph, reproduce, preserve in whole or in part, or identify the item;

(B) transcribe all serial numbers, identification numbers, or other identifying markings; or

(C) prepare, or have an expert prepare, a report identifying the item.

(2) *Notice.* At least 20 days before disposing an item under this rule, the prosecuting agency or law enforcement agency must serve a notice of disposal, together with a

copy of any record of disposal made under (b)(5) to any person and the person's counsel against whom the State has used or may use the item as evidence.

(3) *Examination.* No later than 10 days after the disposal notice is served, the person may request a stay of disposal until after trial or may request permission to examine, test, analyze, or otherwise make his or her own record of disposal of the item.

(4) *Conditions.* The State must permit an examination requested under (b)(3), but may impose reasonable conditions on any examination, testing, or analysis, including a stipulation concerning chain of title.

(5) *Record of Disposal.* The prosecuting agency, law enforcement agency, or the Attorney General must prepare a record of disposal for any item disposed of under (b)(1).

(c) Stay of Disposal. On any party's request or on its own, the court with jurisdiction over the case may stay disposal of any item for a reasonable time. The timely filing of a motion stays the disposal of any item until the court rules.

(d) Use of Record of Disposal. A record of disposal that is made under (b)(5) is admissible for any purpose for which the item itself would be admissible.

Credits

Added Aug. 31, 2017, effective Jan. 1, 2018.

Editors' Notes

HISTORICAL AND STATUTORY NOTES

Former Rule 28.2, relating to disposition of evidence in the custody of the prosecutor or law enforcement agencies, was abrogated effective Jan. 1, 2018. See, now, this rule.

16A A. R. S. Rules Crim. Proc., Rule 28.2, AZ ST RCRP Rule 28.2

Current with amendments received through 08/15/19

Rule 28.3. Retroactive Application

(Refs & Annos)

VII. Post-Verdict Proceedings

Rule 28. Retention and Destruction of Records and Evidence

16A A.R.S. Rules Crim.Proc., Rule 28.3

Rule 28.3. Retroactive Application

The provisions of this rule apply to all records and evidence in the possession of the clerk, prosecuting agency, and law enforcement agency as of the effective date of these rules regardless of the date on which the records were made or the evidence obtained.

Credits

Added Aug. 31, 2017, effective Jan. 1, 2018.

Editors' Notes

HISTORICAL AND STATUTORY NOTES

Former Rule 28.3, relating to retroactive application, was abrogated effective Jan. 1, 2018. See, now, this rule.

16A A. R. S. Rules Crim. Proc., Rule 28.3, AZ ST RCRP Rule 28.3

Current with amendments received through 08/15/19

R. 29, Refs & Annos

VII. Post-Verdict Proceedings

Rule 29. Setting Aside a Conviction

16A A.R.S. Rules Crim.Proc., R. 29, Refs & Annos

16A A. R. S. Rules Crim. Proc., R. 29, Refs & Annos, AZ ST RCRP R. 29, Refs & Annos

Current with amendments received through 08/15/19

Rule 29.1. Grounds; Notice

(Refs & Annos)

VII. Post-Verdict Proceedings

Rule 29. Setting Aside a Conviction (Refs & Annos)

16A A.R.S. Rules Crim.Proc., Rule 29.1

Rule 29.1. Grounds; Notice

(a) Generally. A person who has completed probation or a sentence may apply in writing to the court to set aside a conviction under A.R.S. § 13-907. The court must provide a person with written notice of this opportunity at the time of sentencing.

(b) Sex Trafficking Victims. Under A.R.S. § 13-907.01, a sex trafficking victim may apply in writing to the court to vacate the victim's conviction under A.R.S. § 13-3214, or a city or town ordinance that has the same or substantially similar elements, if the offense was committed before July 24, 2014.

Credits

Added Aug. 31, 2017, effective Jan. 1, 2018. Amended and effective on an emergency basis Aug. 9, 2017, adopted on a permanent basis Jan. 1, 2018. Amended on an emergency basis June 15, 2018, effective Aug. 3, 2018, adopted on a permanent basis Dec. 13, 2018.

Editors' Notes

COMMENT

Rule 29 implements A.R.S. §§ 13-905 to -911. Rule 29.1 implements A.R.S. § 13-907. Upon conviction of a felony, a person is deprived of rights including the right to vote (Ariz. Const. art. 7, § 2); the right to bear arms if the conviction was for a crime of violence (A.R.S. §§ 13-3101 to -3102); the right to serve on a jury (A.R.S. § 21-201); the right to practice a number of professions and occupations, including law (Ariz. Sup. Ct. Rules 51, 52(a), 52(b), and 57(a)--(d)), accounting (A.R.S. § 32-741), and beauty culture (A.R.S. § 32-553); and, if a life sentence is imposed, the rights negated by a declaration of civil death (A.R.S. §§ 13-904, 13-4301).

HISTORICAL AND STATUTORY NOTES

Former Rule 29.1, relating to grounds and notice, was abrogated effective Jan. 1, 2018. See, now, this rule.

16A A. R. S. Rules Crim. Proc., Rule 29.1, AZ ST RCRP Rule 29.1

Current with amendments received through 08/15/19

Rule 29.2. Application

(Refs & Annos)

VII. Post-Verdict Proceedings

Rule 29. Setting Aside a Conviction (Refs & Annos)

16A A.R.S. Rules Crim.Proc., Rule 29.2

Rule 29.2. Application

(a) Contents. An application under this rule must include the applicant's name, address, date of birth, and signature, the offenses for which the applicant was convicted, the place and date of conviction, the sentence imposed, the status of victim restitution payment and other court-ordered monetary obligations, and the relief the applicant is requesting. The applicant must attach to the application any documents and affidavits required by law and may attach other supporting documents and affidavits.

(b) Place of Filing and Filing Fee. The applicant must file an application with the court that sentenced the applicant. The clerk may not charge a fee for filing or docketing an application.

(c) Processing of Application. The court must send a copy of the application to the applicable prosecuting agency no later than 10 days after filing.

(d) Victim Notification. The victim has the right to be present and be heard at any proceeding in which the defendant has filed an application to have a judgment of conviction set aside. If the victim requested postconviction notice, the prosecuting agency must provide the victim with notice of the defendant's application and of the rights provided to the victim. The prosecuting agency must provide notice to the victim of the opportunity to be heard if the victim requested post-conviction notification.

Credits

Added Aug. 31, 2017, effective Jan. 1, 2018. Amended on an emergency basis June 15, 2018, effective Aug. 3, 2018, adopted on a permanent basis Dec. 13, 2018.

Editors' Notes

HISTORICAL AND STATUTORY NOTES

Former Rule 29.2, relating to contents, place of filing, and service of applications, was abrogated effective Jan. 1, 2018. See, now, this rule.

16A A. R. S. Rules Crim. Proc., Rule 29.2, AZ ST RCRP Rule 29.2

Current with amendments received through 08/15/19

Rule 29.3. State's Response

(Refs & Annos)

VII. Post-Verdict Proceedings

Rule 29. Setting Aside a Conviction (Refs & Annos)

16A A.R.S. Rules Crim.Proc., Rule 29.3

Formerly cited as AZ ST RCRP Rule 29.4

Rule 29.3. State's Response

No later than 60 days after the application is filed, the State and victim may file a written response stating their reasons for opposing the application, if any. The State must send a copy of the response to the applicant's attorney or the applicant, if unrepresented.

Credits

Formerly Rule 29.4 added Aug. 31, 2017, effective Jan. 1, 2018. Renumbered Rule 29.3 and amended on an emergency basis June 15, 2018, effective Aug. 3, 2018, adopted on a permanent basis Dec. 13, 2018.

Editors' Notes

HISTORICAL AND STATUTORY NOTES

Former Rule 29.3, relating to hearing date, was abrogated effective Jan. 1, 2018. See, now, this rule.

Former Rule 29.3, relating to hearing date, was abrogated on an emergency basis June 15, 2018, effective Aug. 3, 2018.

16A A. R. S. Rules Crim. Proc., Rule 29.3, AZ ST RCRP Rule 29.3

Current with amendments received through 08/15/19

Rule 29.4. Reply

(Refs & Annos)
VII. Post-Verdict Proceedings

Rule 29. Setting Aside a Conviction (Refs & Annos)

16A A.R.S. Rules Crim.Proc., Rule 29.4

Rule 29.4. Reply

The applicant may file a reply but must do so no later than 15 days after the State's response is filed.

Credits

Added on an emergency basis June 15, 2018, effective Aug. 3, 2018, adopted on a permanent basis Dec. 13, 2018.

Editors' Notes

HISTORICAL AND STATUTORY NOTES

Former Rule 29.4, relating to response by the prosecutor, was abrogated effective Jan. 1, 2018. See, now, this rule.

16A A. R. S. Rules Crim. Proc., Rule 29.4, AZ ST RCRP Rule 29.4

Current with amendments received through 08/15/19

Rule 29.5 Hearing

(Refs & Annos)
VII. Post-Verdict Proceedings

Rule 29. Setting Aside a Conviction (Refs & Annos)

16A A.R.S. Rules Crim.Proc., Rule 29.5

Rule 29.5 Hearing

On either party's request or on its own motion, the court may set a hearing. The hearing must be held no later than 120 days after the application's filing unless the court finds good cause for an extension. The prosecuting agency must provide post-conviction victim notice of the hearing date and the right to be heard, if the victim requested post-conviction notification.

Credits

Added on an emergency basis June 15, 2018, effective Aug. 3, 2018, adopted on a permanent basis Dec. 13, 2018.

Editors' Notes

HISTORICAL AND STATUTORY NOTES

Former Rule 29.5, relating to disposition, was abrogated effective Jan. 1, 2018. See, now, this rule.

16A A. R. S. Rules Crim. Proc., Rule 29.5, AZ ST RCRP Rule 29.5

Current with amendments received through 08/15/19

Rule 29.6 Disposition

(Refs & Annos)

VII. Post-Verdict Proceedings

Rule 29. Setting Aside a Conviction (Refs & Annos)

16A A.R.S. Rules Crim.Proc., Rule 29.6

Formerly cited as AZ ST RCRP Rule 29.7

Rule 29.6 Disposition

(a) Considerations. In determining whether to grant an application, the court must consider the following factors:

(1) the nature and circumstances of the offense the conviction is based on;

(2) the applicant's compliance with the conditions of probation, the sentence imposed, and the Department of Corrections' rules or regulations, if applicable;

(3) any earlier or later convictions;

(4) the victim's input and the status of victim restitution, if any;

(5) the time that has elapsed since the completion of the applicant's sentence;

(6) the applicant's age at the time of conviction; and

(7) any other factor relevant to the application.

(b) Denial. If the court denies an application, its order must state the reasons for the denial in writing and on the record.

(c) Subsequent Application. If an application is denied, the applicant may file a new application after satisfying all requirements or after resolving any other reason for denial.

(d) Order. The clerk must transmit the order to the applicant, the prosecutor, and the Department of Public Safety.

Credits

Formerly Rule 29.5, added Aug. 31, 2017, effective Jan. 1, 2018. Renumbered Rule 29.6 and amended on an emergency basis June 15, 2018, effective Aug. 3, 2018, adopted on a permanent basis Dec. 13, 2018.
Editors' Notes
HISTORICAL AND STATUTORY NOTES
Former Rule 29.6, relating to confidential record, was abrogated effective Jan. 1, 2018. See, now, this rule.
16A A. R. S. Rules Crim. Proc., Rule 29.6, AZ ST RCRP Rule 29.6
Current with amendments received through 08/15/19

Rule 29.7. Special Provisions for Sex Trafficking Victims

(Refs & Annos)
VII. Post-Verdict Proceedings
Rule 29. Setting Aside a Conviction (Refs & Annos)
16A A.R.S. Rules Crim.Proc., Rule 29.7
Formerly cited as AZ ST RCRP Rule 29.6

Rule 29.7. Special Provisions for Sex Trafficking Victims

(a) Confidentiality. If a court grants an application submitted by a sex trafficking victim, all paper and electronic records of the vacated conviction become confidential. The record may be disclosed upon request to the sex trafficking victim but otherwise may be disclosed only by court order for good cause. The court must order that the pertinent law enforcement agencies and prosecuting agencies make notations in their records that the conviction was vacated and the applicant was a crime victim.

(b) Order. The clerk must transmit the order vacating the conviction of a sex trafficking victim to the arresting agency, the prosecuting agency, the Department of Public Safety, and the applicant.
Credits
Formerly Rule 29.6, added Aug. 31, 2017, effective Jan. 1, 2018. Renumbered Rule 29.7 and amended on an emergency basis June 15, 2018, effective Aug. 3, 2018, adopted on a permanent basis Dec. 13, 2018.
Editors' Notes
HISTORICAL AND STATUTORY NOTES
Former Rule 29.6, relating to confidential record, was abrogated effective Jan. 1, 2018. See, now, this rule.
16A A. R. S. Rules Crim. Proc., Rule 29.7, AZ ST RCRP Rule 29.7
Current with amendments received through 08/15/19

VII. Post-Verdict Proceedings
Rule 30. Restoring Civil Rights
                16A A.R.S. Rules Crim.Proc., R. 30, Refs & Annos

16A A. R. S. Rules Crim. Proc., R. 30, Refs & Annos, AZ ST RCRP R. 30, Refs & Annos
Current with amendments received through 08/15/19

                Rule 30.1. Grounds; Notice

(Refs & Annos)
VII. Post-Verdict Proceedings
Rule 30. Restoring Civil Rights (Refs & Annos)
                16A A.R.S. Rules Crim.Proc., Rule 30.1
                Rule 30.1. Grounds; Notice

(a) Automatic Restoration for First Offense. A person who has not previously been convicted of any other felony must automatically be restored any civil rights that were lost or suspended by the conviction, except the right to possess or carry a gun or firearm, if the person:
(1) completes a term of probation or receives an absolute discharge from imprisonment; and
(2) pays any fine or restitution imposed.
(b) Second or Subsequent Offense. A person who has been convicted of 2 or more felonies and whose period of probation has been completed or has received an absolute discharge from imprisonment may have any civil rights that were lost or suspended by the conviction restored by the court. A person whose civil rights were lost or suspended by 2 or more felony convictions in a United States District Court may apply to the superior court in the county in which the person now resides to have the person's civil rights restored.
(c) Gun or Firearm Rights. To restore the right to possess or carry a gun or firearm the person must file an application under Rule 30.2. The following persons may not file to restore the right to possess a gun or firearm:

(1) a person convicted of a dangerous offense under A.R.S. § 13-704;

(2) a person convicted of a serious offense as defined in A.R.S. § 13-706 until 10 years from the date of discharge from probation or from the date of absolute discharge from prison; or

(3) a person convicted of any other felony offense until 2 years from the person's discharge from probation or absolute discharge from prison.

Credits

Added on an emergency basis, effective June 15, 2018, adopted on a permanent basis Dec. 13, 2018.

Editors' Notes

HISTORICAL AND STATUTORY NOTES

Former Rule 30.1, relating to the right to appeal from courts of limited jurisdiction, was abrogated Aug. 31, 2017, effective Jan. 1, 2018.

16A A. R. S. Rules Crim. Proc., Rule 30.1, AZ ST RCRP Rule 30.1

Current with amendments received through 08/15/19

Rule 30.2. Application

(Refs & Annos)

VII. Post-Verdict Proceedings

Rule 30. Restoring Civil Rights (Refs & Annos)

16A A.R.S. Rules Crim.Proc., Rule 30.2

Rule 30.2. Application

(a) Contents. An application under this rule must include the applicant's name, address, date of birth, and signature, the offenses for which the applicant was convicted, the place and date of conviction, the sentence imposed, the status of victim restitution payment and other court-ordered monetary obligations, and the relief the applicant is requesting. The applicant must attach to the application any documents and affidavits required by law and may attach other supporting documents and affidavits.

(b) Place of Filing and Filing Fee. The applicant must file an application with the court that sentenced the applicant. An applicant who was convicted in a United States District Court may apply for restoration of rights in the superior court in the county where the person now resides. The clerk may not charge a fee for filing an application.

(c) Processing of Application. The court must send a copy of the application to the applicable prosecuting agency no later than 10 days of filing.

(d) Victim Notification. The victim has the right to be present and be heard at any proceeding in which the defendant has filed an application to have civil rights restored. If the victim in a state court matter has requested post-conviction notice, the prosecuting agency must provide the victim with notice of the defendant's application and the rights provided to the victim. The prosecuting agency must provide notice to the victim of the opportunity to be heard if the victim requested post-conviction notification.

Credits

Added on an emergency basis, effective June 15, 2018, adopted on a permanent basis Dec. 13, 2018.

Editors' Notes

HISTORICAL AND STATUTORY NOTES

Former Rule 30.2, relating to time for taking appeal from courts of limited jurisdiction and perfection of appeal, was abrogated Aug. 31, 2017, effective Jan. 1, 2018.

16A A. R. S. Rules Crim. Proc., Rule 30.2, AZ ST RCRP Rule 30.2

Current with amendments received through 08/15/19

Rule 30.3. State's Response

(Refs & Annos)

VII. Post-Verdict Proceedings

Rule 30. Restoring Civil Rights (Refs & Annos)

16A A.R.S. Rules Crim.Proc., Rule 30.3

Rule 30.3. State's Response

Within 60 days after the application is filed, the State and victim may file a written response stating their reasons for opposing the application, if any. The State must send a copy of the response to the applicant's attorney or the applicant, if unrepresented.

Credits

Added on an emergency basis, effective June 15, 2018, adopted on a permanent basis Dec. 13, 2018.

Editors' Notes

HISTORICAL AND STATUTORY NOTES

Former Rule 30.3, relating to preparation of record from courts of limited jurisdiction, was abrogated Aug. 31, 2017, effective Jan. 1, 2018.

16A A. R. S. Rules Crim. Proc., Rule 30.3, AZ ST RCRP Rule 30.3

Current with amendments received through 08/15/19

Rule 30.4. Reply

(Refs & Annos)
VII. Post-Verdict Proceedings
Rule 30. Restoring Civil Rights (Refs & Annos)
16A A.R.S. Rules Crim.Proc., Rule 30.4

Rule 30.4. Reply

The applicant may file a reply but must do so no later than 15 days after the State's response is filed.
Credits
Added on an emergency basis, effective June 15, 2018, adopted on a permanent basis Dec. 13, 2018.
Editors' Notes
HISTORICAL AND STATUTORY NOTES
Former Rule 30.4, relating to setting the date for trial in courts of limited jurisdiction, was abrogated Aug. 31, 2017, effective Jan. 1, 2018.
16A A. R. S. Rules Crim. Proc., Rule 30.4, AZ ST RCRP Rule 30.4
Current with amendments received through 08/15/19

Rule 30.5. Hearing

(Refs & Annos)
VII. Post-Verdict Proceedings
Rule 30. Restoring Civil Rights (Refs & Annos)
16A A.R.S. Rules Crim.Proc., Rule 30.5

Rule 30.5. Hearing

On either party's request or on its own, the court may set a hearing. A hearing must be held no later than 120 days after the application's filing, unless the court finds good cause for an extension. The prosecuting agency must provide post-conviction victim notice of the hearing date and the right to be present and heard if the victim requested post-conviction notification.
Credits
Added on an emergency basis, effective June 15, 2018, adopted on a permanent basis Dec. 13, 2018.
Editors' Notes

Former Rule 30.5, relating to appellant's duty to prosecute the appeal in courts of limited jurisdiction, was abrogated Aug. 31, 2017, effective Jan. 1, 2018.

16A A. R. S. Rules Crim. Proc., Rule 30.5, AZ ST RCRP Rule 30.5

Current with amendments received through 08/15/19

Rule 30.6. Disposition

(Refs & Annos)

VII. Post-Verdict Proceedings

Rule 30. Restoring Civil Rights (Refs & Annos)

16A A.R.S. Rules Crim.Proc., Rule 30.6

Rule 30.6. Disposition

(a) Considerations. Whether to restore civil rights shall be in the discretion of the superior court judge.

(b) Additional Considerations for Applications Filed Under A.R.S. § 13-925. On the petition's filing the court must set a hearing. At the hearing, the person must present psychological or psychiatric evidence in support of the petition. The State must provide the court with the person's criminal history records, if any. The court must receive evidence on and consider the following before granting or denying a petition filed by a prohibited possessor under A.R.S. § 13-925:

(1) the circumstances that resulted in the person being a prohibited possessor as defined in A.R.S. § 13-3101(A)(7)(a), or subject to 18 U.S.C. § 922(d)(4) or (g)(4);

(2) the person's record, including the person's mental health record and criminal history record, if any;

(3) the person's reputation based on character witness statements, testimony, or other character evidence;

(4) whether the person is a danger to self or others or has persistent, acute, or grave disabilities or whether the circumstances that led to the original order, adjudication, or finding remain in effect;

(5) any change in the person's condition or circumstances that is relevant to the relief sought; and

(6) any other evidence deemed admissible by the court.

(c) Burden of Proof. The petitioner must prove by clear and convincing evidence the following:

(1) the petitioner is not likely to act in a manner that is dangerous to public safety; and

(2) granting the requested relief is not contrary to the public interest.

(d) Court Findings. At the hearing's conclusion, the court must issue findings of fact and conclusions of law.

(e) Denial. If the court denies an application, its order must state the reasons for the denial in writing, including any statutory requirements the applicant has not met.

(f) Subsequent Application. If an application is denied, the defendant may file a new application after satisfying all requirements or after resolving any other reason for denial.

(g) Order. The clerk must transmit the order to the applicant, the prosecutor, and the Department of Public Safety. If the order is a result of an application filed under A.R.S. § 13-925, a copy of the order must be provided to the Supreme Court and the Department of Public Safety. The Supreme Court and the Department of Public Safety must update, correct, modify, or remove the person's record in any database available to the national instant criminal background check system. Within 10 court days after receiving the notification from the court, the Department of Public Safety must notify the United States Attorney General that the person no longer falls within the provisions of A.R.S.§ 13-3101 (A)(7)(a) or 18 U.S.C. § 922(d)(4) or (g)(4).

Credits

Added on an emergency basis, effective June 15, 2018, adopted on a permanent basis Dec. 13, 2018.

Editors' Notes

HISTORICAL AND STATUTORY NOTES

Former Rule 30.6, relating to stipulation as to questions of law or fact in courts of limited jurisdiction, was abrogated Aug. 31, 2017, effective Jan. 1, 2018.

16A A. R. S. Rules Crim. Proc., Rule 30.6, AZ ST RCRP Rule 30.6

Current with amendments received through 08/15/19

Rule 30.7. Abrogated Aug. 31, 2017, effective Jan. 1, 2018

(Refs & Annos)

VII. Post-Verdict Proceedings

Rule 30. Restoring Civil Rights (Refs & Annos)

16A A.R.S. Rules Crim.Proc., Rule 30.7

Rule 30.7. Abrogated Aug. 31, 2017, effective Jan. 1, 2018

Editors' Notes

HISTORICAL AND STATUTORY NOTES

Repealed Rule 30.7, related to transmittal of fine upon judgment of guilt from courts of limited jurisdiction.

16A A. R. S. Rules Crim. Proc., Rule 30.7, AZ ST RCRP Rule 30.7
Current with amendments received through 08/15/19

Rule 31.1. Scope; Precedence; Definitions

(Refs & Annos)
VIII. Appeal and Other Post-Conviction Relief
Rule 31. Appeals
Section One. General Provisions

16A A.R.S. Rules Crim.Proc., Rule 31.1
Formerly cited as AZ ST RCRP Rule 30.1

Rule 31.1. Scope; Precedence; Definitions

(a) Scope.
(1) *Appeals from Limited Jurisdiction Courts.* The Superior Court Rules of Appellate Procedure-Criminal govern appeals from justice courts and municipal courts.
(2) *Appeals from the Superior Court.* The provisions of Rule 31 govern criminal appeals from the superior court to the Court of Appeals and the Supreme Court.
(b) Precedence of Criminal Appeals. Appeals in criminal cases have precedence over all other appeals except those from juvenile actions or if otherwise provided by law. Capital case appeals have precedence over all other appeals.
(c) Definitions. As used in this rule, the following terms have the following meanings:
(1) *"Appellate clerk"* means the clerk of the court in which an appeal is pending.
(2) *"Appellate court"* means the Supreme Court and the Court of Appeals, Divisions One and Two.
(3) *"Appellant"* is a party that commences an appeal. An appellant also may be a cross-appellee.
(4) *"Appellee"* is a party that responds to an appeal. An appellee also may be a cross-appellant.
(5) *"Decision"* is a written disposition of an appeal, as provided in Rule 31.19.
(6) *"Entry"* of a court order or decision occurs when it is filed by the clerk.
(7) *"Judgment"* is an appealable order, whether identified as a "judgment," an "order," a "pronouncement of sentence," or another term.
Credits
Added by Aug. 31, 2017, effective Jan. 1, 2018.
Editors' Notes
HISTORICAL AND STATUTORY NOTES
Former Rule 31.1, relating to scope of rule, was abrogated effective Jan. 1, 2018.

Rule 31.2. Notice of Appeal or Notice of Cross-Appeal

(Refs & Annos)
VIII. Appeal and Other Post-Conviction Relief
Rule 31. Appeals
Section One. General Provisions

16A A.R.S. Rules Crim.Proc., Rule 31.2
Formerly cited as AZ ST RCRP Rule 30.2

Rule 31.2. Notice of Appeal or Notice of Cross-Appeal

(a) Notice of Appeal or Cross-Appeal.

(1) *Filing a Notice.* Except as provided in (b), a party appeals or cross-appeals a judgment or sentence by signing and filing a notice of appeal or a notice of cross-appeal with the superior court clerk.

(2) *Time for Filing.*

(A) A *notice of appeal* from a judgment of conviction and imposition of sentence must be filed no later than 20 days after the oral pronouncement of sentence.

(B) A notice of appeal from a judgment or order other than (A) must be filed no later than 20 days after entry of the judgment or order.

(C) A *notice of cross-appeal*, if any, must be filed no later than 20 days after the appellant's notice of appeal is filed.

(3) *Delayed Appeal.* A notice of delayed appeal must be filed no later than 20 days after entry of the order granting a delayed appeal under Rule 32.1(f).

(b) Automatic Appeal for a Defendant Sentenced to Death. As provided in Rule 26.15, when a defendant has been sentenced to death, the superior court clerk must file a notice of appeal on the defendant's behalf after the oral pronouncement of sentence. That notice constitutes a notice of appeal by the defendant with respect to all judgments entered and sentences imposed in that case. No later than 10 days after the notice of appeal is filed, the clerk must notify all assigned court reporters or transcribers that they are required to transmit their portions of the certified transcript to the Supreme Court clerk.

(c) Content of the Notice of Appeal or Cross-Appeal.

(1) *The Appeal's Subject.* A notice of appeal or cross-appeal must identify the order, judgment, or sentence that is being appealed.

(2) *Victim's Rights Certification.* If the State's notice of appeal or cross-appeal is based in whole or in part on a victims' rights violation, the State must certify in the

notice of appeal or opening brief that the victim requested the appeal or cross-appeal.

(3) *Other Requirements.* A notice of appeal also must include:

(A) the defendant's name and address;

(B) the name and address of defense counsel, if any;

(C) the name and address (if known) of any co-defendant at trial; and

(D) whether the defendant was indigent when sentenced or when the appealable order was entered.

(d) Joint Notice of Appeal or Cross-Appeal. If two or more defendants are entitled to appeal from judgments, sentences, or orders arising out of the same proceeding, and they have common issues of law and fact, they may file a joint notice of appeal or cross-appeal.

(e) Distribution of Notices by the Superior Court Clerk.

(1) *When a Defendant Appeals.* No later than 8 days after the defendant files a notice of appeal, the superior court clerk must distribute a copy of the notice to:

(A) the prosecuting agency that tried the case;

(B) the attorney general;

(C) the defendant, and each co-defendant at trial who is not a joint-appellant;

(D) defense counsel of record, if any;

(E) the appropriate certified reporter or reporters or, if the record was made by electronic or other means, to the court's designated transcript coordinator; and

(F) the clerk of the proper appellate court.

(2) *When the State Appeals.* No later than 8 days after the State files a notice of appeal or cross-appeal, the superior court clerk must distribute a copy of the notice to:

(A) each defendant and defense counsel of record, if any;

(B) the appropriate certified reporter or reporters, or if the record was made by electronic or other means, to the court's designated transcript coordinator; and

(C) the clerk of the proper appellate court.

(3) *Notice to Unrepresented Defendant.* When distributing the notice of appeal or cross-appeal, the superior court clerk must distribute a notice advising an unrepresented defendant of the right to counsel under Rule 6.

(4) *Notice to the Appellate Court of Pending Post-Trial Motions.* When the superior court clerk sends a notice of appeal or cross-appeal to an appellate court, the clerk must include a copy of any motion filed by a party under Rule 24 that the superior court has not yet decided.

(f) Entry by the Superior Court Clerk. When any party files a notice of appeal or cross-appeal, the superior court clerk must enter in the docket:

(1) whether the defendant was indigent when the appealable order was entered; and

(2) the name and address of each party to whom the clerk distributed copies of the notice of appeal or notice of cross-appeal, and when each notice was distributed.

(g) Assignment of Appellate Case Number.

(1) *Timing.* No later than 10 days after receiving a notice of appeal from the superior court clerk, the appellate clerk must assign an appellate case number to the appeal.

(2) *Case Title.* The appellate clerk must use same case title used in the superior court. If the title does not contain the name of the appellant, the appellate clerk may modify the title. The clerk also must designate the parties as appellants, appellees, cross-appellants, or cross-appellees, as they will appear in the appellate court.

(3) *Notice.* The appellate clerk must promptly notify each individual identified in Rule 31.2(e)(1) or (2) of the assignment of the appellate case number.

(h) Amended Notice. If the superior court enters an order granting or denying relief under Rule 24 after a notice of appeal or cross-appeal has been filed, a party seeking review of the order must file an amended notice no later than 20 days after entry of the order.

Credits

Added by Aug. 31, 2017, effective Jan. 1, 2018. Amended effective Jan. 16, 2019.

Editors' Notes

HISTORICAL AND STATUTORY NOTES

Former Rule 31.2, relating to notice of appeal, automatic appeal, and joint appeals, was abrogated effective Jan. 1, 2018.

16A A. R. S. Rules Crim. Proc., Rule 31.2, AZ ST RCRP Rule 31.2

Current with amendments received through 08/15/19

Rule 31.3. Suspension of These Rules; Suspension of an Appeal; Computation of Time; Modifying a...

(Refs & Annos)

VIII. Appeal and Other Post-Conviction Relief

Rule 31. Appeals

Section One. General Provisions

16A A.R.S. Rules Crim.Proc., Rule 31.3

Rule 31.3. Suspension of These Rules; Suspension of an Appeal; Computation of Time; Modifying a Deadline

(a) Suspension of Rule 31. For good cause, an appellate court, on motion or on its own, may suspend any provision of this rule in a particular case, and may order such proceedings as the court directs.

(b) Suspension of an Appeal.

(1) *Generally.* An appellate court on motion or on its own may suspend an appeal if a motion under Rule 24 or a petition under Rule 32 is pending to permit the superior court to decide those matters.

(2) *Notice.* If an appeal is suspended, the appellate clerk must notify the parties, the superior court clerk, and, if certified transcripts have not yet been filed, the certified reporters or transcribers.

(3) *Later Notification.* No later than 20 days after the superior court's decision on the Rule 24 motion or Rule 32 petition, the appellant must file with the appellate clerk either a notice of reinstatement of the appeal or a motion to dismiss the appeal under Rule 31.24(b), and must serve a copy of such documents on all persons entitled to notice under (b)(2).

(c) New Matters. Other than a petition for post-conviction relief that is not otherwise precluded under Rule 32.2, a party to an appeal may not, without the appellate court's consent, file any new matter in the superior court later than 15 days after the appellate clerk distributes a notice under Rule 31.9(e) that the record on appeal has been filed.

(d) Computation of Time. Rule 1.3(a) governs the computation of any time period in Rule 31, an appellate court order, or a statute regarding a criminal appeal, except that 5 calendar days are not added to the time for responding to an electronically served document.

(e) Modifying a Deadline. A party seeking to modify a deadline in the appellate court must obtain an appellate court order authorizing the modified deadline. For good cause and after considering the rights of the victim, an appellate court may shorten or extend the time for doing any act required by Rule 31, a court order, or an applicable statute.

Credits

Added by Aug. 31, 2017, effective Jan. 1, 2018.

Editors' Notes

COMMENT

Rule 31.3(d). On January 1, 2016, Rule 5(a) of the Arizona Rules of Civil Appellate Procedure was amended to provide that 5 additional days are not added to the time to respond to a brief, motion, or other document if it is electronically served. A similar provision appears in Rule 31.3(d) to ensure that the computation of time is the same in criminal and civil appeals.

HISTORICAL AND STATUTORY NOTES

Former Rule 31.3, relating to time for taking appeal, was abrogated effective Jan. 1, 2018. See, now, this rule.

16A A. R. S. Rules Crim. Proc., Rule 31.3, AZ ST RCRP Rule 31.3

Current with amendments received through 08/15/19

Rule 31.4. Consolidation of Appeals

(Refs & Annos)
VIII. Appeal and Other Post-Conviction Relief
Rule 31. Appeals
Section One. General Provisions

16A A.R.S. Rules Crim.Proc., Rule 31.4

Rule 31.4. Consolidation of Appeals

(a) Consolidation by Appellate Court Order. On motion, by stipulation, or on its own, an appellate court may order appeals or cross-appeals consolidated at any time:

(1) if those appeals or cross-appeals raise a common question of law or fact; and

(2) the court has given the parties an opportunity to object.

(b) Consolidation with the Appeal of a Post-Judgment Proceeding. Unless good cause exists not to do so, an appellate court must consolidate an appeal from a judgment or sentence with an appeal from a final decision on a Rule 24 motion or a petition for review from a final decision on a Rule 32 petition if the motion or petition was filed:

(1) before a notice of appeal is filed; or

(2) while an appeal is pending and the motion or petition was decided while the appeal is stayed.

Credits

Added by Aug. 31, 2017, effective Jan. 1, 2018.

Editors' Notes

HISTORICAL AND STATUTORY NOTES

Former Rule 31.4, relating to motion to stay appeal, notice of reinstatement of appeal, consolidation of appeals, was abrogated effective Jan. 1, 2018. See, now, this rule.

16A A. R. S. Rules Crim. Proc., Rule 31.4, AZ ST RCRP Rule 31.4

Current with amendments received through 08/15/19

Rule 31.5. Appointment of Counsel on Appeal; Waiver of the Right to Appellate Counsel

(Refs & Annos)
VIII. Appeal and Other Post-Conviction Relief
Rule 31. Appeals
Section One. General Provisions

16A A.R.S. Rules Crim.Proc., Rule 31.5

Rule 31.5. Appointment of Counsel on Appeal; Waiver of the Right to Appellate Counsel

(a) Determination that the Defendant Is Indigent.

(1) *If Indigent in Superior Court.* A defendant who was indigent when sentenced may proceed on appeal as indigent without further authorization, unless after a notice of appeal is filed, the superior court finds that the defendant is financially able to employ counsel and pay for a certified copy of the record on appeal, including a certified transcript.

(2) *If Not Indigent in Superior Court.* A defendant who was not indigent when sentenced may proceed as indigent on appeal by filing in the superior court a request to proceed as indigent, together with a completed sworn questionnaire required under Rule 6.4(a). The superior court clerk must immediately provide a copy of the defendant's request and questionnaire to the State. The superior court may require the defendant to appear for an inquiry into his or her ability to pay. The court must promptly grant or deny the defendant's request.

(3) *Definition of "Indigent."* The term "indigent" is defined in Rule 6.1(b).

(b) Contribution by the Defendant. The superior court may order an indigent defendant to contribute to the costs of appeal and the services of counsel in the manner provided in Rule 6.4(c).

(c) Motion in the Appellate Court. If the superior court finds that a defendant is not entitled to proceed as indigent, the defendant may file a motion in the appellate court for permission to proceed as indigent, together with a copy of the sworn questionnaire required by (a)(2). The appellate court, or a single judge of that court, must promptly rule on the motion.

(d) Notice of an Order to Proceed as Indigent. The clerk of the court that enters an order allowing a defendant to proceed as indigent on appeal must send a copy of that order to:

(1) the superior court clerk or the appellate clerk, as the case may be;

(2) the parties; and

(3) the appropriate certified reporters or, if the record was made by electronic or other means, the court's designated transcript coordinator.

(e) Appointment of Counsel. If a court allows a defendant's appointed attorney to withdraw, the superior court or the appellate court must appoint new counsel if the defendant is legally entitled to counsel on appeal.

(f) Waiver of Right to Counsel.

(1) *Filing Deadline.* A defendant may waive the right to appellate counsel by filing a written waiver no later than 30 days after filing a notice of appeal.

(2) *Where to File.* If the waiver is filed before or when the defendant files a notice of appeal, the waiver must be filed with the superior court clerk. If the waiver is filed after filing a notice of appeal, the waiver must be filed with the superior court clerk and the appellate clerk.

(3) *Superior Court Determination.* If the superior court determines that the defendant's waiver of the right to appellate counsel is made knowingly, intelligently, and voluntarily, the defendant will be allowed to represent himself or herself on appeal.

(4) *Advisory Counsel.* The superior court or the appellate court may appoint advisory counsel for a self-represented defendant during any stage of the appellate proceedings. Advisory counsel must be given notice of all matters for which the defendant is entitled to notice.

(5) *Withdrawal of Waiver.* In the interest of justice, the appellate court may grant a defendant's written request to withdraw a waiver of the right to appellate counsel. The defendant is not entitled to repeat any proceeding previously held or waived merely because counsel is later appointed or retained.

Credits

Added by Aug. 31, 2017, effective Jan. 1, 2018.

Editors' Notes

HISTORICAL AND STATUTORY NOTES

Former Rule 31.5, relating to Appointment of counsel for appeal, waiver to right to appellate counsel, was abrogated effective Jan. 1, 2018. See, now, this rule.

16A A. R. S. Rules Crim. Proc., Rule 31.5, AZ ST RCRP Rule 31.5

Current with amendments received through 08/15/19

Rule 31.6. Filing Documents with an Appellate Court; Document Format; Service and Proof of Serv...

(Refs & Annos)

VIII. Appeal and Other Post-Conviction Relief

Rule 31. Appeals

Section One. General Provisions

16A A.R.S. Rules Crim.Proc., Rule 31.6

Rule 31.6. Filing Documents with an Appellate Court; Document Format; Service and Proof of Service

(a) Filing. Documents filed in an appellate court must be filed with the appellate clerk. Rule 1.7(b) defines when a document is deemed filed.

(b) Document Format. Documents filed with the appellate clerk other than briefs must comply with the formatting requirements of Rule 1.6, except that every typed document and footnote must use at least a 14-point typeface. Briefs must comply with the formatting requirements in Rule 31.12(b).

(c) Service and Proof of Service. If a party files a document other than a brief with the appellate clerk, the party must serve a copy of the document on the same day on all other parties as provided in Rule 1.7(c) unless the filing party shows a need for confidentiality. Rule 31.13(d) governs service of briefs. The appellate clerk may permit a document to be filed without a proof of service, but the filing party must file one no later than 5 days after filing the document.

(d) Word Limits. Word limits specified in Rules 31.12(a), 31.14(a), 31.18(d), 31.20(e), and 31.21(g) include footnotes and quotations, but do not include the cover page, the caption, the table of contents, the table of citations, paragraph numbers appearing at the beginning of each paragraph (if any), the date and signature block, a certificate of service, a certificate of compliance, or any appendix.

Credits

Added by Aug. 31, 2017, effective Jan. 1, 2018.

Editors' Notes

HISTORICAL AND STATUTORY NOTES

Former Rule 31.6, relating to stay of execution of sentence and credit pending appeal, was abrogated effective Jan. 1, 2018. See, now, AZ ST RCRP Rule 31.7.

16A A. R. S. Rules Crim. Proc., Rule 31.6, AZ ST RCRP Rule 31.6

Current with amendments received through 08/15/19

Rule 31.7. Stay of Proceedings

(Refs & Annos)

VIII. Appeal and Other Post-Conviction Relief

Rule 31. Appeals

Section One. General Provisions

16A A.R.S. Rules Crim.Proc., Rule 31.7

Formerly cited as AZ ST RCRP Rule 31.6

Rule 31.7. Stay of Proceedings

(a) During a Defendant's Appeal.

(1) *Sentence of Imprisonment; Credit.* If a defendant is released from custody pending appeal under Rule 7.2(c), a sentence of imprisonment is stayed pending appeal. A defendant who remains in custody during an appeal's pendency must receive credit for the time of incarceration pending the appeal's disposition.

(2) *Sentence of a Fine.* A sentence to pay a fine is stayed pending appeal.

(b) During an Appeal by the State. An appeal by the State does not stay an order in favor of the defendant, except when the State appeals from:

(1) an order granting a new trial; or

(2) an order granting a motion to suppress that directs the return of seized evidence.

Credits

Added by Aug. 31, 2017, effective Jan. 1, 2018.

Editors' Notes

HISTORICAL AND STATUTORY NOTES

Former Rule 31.7, relating to docketing in the appellate court, and designation of the parties, was abrogated effective Jan. 1, 2018. See, now, AZ ST RCRP Rule 31.6.

16A A. R. S. Rules Crim. Proc., Rule 31.7, AZ ST RCRP Rule 31.7

Current with amendments received through 08/15/19

Rule 31.8. The Record on Appeal

(Refs & Annos)

VIII. Appeal and Other Post-Conviction Relief

Rule 31. Appeals

Section Two. The Record on Appeal; Briefs and Argument

16A A.R.S. Rules Crim.Proc., Rule 31.8

Rule 31.8. The Record on Appeal

(a) Composition of the Record on Appeal.

(1) *Generally.* The record on appeal consists of:

(A) all documents (including minute entries, exhibit lists, transcripts, and other items) filed in the superior court on or before the effective date of the filing of a notice of appeal, a notice of cross-appeal, or an amended notice of appeal;

(B) the index prepared under Rule 31.9(b);

(C) all documents, papers, books, and photographs introduced into evidence; and

(D) certified transcripts of oral proceedings, as provided in Rule 31.8(b).

(2) *Additions and Deletions.*

(A) By Appellant. No later than 30 days after filing a notice of appeal, the appellant may file with the superior court clerk a designation to include in the record any item not within (a)(1)(C) that the appellant deems necessary, and to delete from the record all the documents, papers, books, and photographs the appellant deems unnecessary.

(B) By Appellee. No later than 30 days after the opening brief is filed, the appellee may file with the superior court clerk a designation to include in the record any item not within (a)(1)(C) that the appellee deems necessary, and any document, paper, book, or photograph deleted by the appellant. The superior court clerk must supplement the record accordingly.

(C) By the Appellate Court. An exhibit other than those listed in (a)(1)--including the excised portion, if any, of a presentence, diagnostic, or mental health report--may be added to the record on appeal only by order of the appellate court. The court may enter such an order at any time.

(D) Notice to Other Parties. An appellant or appellee must serve any designation or request made under this rule on all other parties when the party submits the designation or request.

(b) Certified Transcripts.

(1) *Generally.* The record on appeal includes certified transcripts as follows:

(A) if the defendant is sentenced to death, the record on appeal must include a certified transcript of all recorded proceedings, including grand jury proceedings; and

(B) in all other cases, the record on appeal must include a certified transcript of the following proceedings:

(i) any voluntariness hearing or hearing to suppress the use of evidence;

(ii) all trial proceedings, excluding the record of voir dire unless a party specifically designates it;

(iii) any aggravation or mitigation hearing;

(iv) proceedings for the entry of judgment and sentence; and

(v) any probation violation proceeding.

(2) *Additions and Deletions.*

(A) By Appellant. No later than 30 days after filing a notice of appeal, the appellant may request from the certified court reporter or, if the record was made by electronic or other means, the court's designated transcript coordinator:

(i) a certified transcript of any proceeding not automatically included under (b)(1); and

(ii) to exclude from a certified transcript any portion of the proceedings the appellant deems unnecessary for a proper hearing of the appeal.

(B) By Appellee. No later than 30 days after the opening brief is filed, the appellee may request from the certified court reporter or, if the record was made by electronic or other means, the court's designated transcript coordinator, a certified transcript of:

(i) any portion of a proceeding deleted by the appellant; and

(ii) a proceeding not automatically included under (b)(1).

(C) Untimely Request. For good cause shown, a party may request an addition to the record under (b)(2)(A) and (B).

(D) Notice to Other Parties. An appellant or appellee must serve any designation or request made under this rule on all other parties when the party submits the designation or request.

(c) Authorized Transcriber: Time to Prepare, and Payment Arrangements for, Certified Transcripts.

(1) *Generally.* Every transcript in the record on appeal must be prepared by an authorized transcriber. An "authorized transcriber" as used in this rule means a certified reporter or a transcriber under contract with an Arizona court. There may be multiple authorized transcribers for a single case.

(2) *Court Reporter.* If a certified reporter attended a proceeding in the superior court, a party must order a certified transcript of proceedings directly from that reporter.

(3) *Audio or Video Recording.* If the superior court created only an audio or audio-video recording of the proceeding, a party must order a certified transcript of the proceeding directly from an authorized transcriber. Unless the ordering party is an indigent defendant, the superior court will furnish the transcriber with a copy of the designated electronic recording upon receiving a notice from the transcriber that the transcriber has reached a satisfactory arrangement for payment. All parties to the appeal must cooperate with the transcriber by providing information that is necessary to facilitate transcription.

(4) *Time to Prepare.* The authorized transcriber must prepare the certified transcript promptly upon receiving a notice of appeal either:

(A) by the State; or

(B) by the defendant if the notice indicates that the defendant was represented by appointed counsel when found guilty or when sentenced.

(5) *Non-Indigent Defendant.* No later than 5 days after filing a notice of appeal or after the denial of a request during the appeal to proceed as indigent, a non-indigent defendant must make payment arrangements with the authorized transcriber for the certified transcript. The authorized transcriber then must promptly prepare the certified transcript. The authorized transcriber must notify the appellate court if the defendant fails to make satisfactory payment arrangements within the prescribed time.

(6) *Additions and Deletions.* The authorized transcriber must promptly add or delete any portions requested by the parties. Non-indigent defendants must pay for all portions of the record on appeal and certified transcripts that they have designated or requested.

(d) Authorized Transcriber: Manner of Delivering Transcripts.

(1) *Delivery to the Appellate and Trial Courts.* The authorized transcriber must file a certified electronic transcript of proceedings with the appellate and trial court

clerks within the time allowed for the superior court clerk to transmit the record to the appellate court under Rule 31.9(c).

(2) *Delivery to the State.*

(A) If an Appellee. If the State is the appellee, the authorized transcriber must deliver an electronic copy of the certified transcript to the Attorney General and the appropriate county attorney's office, if any.

(B) If an Appellant. If the State is the appellant, the authorized transcriber must deliver an electronic copy of the certified transcript to the agency that prosecuted the case in the superior court.

(3) *Delivery to the Defendant.*

(A) Electronic. The authorized transcriber must submit the electronic transcript for the defendant to the superior court clerk, who will provide the electronic transcript to the defendant's appellate counsel or to the defendant, if self-represented.

(B) Paper. If defense counsel or a self-represented defendant requires or requests a paper transcript rather than an electronic transcript, the authorized transcriber must submit the defendant's paper copy to the superior court clerk, who will transmit the copy to the defendant's appellate counsel or to the defendant, if self-represented.

(C) Exception. If a local rule or administrative order prescribes a procedure different from (d)(3)(A) or (B), the authorized transcriber must distribute the defendant's copy as provided in that rule or order.

(4) *Notice of Service.* The authorized transcriber must file with the appellate court a notice of service of the certified transcript. The notice must state when and on whom service was made.

(e) Narrative Statement if No Record Is Available.

(1) *Clerk's Duty.* If the court did not make a record of evidence or of an oral proceeding at trial, or if the transcript is unavailable, the superior court clerk must promptly notify the parties and the appellate clerk.

(2) *Narrative Statement.*

(A) Preparation. If no record of evidence or transcript of an oral proceeding is available, the appellant may prepare and file a narrative statement of the evidence or proceeding from the best available means, including the appellant's recollection.

(B) Filing and Service. The appellant must file the narrative statement in the superior court no later than 30 days after filing a notice of appeal and must serve it on all other parties.

(C) Objections. Any other party may file objections or proposed amendments to the narrative statement no later than 10 days after the statement is served.

(D) If the Appellant Does Not File a Statement. If the appellant does not file a narrative statement within the time specified in (2)(B), any other party may prepare, file, and serve such a narrative statement. The appellant may file objections or proposed amendments to that statement no later than 10 days after the statement is served.

(E) Court Review and Transmittal. After considering a narrative statement and any objections or proposed amendments, the superior court must settle and approve the narrative statement. The superior court clerk must then include it in the record transmitted to the appellate court under Rule 31.9(c).

(f) Agreed Statement.

(1) *Generally.* Instead of providing a transcript of oral proceedings to the appellate court, the parties may prepare an agreed statement that contains the evidence or proceedings that are essential to a decision of the issues presented by the appeal, and submit the statement to the superior court for settlement and approval. The agreed statement must include a statement of the issues the appellant and any cross-appellant intend to present on the appeal.

(2) *Notice.* The parties must notify the superior court clerk and authorized transcribers at the earliest practical time of the parties' intent to submit an agreed statement.

(3) *Filing.* The parties must file the agreed statement in the superior court no later than 30 days after a notice of appeal is filed.

(4) *Court Review and Transmittal.* The superior court may make any additions and corrections it considers necessary to the issues presented by the appeal. The superior court clerk will then include the agreed statement, as corrected and modified by the court, in the record transmitted to the appellate court under Rule 31.9(c).

(g) Correcting or Modifying the Record.

(1) *Generally.* If anything material to either party is omitted from or misstated in the record, the omission or misstatement may be corrected and a supplemental record may be certified and forwarded:

(A) on stipulation of the parties; or

(B) by the superior court before or after the record has been forwarded.

(2) *Superior Court Review.* If a dispute arises about whether the record accurately discloses what occurred in the superior court, the dispute must be submitted to and settled by the superior court and the record conformed accordingly.

(3) *Appellate Court Review.* The parties must present all other questions as to the form and content of the record to the appellate court.

(4) *Order to Correct the Record.* The appellate court may order the parties to correct an omission or misstatement in the record.

Credits

Added by Aug. 31, 2017, effective Jan. 1, 2018.

Editors' Notes

HISTORICAL AND STATUTORY NOTES

Former Rule 31.8, relating to the record on appeal, transcript, duty of the authorized transcriber, was abrogated effective Jan. 1, 2018. See, now, this rule.

16A A. R. S. Rules Crim. Proc., Rule 31.8, AZ ST RCRP Rule 31.8

Current with amendments received through 08/15/19

Rule 31.9. Transmission of the Record to the Appellate Court

(Refs & Annos)

VIII. Appeal and Other Post-Conviction Relief

Rule 31. Appeals

Section Two. The Record on Appeal; Briefs and Argument

16A A.R.S. Rules Crim.Proc., Rule 31.9

Rule 31.9. Transmission of the Record to the Appellate Court

(a) Transcripts. The authorized transcriber provides transcripts of superior court proceedings to the appellate court as provided in Rule 31.8(d).

(b) Official Documents; Index. After a party files a notice of appeal, the superior court clerk must prepare a numerical index of the documents in the superior court's file (the *"index"*). The superior court clerk must promptly distribute a copy of the index to every party to the superior court judgment that is the subject of the appeal.

(c) Electronic Transmission by the Superior Court Clerk.

(1) *Generally.* No later than 45 days after a notice of appeal is filed, the superior court clerk must electronically transmit to the appellate clerk, and make available to all parties:

(A) all documents filed in the superior court before the effective date of the filing of the notice of appeal, a notice of cross-appeal, or an amended notice of appeal, including minute entries, notices of appeal and cross-appeal, and the index;

(B) every exhibit listed or designated under Rule 31.8(a) in paper, electronic, or photographic form, unless relieved by the appellate court of an obligation to do so; and

(C) any other items requested by the appellate clerk.

(2) *Extension and Reduction of Time.* For good cause and after considering the rights of the victim, the appellate court may grant one 20-day extension for transmitting the record on appeal. The appellate court also may order the superior court clerk to transmit the electronic record, or a portion of the record, at an earlier time or it may order physical transmission of the entire record or portions of the record under (d). The appellate clerk must distribute a copy of any order entered under this rule to the parties, the superior court clerk, and to the requesting authorized transcriber.

(3) *Supplementation.* At any time during the appeal, the appellate court may direct the superior court clerk by an order or written request to transmit portions of the record that were not included in previous transmissions.

(d) Physical Transmission by the Superior Court Clerk. The superior court clerk must notify the appellate clerk and the parties to the appeal of any items in the superior court's record of a size, bulk, or condition that makes their electronic transmission impractical. If any of those items are necessary for a determination of issues raised on appeal, the appellate court, on motion or on its own, may order that the superior court clerk transmit to the appellate court any or all of these items in physical form. Alternatively, the parties may stipulate to the method of transmitting the item.

(e) Notice that the Record Was Received. When the appellate clerk receives all of the record on appeal, the appellate clerk must promptly give all parties notice of that fact and the date on which the clerk received the complete record.

Credits

Added by Aug. 31, 2017, effective Jan. 1, 2018.

Editors' Notes

HISTORICAL AND STATUTORY NOTES

Former Rule 31.9, relating to transmission of the record, was abrogated effective Jan. 1, 2018. See, now, this rule.

16A A. R. S. Rules Crim. Proc., Rule 31.9, AZ ST RCRP Rule 31.9

Current with amendments received through 08/15/19

Rule 31.10. Content of Briefs

(Refs & Annos)

VIII. Appeal and Other Post-Conviction Relief

Rule 31. Appeals

Section Two. The Record on Appeal; Briefs and Argument

16A A.R.S. Rules Crim.Proc., Rule 31.10

Formerly cited as AZ ST RCRP Rule 31.13

Rule 31.10. Content of Briefs

(a) Appellant's Opening Brief. An appellant's opening brief must set forth under headings and in the following suggested order the items listed below, except for items (4) and (9), which are optional:

(1) a *"table of contents"* with page references. If the brief is filed electronically, if feasible, the table of contents should include bookmarks to sections of the brief described in items (2) through (9) below.

(2) a *"table of citations"* that alphabetically arranges and indexes the cases, statutes and other authorities cited in the brief, and that refers to the pages of the brief on which each citation appears.

(3) a *"statement of the issues"* presented for review. The statement of issues presented for review includes every subsidiary issue fairly comprised within the statement.

(4) a short *"introduction."*

(5) a *"statement of the case"* that concisely states the nature of the case, the course of the proceedings, the disposition in the court from which the appeal is taken, and the basis of the appellate court's jurisdiction. The statement must include appropriate references to the record.

(6) a *"statement of facts"* that are relevant to the issues presented for review, with appropriate references to the record. A party may combine a statement of facts with a statement of the case.

(7) an *"argument"* that contains:

(A) appellant's contentions with supporting reasons for each contention, and with citations of legal authorities and appropriate references to the portions of the record on which the appellant relies. The argument may include a summary.

(B) for each issue, references to the record on appeal where the issue was raised and ruled on, and the applicable standard of appellate review with citation to supporting legal authority.

(8) a short *"conclusion"* stating the precise relief sought.

(9) an *"appendix,"* as provided in Rule 31.11.

(b) Appellee's Answering Brief. The appellee's answering brief must follow the requirements of Rule 31.10(a), except that it does not need to include a statement of the case, a statement of facts, or a statement of the issues, unless the appellee finds the appellant's statements to be insufficient or incorrect.

(c) Reply Brief. If the appellant files a reply brief, it must be strictly confined to the rebuttal of points made in the appellee's answering brief. A party may file additional briefs other than a reply only with the appellate court's permission.

(d) References to the Record. In any brief, references to evidence or other parts of the record must include a citation to the index, exhibit, or page of a certified transcript, authorized transcription, narrative statement, or agreed statement where such evidence or other material appears. In Division One, a brief may cite to a document in the appendix in lieu of citing to the record, but only if the table of contents of the appendix complies with the requirements of Rule 31.11(c). If a party refers to a video or audio recording, the party must provide specific, time-coded references to the relevant portions of the recording.

(e) References to Parties. In briefs and at oral argument, parties should minimize use of the terms "appellant" and "appellee." For clarity, briefs should use the parties' actual names or the designations used in the superior court proceeding, or such descriptive terms as "the defendant" or "the State."

(f) Substitute Victim Identifier. Appellate briefs must use a victim identifier in place of the victim's name in any case in which the defendant was charged with an offense listed in A.R.S. §§ 13-1401 et seq., 13-3201 et seq., 13-3501 et seq., or 13-3551 et seq., or in any case in which the victim was a juvenile at the time of the offense. For purposes of this rule, "victim identifier" means a victim's initials, a pseudonym, or other substitute for the victim's actual name.

(g) References to Case Law. Citation of Arizona case law must be to the volume, page number and, if available, the paragraph number, of the official Arizona reporters. Citation of non-Arizona case law must be to the volume and page number of the applicable regional or federal reporter.

(h) Briefs in Cases Involving Cross-Appeals. If a cross-appeal is filed, the combined brief under Rule 31.13(a)(4) must include a statement of the issues that are presented in the cross-appeal.

(i) Briefs Involving Multiple Appellants or Appellees. In cases involving more than one appellant or more than one appellee, including consolidated cases, multiple parties may join in a single brief, or an appellant or appellee may adopt by reference any part of the brief of another party. Parties having contentions in common must make a good faith effort to join in a single brief. If there is a contention common to other parties, the filing party must make a good faith effort to adopt by reference the pertinent part of the previously filed brief of another party.

(j) Briefs of Amicus Curiae. A brief of amicus curiae must comply with Rule 31.10(a)(1), (2), (3), (7), (8), and (9), and Rule 31.15.

(k) Non-Compliance. The appellate court may strike a brief or other filing that does not substantially conform to the requirements of these rules.

Credits

Added by Aug. 31, 2017, effective Jan. 1, 2018.

Editors' Notes

HISTORICAL AND STATUTORY NOTES

Former Rule 31.10, relating to filing of the record, was abrogated effective Jan. 1, 2018. See, now, AZ ST RCRP Rule 31.13.

16A A. R. S. Rules Crim. Proc., Rule 31.10, AZ ST RCRP Rule 31.10

Current with amendments received through 08/15/19

Rule 31.11. Appendix

(Refs & Annos)

VIII. Appeal and Other Post-Conviction Relief

Rule 31. Appeals
Section Two. The Record on Appeal; Briefs and Argument
16A A.R.S. Rules Crim.Proc., Rule 31.11
Formerly cited as AZ ST RCRP Rule 31.13
Rule 31.11. Appendix

(a) Applicability. A party may file an appendix with the party's brief in the Supreme Court and in Division One of the Court of Appeals. A party's appendix must be filed by the same method--paper or electronic--as the party's brief. An electronically filed brief in Division Two of the Court of Appeals must include electronic links when citing to the record on appeal and the brief must not include an appendix. A party may file an appendix in Division Two only if filing a paper brief.

(b) Content of the Appendix. The appendix should include only those portions of the record and legal authorities that are cited in the briefs and that are essential to decide an issue on appeal.

(c) Table of Contents. If there is more than a single item in the appendix, the appendix must begin with a table of contents that identifies each item included in the appendix. The table of contents must identify items in both of the following ways:

(1) *Location in the Record.* If the item is included in the record on appeal, the table of contents must identify where each item is located in the record--by item number in the clerk's index (see Rule 31.9(b)), by transcript date, or by exhibit number, as appropriate.

(2) *Location in the Appendix.* The table of contents also must identify the item's location in the appendix by page number, or by volume and page number.

(d) Appendix Filed Electronically. A party that electronically files a brief may file a separate appendix or may file a combined brief and appendix as a single document, with the appendix following the brief. A combined filing must not exceed the size limits of the filing portal.

(1) *Page Numbering.* The pages in an appendix must be numbered sequentially. An appendix page number should match the electronic page number of the viewing software. If a party files a combined brief and appendix, the first page of the appendix must include a number sequential to the last page of the brief. For a separately filed appendix, the numbers should start with the cover page of the appendix.

(2) *Multiple Volumes.* If a separate appendix is more than one volume, page numbering should restart for each volume and include an identifier that distinguishes each volume (e.g., APPV1-001, APPV2-001).

(3) *Bookmarks and Hyperlinks.* Each item in the appendix table of contents must include a bookmark or hyperlink to the item in the appendix. If feasible, a combined brief and appendix filed as a single document must contain bookmarks or hyperlinks to items in the appendix when these items are cited in the brief.

(e) Appendix Filed in Paper.

(1) *Page Numbering.* Pages of the appendix must be numbered sequentially, beginning with the appendix cover page.

(2) *Combined Filing.* A party that files a brief in paper form may file a combined brief and appendix. If combined, the appendix must be located after the brief, and a blank page of distinctive color must separate the last page of the brief from the first page of the appendix.

(3) *Separate Filing.* A party filing a paper appendix that is not combined with the brief must securely bind the appendix (for example, the pages of the appendix may be clipped or banded), but the binding must not use adhesives. The Supreme Court and Division One discourage the use of devices such as staples or two-pronged fasteners that perforate the pages of the appendix.

Credits

Added by Aug. 31, 2017, effective Jan. 1, 2018.

Editors' Notes

HISTORICAL AND STATUTORY NOTES

Former Rule 31.11, relating to perfection of the appeal, was abrogated effective Jan. 1, 2018. See, now, AZ ST RCRP Rule 31.13.

16A A. R. S. Rules Crim. Proc., Rule 31.11, AZ ST RCRP Rule 31.11

Current with amendments received through 08/15/19

Rule 31.12. Length and Form of Briefs

(Refs & Annos)

VIII. Appeal and Other Post-Conviction Relief

Rule 31. Appeals

Section Two. The Record on Appeal; Briefs and Argument

16A A.R.S. Rules Crim.Proc., Rule 31.12

Formerly cited as AZ ST RCRP Rule 31.13

Rule 31.12. Length and Form of Briefs

(a) Length of Briefs.

(1) *Opening/Answering Briefs.* Opening briefs and answering briefs must not exceed 14,000 words.

(2) *Reply Briefs.* Reply briefs must not exceed 7,000 words.

(3) *Combined Briefs.* If a party is filing a combined brief involving a cross-appeal, each separate portion of the combined brief must not exceed the number of words that each of the separate briefs may contain.

(4) *Amicus Curiae Briefs.* Amicus curiae briefs or responses to amicus curiae briefs must not exceed 12,000 words.

(5) *Certificate of Compliance.* Every brief must be accompanied by a certificate that confirms compliance with the word limits in (a)(1)-(4). Form 30 is a template certificate of compliance. A party preparing a certificate of compliance may rely on the word count of the word processing system used to prepare the brief if it counts the required words, including any footnotes.

(b) Format. Paper and electronic briefs must comply with the format requirements of Rule 1.6(b)-(c), except that the text and any footnotes in a typed brief must use at least a 14-point typeface. The first page of the brief must contain a caption that includes the information specified in Rule 1.6(a).

(c) Paper Filing.

(1) *Binding.* A party must securely bind a paper brief, for example by clipping or banding the pages, but the binding must not use adhesives. The Supreme Court and Division One discourage the use of devices such as staples or two-pronged fasteners that perforate the pages of the brief.

(2) *Cover Page.* A paper brief must have a separate cover page that contains the caption.

Credits

Added by Aug. 31, 2017, effective Jan. 1, 2018.

Editors' Notes

HISTORICAL AND STATUTORY NOTES

Former Rule 31.12, relating to form of motions, was abrogated effective Jan. 1, 2018. See, now, AZ ST RCRP Rule 31.13.

Former Rule 31.12, relating to authorized an appellant or cross-appellant to file a request to file a request to file a brief and required that the request be supported by a statement of the issues, was deleted effective Aug. 1, 1975.

16A A. R. S. Rules Crim. Proc., Rule 31.12, AZ ST RCRP Rule 31.12

Current with amendments received through 08/15/19

Rule 31.13. Due Dates; Filing and Service of Briefs

(Refs & Annos)

VIII. Appeal and Other Post-Conviction Relief

Rule 31. Appeals

Section Two. The Record on Appeal; Briefs and Argument

Rule 31.13. Due Dates; Filing and Service of Briefs

(a) Time for Filing a Brief in a Noncapital Case.

(1) *Opening Brief.* The appellant must file an opening brief no later than 40 days after the appellate clerk mails or otherwise distributes an initial notice under Rule 31.9(e). If an appellant does not timely file an opening brief, the appellate court may dismiss the appeal on motion or on its own.

(2) *Answering Brief.* The appellee must file an answering brief no later than 40 days after the appellant's brief is served. If the appellee does not timely file an answering brief, the appellate court may deem the appeal submitted for decision based on the opening brief and the record.

(3) *Reply Brief.* The appellant may file a reply brief no later than 20 days after the answering brief is served. In lieu of filing a reply brief, the appellant may file a notice that the appellant will not be filing a reply brief.

(4) *Combined Brief on Cross-Appeal.* A cross-appealing party must file a combined answering brief on appeal and opening brief on cross-appeal no later than 40 days after the appellant's opening brief is served. The appellant/cross-appellee must then file a combined reply brief on appeal and answering brief on cross-appeal no later than 40 days after service of the combined answering brief on appeal/opening brief on cross-appeal.

(5) *Reply Brief on Cross-Appeal.* The cross-appellant may file a reply brief no later than 20 days after the cross-appellee's combined brief is served. The reply brief must address only matters raised in the answering brief on cross-appeal. In lieu of filing a reply brief, the cross-appellant may file a notice that the cross-appellant will not be filing a reply brief.

(6) *Amicus Curiae Brief.* An amicus curiae must file its brief by the deadlines provided in Rule 31.15(c) or (d).

(7) *Response to Amicus Curiae Brief.* A party may respond to an amicus curiae brief. If the amicus curiae files a brief with the consent of the parties or if a government entity or agency files an amicus curiae brief, a party has 30 days after the brief is served to file a response. If the appellate court grants a motion for leave to file an amicus curiae brief that has been lodged with the appellate court, a party has 30 days from entry of that order to file a response.

(b) "At Issue." The appeal will be deemed to be "at issue" when the final reply brief or a notice that no reply brief will be submitted is filed, or when the reply brief is due, whichever is earlier.

(c) Manner of Filing Briefs.

(1) *Electronic Filing.* If a party is represented by counsel, the party must file a brief electronically. Electronic filing of a brief is timely only if the appellate clerk actually receives it within the time allowed for filing.

(2) *Paper Filing.* A defendant may file a paper brief only if self-represented. The filing of a paper brief is timely if:

(A) the filing party places the brief in the United States Postal Service mail within the time allowed for filing;

(B) the filing party delivers the brief to a third-party commercial carrier within the time allowed for filing, for the carrier's delivery to the appellate clerk within 3 calendar days;

(C) the filing party hand-delivers the brief to the appellate clerk within the time allowed for filing; or

(D) if the party is incarcerated, the party delivers the brief to jail or prison authorities for mailing within the time allowed for filing.

(d) Service of Briefs and Appendices.

(1) *Service.* A party must serve a brief and any separate appendix on all other parties to the appeal, as provided in Rule 1.7(c). A party that files a paper brief or separate paper appendix must serve two copies of the brief and appendix on every separately represented party. If a party files an electronic brief or appendix that includes bookmarks or hyperlinks, the party must serve on all other parties to the appeal an electronic copy of the brief or appendix that contains the same functioning bookmarks or hyperlinks.

(2) *Certificate of Service.*

(A) Generally. The party serving the brief and any separate appendix must file a certificate of service with the appellate clerk, as provided in Rule 1.7(c)(3). The filing party also must serve this certificate on all other parties.

(B) Mailing or Carrier Delivery. If a brief is filed under (c)(2)(A) or (B), the certificate also must include the date the brief was delivered to the commercial carrier or placed in the United States Postal Service mail.

(C) Hand Delivery. If a brief is filed under (c)(2)(C), the certificate also must include the date of delivery to the clerk.

(D) Delivery to Prison Authorities. If a brief is filed under (c)(2)(D), the certificate also must include the date the brief was delivered to jail or prison authorities for mailing.

(e) Extension of Time to File a Brief.

(1) *Extension Due to Transcript Unavailability.*

(A) Generally. If a party moves to extend the time for filing a brief based on a transcript's unavailability, the motion must:

(i) certify that the party timely ordered and, if applicable, made payment arrangements for the transcript under Rule 31.8(c);

(ii) provide the reason for the reporter's or transcriber's inability to have the transcript completed; and

(iii) state the reporter's or transcriber's estimated date of completing and filing the transcript.

(B) Order. If the appellate court grants a motion to extend time based on a transcript's unavailability, it will extend the time for filing the brief to 30 days after the transcript's estimated filing date.

(2) *Extensions for Other Reasons.* A motion or stipulation to extend the time for filing a brief for any reason other than a transcript's unavailability must comply with Rule 31.3(e).

Credits

Added by Aug. 31, 2017, effective Jan. 1, 2018.

Editors' Notes

HISTORICAL AND STATUTORY NOTES

Former Rule 31.13, relating to appellate briefs, was abrogated effective Jan. 1, 2018. See, now, this rule and AZ ST RCRP Rules 31.10, 31.11, 31.12, 31.14.

16A A. R. S. Rules Crim. Proc., Rule 31.13, AZ ST RCRP Rule 31.13

Current with amendments received through 08/15/19

Rule 31.14. Provisions Applicable Only to Briefs in Capital Case Appeals

(Refs & Annos)

VIII. Appeal and Other Post-Conviction Relief

Rule 31. Appeals

Section Two. The Record on Appeal; Briefs and Argument

16A A.R.S. Rules Crim.Proc., Rule 31.14

Formerly cited as AZ ST RCRP Rule 31.13

Rule 31.14. Provisions Applicable Only to Briefs in Capital Case Appeals

(a) Length of Briefs. Opening briefs and answering briefs in a capital case appeal must not exceed 28,000 words. Reply briefs must not exceed 14,000 words.

(b) Time for Filing. An opening brief in a capital case must be filed no later than 90 days after the court issues a notice that the record is complete. An answering brief must be filed no later than 60 days after the appellant's brief is served. A reply brief must be filed no later than 30 days after the appellee's brief is served.

(c) Request for an Extension of Time to File a Brief.

(1) *Factors a Court Must Consider.* In ruling on any request for an extension of a time limit to file a brief, the court must consider the rights of the defendant and the rights of the victim to a prompt and final conclusion of the case.

(2) *Notice to the Victim.*

(A) Generally. If the victim in a capital case has filed a notice of appearance as provided in A.R.S. § 13-4042, a party requesting an extension of time to file a brief must provide notice of the request to the victim.

(B) Who Must Receive Notice.

(i) The victim may specify in the notice of appearance whether notification should be provided directly to the victim or to another person, including the prosecutor.

(ii) Unless the victim specifies a different method in the notice of appearance, notice must be provided through the prosecutor's office handling the appeal.

(C) Timing.

(i) If the victim has requested direct notification, the party requesting an extension of time must provide notice to the victim no later than 24 hours after filing the request.

(ii) If the prosecutor has the duty to notify the victim on behalf of the defendant, the prosecutor must provide notice to the victim no later than 24 hours after receiving the request.

(D) Manner of Providing Notice.

(i) The victim's notice of appearance may specify whether notice must be provided electronically, by telephone, or by regular mail.

(ii) Notice must be provided in the manner specified in the victim's notice of appearance. If no method is specified, notice must be provided by regular mail.

Credits

Added by Aug. 31, 2017, effective Jan. 1, 2018.

Editors' Notes

HISTORICAL AND STATUTORY NOTES

Former Rule 31.14, relating to request for oral argument, and precedence of criminal appeals, was abrogated effective Jan. 1, 2018. See, now, AZ ST RCRP Rule 31.17.

16A A. R. S. Rules Crim. Proc., Rule 31.14, AZ ST RCRP Rule 31.14

Current with amendments received through 08/15/19

Rule 31.15. Amicus Curiae

(Refs & Annos)

VIII. Appeal and Other Post-Conviction Relief

Rule 31. Appeals

Section Two. The Record on Appeal; Briefs and Argument

16A A.R.S. Rules Crim.Proc., Rule 31.15

Formerly cited as AZ ST RCRP Rule 31.25

Rule 31.15. Amicus Curiae

(a) Generally. Amicus curiae is not a party to the appeal and must be independent of any party to the appeal. Counsel for a party may not author an amicus curiae brief in whole or in part.

(b) Requirements for Filing.

(1) *Allowance.* An applicant may file a brief as amicus curiae only if:

(A) the brief is filed with the parties' written consent, which is separately filed;

(B) the applicant is the State of Arizona or an officer or agency of the State of Arizona, or is an Arizona county, city, or town; or

(C) the appellate court grants a motion to file it.

(2) *Motion to File.*

(A) Requirements. If an applicant files a motion to file a brief as amicus curiae, the applicant must lodge the brief with the motion. The motion must identify the interest of the applicant, state that the applicant has read the relevant brief, petition, or motion, and state the reasons why the appellate court's acceptance of applicant's brief as amicus curiae would be desirable.

(B) Grounds for Granting a Motion. An appellate court may grant a motion to permit the filing of an amicus curiae brief if:

(i) a party has incompetent representation or is self-represented;

(ii) amicus curiae has an interest in another case that the decision in the present case may affect; or

(iii) amicus curiae can provide information, perspective, or argument that can help the appellate court beyond the help that the parties' lawyers provide.

(3) *Disclosure of Sponsor.* Amicus curiae's brief must clearly identify the group or organization sponsoring the brief and the interests of the sponsoring entity in the outcome of the appeal.

(4) *Other Requirements.* Except as these rules provide otherwise, briefs and other documents filed by amicus curiae must comply with the form, formatting, filing, certification of compliance, and service requirements applicable to briefs and other documents filed by parties.

(c) Time to File or Submit Amicus Curiae Briefs in the Court of Appeals. In a case that is not a special action, a person filing a brief as amicus curiae in the Court of Appeals must file the brief, or lodge the brief with a motion, no later than 21 days after the deadline for filing the final reply brief.

(d) Time to File Amicus Curiae Briefs in the Supreme Court. An applicant seeking to file a brief as amicus curiae in the Supreme Court must file the brief as provided in this rule.

(1) *Briefs Filed Before a Decision by the Supreme Court to Grant Review.* Unless the Supreme Court orders otherwise, applicants must file (or, if by motion, lodge) amicus curiae briefs in support of a petition for review or a response to a petition for

review no later than 21 days after the filing of the response or, if none is filed, the deadline for filing the response to the petition for review. Amicus curiae briefs must comply with the form and length requirements of Rule 31.21(g), exclusive of any appendix.

(2) *Briefs Filed After the Supreme Court Grants Review.* After the Supreme Court grants review, and unless the Court orders otherwise, amicus curiae must file (or, if by motion, lodge) a brief no later than 10 days after the date ordered by the Court for the parties to file supplemental briefs. Amicus curiae briefs must not exceed the word or page limitation imposed for the parties' supplemental briefs.

(3) *Briefs Filed in Direct Appeals in Capital Cases.* In a direct appeal in a capital case that is not a special action, a person filing a brief as amicus curiae in the Supreme Court must file the brief, or lodge the brief with a motion, no later than 21 days after the deadline for filing the final reply brief.

(e) Oral Argument. Amicus curiae may participate in oral argument only with the appellate court's permission.

Credits

Added by Aug. 31, 2017, effective Jan. 1, 2018.

Editors' Notes

HISTORICAL AND STATUTORY NOTES

Former Rule 31.15, relating to motion to dismiss, was abrogated effective Jan. 1, 2018. See, now, AZ ST RCRP Rule 31.24.

16A A. R. S. Rules Crim. Proc., Rule 31.15, AZ ST RCRP Rule 31.15

Current with amendments received through 08/15/19

Rule 31.16. Supplemental Citation of Legal Authority

(Refs & Annos)

VIII. Appeal and Other Post-Conviction Relief

Rule 31. Appeals

Section Two. The Record on Appeal; Briefs and Argument

16A A.R.S. Rules Crim.Proc., Rule 31.16

Formerly cited as AZ ST RCRP Rule 31.22

Rule 31.16. Supplemental Citation of Legal Authority

(a) Generally. A party may file a notice of supplemental legal authority at any time before the court enters its decision. If the court has set oral argument, the notice should be filed at least 5 days before argument, unless the party shows good cause for a later filing.

(b) Form. The notice of supplemental legal authority must state concisely and without argument the legal proposition supported by the supplemental authority. The notice also must clearly identify the page numbers of the party's brief that the party intends to supplement and the relevant pages of the supplemental authority.
Credits
Added by Aug. 31, 2017, effective Jan. 1, 2018.
Editors' Notes
HISTORICAL AND STATUTORY NOTES
Former Rule 31.16, relating to appeal by state is inoperative to stay order in favor of defendant, was abrogated effective Jan. 1, 2018. See, now, AZ ST RCRP Rule 31.22.
16A A. R. S. Rules Crim. Proc., Rule 31.16, AZ ST RCRP Rule 31.16
Current with amendments received through 08/15/19

Rule 31.17. Oral Argument in the Court of Appeals

(Refs & Annos)
VIII. Appeal and Other Post-Conviction Relief
Rule 31. Appeals
Section Two. The Record on Appeal; Briefs and Argument
16A A.R.S. Rules Crim.Proc., Rule 31.17
Formerly cited as AZ ST RCRP Rule 31.14

Rule 31.17. Oral Argument in the Court of Appeals

(a) Request for Oral Argument.
(1) *Request.* A party may file a separate request for oral argument no later than 10 days after the due date for the final reply brief, or no later than 10 days after the date the appellant or cross-appellant actually files the final reply brief, whichever is earlier. A party requesting extended oral argument must state the reasons as part of the request.
(2) *Order and Notice.* If the Court of Appeals grants a request for oral argument, or if the Court of Appeals orders oral argument on its own, the Court of Appeals clerk will notify the parties of the time and place for oral argument and the allocation of time for each side. The Court of Appeals clerk will provide the notice at least 20 days before the date set for oral argument.
(b) Declining a Request for Oral Argument.
(1) *Generally.* Notwithstanding a party's request under (a)(1), the Court of Appeals may decide an appeal without oral argument if it determines that:
(A) the appeal is frivolous;

(B) the Court of Appeals has recently decided in another case the dispositive issues presented; or

(C) the briefs and record adequately present the facts and legal arguments, and oral argument would not significantly aid the decisional process.

(2) *Notice.* The Court of Appeals clerk must give the parties prompt written notice if the Court of Appeals determines the case will be submitted without the requested oral argument.

Credits

Added by Aug. 31, 2017, effective Jan. 1, 2018.

Editors' Notes

HISTORICAL AND STATUTORY NOTES

Former Rule 31.17, relating to disposition and ancillary orders, was abrogated effective Jan. 1, 2018. See, now, AZ ST RCRP Rule 31.23.

16A A. R. S. Rules Crim. Proc., Rule 31.17, AZ ST RCRP Rule 31.17

Current with amendments received through 08/15/19

Rule 31.18. Petition for Transfer

(Refs & Annos)

VIII. Appeal and Other Post-Conviction Relief

Rule 31. Appeals

Section Three. Appellate Court Procedures and Decisions

16A A.R.S. Rules Crim.Proc., Rule 31.18

Rule 31.18. Petition for Transfer

(a) Grounds for Transfer. The Supreme Court may permit the transfer of an appeal pending in the Court of Appeals to the Supreme Court if:

(1) the appeal requests that a decision of the Supreme Court be overruled or qualified;

(2) there are conflicting Court of Appeals decisions concerning an issue on appeal; or

(3) other extraordinary circumstances justify transfer.

(b) Transfer on Petition of a Party. A party to a case that is pending before the Court of Appeals may request the Supreme Court to transfer the case by filing a petition with the Supreme Court clerk on or before the date the appeal is at issue under Rule 31.13(b).

(c) Transfer on Petition by the Court of Appeals. The chief judge of the division of the Court of Appeals in which the appeal is pending may request transfer of the case by filing a petition with the Supreme Court at any time after the appeal is at issue under Rule 31.13(b).

(d) Form of a Petition. A petition filed under (b) must be no more than 1,400 words, must be in the form required by Rule 31.6(b), and must concisely explain why the Supreme Court should take jurisdiction of the case. The petitioner must serve a copy of the petition on each of the parties.

(e) Response to Petition. A party may file a response to a petition to transfer no later than 5 days after the petition is served. The length of a response and its form must be the same as required for a petition under (d).

(f) Transfer on Motion of the Supreme Court. On its own motion, the Supreme Court may order the transfer of a case pending before the Court of Appeals to the Supreme Court. The Supreme Court also may transfer a case filed in that court to the Court of Appeals.

Credits

Added by Aug. 31, 2017, effective Jan. 1, 2018.

Editors' Notes

HISTORICAL AND STATUTORY NOTES

Former Rule 31.18, relating to motions for reconsideration, was abrogated effective Jan. 1, 2018. See, now, AZ ST RCRP Rule 31.20.

16A A. R. S. Rules Crim. Proc., Rule 31.18, AZ ST RCRP Rule 31.18

Current with amendments received through 08/15/19

Rule 31.19. An Appellate Court's Orders and Decisions

(Refs & Annos)

VIII. Appeal and Other Post-Conviction Relief

Rule 31. Appeals

Section Three. Appellate Court Procedures and Decisions

16A A.R.S. Rules Crim.Proc., Rule 31.19

Rule 31.19. An Appellate Court's Orders and Decisions

(a) Notice of an Order or a Decision. When an appellate court enters an order or a decision, the appellate clerk must promptly notify all parties and amicus curiae by mail or electronic distribution. The notice must state the date the appellate court filed the order or decision, and the appellate clerk must include with the notice a copy of the order or decision or a hyperlink to the order or decision. The appellate clerk must note the date of mailing or electronic distribution in the appellate court's docket.

(b) Order Pending a Decision. An appellate court may issue any order during the course of an appeal that it deems necessary or appropriate to facilitate or expedite the appeal's consideration.

(c) Decision. The appellate court may reverse, affirm, or modify the action of a lower court, and it may issue any necessary and appropriate order in connection with its decision.

(d) Modification of a Judgment upon Finding of Insufficient Evidence at Trial. An appellate court may modify a judgment to one of conviction for a lesser-included offense and remand the case for resentencing if:

(1) the evidence introduced at trial is not legally sufficient to establish the defendant's guilt for the offense for which the defendant was convicted; but

(2) the evidence is legally sufficient to establish defendant's guilt of a necessarily lesser-included offense.

(e) Publication of Decisions; Depublication; Decisions as Precedent. Supreme Court Rule 111 governs the types of dispositions, the publication of decisions, depublication, and the precedential effect of decisions.

(f) Partial Publication. If an appellate court concludes that only a portion of its decision meets the criteria for publication as an opinion, the court may issue that portion of the decision as a published opinion and the remainder of the decision as a separate memorandum decision not intended for publication.

Credits

Added by Aug. 31, 2017, effective Jan. 1, 2018.

Editors' Notes

HISTORICAL AND STATUTORY NOTES

Former Rule 31.19, relating to petitions for review, was abrogated effective Jan. 1, 2018. See, now, AZ ST RCRP Rule 31.21.

16A A. R. S. Rules Crim. Proc., Rule 31.19, AZ ST RCRP Rule 31.19

Current with amendments received through 08/15/19

Rule 31.20. Motion for Reconsideration

(Refs & Annos)

VIII. Appeal and Other Post-Conviction Relief

Rule 31. Appeals

Section Three. Appellate Court Procedures and Decisions

16A A.R.S. Rules Crim.Proc., Rule 31.20

Formerly cited as AZ ST RCRP Rule 31.18

Rule 31.20. Motion for Reconsideration

(a) Purpose and Necessity. A party may file a motion for reconsideration requesting an appellate court to reconsider whether its decision contained erroneous determinations of fact or law. A party need not file a motion for reconsideration in the Court of Appeals before filing a petition for review under Rule 31.21.

(b) Required Showing. A motion for reconsideration must state with particularity the points of law or fact that the party believes the appellate court has erroneously determined, or any changes in the law after briefing or oral argument that may entitle the party to relief.

(c) Filing and Timing. A party desiring reconsideration of a decision must file a motion for reconsideration in the appellate court no later than 15 days after entry of the decision. A motion to extend this deadline must be filed in the appellate court that issued the decision. A party may amend a motion for reconsideration only with the court's permission.

(d) Response. A party may not file a response to a motion for reconsideration unless requested by the appellate court to do so, but the court will not grant the motion without requesting the opposing party to file a response.

(e) Form and Length. A motion for reconsideration or a response to a motion for reconsideration must comply with Rule 31.6(b). A motion for reconsideration or a response to a motion for reconsideration may not exceed 3,500 words. A certificate of compliance, as provided in Form 30, must accompany a motion for reconsideration or a response. A party preparing this certificate may rely on the word count of the word processing system used to prepare the motion or response if it counts the required words including any footnotes.

(f) Motions Not Permitted. Unless permitted by specific appellate court order, no party may file a motion for reconsideration of an order denying a motion for reconsideration, an order denying a petition for review by the Supreme Court, or an order declining to accept jurisdiction of a petition for special action.

Credits

Added by Aug. 31, 2017, effective Jan. 1, 2018.

Editors' Notes

HISTORICAL AND STATUTORY NOTES

Former Rule 31.20, relating to suspension of the rules, was abrogated effective Jan. 1, 2018. See, now, AZ ST RCRP Rule 31.18.

16A A. R. S. Rules Crim. Proc., Rule 31.20, AZ ST RCRP Rule 31.20

Current with amendments received through 08/15/19

Rule 31.21. Petition for Review

(Refs & Annos)

VIII. Appeal and Other Post-Conviction Relief

Rule 31. Appeals

Section Three. Appellate Court Procedures and Decisions
16A A.R.S. Rules Crim.Proc., Rule 31.21
Formerly cited as AZ ST RCRP Rule 31.19
Rule 31.21. Petition for Review

(a) Purpose. A party may ask the Supreme Court to review a decision of the Court of Appeals by filing a petition for review.

(b) Place and Time for Filing.

(1) *Place for Filing.* Any petition for review, cross-petition for review, response to a petition for review or cross-petition for review, or motion to extend the time for filing any of these documents, must be filed with the Supreme Court clerk.

(2) *Timing.*

(A) Petition. A party must file a petition for review no later than 30 days after the Court of Appeals enters its decision, unless a party files a timely motion for reconsideration in the Court of Appeals and, in that event, a party must file a petition for review no later than 15 days after the motion's final disposition.

(B) Cross-Petition. A party may file a cross-petition for review no later than 15 days after service of a petition for review or no later than 30 days after the Court of Appeals enters its decision, whichever is later.

(c) Stay Pending Motion for Reconsideration.

(1) *Generally.* A petition for review is automatically stayed if the petition is filed before the Court of Appeals decides a timely filed motion for reconsideration.

(2) *Duration of the Stay.*

(A) If the Motion Is Denied. If the Court of Appeals denies the motion for reconsideration, the stay remains in effect until the Court of Appeals clerk notifies the parties and the Supreme Court clerk that the Court of Appeals has denied the motion.

(B) If the Motion Is Granted. If the Court of Appeals grants the motion for reconsideration, the stay remains in effect until the Court of Appeals has made a final disposition.

(3) *Timing for Response or Cross-Petition.* The time for filing a response to a petition for review, or a cross-petition, is computed as if that petition's filing occurred on the date the stay is lifted, as described in (c)(2).

(4) *Mootness.* If a petition or cross-petition becomes moot because of the final disposition of a motion for reconsideration by the Court of Appeals, the petitioner or cross-petitioner must promptly file a written notice of mootness with the Supreme Court clerk.

(d) Contents.

(1) *Generally.* A petition or cross-petition must contain concise statements of the following:

(A) the issues that were decided by the Court of Appeals that the petitioner is presenting for Supreme Court review. The petition must also list, separately and without argument, additional issues presented to, but not decided by, the Court of Appeals that the Supreme Court may need to decide if review is granted.

(B) the facts material to a consideration of the issues presented to the Supreme Court for review, with appropriate references to the record on appeal. No evidentiary matter should be included if it is not material to proper consideration of the issues. If an evidentiary matter is material, the party must include a reference to the record where that evidence appears, as provided in Rule 31.10(d).

(C) the reasons the petition should be granted, which may include, among others, that no Arizona decision controls the point of law in question, that a decision of the Supreme Court should be overruled or qualified, that there are conflicting decisions by the Court of Appeals, or that important issues of law have been incorrectly decided.

(2) *Attachments.* A copy of the Court of Appeals' decision must accompany the petition. If the Court of Appeals' decision is an order declining to accept jurisdiction of a special action, a copy of the superior court's decision that was the subject of the special action also must accompany the petition.

(e) Appendix.

(1) *Necessity.* If there are documents in the record on appeal that are necessary for determination of the issues raised by the petition or cross-petition, and hyperlinking to the record is unavailable, the petitioner and cross-petitioner must file with the petition or cross-petition an appendix that contains only those documents.

(2) *Form.* An appendix must comply with the requirements of Rule 31.11.

(f) Response and Reply.

(1) *Timing and Necessity.* A party may respond to a petition or cross-petition by filing a response with the Supreme Court clerk no later than 30 days after service of the petition or cross-petition. A party's failure to file a response to a petition or cross-petition will not be treated as an admission that the Supreme Court should grant the petition or cross-petition.

(2) *Additional Issues.* A response must list, separately and without argument, any additional issues not listed by the petitioner that the parties presented to the Court of Appeals but were not decided and that the Supreme Court may need to decide if it grants review.

(3) *Appendix.* The response may include an appendix as provided in (e), but the appendix to the response may only include documents that were not within the appendix to the petition or cross-petition.

(4) *Reply.* The petitioner or cross-petitioner may not file a reply unless the Supreme Court enters an order specifically authorizing it, and then the petitioner or cross-petitioner must file the reply within the time set by that order.

(g) Form and Length of Petition, Cross-Petition, and Responses.

(1) *Form.* The caption of the petition must designate the parties as designated in the caption of filings in the Court of Appeals. The formatting requirements of Rule 31.6(b) apply to a petition, a cross-petition, and a response to a petition or cross-petition.

(2) *Length.* A petition, a cross-petition, or a response to a petition or cross-petition must not exceed 3,500 words. A cross-petition combined with a response to a petition may not exceed 6,500 words.

(3) *Certificate of Compliance.* A petition, a cross-petition, or a response to a petition or cross-petition must include a certificate of compliance as shown in Form 30. A party preparing this certificate may rely on the word count of the processing system used to prepare the petition, cross-petition, or response.

(h) Service. A party filing a petition, a cross-petition, a response, a reply, or an appendix must serve a copy of the document in the manner provided in Rule 31.13(d) on all parties who were entitled to service in the Court of Appeals. The party also must file and serve a certificate of service in the manner provided in Rule 31.13(d)(2).

(i) Order Denying Review. The Supreme Court clerk must promptly notify the parties and the Court of Appeals clerk if the Supreme Court has denied a petition or cross-petition for review. An order of the Supreme Court denying review must identify those Supreme Court justices, if any, who voted to grant review.

(j) Order Granting Review.

(1) *Notice.* The Supreme Court clerk must promptly notify the parties and the Court of Appeals clerk if the Supreme Court grants a petition or cross-petition for review.

(2) *Issues.* A Supreme Court order granting review must specify the issue or issues the Supreme Court will review, and whether it will consider issues raised in, but not decided by, the Court of Appeals.

(3) *Supplemental Briefs and Oral Argument.* The Supreme Court may permit the parties to file supplemental briefs, or it may set oral argument, or both. Unless otherwise ordered, oral argument may not be scheduled less than 30 days after entry of a written notice of oral argument or, if supplemental briefs are permitted, less than 30 days after the deadline for filing supplemental briefs.

(4) *Motion for Supplementation or Oral Argument.* If an order granting review does not provide for supplemental briefs or oral argument, any party may file a motion specifying the reasons that supplementation or oral argument, or both, would be appropriate. A party must file this motion no later than 15 days after the Supreme Court clerk sends notice to the parties of the order granting review.

(k) Availability of the Remaining Record. The Court of Appeals clerk must make the remaining record available to the Supreme Court clerk upon notification that the Supreme Court has granted a petition or cross-petition for review.

(l) Disposition. If the Supreme Court grants review, it may decide the appeal in any manner specified in Rule 31.19(c) or (d). Additionally, the Supreme Court may do the following:

(1) remand the appeal to the Court of Appeals for reconsideration in light of specified authority;

(2) if issues were raised in, and not decided by, the Court of Appeals, the Supreme Court may consider and decide those issues, remand the appeal to the Court of Appeals to decide them, or dispose of those issues as deemed appropriate; or

(3) if the parties by agreement resolve the appeal after a petition for review is filed, the Supreme Court may vacate the disposition of the Court of Appeals or order depublication of an opinion of the Court of Appeals.

Credits

Added by Aug. 31, 2017, effective Jan. 1, 2018.

Editors' Notes

HISTORICAL AND STATUTORY NOTES

Former Rule 31.21, relating to manner of filing and service, and copies, was abrogated effective Jan. 1, 2018. See, now, AZ ST RCRP Rule 31.19.

16A A. R. S. Rules Crim. Proc., Rule 31.21, AZ ST RCRP Rule 31.21

Current with amendments received through 08/15/19

Rule 31.22. Appellate Court Mandates

(Refs & Annos)

VIII. Appeal and Other Post-Conviction Relief

Rule 31. Appeals

Section Three. Appellate Court Procedures and Decisions

16A A.R.S. Rules Crim.Proc., Rule 31.22

Formerly cited as AZ ST RCRP Rule 31.23

Rule 31.22. Appellate Court Mandates

(a) Definition. The mandate is the final order of the appellate court, which may command another appellate court, superior court, or agency to take further proceedings or to enter a certain disposition of a case. An appellate court retains jurisdiction of an appeal until it issues the mandate.

(b) Generally. Except in a capital case appeal in which the Supreme Court has affirmed a death sentence, an appellate court will issue the mandate in an appeal as follows:

(1) if the parties did not file a petition for review, the Court of Appeals clerk will issue the mandate when the time expires for filing the petition for review;

(2) if a party filed a petition for review, the Court of Appeals clerk will issue the mandate 15 days after the clerk receives a Supreme Court order denying the petition for review; and

(3) when the Supreme Court has filed any disposition that requires the issuance of a mandate, the Supreme Court clerk will issue the mandate 15 days after the disposition is filed, or, if a party files a motion for reconsideration, 15 days after the motion's final disposition.

(c) Capital Case Appeals.

(1) *Generally.* In an appeal in which the Supreme Court has affirmed a death sentence, the Supreme Court clerk will issue the mandate:

(A) when the time expires for filing a petition for writ of certiorari in the United States Supreme Court challenging the decision affirming the defendant's conviction or sentence on direct appeal; or

(B) if the defendant has filed a petition for writ of certiorari, when the Supreme Court clerk receives notice from the United States Supreme Court of a denial of the petition or, in a case in which the United States Supreme Court grants the petition, receives notice that the United States Supreme Court has issued its mandate.

(2) *Petition for Rehearing.* If the defendant files a petition for rehearing of a denial of a petition for writ of certiorari, the petition for rehearing does not stay or otherwise delay the Supreme Court clerk's issuance of the mandate.

(d) Return of Papers. After the appellate court issues the mandate:

(1) the appellate clerk will return to the superior court clerk or other transmitting body any original exhibit or record provided to the appellate court under Rule 31.9; and

(2) the appellate clerk may destroy copies of the record as authorized by rule or appellate court administrative order.

(e) Stay of Mandate Pending Application for Writ of Certiorari.

(1) *Request for Stay.* A party may request an appellate court to stay issuance of the mandate pending application to the United States Supreme Court for a writ of certiorari as follows:

(A) a party may file an application for a stay of issuance of the mandate with the Arizona Supreme Court clerk no later than 15 days after the filing of the Court's opinion, memorandum decision, or order denying a motion for reconsideration; or

(B) a party may file an application for a stay of issuance of the mandate with the Court of Appeals clerk no later than 15 days after the Arizona Supreme Court enters an order denying a petition for review, or no later than 15 days in any other situation requiring the Court of Appeals to issue a mandate.

(2) *Duration.* A stay may not exceed 90 days unless the appellate court extends the time for good cause. If, during this stay period, a party files a notice with the appellate clerk stating that the party has filed a petition for a writ of certiorari, the stay will continue until the appellate clerk receives notice from the United States Supreme Court of the denial of the petition or, in a case in which the United States Supreme Court grants the petition, receives notice that the United States Supreme Court has issued its mandate.

(f) Mandates from the United States Supreme Court. Upon receiving a mandate from the United States Supreme Court, an Arizona appellate court will take action consistent with that mandate, including issuing its own mandate to the superior court that entered the original judgment. The Arizona appellate court's mandate will contain a verbatim recital of the United States Supreme Court mandate and command the superior court to take action as provided in the mandate.

Credits

Added by Aug. 31, 2017, effective Jan. 1, 2018.

Editors' Notes

HISTORICAL AND STATUTORY NOTES

Former Rule 31.22, relating to supplemental citation of legal authority, was abrogated effective Jan. 1, 2018. See, now, AZ ST RCRP Rule 31.16.

16A A. R. S. Rules Crim. Proc., Rule 31.22, AZ ST RCRP Rule 31.22

Current with amendments received through 08/15/19

Rule 31.23. Warrant of Execution

(Refs & Annos)

VIII. Appeal and Other Post-Conviction Relief

Rule 31. Appeals

Section Three. Appellate Court Procedures and Decisions

16A A.R.S. Rules Crim.Proc., Rule 31.23

Formerly cited as AZ ST RCRP Rule 31.17

Rule 31.23. Warrant of Execution

(a) Issuance of Warrant. After affirming a death sentence, the Supreme Court must issue a warrant of execution if the State files a notice stating that:

(1) the defendant has not filed a first Rule 32 petition for post-conviction relief and the time for filing a petition has expired;

(2) the defendant has not filed a petition for review seeking review of a superior court denial of the defendant's first Rule 32 petition for post-conviction relief and the time for filing a petition for review has expired; or

(3) the defendant has not initiated habeas corpus proceedings in federal district court within 15 days after the Supreme Court's denial of a petition for review seeking review of the denial of the defendant's first Rule 32 petition for post-conviction relief.

(b) Post-Habeas Warrant. On the State's motion, the Supreme Court must issue a warrant of execution when federal habeas corpus proceedings and habeas appellate review conclude.

(c) Date and Time of Execution. The warrant of execution must specify an execution date that is 35 days after the warrant's issuance. If the Supreme Court finds that it is impracticable to carry out an execution on that date, it may extend the execution date but may not extend it more than 60 days after the warrant's issuance. Additionally, the warrant must:

(1) state the date for starting the execution time period;

(2) state that the warrant is valid for 24 hours beginning at an hour to be designated by the director of the Arizona Department of Corrections;

(3) order the director to provide written notice of the designated hour of execution to the Supreme Court and each party at least 20 calendar days before the execution date; and

(4) authorize the director to carry out the execution at any time during the warrant's duration.

(d) Return on Warrant. The director of the Arizona Department of Corrections must make a return on the warrant to the Supreme Court showing the manner and time of execution.

Credits

Added by Aug. 31, 2017, effective Jan. 1, 2018.

Editors' Notes

HISTORICAL AND STATUTORY NOTES

Former Rule 31.23, relating to issuance of mandates by appellate courts and mandates from the United States Supreme Court, was abrogated effective Jan. 1, 2018. See, now, AZ ST RCRP Rule 31.22.

16A A. R. S. Rules Crim. Proc., Rule 31.23, AZ ST RCRP Rule 31.23

Current with amendments received through 08/15/19

Rule 31.24. Voluntary Dismissal

(Refs & Annos)

VIII. Appeal and Other Post-Conviction Relief
Rule 31. Appeals
Section Three. Appellate Court Procedures and Decisions
16A A.R.S. Rules Crim.Proc., Rule 31.24
Formerly cited as AZ ST RCRP Rule 31.15

Rule 31.24. Voluntary Dismissal

(a) Dismissal by the Superior Court. If the appellate clerk has not assigned an appellate case number under Rule 31.2(g), the superior court may dismiss the appeal on the filing of a stipulation signed by all parties, or on the appellant's motion with notice to all parties.

(b) Dismissal by the Appellate Court. An appellate clerk may dismiss an appeal if the parties file a signed stipulation requesting dismissal. The appellate clerk, however, may not issue a mandate or other process without an order from the appellate court. The appellant also may file a motion to dismiss the appeal, which the appellate court may grant on terms as agreed to by the parties or as determined by the appellate court.

Credits

Added by Aug. 31, 2017, effective Jan. 1, 2018.

Editors' Notes

HISTORICAL AND STATUTORY NOTES

Former Rule 31.24, relating to citation of memorandum decisions, was abrogated effective Jan. 1, 2018. See, now, AZ ST RCRP Rule 31.15.

16A A. R. S. Rules Crim. Proc., Rule 31.24, AZ ST RCRP Rule 31.24

Current with amendments received through 08/15/19

Rule 31.25. Abrogated Aug. 31, 2017, effective Jan. 1, 2018

(Refs & Annos)
VIII. Appeal and Other Post-Conviction Relief
Rule 31. Appeals
Section Three. Appellate Court Procedures and Decisions
16A A.R.S. Rules Crim.Proc., Rule 31.25

Rule 31.25. Abrogated Aug. 31, 2017, effective Jan. 1, 2018

Editors' Notes

HISTORICAL AND STATUTORY NOTES

The abrogated rule related to amicus curiae filings. See, now, AZ ST RCRP Rule 31.15.

16A A. R. S. Rules Crim. Proc., Rule 31.25, AZ ST RCRP Rule 31.25
Current with amendments received through 08/15/19

Rule 31.26. Abrogated Aug. 31, 2017, effective Jan. 1, 2018

(Refs & Annos)
VIII. Appeal and Other Post-Conviction Relief
Rule 31. Appeals
Section Three. Appellate Court Procedures and Decisions
16A A.R.S. Rules Crim.Proc., Rule 31.26

Rule 31.26. Abrogated Aug. 31, 2017, effective Jan. 1, 2018

Editors' Notes
HISTORICAL AND STATUTORY NOTES
The abrogated rule related to partial publication.
16A A. R. S. Rules Crim. Proc., Rule 31.26, AZ ST RCRP Rule 31.26
Current with amendments received through 08/15/19

Rule 31.27. Abrogated Aug. 31, 2017, effective Jan. 1, 2018

(Refs & Annos)
VIII. Appeal and Other Post-Conviction Relief
Rule 31. Appeals
Section Three. Appellate Court Procedures and Decisions
16A A.R.S. Rules Crim.Proc., Rule 31.27

Rule 31.27. Abrogated Aug. 31, 2017, effective Jan. 1, 2018

Editors' Notes
HISTORICAL AND STATUTORY NOTES
The abrogated rule related to extensions of time and notification of victims.
16A A. R. S. Rules Crim. Proc., Rule 31.27, AZ ST RCRP Rule 31.27
Current with amendments received through 08/15/19

R. 32, Refs & Annos

VIII. Appeal and Other Post-Conviction Relief

Rule 32. Post-Conviction Relief
16A A.R.S. Rules Crim.Proc., R. 32, Refs & Annos

16A A. R. S. Rules Crim. Proc., R. 32, Refs & Annos, AZ ST RCRP R. 32, Refs & Annos
Current with amendments received through 08/15/19

Rule 32.1. Scope of Remedy

(Refs & Annos)
VIII. Appeal and Other Post-Conviction Relief
Rule 32. Post-Conviction Relief (Refs & Annos)
16A A.R.S. Rules Crim.Proc., Rule 32.1
Rule 32.1. Scope of Remedy

Petition for Relief. Subject to Rules 32.2 and 32.4(a)(2), a defendant convicted of, or sentenced for, a criminal offense may file a notice of post-conviction relief, without paying any fee, to request appropriate relief under this rule.

Of-Right Petition. A defendant who pled guilty or no contest, or who admitted a probation violation, or who had an automatic probation violation based on a plea of guilty or no contest, may file an of-right notice of post-conviction relief. After the court's final order or mandate in a Rule 32 of-right proceeding, the defendant also may file an of-right notice challenging the effectiveness of Rule 32 counsel in the first of-right proceeding.

Grounds for Relief. Grounds for relief are:

(a) the defendant's conviction was obtained or the sentence was imposed in violation of the United States or Arizona constitutions;

(b) the court did not have jurisdiction to render a judgment or to impose a sentence on the defendant;

(c) the sentence imposed exceeds the maximum authorized by law, or is otherwise not in accordance with the sentence authorized by law;

(d) the defendant continues to be in custody after his or her sentence expired;

(e) newly discovered material facts probably exist and those facts probably would have changed the verdict or sentence.

Newly discovered material facts exist if:

(1) the facts were discovered after the trial or sentencing;

(2) the defendant exercised due diligence in discovering these facts; and

(3) the newly discovered facts are material and not merely cumulative or used solely for impeachment, unless the impeachment evidence substantially undermines testimony that was of critical significance such that the evidence probably would have changed the verdict or sentence.

(f) the failure to file a notice of post-conviction relief of-right or a notice of appeal within the required time was not the defendant's fault;

(g) there has been a significant change in the law that, if applied to the defendant's case, would probably overturn the defendant's conviction or sentence; or

(h) the defendant demonstrates by clear and convincing evidence that the facts underlying the claim would be sufficient to establish that no reasonable fact-finder would find the defendant guilty beyond a reasonable doubt, or that the death penalty would not have been imposed.

Credits

Added by Aug. 31, 2017, effective Jan. 1, 2018.

Editors' Notes

COMMENT

Rule 32.1(a). Most traditional collateral attacks are encompassed within this provision. Claims of denial of counsel, of incompetency of counsel, and of violation of other rights based on the federal or Arizona constitutions are included.

Rule 32.1(b). This provision retains the basic attack on jurisdiction universally recognized as a ground for collateral attack.

Rule 32.1(c). This provision is intended to allow an attack on a sentence even though the petitioner does not contest the validity of the underlying conviction.

Rule 32.1(d). This provision is not intended to include attacks on the conditions of imprisonment or on correctional practices or prison rules. It is intended to include claims of more traditional types--*e.g.,* miscalculation of sentence, questions of computation of good time--which result in the defendant remaining in custody when he should be free. Appeals from the conviction and imposition of probation must be filed no later than 20 days of the entry of judgment and sentence. *See* Rules 26.1, 26.16(a), and 31.2.

Rule 32.1(f). This provision includes the situation in which the defendant fails to appeal because the trial court, despite the requirements of Rule 26.11(a)(1), did not advise him of his appeal rights, and the situation in which the defendant intended to appeal and thought timely appeal had been filed by his attorney when in reality it had not.

Rule 32.1(h). This claim is independent of a claim under Rule 32.1(e). A defendant who establishes a claim of newly discovered evidence does not need to comply with the requirements of Rule 32.1(h).

HISTORICAL AND STATUTORY NOTES

Former Rule 32.1, relating to scope of remedy, was abrogated effective Jan. 1, 2018. See, now, this rule.

16A A. R. S. Rules Crim. Proc., Rule 32.1, AZ ST RCRP Rule 32.1

Current with amendments received through 08/15/19

Rule 32.2. Preclusion of Remedy

(Refs & Annos)

VIII. Appeal and Other Post-Conviction Relief

Rule 32. Post-Conviction Relief (Refs & Annos)

16A A.R.S. Rules Crim.Proc., Rule 32.2

Rule 32.2. Preclusion of Remedy

(a) Preclusion. A defendant is precluded from relief under Rule 32 based on any ground:

(1) still raisable on direct appeal under Rule 31 or in a post-trial motion under Rule 24;

(2) finally adjudicated on the merits in an appeal or in any previous collateral proceeding; or

(3) waived at trial, on appeal, or in any previous collateral proceeding.

(b) Exceptions. Rule 32.2(a) does not apply to claims for relief based on Rule 32.1(d) through (h). A claim under Rule 32.1(d) through (h) that defendant raises in a successive or untimely post-conviction notice must include the specific exception to preclusion and explain the reasons for not raising the claim in a previous notice or petition, or for not raising the claim in a timely manner. If the notice does not identify a specific exception or provide reasons why defendant did not raise the claim in a previous petition or in a timely manner, the court may summarily dismiss the notice.

(c) Standard of Proof. The State must plead and prove any ground of preclusion by a preponderance of the evidence. A court may determine that an issue is precluded even if the State does not raise preclusion.

Credits

Added by Aug. 31, 2017, effective Jan. 1, 2018.

Editors' Notes

HISTORICAL AND STATUTORY NOTES

Former Rule 32.2, relating to preclusion of remedy, was abrogated effective Jan. 1, 2018. See, now, this rule.

16A A. R. S. Rules Crim. Proc., Rule 32.2, AZ ST RCRP Rule 32.2

Current with amendments received through 08/15/19

Rule 32.3. Nature of a Post-Conviction Proceeding and Relation to Other Remedies

(Refs & Annos)
VIII. Appeal and Other Post-Conviction Relief
Rule 32. Post-Conviction Relief (Refs & Annos)

16A A.R.S. Rules Crim.Proc., Rule 32.3

Rule 32.3. Nature of a Post-Conviction Proceeding and Relation to Other Remedies

(a) Generally. A post-conviction proceeding is part of the original criminal action and is not a separate action. It displaces and incorporates all trial court post-trial remedies except those obtainable by post-trial motions and habeas corpus.

(b) Habeas Corpus. If a court having jurisdiction over a defendant's person receives an application for a writ of habeas corpus raising any claim that attacks the validity of the defendant's conviction or sentence, and if that court is not the court that convicted or sentenced the defendant, it must transfer the application to the court where the defendant was convicted or sentenced. The court to which the application is transferred must treat the application as a Rule 32 petition for post-conviction relief, and the court and all parties must apply Rule 32's procedures.

Credits

Added by Aug. 31, 2017, effective Jan. 1, 2018.

Editors' Notes

COMMENT

This rule provides that all Rule 32 proceedings are to be treated as criminal actions. The characterization of the proceeding as criminal assures compensation for appointed counsel and the applicability of criminal standards for admissibility of evidence at an evidentiary hearing except as otherwise provided.

Rule 32 does not restrict the scope of the writ of habeas corpus under Ariz. Const. art. 2, § 14. *See* A.R.S. §§ 13-4121 et seq. (statutes governing habeas corpus). The rule is intended to provide a standard procedure for accomplishing the objectives of all constitutional, statutory, or common law post-trial writs and remedies except a writ of habeas corpus.

HISTORICAL AND STATUTORY NOTES

Former Rule 32.3, relating to nature of proceeding and relation to other remedies, was abrogated effective Jan. 1, 2018. See, now, this rule.

16A A. R. S. Rules Crim. Proc., Rule 32.3, AZ ST RCRP Rule 32.3

Current with amendments received through 08/15/19

Rule 32.4. Filing of Notice and Petition, and Other Initial Proceedings

(Refs & Annos)
VIII. Appeal and Other Post-Conviction Relief
Rule 32. Post-Conviction Relief (Refs & Annos)

16A A.R.S. Rules Crim.Proc., Rule 32.4

Rule 32.4. Filing of Notice and Petition, and Other Initial Proceedings

(a) Notice of Post-Conviction Relief.
(1) *Filing.* A defendant starts a post-conviction proceeding by filing a notice of post-conviction relief in the court where the defendant was convicted. The court must make "notice" forms available for defendants' use.
(2) *Time for Filing.*
(A) Generally. In filing a notice, a defendant must follow the deadlines set forth in this rule. These deadlines do not apply to claims under Rule 32.1(d) through (h).
(B) Time for Filing a Notice in a Capital Case. In a capital case, the Supreme Court clerk must expeditiously file a notice of post-conviction relief with the trial court upon the issuance of the mandate affirming the defendant's conviction and sentence on direct appeal.
(C) Time for Filing a Notice in an Of-Right Proceeding. In a Rule 32 of-right proceeding, a defendant must file the notice no later than 90 days after the entry of judgment and sentence. A defendant may raise an of-right claim of ineffective assistance of Rule 32 counsel in a successive Rule 32 notice if it is filed no later than 30 days after the final order or mandate in the defendant's of-right petition for post-conviction relief.
(D) Time for Filing a Notice in Other Noncapital Cases. In all other noncapital cases, a defendant must file a notice no later than 90 days after the entry of judgment and sentence or no later than 30 days after the issuance of the order and mandate in the direct appeal, whichever is later.
(3) *Content of the Notice.* The notice must contain the caption of the original criminal case or cases to which it pertains and the other information shown in Rule 41, Form 24(b).
(4) *Duty of the Clerk upon Receiving a Notice.*
(A) Generally. Upon receiving a notice from a defendant or the Supreme Court, the superior court clerk must file it in the record of each original case to which it pertains. Unless the court summarily dismisses the notice, the clerk must promptly send copies of the notice to the defendant, defense counsel, the prosecuting attorney's office, and the Attorney General. If the conviction occurred in a limited jurisdiction court, the clerk for the limited jurisdiction court must send a copy of the

notice to the prosecuting attorney who represented the State at trial, and to a defense counsel or a defendant, if self-represented. In either court, the clerk must note in the record the date and manner of sending copies of the notice.

(B) Notice to an Appellate Court. If an appeal of the defendant's conviction or sentence is pending, the clerk must send a copy of the notice of post-conviction relief to the appropriate appellate court no later than 5 days of its filing, and must note in the record the date and manner of sending the copy.

(5) *Duty of the State upon Receiving a Notice.* Upon receiving a copy of a notice, the State must notify any victim who has requested notification of post-conviction proceedings.

(b) Appointment of Counsel.

(1) *Capital Cases.* After the Supreme Court has affirmed a capital defendant's conviction and sentence, it must appoint counsel who meets the standards of Rules 6.5 and 6.8 and A.R.S. § 13-4041. Alternatively, the Supreme Court may authorize the presiding judge of the county where the case originated to appoint counsel. If the presiding judge makes an appointment, the court must file a copy of the appointment order with the Supreme Court. If a capital defendant files a successive notice, the presiding judge must appoint the defendant's previous post-conviction counsel, unless the defendant waives counsel or there is good cause to appoint another qualified attorney who meets the standards of Rules 6.5 and 6.8 and A.R.S. § 13-4041.

(2) *Noncapital Cases.* No later than 15 days after the filing of a notice of a defendant's timely or first Rule 32 proceeding, the presiding judge must appoint counsel for the defendant if: (A) the defendant requests it; and (B) the judge has previously determined that the defendant is indigent or the defendant has completed an affidavit of indigency. Upon the filing of all other notices in a noncapital case, the presiding judge may appoint counsel for an indigent defendant if requested.

(c) Time for Filing a Petition for Post-Conviction Relief.

(1) *Capital Cases.*

(A) Filing Deadline for First Petition. In a capital case, the defendant must file a petition no later than 12 months after the first notice is filed.

(B) Filing Deadline for Any Successive Petition. On a successive notice in a capital case, the defendant must file the petition no later than 30 days after the notice is filed.

(C) Time Extensions. For good cause, the court may grant a capital defendant one 60-day extension in which to file a petition. For good cause and after considering the rights of the victim, the court may grant additional 30-day extensions for good cause.

(D) Notice of Status. The defendant must file a notice in the Supreme Court advising the Court of the status of the proceeding if a petition is not filed:

(i) within 12 months after counsel is appointed; or

(ii) if the defendant is proceeding without counsel, within 12 months after the notice is filed or the court denies the defendant's request for appointed counsel, whichever is later.

The defendant must file a status report in the Supreme Court every 60 days until a petition is filed.

(2) *Noncapital Cases.*

(A) Filing Deadline. In a noncapital case, appointed counsel must file a petition no later than 60 days after the date of appointment. A defendant without counsel must file a petition no later than 60 days after the notice is filed or the court denies the defendant's request for appointed counsel, whichever is later.

(B) Time Extensions. For good cause and after considering the rights of the victim, the court may grant a defendant in a noncapital case a 30-day extension to file the petition. The court may grant additional 30-day extensions only on a showing of extraordinary circumstances.

(d) Duty of Counsel; Extension of Time for the Defendant.

(1) *Duty.* In a Rule 32 proceeding, counsel must investigate the defendant's case for any and all colorable claims.

(2) *If Counsel Finds No Colorable Claims.*

(A) Counsel's Notice. In an of-right proceeding, if counsel determines there are no colorable claims, counsel must file a notice advising the court of this determination. The notice should include a summary of the facts and procedural history of the case, including appropriate citations to the record. The notice also must identify the specific materials that counsel reviewed, the date when counsel provided the record to the defendant, and the contents of the record provided. After counsel files a notice, counsel's role is limited to acting as advisory counsel until the trial court's final determination in the Rule 32 proceeding unless the court orders otherwise.

(B) Defendant's Pro Se Petition. Upon receipt of counsel's notice, the court must allow the defendant to file a petition on his or her own behalf, and extend the time for filing a petition by 45 days from the date counsel filed the notice. The court may grant additional extensions only on a showing of extraordinary circumstances.

(e) Transcript Preparation.

(1) *Requests for Transcripts.* If the trial court proceedings were not transcribed, the defendant may request that certified transcripts be prepared. The court or clerk must provide a form for the defendant to make this request.

(2) *Order.* The court must promptly review the defendant's request and order the preparation of only those transcripts it deems necessary for resolving issues the defendant will raise in the petition.

(3) *Deadline.* Certified transcripts must be prepared and filed no later than 60 days after the entry of the order granting the request.

(4) *Cost.* If the defendant is indigent, the transcripts must be prepared at county expense.

(5) *Extending the Deadline for Filing a Petition.* If a defendant requests the preparation of certified transcripts, the defendant's deadline for filing a petition under (c) is extended by the time between the request and either the transcripts' final preparation or the court's denial of the request.

(f) Assignment of a Judge. The presiding judge must, if possible, assign a proceeding for post-conviction relief to the sentencing judge. If the sentencing judge's testimony will be relevant, the case must be reassigned to another judge.

(g) Stay of Execution of a Death Sentence on a Successive Petition. Once the defendant has received a sentence of death and the Supreme Court has fixed the time for executing the sentence, the trial court may not grant a stay of execution if the defendant files a successive petition. In those circumstances, the defendant must file an application for a stay with the Supreme Court, and the application must show with particularity any claims that are not precluded under Rule 32.2. If the Supreme Court grants a stay, the Supreme Court clerk must notify the defendant, the Attorney General, and the Director of the State Department of Corrections.

Credits

Added by Aug. 31, 2017, effective Jan. 1, 2018.

Editors' Notes

COMMENT

Rule 32.4(a). If a petition is filed while an appeal is pending, the appellate court, under Rule 31.3(b), may stay the appeal until the petition is adjudicated. Any appeal from the decision on the petition will then be joined with the appeal from the judgment or sentence. *See* Rule 31.4(b) (requiring consolidation unless good cause exists not to do so).

HISTORICAL AND STATUTORY NOTES

Former Rule 32.4, relating to commencement of proceedings, was abrogated effective Jan. 1, 2018. See, now, this rule.

16A A. R. S. Rules Crim. Proc., Rule 32.4, AZ ST RCRP Rule 32.4

Current with amendments received through 08/15/19

Rule 32.5. Contents of a Petition for Post-Conviction Relief

(Refs & Annos)

VIII. Appeal and Other Post-Conviction Relief

Rule 32. Post-Conviction Relief (Refs & Annos)

16A A.R.S. Rules Crim.Proc., Rule 32.5

Rule 32.5. Contents of a Petition for Post-Conviction Relief

(a) Form of Petition. A petition for post-conviction relief should contain the information shown in Rule 41, Form 25, and must include a memorandum that contains citations to relevant portions of the record and to relevant legal authorities.

(b) Length of Petition. In Rule 32 of-right and noncapital cases, the petition must not exceed 28 pages. The State's response must not exceed 28 pages, and defendant's reply, if any, must not exceed 11 pages. In capital cases, the petition must not exceed 80 pages. The State's response must not exceed 80 pages, and defendant's reply must not exceed 40 pages.

(c) Declaration. A petition by a self-represented defendant must include a declaration stating under penalty of perjury that the information contained in the petition is true to the best of the defendant's knowledge and belief. The declaration must identify facts that are within the defendant's personal knowledge separately from other factual allegations.

(d) Attachments. The defendant must attach to the petition any affidavits, records, or other evidence currently available to the defendant supporting the petition's allegations.

(e) Effect of Non-Compliance. The court will return to the defendant any petition that fails to comply with this rule, with an order specifying how the petition fails to comply. The defendant has 40 days after that order is entered to revise the petition to comply with this rule, and to return it to the court for refiling. If the defendant does not return the petition within 40 days, the court may dismiss the proceeding with prejudice. The State's time to respond to a refiled petition begins on the date of refiling.

Credits

Added by Aug. 31, 2017, effective Jan. 1, 2018.

Editors' Notes

HISTORICAL AND STATUTORY NOTES

Former Rule 32.5, relating to contents of petition, was abrogated effective Jan. 1, 2018. See, now, this rule.

16A A. R. S. Rules Crim. Proc., Rule 32.5, AZ ST RCRP Rule 32.5

Current with amendments received through 08/15/19

Rule 32.6. Response and Reply; Amendments; Review

(Refs & Annos)

VIII. Appeal and Other Post-Conviction Relief

Rule 32. Post-Conviction Relief (Refs & Annos)

16A A.R.S. Rules Crim.Proc., Rule 32.6

Rule 32.6. Response and Reply; Amendments; Review

(a) State's Response. The State must file its response no later than 45 days after the defendant files the petition. The court may grant the State a 30-day extension to file its response for good cause, and may grant the State additional extensions only on a showing of extraordinary circumstances and after considering the rights of the victim. The State's response must include a memorandum that contains citations to relevant portions of the record and to relevant legal authorities, and must attach any affidavits, records, or other evidence that contradicts the petition's allegations.

(b) Defendant's Reply. No later than 15 days after a response is served, the defendant may file a reply. The court may for good cause grant an extension of time.

(c) Amending the Petition. After the filing of a post-conviction relief petition, the court may permit amendments only for good cause.

(d) Review and Further Proceedings.

(1) *Summary Disposition.* If, after identifying all precluded and untimely claims, the court determines that no remaining claim presents a material issue of fact or law that would entitle the defendant to relief under this rule, the court must summarily dismiss the petition.

(2) *Setting a Hearing.* If the court does not summarily dismiss the petition, it must set a status conference or hearing within 30 days on those claims that present a material issue of fact. The court also may set a hearing on those claims that present only a material issue of law.

(3) *Notice to Victim.* If a hearing is ordered, the State must notify any victim of the time and place of the hearing if the victim has requested such notice under a statute or court rule relating to victims' rights.

Credits

Added by Aug. 31, 2017, effective Jan. 1, 2018.

Editors' Notes

HISTORICAL AND STATUTORY NOTES
Former Rule 32.6, relating to additional pleadings, summary disposition, and amendments, was abrogated effective Jan. 1, 2018. See, now, this rule.
16A A. R. S. Rules Crim. Proc., Rule 32.6, AZ ST RCRP Rule 32.6
Current with amendments received through 08/15/19

Rule 32.7. Informal Conference

(Refs & Annos)

VIII. Appeal and Other Post-Conviction Relief

Rule 32. Post-Conviction Relief (Refs & Annos)

16A A.R.S. Rules Crim.Proc., Rule 32.7

Rule 32.7. Informal Conference

(a) Generally. At any time, the court may hold an informal conference to expedite a proceeding for post-conviction relief.

(b) Capital Cases. In a capital case, the court must hold an informal conference no later than 90 days after counsel is appointed on the first notice of a petition for post-conviction relief.

(c) The Defendant's Presence. The defendant need not be present at an informal conference if defense counsel is present.

Credits

Added by Aug. 31, 2017, effective Jan. 1, 2018.

Editors' Notes

HISTORICAL AND STATUTORY NOTES

Former Rule 32.7, relating to informal conference, was abrogated effective Jan. 1, 2018. See, now, this rule.

16A A. R. S. Rules Crim. Proc., Rule 32.7, AZ ST RCRP Rule 32.7

Current with amendments received through 08/15/19

Rule 32.8. Evidentiary Hearing

(Refs & Annos)

VIII. Appeal and Other Post-Conviction Relief

Rule 32. Post-Conviction Relief (Refs & Annos)

16A A.R.S. Rules Crim.Proc., Rule 32.8

Rule 32.8. Evidentiary Hearing

(a) Rights Attendant to the Hearing; Location; Record. The defendant is entitled to a hearing to determine issues of material fact, and has the right to be present and to subpoena witnesses for the hearing. The court may order the hearing to be held at the defendant's place of confinement if facilities are available and after giving at least 15 days' notice to the officer in charge of the confinement facility. In superior court proceedings, the court must make a verbatim record.

(b) Evidence. The Arizona Rules of Evidence applicable to criminal proceedings apply at the hearing, except that the defendant may be called to testify.

(c) Burden of Proof. The defendant has the burden of proving factual allegations by a preponderance of the evidence. If the defendant proves a constitutional violation, the State has the burden of proving beyond a reasonable doubt that the violation was harmless.

(d) Decision.

(1) *Findings and Conclusions.* The court must make specific findings of fact and expressly state its conclusions of law relating to each issue presented.

(2) *Decision in the Defendant's Favor.* If the court finds in the defendant's favor, it must enter appropriate orders concerning:

(A) the conviction, sentence, or detention;

(B) any further proceedings, including a new trial and conditions of release; and

(C) other matters that may be necessary and proper.

(e) Transcript. On a party's request, the court must order the preparation of a certified transcript of the evidentiary hearing. The request must be made within the time allowed for filing a petition for review. If the defendant is indigent, preparation of the evidentiary hearing transcript will be at county expense.

Credits

Added by Aug. 31, 2017, effective Jan. 1, 2018.

Editors' Notes

HISTORICAL AND STATUTORY NOTES

Former Rule 32.8, relating to evidentiary hearing, was abrogated effective Jan. 1, 2018. See, now, this rule.

16A A. R. S. Rules Crim. Proc., Rule 32.8, AZ ST RCRP Rule 32.8

Current with amendments received through 08/15/19

Rule 32.9. Review

(Refs & Annos)

VIII. Appeal and Other Post-Conviction Relief

Rule 32. Post-Conviction Relief (Refs & Annos)

16A A.R.S. Rules Crim.Proc., Rule 32.9

Rule 32.9. Review

(a) Filing of a Motion for Rehearing.

(1) *Timing and Content.* No later than 15 days after entry of the trial court's final decision on a petition, any party aggrieved by the decision may file a motion for rehearing. The motion must state in detail the grounds of the court's alleged errors.

(2) *Response and Reply.* An opposing party may not file a response to a motion for rehearing unless the court requests one, but the court may not grant a motion for

rehearing without requesting and considering a response. If a response is filed, the moving party may file a reply no later than 10 days after the response is served.
(3) *Effect on Appellate Rights.* Filing of a motion for rehearing is not a prerequisite to filing a petition for review under (c).
(b) Disposition if Motion Granted. If the court grants the motion for rehearing, it may either amend its previous ruling without a hearing, or grant a new hearing and then either amend or reaffirm its previous ruling. In either case, it must state its reasons for amending a previous ruling. The State must notify the victim of any action taken by the court if the victim has requested notification.
(c) Petition and Cross-Petition for Review.
(1) *Time and Place for Filing.*
(A) Petition. No later than 30 days after the entry of the trial court's final decision on a petition or a motion for rehearing, an aggrieved party may petition the appropriate appellate court for review of the decision.
(B) Cross-Petition. The opposing party may file a cross-petition for review no later than 15 days after a petition for review is served.
(C) Place for Filing. The parties must file the petition for review, cross-petition, and all responsive filings with the appellate court and not the trial court.
(D) Computation of Time and Modifying Deadlines. Rule 31.3(d) governs the computation of any appellate court deadline in this rule, and an appellate court may modify any deadline in accordance with Rule 31.3(e).
(2) *Notice of Filing and Additional Record Designation.* No later than 3 days after a petition or cross-petition for review is filed, the petitioner and cross-petitioner must file with the trial court a "notice of filing." The notice of filing may designate additional items for the record described in (e). These items may include additional certified transcripts of trial court proceedings prepared under Rule 32.4(e), or that were otherwise available to the trial court and the parties, and are material to the issues raised in the petition for review.
(3) *Motions.* Motions for extensions of time to file petitions or cross-petitions for review must be filed with the trial court, which must decide the motions promptly. The parties must file all other motions in the appellate court.
(4) *Form and Contents of a Petition or Cross-Petition for Review.*
(A) Form and Length. Petitions and cross-petitions for review, along with other documents filed with the appellate clerk, must comply with the formatting requirements of Rule 31.6(b). The petition or cross-petition must contain a caption with the name of the appellate court, the title of the case, a space for the appellate court case number, the trial court case number, and a brief descriptive title. The caption must designate the parties as they appear in the trial court's caption. The petition or cross-petition must not exceed 6,000 words if typed or 22 pages if handwritten, exclusive of an appendix and copies of the trial court's rulings.

(B) Contents. A petition or cross-petition for review must contain:

(i) copies of the trial court's rulings entered under Rules 32.6(d), 32.8(d) and 32.9(b);

(ii) a statement of issues the trial court decided that the defendant is presenting for appellate review;

(iii) a statement of material facts concerning the issues presented for review, including specific references to the record for each material fact; and

(iv) reasons why the appellate court should grant the petition, including citations to supporting legal authority, if known.

(C) Effect of a Motion for Rehearing. The filing of a motion for rehearing under (a) does not limit the issues a party may raise in a petition or cross-petition for review.

(D) Waiver. A party's failure to raise any issue that could be raised in the petition or cross-petition for review constitutes a waiver of appellate review of that issue.

(5) *Appendix Accompanying Petition or Cross-Petition.*

(A) Generally. Unless otherwise ordered, a petition or cross-petition may be accompanied by an appendix. The petition or cross-petition must not incorporate any document by reference, except the appendix. An appendix that exceeds 15 pages in length, exclusive of the trial court's rulings, must be submitted separately from the petition or cross-petition.

(B) Capital Cases. In capital cases, the parties must submit an appendix that supports all of the petition's references to the trial court record, with copies of supporting portions of the record.

(C) Noncapital Cases. In non-capital cases, an appendix is not required, but the petition must contain specific references to the record to support all material factual statements.

(6) *Service; Response; Reply.*

(A) Service. A party filing a petition, cross-petition, appendix, response, reply, or a related filing must serve a copy of the filing on all other parties. The serving party must file a certificate of service complying with Rule 1.7(c)(3), identifying who was served and the date and manner of service.

(B) Response. No later than 30 days after a petition or cross-petition is served, a party opposing the petition or cross-petition may file a response. The response must not exceed 6,000 words if typed and 22 pages if handwritten, exclusive of an appendix, and must comply with the form requirements in (c)(4)(A). An appendix to a response must comply with the form and substantive requirements in (c)(5).

(C) Reply. No later than 10 days after a response is served, a party may file a reply. The reply is limited to matters addressed in the response and may not exceed 3,000 words if typed and 11 pages if handwritten. It also must comply with the form requirements in (c)(4)(A), and may not include an appendix.

(7) *Amicus Curiae.* Rules 31.13(a)(7) and 31.15 govern filing and responding to an amicus curiae brief.

(d) Stay Pending Review. The State's filing of a motion for rehearing or a petition for review of an order granting a new trial automatically stays the order until appellate review is completed. For any relief the trial court grants to a defendant other than a new trial, granting a stay pending further review is within the discretion of the trial court or the appellate court.

(e) Transmitting the Record to the Appellate Court.

(1) *In Noncapital Cases.* No later than 45 days after receiving a notice of filing under (c)(2), the trial court clerk must transmit the record, including the trial court file and transcripts filed in the trial court, to the appellate court.

(2) *In Capital Cases.* The trial court clerk may transmit the record of post-conviction proceedings to the appellate court only if the appellate court requests it. The record includes copies of the notice of post-conviction relief, the petition for post-conviction relief, response and reply, all motions and responsive pleadings, all minute entries and orders issued in the post-conviction proceedings, transcripts filed in the trial court, and any exhibits admitted by the trial court in the post-conviction proceedings.

(f) Disposition. The appellate court may grant review of the petition and may order oral argument. Upon granting review, the court may grant or deny relief and issue other orders it deems necessary and proper.

(g) Reconsideration or Review of an Appellate Court Decision. The provisions in Rules 31.20 and 31.21 relating to motions for reconsideration and petitions for review in criminal appeals govern motions for reconsideration and petitions for review of an appellate court decision entered under (f).

(h) Return of the Record. After a petition for review is resolved, the appellate clerk must return the record to the trial court clerk for retention.

(i) Notice to the Victim. Upon the victim's request, the State must notify the victim of any action taken by the appellate court.

Credits

Added by Aug. 31, 2017, effective Jan. 1, 2018.

Editors' Notes

HISTORICAL AND STATUTORY NOTES

Former Rule 32.9, relating to review, was abrogated effective Jan. 1, 2018. See, now, this rule.

16A A. R. S. Rules Crim. Proc., Rule 32.9, AZ ST RCRP Rule 32.9

Current with amendments received through 08/15/19

Rule 32.10. Review of an Intellectual Disability Determination in Capital Cases

(Refs & Annos)

VIII. Appeal and Other Post-Conviction Relief
Rule 32. Post-Conviction Relief (Refs & Annos)

16A A.R.S. Rules Crim.Proc., Rule 32.10

Rule 32.10. Review of an Intellectual Disability Determination in Capital Cases

No later than 10 days after the trial court makes a finding on intellectual disability, the State or the defendant may file with the Court of Appeals a petition for special action challenging the finding. The Rules of Procedure for Special Actions govern the special action, except the Court of Appeals must accept jurisdiction and decide any issue raised.

Credits

Added by Aug. 31, 2017, effective Jan. 1, 2018.

Editors' Notes

HISTORICAL AND STATUTORY NOTES

Former Rule 32.10, relating to review of intellectual disability determination, was abrogated effective Jan. 1, 2018. See, now, this rule.

Former Rule 32.10, was deleted effective Dec. 1, 1992, nunc pro tunc effective Sept. 30, 1992.

16A A. R. S. Rules Crim. Proc., Rule 32.10, AZ ST RCRP Rule 32.10

Current with amendments received through 08/15/19

Rule 32.11. Extensions of Time; Victim Notice and Service

(Refs & Annos)

VIII. Appeal and Other Post-Conviction Relief

Rule 32. Post-Conviction Relief (Refs & Annos)

16A A.R.S. Rules Crim.Proc., Rule 32.11

Rule 32.11. Extensions of Time; Victim Notice and Service

(a) Notice to the Victim. If the victim in a capital case has filed a notice of appearance under A.R.S. § 13-4234.01, a party requesting an extension of time to file a brief must serve or otherwise provide notice of the request to the victim.

(b) Manner and Timing of Service or Notice.

(1) *Victim's Choice of the Manner of Service.* The victim may specify in the notice of appearance whether the service of the request should be to the victim or whether it should go to another person, including the prosecutor, and whether service of the notice should be electronic, by telephone, or by regular mail. Service must be made in the manner specified in the victim's notice of appearance or, if no method is specified, by regular mail. If the victim has requested direct notification, the party

requesting an extension of time must serve the victim with notice no later than 24 hours after filing the request.

(2) *Service Through the Prosecutor.* If the victim has not specified a method of service or if the victim has requested service through the prosecutor, the party requesting the extension of time must serve the prosecutor's office handling the post-conviction proceeding. If the prosecutor has the duty to notify the victim on behalf of the defendant, the prosecutor must do so no later than 24 hours after receiving the request.

(c) Victim's Response. A victim may file a response to the request no later than 10 days after it is served.

(d) Factors. In ruling on any request for an extension of time to file a brief, the court must consider the rights of the defendant and the victim to a prompt and final conclusion of the case.

Credits

Added by Aug. 31, 2017, effective Jan. 1, 2018.

Editors' Notes

HISTORICAL AND STATUTORY NOTES

Former Rule 32.11, relating to extension of time and notification of victims, was abrogated effective Jan. 1, 2018. See, now, this rule.

16A A. R. S. Rules Crim. Proc., Rule 32.11, AZ ST RCRP Rule 32.11

Current with amendments received through 08/15/19

Rule 32.12. Post-Conviction Deoxyribonucleic Acid Testing

(Refs & Annos)

VIII. Appeal and Other Post-Conviction Relief

Rule 32. Post-Conviction Relief (Refs & Annos)

16A A.R.S. Rules Crim.Proc., Rule 32.12

Rule 32.12. Post-Conviction Deoxyribonucleic Acid Testing

(a) Generally. Any person who has been convicted and sentenced for a felony offense may petition the court at any time for forensic deoxyribonucleic acid (DNA) testing of any evidence:

(1) in the possession or control of the court or the State;

(2) related to the investigation or prosecution that resulted in the judgment of conviction; and

(3) that may contain biological evidence.

(b) Manner of Filing; Response. The defendant must file the petition under the same criminal cause number as the felony conviction, and the clerk must distribute it in the manner provided in Rule 32.4(a)(4). The State must respond to the petition no later than 45 days after it is served.

(c) Appointment of Counsel. The court may appoint counsel for an indigent defendant at any time during proceedings under this rule.

(d) Court Orders.

(1) *Mandatory Testing.* After considering the petition and the State's response, the court must order DNA testing if the court finds that:

(A) a reasonable probability exists that the defendant would not have been prosecuted or convicted if exculpatory results had been obtained through DNA testing;

(B) the evidence is still in existence; and

(C) the evidence was not previously subjected to DNA testing, or the evidence was not subjected to the type of DNA testing that defendant now requests and the requested testing may resolve an issue not resolved by previous testing.

(2) *Discretionary Testing.* After considering the petition and the State's response, the court may order DNA testing if the court finds that (d)(1)(B) and (C) apply, and that a reasonable probability exists that either:

(A) the defendant's verdict or sentence would have been more favorable if the results of DNA testing had been available at the trial leading to the judgment of conviction; or

(B) DNA testing will produce exculpatory evidence.

(3) *Laboratory; Costs.* If the court orders testing under (d)(1) or (2), the court must select an accredited laboratory to conduct the testing. The court may require the defendant to pay the costs of testing.

(4) *Other Orders.* The court may enter any other appropriate orders, including orders requiring elimination samples from third parties and designating:

(A) the type of DNA analysis to be used;

(B) the procedures to be followed during the testing; and

(C) the preservation of some of the sample for replicating the testing.

(e) Test Results.

(1) *Earlier Testing.* If the State or defense counsel has previously subjected evidence to DNA testing, the court may order the party to provide all other parties and the court with access to the laboratory reports prepared in connection with that testing, including underlying data and laboratory notes.

(2) *Testing Under this Rule.* If the court orders DNA testing under this rule, the court must order the production to all parties of any laboratory reports prepared in connection with the testing and may order the production of any underlying data and laboratory notes.

(f) Preservation of Evidence. If a defendant files a petition under this rule, the court must order the State to preserve during the pendency of the proceeding all evidence in the State's possession or control that could be subjected to DNA testing. The State must prepare an inventory of the evidence and submit a copy of the inventory to the defendant and the court. If evidence is destroyed after the court orders its preservation, the court may impose appropriate sanctions, including criminal contempt, for a knowing violation.

(g) Unfavorable Test Results. If the results of the post-conviction DNA testing are not favorable to the defendant, the court must dismiss without a hearing any DNA-related claims asserted under Rule 32.1. The court may make further orders as it deems appropriate, including orders:

(1) notifying the Board of Executive Clemency or a probation department;

(2) requesting to add the defendant's sample to the federal combined DNA index system offender database; or

(3) notifying the victim or the victim's family.

(h) Favorable Test Results. Notwithstanding any other provision of law that would bar a hearing as untimely, the court must order a hearing and make any further orders that are required by statute or the Arizona if the results of the post-conviction DNA testing are favorable to the defendant. If there are no material issues of fact, the hearing need not be an evidentiary hearing, but the court must give the parties an opportunity to argue why the defendant should or should not be entitled to relief under Rule 32.1 as a matter of law.

Credits

Added by Aug. 31, 2017, effective Jan. 1, 2018.

Editors' Notes

HISTORICAL AND STATUTORY NOTES

Former Rule 32.12, relating to post-conviction deoxyribonucleic acid testing, was abrogated effective Jan. 1, 2018.

16A A. R. S. Rules Crim. Proc., Rule 32.12, AZ ST RCRP Rule 32.12

Current with amendments received through 08/15/19

R. 33, Refs & Annos

VIII. Appeal and Other Post-Conviction Relief

Rule 33. Criminal Contempt

16A A.R.S. Rules Crim.Proc., R. 33, Refs & Annos

16A A. R. S. Rules Crim. Proc., R. 33, Refs & Annos, AZ ST RCRP R. 33, Refs & Annos

Current with amendments received through 08/15/19

Rule 33.1. Definition

(Refs & Annos)
VIII. Appeal and Other Post-Conviction Relief
Rule 33. Criminal Contempt (Refs & Annos)
16A A.R.S. Rules Crim.Proc., Rule 33.1

Rule 33.1. Definition

A court may hold a person in contempt of court if the person:

(a) willfully disobeys a lawful writ, process, order, or judgment of a court by doing or not doing an act or thing forbidden or required; or

(b) willfully engages in any other unreasonable conduct that obstructs the administration of justice or lessens the court's dignity and authority.

Credits

Added by Aug. 31, 2017, effective Jan. 1, 2018.

Editors' Notes

COMMENT

This rule is applicable to all types of contempt except the comparatively narrow class of direct criminal contempts covered by A.R.S. §§ 12-861 to -863 which must be prosecuted according to the terms of those statutes.

Rule 33.1 defines criminal contempt. The definition derives from A.R.S. § 12-861 and the Arizona Supreme Court's statements in *Ong Hing v. Thurston*, 101 Ariz. 92, 96, 416 P.2d 416, 420 (1966). This definition, and the succeeding sections, apply only to criminal contempt. Civil contempt, which is possible in a criminal case (such as in the case of a witness who refuses to submit to a deposition) is not treated in this rule. The general distinction between civil and criminal contempt is the purpose for which the punishment is imposed. A person is imprisoned for civil contempt to force compliance with a lawful order of the court; that person holds the keys to the jail and can gain release at any time by complying with the order. *See Shillitani v. United States*, 384 U.S. 364, 370-71 (1966). A criminal contempt citation, on the other hand, is intended to vindicate the dignity of the court. It is a criminal offense for which a specific punishment is meted out, over which the defendant has no control. *See United States v. Barnett*, 376 U.S. 681, 692-94 (1964).

HISTORICAL AND STATUTORY NOTES

Former Rule 33.1, relating to definition, was abrogated effective Jan. 1, 2018. See, now, this rule.

16A A. R. S. Rules Crim. Proc., Rule 33.1, AZ ST RCRP Rule 33.1

Current with amendments received through 08/15/19

Rule 33.2. Summary Disposition of Contempt

(Refs & Annos)
VIII. Appeal and Other Post-Conviction Relief
Rule 33. Criminal Contempt (Refs & Annos)
16A A.R.S. Rules Crim.Proc., Rule 33.2

Rule 33.2. Summary Disposition of Contempt

(a) Citation. The court may summarily find a person in contempt if the person commits a criminal contempt in the court's presence. The court must immediately notify the person of this finding, and prepare and file a written order reciting the grounds for the finding, including a statement that the court saw or heard the conduct constituting the contempt.

(b) Procedure. The court must inform the person of the specific conduct on which the citation is based. The court must also provide the person a brief opportunity to present evidence or argument regarding the punishment the court will impose. The court may not impose punishment during the course of the proceeding at which the contempt occurs, unless prompt punishment is imperative.

(c) Punishment. The court may not punish a person under this rule by imprisonment for longer than 6 months, or by a fine greater than $300, or both, unless the person either has been found guilty of contempt by a jury or has waived the right to a jury trial.

Credits

Added by Aug. 31, 2017, effective Jan. 1, 2018.

Editors' Notes

HISTORICAL AND STATUTORY NOTES

Former Rule 33.2, relating to summary procedure, was abrogated effective Jan. 1, 2018. See, now, this rule.

16A A. R. S. Rules Crim. Proc., Rule 33.2, AZ ST RCRP Rule 33.2

Current with amendments received through 08/15/19

Rule 33.3. Disposition of Contempt by Notice and Hearing

(Refs & Annos)
VIII. Appeal and Other Post-Conviction Relief
Rule 33. Criminal Contempt (Refs & Annos)
16A A.R.S. Rules Crim.Proc., Rule 33.3

Rule 33.3. Disposition of Contempt by Notice and Hearing

Except as provided by law or Rule 33.2, the court may not find a person in criminal contempt without notifying the person of the charge and holding a hearing. The court must set the hearing on a date that will allow the person reasonable time to prepare a defense. The notice of hearing must state the hearing's time and place, and the essential facts constituting the charged contempt. A court may give the notice orally in open court in the presence of the person charged or by an order to show cause. The person charged with contempt has the right to subpoena witnesses for the hearing, and to release under Rule 7 pending the hearing.

Credits

Added by Aug. 31, 2017, effective Jan. 1, 2018.

Editors' Notes

COMMENT

Rule 33.3 does not apply to the class of indirect contempts covered by A.R.S. §§ 12-861 to -863, which must be prosecuted according to the terms of those statutes. *See State v. Cohen*, 15 Ariz. App. 436, 439, 489 P.2d 283, 286 (1971) (discussing statutory requirements).

HISTORICAL AND STATUTORY NOTES

Former Rule 33.3, relating to disposition of other contempts, notice, and hearing, was abrogated effective Jan. 1, 2018. See, now, this rule.

16A A. R. S. Rules Crim. Proc., Rule 33.3, AZ ST RCRP Rule 33.3

Current with amendments received through 08/15/19

Rule 33.4. Jury Trial; Disqualification of the Citing Judge

(Refs & Annos)

VIII. Appeal and Other Post-Conviction Relief

Rule 33. Criminal Contempt (Refs & Annos)

16A A.R.S. Rules Crim.Proc., Rule 33.4

Rule 33.4. Jury Trial; Disqualification of the Citing Judge

(a) Jury Trial. The court may not punish a person under this rule by imprisonment for longer than 6 months, or by a fine greater than $300, or both, unless the person either has been found guilty of contempt by a jury or has waived the right to a jury trial.

(b) Disqualification of Judge. Unless prompt punishment is imperative, the citation must be transferred to another judge if the unreasonable conduct involves gross disrespect or a personal attack on the citing judge's character, or if the citing judge's conduct is so integrated with the contempt that the citing judge contributed to or was otherwise involved in it. Should the matter be transferred, any prior adjudication of guilt is void and the judge to whom the citation is transferred must hold a hearing to determine the person's guilt and punishment.

Credits

Added by Aug. 31, 2017, effective Jan. 1, 2018.

Editors' Notes

COMMENT

The self-disqualification of the judge required by this rule does not give the contemnor a pre-sentence challenge of the judge under Rule 10.2.

HISTORICAL AND STATUTORY NOTES

Former Rule 33.4, relating to jury trial and disqualification of a judge, was abrogated effective Jan. 1, 2018. See, now, this rule.

16A A. R. S. Rules Crim. Proc., Rule 33.4, AZ ST RCRP Rule 33.4

Current with amendments received through 08/15/19

Rule 34. Subpoenas

(Refs & Annos)

IX. Miscellaneous

Rule 34. Subpoenas

16A A.R.S. Rules Crim.Proc., Rule 34

Rule 34. Subpoenas

(a) Generally. The process by which attendance of a witness before a court or magistrate is required is a subpoena. The subpoena must be substantially in the form shown in Rule 41, Form 27(a).

(b) Alternative Form of Subpoena. If requested, a subpoena requiring a person to appear at a criminal proceeding may allow the person to appear in court on 30 minutes notice. If the subpoenaed person agrees to this option, the person must promise to appear when called and provide on the return of service a telephone number where the person can be contacted during regular court hours on the appearance date. The alternative subpoena must be substantially in the form shown in Rule 41, Form 27(b).

(c) Multiple Subpoenas. A person served with two or more subpoenas that require simultaneous attendance in different courts must honor them in the following order: United States District Court, Superior Court, Justice of the Peace Court, and

Municipal Court, and then must honor them based on the date of service. The person must immediately notify the parties requesting the subpoenas of the conflict.

(d) ADA Notification. The subpoena must state that "Requests for reasonable accommodation for persons with disabilities must be made to the court by parties at least 3 working days in advance of a scheduled court proceeding."

Credits

Added by Aug. 31, 2017, effective Jan. 1, 2018.

Editors' Notes

COMMENT

This rule supplements the statutory provisions governing criminal subpoenas. *See* A.R.S. §§ 13-4071 to -4075 and 13-4077.

HISTORICAL AND STATUTORY NOTES

Former Rule 34, relating to subpoenas, was abrogated effective Jan. 1, 2018. See, now, this rule.

16A A. R. S. Rules Crim. Proc., Rule 34, AZ ST RCRP Rule 34

Current with amendments received through 08/15/19

Rules 35.1 to 35.7. Abrogated Aug. 31, 2017, effective Jan. 1, 2018.

(Refs & Annos)

IX. Miscellaneous

Rule 35. [Reserved]

16A A.R.S. Rules Crim.Proc., R. 35.1 to 35.7

Rules 35.1 to 35.7. Abrogated Aug. 31, 2017, effective Jan. 1, 2018.

Editors' Notes

HISTORICAL AND STATUTORY NOTES

Abrogated Rule 35.1 related to motions, form, content, and rights of reply. See, now, AZ ST RCRP Rule 1.9.

Abrogated Rule 35.2 related to a hearing and oral argument. See, now, AZ ST RCRP Rule 1.9.

Abrogated Rule 35.3 related to requests, form, content, right of reply and hearing. See, now, AZ ST RCRP Rule 1.9.

Abrogated Rule 35.4 related to waiver of formal requirements. See, now, AZ ST RCRP Rule 1.9.

Abrogated Rule 35.5 related to service and filing. See, now, AZ ST RCRP Rule 1.7.

Abrogated Rule 35.6 related to notice of orders. See, now, AZ ST RCRP Rule 1.8.

Abrogated Rule 35.7 related to proposed orders. See, now, AZ ST RCRP Rule 1.9.

16A A. R. S. Rules Crim. Proc., R. 35.1 to 35.7, AZ ST RCRP R. 35.1 to 35.7

Current with amendments received through 08/15/19

Rules 35.1 to 35.7. Abrogated Aug. 31, 2017, effective Jan. 1, 2018.

(Refs & Annos)
IX. Miscellaneous
Rule 35. [Reserved]

16A A.R.S. Rules Crim.Proc., R. 35.1 to 35.7

Rules 35.1 to 35.7. Abrogated Aug. 31, 2017, effective Jan. 1, 2018.

Editors' Notes
HISTORICAL AND STATUTORY NOTES
Abrogated Rule 35.1 related to motions, form, content, and rights of reply. See, now, AZ ST RCRP Rule 1.9.
Abrogated Rule 35.2 related to a hearing and oral argument. See, now, AZ ST RCRP Rule 1.9.
Abrogated Rule 35.3 related to requests, form, content, right of reply and hearing. See, now, AZ ST RCRP Rule 1.9.
Abrogated Rule 35.4 related to waiver of formal requirements. See, now, AZ ST RCRP Rule 1.9.
Abrogated Rule 35.5 related to service and filing. See, now, AZ ST RCRP Rule 1.7.
Abrogated Rule 35.6 related to notice of orders. See, now, AZ ST RCRP Rule 1.8.
Abrogated Rule 35.7 related to proposed orders. See, now, AZ ST RCRP Rule 1.9.
16A A. R. S. Rules Crim. Proc., R. 35.1 to 35.7, AZ ST RCRP R. 35.1 to 35.7
Current with amendments received through 08/15/19

Rules 35.1 to 35.7. Abrogated Aug. 31, 2017, effective Jan. 1, 2018.

(Refs & Annos)
IX. Miscellaneous
Rule 35. [Reserved]

16A A.R.S. Rules Crim.Proc., R. 35.1 to 35.7

Rules 35.1 to 35.7. Abrogated Aug. 31, 2017, effective Jan. 1, 2018.

Editors' Notes
HISTORICAL AND STATUTORY NOTES

Abrogated Rule 35.1 related to motions, form, content, and rights of reply. See, now, AZ ST RCRP Rule 1.9.

Abrogated Rule 35.2 related to a hearing and oral argument. See, now, AZ ST RCRP Rule 1.9.

Abrogated Rule 35.3 related to requests, form, content, right of reply and hearing. See, now, AZ ST RCRP Rule 1.9.

Abrogated Rule 35.4 related to waiver of formal requirements. See, now, AZ ST RCRP Rule 1.9.

Abrogated Rule 35.5 related to service and filing. See, now, AZ ST RCRP Rule 1.7.

Abrogated Rule 35.6 related to notice of orders. See, now, AZ ST RCRP Rule 1.8.

Abrogated Rule 35.7 related to proposed orders. See, now, AZ ST RCRP Rule 1.9.

16A A. R. S. Rules Crim. Proc., R. 35.1 to 35.7, AZ ST RCRP R. 35.1 to 35.7

Current with amendments received through 08/15/19

Rules 35.1 to 35.7. Abrogated Aug. 31, 2017, effective Jan. 1, 2018.

(Refs & Annos)

IX. Miscellaneous

Rule 35. [Reserved]

16A A.R.S. Rules Crim.Proc., R. 35.1 to 35.7

Rules 35.1 to 35.7. Abrogated Aug. 31, 2017, effective Jan. 1, 2018.

Editors' Notes

HISTORICAL AND STATUTORY NOTES

Abrogated Rule 35.1 related to motions, form, content, and rights of reply. See, now, AZ ST RCRP Rule 1.9.

Abrogated Rule 35.2 related to a hearing and oral argument. See, now, AZ ST RCRP Rule 1.9.

Abrogated Rule 35.3 related to requests, form, content, right of reply and hearing. See, now, AZ ST RCRP Rule 1.9.

Abrogated Rule 35.4 related to waiver of formal requirements. See, now, AZ ST RCRP Rule 1.9.

Abrogated Rule 35.5 related to service and filing. See, now, AZ ST RCRP Rule 1.7.

Abrogated Rule 35.6 related to notice of orders. See, now, AZ ST RCRP Rule 1.8.

Abrogated Rule 35.7 related to proposed orders. See, now, AZ ST RCRP Rule 1.9.

16A A. R. S. Rules Crim. Proc., R. 35.1 to 35.7, AZ ST RCRP R. 35.1 to 35.7

Current with amendments received through 08/15/19

Rules 35.1 to 35.7. Abrogated Aug. 31, 2017, effective Jan. 1, 2018.

(Refs & Annos)
IX. Miscellaneous
Rule 35. [Reserved]

16A A.R.S. Rules Crim.Proc., R. 35.1 to 35.7

Rules 35.1 to 35.7. Abrogated Aug. 31, 2017, effective Jan. 1, 2018.

Editors' Notes

HISTORICAL AND STATUTORY NOTES

Abrogated Rule 35.1 related to motions, form, content, and rights of reply. See, now, AZ ST RCRP Rule 1.9.

Abrogated Rule 35.2 related to a hearing and oral argument. See, now, AZ ST RCRP Rule 1.9.

Abrogated Rule 35.3 related to requests, form, content, right of reply and hearing. See, now, AZ ST RCRP Rule 1.9.

Abrogated Rule 35.4 related to waiver of formal requirements. See, now, AZ ST RCRP Rule 1.9.

Abrogated Rule 35.5 related to service and filing. See, now, AZ ST RCRP Rule 1.7.

Abrogated Rule 35.6 related to notice of orders. See, now, AZ ST RCRP Rule 1.8.

Abrogated Rule 35.7 related to proposed orders. See, now, AZ ST RCRP Rule 1.9.

16A A. R. S. Rules Crim. Proc., R. 35.1 to 35.7, AZ ST RCRP R. 35.1 to 35.7

Current with amendments received through 08/15/19

Rule 36. [RESERVED]

(Refs & Annos)
IX. Miscellaneous
Rule 36. [Reserved]

16A A.R.S. Rules Crim.Proc., Rule 36

Rule 36. [RESERVED]

16A A. R. S. Rules Crim. Proc., Rule 36, AZ ST RCRP Rule 36

Current with amendments received through 08/15/19

Rule 37.1. Final Disposition Report

(Refs & Annos)

IX. Miscellaneous
Rule 37. Report of Court Dispositions

16A A.R.S. Rules Crim.Proc., Rule 37.1

Rule 37.1. Final Disposition Report

(a) Definition of "Final Disposition Report." A "final disposition report" is a report on a Supreme Court approved form that a court must provide to the Department of Public Safety, which contains details regarding the disposition of a criminal proceeding. The report may be created and transmitted electronically.

(b) Scope. The court must submit a final disposition report to the Department of Public Safety's central state repository in every criminal case if the defendant was fingerprinted as a result of the charge or incarcerated.

(c) Timing. The court must send a final disposition report to the Department of Public Safety's central state repository no later than 10 days after the final disposition of a criminal proceeding.

Credits

Added by Aug. 31, 2017, effective Jan. 1, 2018.

Editors' Notes

HISTORICAL AND STATUTORY NOTES

Former Rule 37.1, relating to scope, was abrogated effective Jan. 1, 2018. See, now, this rule.

16A A. R. S. Rules Crim. Proc., Rule 37.1, AZ ST RCRP Rule 37.1

Current with amendments received through 08/15/19

Rule 37.2. State's Duty to File a Disposition Form with the Court

(Refs & Annos)
IX. Miscellaneous
Rule 37. Report of Court Dispositions

16A A.R.S. Rules Crim.Proc., Rule 37.2

Rule 37.2. State's Duty to File a Disposition Form with the Court

(a) Generally. When the State files a criminal charge against a defendant who was fingerprinted or incarcerated following an arrest, the State must complete the applicable portions of the disposition form and forward it to the court.

(1) *When Filing a Complaint.* If the State files a complaint, the State must attach a disposition form to the complaint. If a magistrate holds the defendant to answer before the superior court, the magistrate must forward the disposition form with the records listed in Rule 5.6 to the superior court.

(2) *When Filing an Indictment or Information.* The State must complete the disposition form when it files an indictment or information in the superior court and forward it to the court.

(b) When the Defendant Is Fingerprinted. No later than 5 days after the defendant is fingerprinted under Rule 3.2(b), the State must forward a disposition form to the same court where the complaint, information, or indictment was filed.

Credits

Added by Aug. 31, 2017, effective Jan. 1, 2018.

Editors' Notes

HISTORICAL AND STATUTORY NOTES

Former Rule 37.2, relating to initiation of report, was abrogated effective Jan. 1, 2018. See, now, this rule.

16A A. R. S. Rules Crim. Proc., Rule 37.2, AZ ST RCRP Rule 37.2

Current with amendments received through 08/15/19

Rule 37.3. Reporting Procedure

(Refs & Annos)

IX. Miscellaneous

Rule 37. Report of Court Dispositions

16A A.R.S. Rules Crim.Proc., Rule 37.3

Rule 37.3. Reporting Procedure

(a) In the Superior Court. If the final disposition of a case occurs in superior court, the clerk must complete the disposition form and forward it to the Department of Public Safety's central state repository. The clerk must retain a copy of the completed disposition form in the court's file.

(b) In a Limited Jurisdiction Court. If the final disposition of a case occurs in a limited jurisdiction court, the magistrate must retain the disposition form until the clerk has transmitted the record on appeal or the time for an appeal has expired. If the clerk has transmitted the record on appeal, the magistrate must forward the disposition form to the court where the appeal is pending. If the time for appeal has expired and no timely notice of appeal was filed, the magistrate must forward the disposition form to the Department of Public Safety's central state repository.

Credits

Added by Aug. 31, 2017, effective Jan. 1, 2018.

Editors' Notes

HISTORICAL AND STATUTORY NOTES

Former Rule 37.3, relating to reporting procedure, was abrogated effective Jan. 1, 2018. See, now, this rule.

16A A. R. S. Rules Crim. Proc., Rule 37.3, AZ ST RCRP Rule 37.3

Current with amendments received through 08/15/19

Rule 37.4. Procedure on Appeal

(Refs & Annos)

IX. Miscellaneous

Rule 37. Report of Court Dispositions

16A A.R.S. Rules Crim.Proc., Rule 37.4

Rule 37.4. Procedure on Appeal

(a) In the Superior Court. When the superior court clerk transmits the record on appeal, the court must forward a copy of the disposition form to the appellate court.

(b) Reversed or Remanded Case. If the appellate court reverses a conviction or remands a case for a new trial or a new proceeding, the appellate court must forward to the Department of Public Safety's central state repository a copy of the disposition form that notes the change in the status of the disposition.

(c) New Proceedings. If an appellate court remands a case for a new trial or a new proceeding, the State must forward a new disposition form to the trial court.

Credits

Added by Aug. 31, 2017, effective Jan. 1, 2018.

Editors' Notes

HISTORICAL AND STATUTORY NOTES

Former Rule 37.4, relating to procedure on appeal, was abrogated effective Jan. 1, 2018. See, now, this rule.

16A A. R. S. Rules Crim. Proc., Rule 37.4, AZ ST RCRP Rule 37.4

Current with amendments received through 08/15/19

Rule 37.5. Abrogated Aug. 1, 2017, effective Jan. 1, 2018.

(Refs & Annos)

IX. Miscellaneous

Rule 37. Report of Court Dispositions

16A A.R.S. Rules Crim.Proc., Rule 37.5

Rule 37.5. Abrogated Aug. 1, 2017, effective Jan. 1, 2018.

Rule 38.1. Application for a Suspension Order

(Refs & Annos)
IX. Miscellaneous
Rule 38. Suspension of Prosecution for a Deferred Prosecution Programs
16A A.R.S. Rules Crim.Proc., Rule 38.1

Rule 38.1. Application for a Suspension Order

(a) Generally. After filing a complaint, indictment, or information, but before adjudication, the State may file a motion requesting that the court suspend further proceedings to allow a defendant to participate in a deferred prosecution program.
(b) Motion's Content. The motion must state facts establishing that the defendant is legally eligible for participation in a deferred prosecution program. The motion must be accompanied by the defendant's signed consent agreeing to participate in the program. The consent also must be signed by defense counsel, if any.
(c) Suspension Order. After reviewing the motion and the defendant's signed consent, and upon finding the defendant legally eligible for a deferred prosecution program, the court must suspend further proceedings for the period specified in the motion, not exceeding two years. If the defendant is in custody, the court may order the defendant's release.

Credits
Added by Aug. 31, 2017, effective Jan. 1, 2018.

Rule 38.2. Resuming Prosecution

(Refs & Annos)

IX. Miscellaneous
Rule 38. Suspension of Prosecution for a Deferred Prosecution Programs
16A A.R.S. Rules Crim.Proc., Rule 38.2

Rule 38.2. Resuming Prosecution

(a) Notice of Failure to Fulfill Deferred Prosecution Conditions. If the State is not satisfied that the defendant has fulfilled the conditions of the deferred prosecution program, it may file a written notice to that effect and request that the court vacate its order suspending prosecution. The State must serve a copy of the notice on the defendant.

(b) Order to Resume Prosecution. After receiving a notice of the defendant's failure to fulfill the deferred prosecution conditions, the court must vacate the suspension order and order that the prosecution resume. The court must mail a copy of the order to the defendant and defense counsel, if any.

(c) Time for Trial. Subject to Rule 8.4 and irrespective of the phase of the case when the prosecution was suspended, the defendant must be tried no later than 90 days after the filing of the order to resume prosecution.

Credits
Added by Aug. 31, 2017, effective Jan. 1, 2018.

Editors' Notes
HISTORICAL AND STATUTORY NOTES
Former Rule 38.2, relating to resumption of prosecution, was abrogated effective Jan. 1, 2018. See, now, this rule.
16A A. R. S. Rules Crim. Proc., Rule 38.2, AZ ST RCRP Rule 38.2
Current with amendments received through 08/15/19

Rule 38.3. Dismissal of Prosecution

(Refs & Annos)
IX. Miscellaneous
Rule 38. Suspension of Prosecution for a Deferred Prosecution Programs
16A A.R.S. Rules Crim.Proc., Rule 38.3

Rule 38.3. Dismissal of Prosecution

(a) At the End of Two Years. Two years after an order suspending prosecution is filed, the court may order the prosecution dismissed without prejudice.

(b) On Successful Completion. If the State notifies the court that the defendant has satisfactorily completed the terms of the deferred prosecution program, the court must order a dismissal of the charges.

Credits

Added by Aug. 31, 2017, effective Jan. 1, 2018.

Editors' Notes

HISTORICAL AND STATUTORY NOTES

Former Rule 38.3, relating to dismissal of prosecution, was abrogated effective Jan. 1, 2018. See, now, this rule.

16A A. R. S. Rules Crim. Proc., Rule 38.3, AZ ST RCRP Rule 38.3

Current with amendments received through 08/15/19

Rule 39. Victims' Rights

(Refs & Annos)

IX. Miscellaneous

Rule 39. Victims' Rights

16A A.R.S. Rules Crim.Proc., Rule 39

Rule 39. Victims' Rights

(a) Definitions and Limitations.

(1) *Criminal Proceeding.* As used in this rule, a "criminal proceeding" is any matter scheduled and held before a trial court, telephonically or in person, at which the defendant has the right to be present, including any post-conviction matter.

(2) *Identifying and Locating Information.* As used in this rule, "identifying and locating information" includes a person's date of birth, social security number, official state or government issued driver license or identification number, the person's address, telephone number, email addresses, and place of employment.

(3) *Limitations.*

(A) Cessation of Victim Status. A victim retains the rights provided in these rules until the rights are no longer enforceable under A.R.S. §§ 13-4402 and 13-4402.01.

(B) Legal Entities. The victim's rights of any corporation, partnership, association, or other similar legal entity are limited as provided in statute.

(b) Victims' Rights. These rules must be construed to preserve and protect a victim's rights to justice and due process. Notwithstanding the provisions of any other rule, a victim has and is entitled to assert each of the following rights:

(1) the right to be treated with fairness, respect and dignity, and to be free from intimidation, harassment, or abuse, throughout the criminal justice process;

(2) the right to notice regarding the rights available to a victim under this rule and any other provision of law, and the court must prominently post or read the statement of rights in accordance with A.R.S. § 13-4438;

(3) upon request, the right to reasonable notice of the date, time, and place of any criminal proceeding in accordance with A.R.S. § 13-4409;

(4) the right to be present at all criminal proceedings;

(5) upon request, the right to be informed of any permanent or temporary release or any proposed release of the defendant;

(6) upon request, the right to confer with the State regarding:

(A) any decision about the preconviction release of the defendant;

(B) any pretrial resolution including any diversion program or plea offer;

(C) a decision not to initiate a criminal prosecution or to dismiss charges; and

(D) the trial, before the trial begins;

(7) upon request, the right to notice of and to be heard at any criminal proceeding involving:

(A) the initial appearance;

(B) the accused's post-arrest release or release conditions;

(C) a proposed suspension of Rule 8 or a continuance of a trial date;

(D) the court's consideration of a negotiated plea resolution;

(E) sentencing;

(F) the modification of any term of probation that will substantially affect the victim's safety, the defendant's contact with the victim, or restitution;

(G) the early termination of probation;

(H) a probation revocation disposition; and

(I) post-conviction release.

(8) the right to be accompanied at any interview, deposition, or criminal proceeding by a parent or other relative, or by an appropriate support person named by a victim, including a victim's caseworker or advocate, unless testimony of the person accompanying the victim is required in the case. If the court finds that a party's claim that a person is a prospective witness is not made in good faith, it may impose sanctions, including holding counsel in contempt;

(9) if the victim is eligible, the right to the assistance of a facility dog when testifying as provided in A.R.S. § 13-4442;

(10) the right to refuse to testify regarding any identifying or locating information unless the court orders disclosure after finding a compelling need for the information, and any proceeding on any motion to require such testimony must be in camera;

(11) the right to require the prosecutor to withhold, during discovery and other proceedings, the victim's identifying and locating information.

(A) Exception. A court may order disclosure of the victim's identifying and locating information as necessary to protect the defendant's constitutional rights. If disclosure is made to defense counsel, counsel must not disclose the information to any person other than counsel's staff and designated investigator, and must not convey the information to the defendant without prior court authorization.

(B) Redactions. Rule 15.5(e) applies to information withheld under this rule;

(12) the right to refuse an interview, deposition, or other discovery request by the defendant, the defendant's attorney, or other person acting on the defendant's behalf, and:

(A) the defense must communicate requests to interview a victim to the prosecutor, not the victim;

(B) a victim's response to such requests must be communicated through the prosecutor; and

(C) if there is any comment or evidence at trial regarding a victim's refusal to be interviewed, the court must instruct the jury that a victim has the right under the Arizona Constitution to refuse an interview;

(13) at any interview or deposition conducted by defense counsel, the right to condition the interview or deposition on specification of a reasonable date, time, duration, and location of the interview or deposition, including a requirement that it be held at the victim's home, at the prosecutor's office, or at an appropriate location in the courthouse;

(14) the right to terminate an interview at any time or refuse to answer any question during the interview;

(15) the right to a copy of any presentence report provided to the defendant except those parts that are excised by the court or are confidential by law;

(16) the right to be informed of the disposition of the case;

(17) the right to a speedy trial or disposition and a prompt and final conclusion of the case after conviction and sentence; and

(18) the right to be informed of a victim's right to restitution upon conviction of the defendant, of the items of loss included within the scope of restitution, and of the procedures for invoking the right.

(c) Exercising the Right to Be Heard.

(1) *Nature of the Right.* If a victim exercises the right to be heard, the victim does not do so as a witness and the victim is not subject to cross-examination. A victim is not required to disclose any statement to any party and is not required to submit any written statement to the court. The court must give any party the opportunity to explain, support, or refute the victim's statement. This subsection does not apply to victim impact statements made in a capital case under A.R.S. § 13-752(R).

(2) *Victims in Custody.* If a victim is in custody for an offense, the victim's right to be heard under this rule is satisfied by affording the victim the opportunity to submit a written statement.

(3) *Victims Not in Custody.* A victim who is not in custody may exercise the right to be heard under this rule through an oral statement or by submitting a written or recorded statement.

(4) *At Sentencing.* The right to be heard at sentencing allows the victim to present evidence, information, and opinions about the criminal offense, the defendant, the sentence, or restitution. The victim also may submit a written or oral impact statement to the probation officer for use in any presentence report.

(d) Assistance and Representation.

(1) *Right to Prosecutor's Assistance.* A victim has the right to the prosecutor's assistance in asserting rights enumerated in this rule or otherwise provided by law. The prosecutor must inform a victim of these rights and provide a victim with notices and information that a victim is entitled to receive from the prosecutor by these rules and by law.

(2) *Standing.* The prosecutor has standing in any criminal proceeding, upon the victim's request, to assert any of the rights to which a victim is entitled by this rule or by any other provision of law.

(3) *Conflicts.* If any conflict arises between the prosecutor and a victim in asserting the victim's rights, the prosecutor must advise the victim of the right to seek independent legal counsel and provide contact information for the appropriate state or local bar association.

(4) *Representation by Counsel.* In asserting any of the rights enumerated in this rule or provided by any other provision of law, a victim has the right to be represented by personal counsel of the victim's choice. After a victim's counsel files a notice of appearance, all parties must endorse the victim's counsel on all pleadings. When present, the victim's counsel must be included in all bench conferences and in chambers meetings with the trial court that directly involve the victim's constitutional rights. At any proceeding to determine restitution, the victim has the right to present information and make argument to the court personally or through counsel.

(e) Victim's Duties.

(1) *Generally.* Any victim desiring to claim the notification rights and privileges provided in this rule must provide his or her full name, address, and telephone number to the entity prosecuting the case and to any other entity from which the victim requests notice, and to keep this information current.

(2) *Legal Entities.*

(A) Designation of a Representative. If a victim is a corporation, partnership, association, or other legal entity that has requested notice of the hearings to which it is entitled by law, that legal entity must promptly designate a representative by giving notice to the prosecutor and to any other entity from which the victim requests notice. The notice must include the representative's address and telephone number.

(B) Notice. The prosecutor must notify the defendant and the court if the prosecutor receives notice under (e)(2)(A).

(C) Effect. After notice is provided under (e)(2)(B), only the representative designated under (e)(2)(A) may assert the victim's rights on behalf of the legal entity.

(D) Changes in Designation. The legal entity must provide any change in designation in writing to the prosecutor and to any other entity from which the victim requests notice. The prosecutor must notify the defendant and court of any change in designation.

(f) Waiver. A victim may waive the rights and privileges enumerated in this rule. A prosecutor or a court may consider a victim's failure to provide a current address and telephone number, or a legal entity's failure to designate a representative, to be a waiver of notification rights under this rule.

(g) Court Enforcement of Victim Notice Requirements.

(1) *Court's Duty to Inquire.* At the beginning of any proceeding that takes place more than 7 days after the filing of charges by the State and at which the victim has a right to be heard, the court must inquire of the State or otherwise determine whether the victim has requested notice and has been notified of the proceeding.

(2) *If the Victim Has Been Notified.* If the victim has been notified as requested, the court must further inquire of the State whether the victim is present. If the victim is present and the State advises the court that the victim wishes the court to address the victim, the court must inquire whether the State has advised the victim of their rights. If not, the court must recess the hearing and the State must immediately comply with (d)(1).

(3) *If the Victim Has Not Been Notified.* If the victim has not been notified as requested, the court may not proceed unless public policy, the specific provisions of a statute, or the interests of due process require otherwise. In the absence of such considerations, the court may reconsider any ruling made at a proceeding at which the victim did not receive notice as requested.

(h) Appointment of Victim's Representative. Upon request, the court must appoint a representative for a minor victim or for an incapacitated victim, as provided in A.R.S. § 13-4403. The court must notify the parties if it appoints a representative.

Credits

Added by Aug. 31, 2017, effective Jan. 1, 2018.

Editors' Notes

HISTORICAL AND STATUTORY NOTES

Former Rule 39, relating to victims' rights, was abrogated effective Jan. 1, 2018. See, now, this rule.

Rule 40. Transfer for Juvenile Prosecution

(Refs & Annos)
IX. Miscellaneous
Rule 40. Transfer for Juvenile Prosecution
16A A.R.S. Rules Crim.Proc., Rule 40

Rule 40. Transfer for Juvenile Prosecution

(a) Scope. This rule applies to defendants who are eligible for transfer to juvenile court under A.R.S. § 13-504.

(b) Initiation. The court must hold a hearing to determine whether prosecution of a defendant should be transferred to juvenile court if:

(1) the defendant files a motion requesting transfer; or

(2) the court enters an order stating that a transfer hearing is being set in the court's discretion or is required by law.

(c) Contents of Motion and Court Order. The motion or order under (b) must designate the offense or offenses that are the subject of the transfer hearing.

(d) Timing.

(1) *Request for Transfer.* A motion for transfer or a court order setting a transfer hearing must be filed no later than 45 days after the arraignment date.

(2) *Hearing Date.* The court must hold a transfer hearing no later than 45 days after a motion or order is filed under (b). The court may continue the hearing for good cause.

(e) Disclosure. Setting a hearing under (d)(2) does not suspend the parties' Rule 15 disclosure duties.

(f) Transfer Investigation. After the court sets a transfer hearing, it may order the adult or juvenile probation departments to conduct a transfer investigation and prepare a written report that addresses issues the court will consider at the transfer hearing. The adult and juvenile probation departments may confer as necessary to complete the investigation. The court must provide a copy of the report to all parties at least 5 days before the hearing, unless the parties waive the deadline.

(g) Prior Transfer. The court may waive the provisions of (f) if an Arizona court has previously transferred the defendant for juvenile prosecution. The court may consider, and must provide to the parties, any prior orders of transfer, probation reports, or reports pertaining to physical, psychological, or psychiatric evaluations introduced into evidence in a prior transfer proceeding.

(h) Transfer Hearing. At a transfer hearing, the court must determine whether the defendant has shown by clear and convincing evidence that public safety and the rehabilitation of the defendant, if adjudicated delinquent in juvenile court, would be best served by transferring the prosecution to juvenile court. The court must consider those factors provided in A.R.S. § 13-504(D).

(i) Privilege.

(1) *Statements About Events Relating to Charged Offenses.* Unless the defendant consents, the defendant's statements obtained under (f), or evidence resulting from those statements, concerning the events that form the basis of the charges against the defendant are inadmissible in any proceeding to determine the defendant's guilt of those charges.

(2) *Statements About Other Events or Transactions.* Unless the defendant consents, the defendant's statements obtained under (f), or evidence resulting from those statements, concerning any other events or transactions are inadmissible in any proceeding to determine the defendant's guilt of other offenses based on those events or transactions.

(3) *Right to Remain Silent.* A defendant's decision to testify at the transfer hearing does not waive the defendant's right to remain silent during the trial or adjudication hearing. Neither the fact that the defendant testified at the transfer hearing nor the defendant's testimony at the hearing may be mentioned to the trier of fact unless the defendant testifies at trial concerning the same matters.

(j) Order of Transfer. After the transfer hearing, the court must determine with all possible speed whether to transfer the defendant to juvenile court. It must state its reasons in writing in a minute entry or order, and may not take any other action in the case until it makes this determination.

(k) Further Juvenile Proceedings. If the court orders the defendant's transfer for juvenile prosecution, the indictment or information will serve as the juvenile petition for the transferred charges. No later than 48 hours after the order transferring prosecution is entered, the clerk must file a copy of the indictment or information in the juvenile court.

(l) Release. If the court orders the defendant's transfer for juvenile prosecution, the court must determine if the defendant should be released or detained in a juvenile detention facility pending further proceedings. In making the release determination, the court must consider the factors listed in Rule 23(D), Rules of Procedure for the Juvenile Court.

Credits

Added by Aug. 31, 2017, effective Jan. 1, 2018.

Editors' Notes

HISTORICAL AND STATUTORY NOTES

Former Rule 40, relating to transfer for juvenile prosecution, was abrogated effective Jan. 1, 2018. See, now, this rule.

16A A. R. S. Rules Crim. Proc., Rule 40, AZ ST RCRP Rule 40

Current with amendments received through 08/15/19

Rule 41. Forms

(Refs & Annos)

IX. Miscellaneous

Rule 41. Forms

16A A.R.S. Rules Crim.Proc., Rule 41

Rule 41. Forms

Arizona courts are required to use Form 2 (arrest warrant). The other forms in the following Appendix are recommended for use in Arizona courts and are sufficient to meet the requirements of these rules.

Credits

Added by Aug. 31, 2017, effective Jan. 1, 2018.

Editors' Notes

HISTORICAL AND STATUTORY NOTES

Former Rule 41, relating to forms, was repealed effective Jan. 1, 2018.

16A A. R. S. Rules Crim. Proc., Rule 41, AZ ST RCRP Rule 41

Current with amendments received through 08/15/19

Form 1. Reserved

(Refs & Annos)

IX. Miscellaneous

Rule 41. Forms

Forms

16A A.R.S. Rules Crim.Proc., Form 1

Form 1. Reserved

Editors' Notes

HISTORICAL NOTES

Former Form 1 was abrogated effective January 1, 2008.

16A A. R. S. Rules Crim. Proc., Form 1, AZ ST RCRP Form 1

Current with amendments received through 08/15/19

Form 2. Abrogated April 11, 2016, effective July 1, 2016

(Refs & Annos)
IX. Miscellaneous
Rule 41. Forms
Forms

16A A.R.S. Rules Crim.Proc., Form 2

Form 2. Abrogated April 11, 2016, effective July 1, 2016

Editors' Notes

HISTORICAL NOTES

Former Form 2, relating to arrest warrant, was added Aug. 27, 2015, effective Jan. 1, 2016.

16A A. R. S. Rules Crim. Proc., Form 2, AZ ST RCRP Form 2

Current with amendments received through 08/15/19

Form 2(a). Arrest Warrant: Superior Court

(Refs & Annos)
IX. Miscellaneous
Rule 41. Forms
Forms

16A A.R.S. Rules Crim.Proc., Form 2(a)

Form 2(a). Arrest Warrant: Superior Court

_____COURT _____County, Arizona

STATE OF ARIZONA	Plaintiff		ARREST WARRANT
-vs			
			CASE NO.
_____			
Defendant(s) (First, MI, Last) *Address			

TO: ANY AUTHORIZED LAW ENFORCEMENT OFFICER,

YOU ARE COMMANDED to arrest and bring the defendant before this court. If this court is unavailable or if the arrest is made in another county, you shall take the defendant before the nearest or most accessible Magistrate. The defendant is accused of an offense or violation based on the following:

[List reason for issuing the warrant] [Include interstate compact statement for probation violations]

This offense or violation is briefly described as follows:

Offense Date	Statute/Rule & Literal Description	Class
_____	_____	_____

The defendant may be released if a $_____ _[secured appearance] [cash] [unsecured appearance]_ bond is posted by or on behalf of the accused OR

☐ _The defendant is not eligible for release on bond. [Explain – add additional orders of the court]_
[Add fingerprint instruction if known – 01 criminal history, 04 ID print, 09 civil]

☐ Yes   ☐ No   ☐ Unknown The offense is, or is materially related to, a victims' rights applicable offense.

_BY ORDER OF: The Honorable _____, Judge of _____ Court. [If signed by the Deputy Clerk]_

Date _____

_____ [Printed name of the Judge or Deputy Clerk of Superior Court]

SEX:	RACE:	DOB:	HGT:	WGT:	EYES:	HAIR:
ADDRESS: [:TYPE____]						
COURT ORI:		WARRANT #: *		EXTRADITION: *		
DL#: *		STATE: *		PURGE DATE: *		
LE AGENCY: [Arresting Agency]		CITATION #: *		DR #: *		

[*optional information can vary by court and may include the last four digits of the defendant's SSN]

CERTIFICATE OF EXECUTION

I certify that the defendant was arrested at _____ a.m./p.m. on _____ _____, 20_____,
                                                                                    (month)   (day)   (year)
and presented defendant before Judge _____ at _____.

_____
Date

_____
Agency

_____
Deputy Sheriff / Officer   Badge #

303

Credits

Added effective April 11, 2016, where available, mandatorily effective July 1, 2016.

Editors' Notes

HISTORICAL AND STATUTORY NOTES

Former Rule 2(a), relating to arrest warrant, was abrogated effective January 1, 2016.

16A A. R. S. Rules Crim. Proc., Form 2(a), AZ ST RCRP Form 2(a)

Current with amendments received through 08/15/19

Form 2(b). Arrest Warrant: Limited Jurisdiction Courts

(Refs & Annos)

IX. Miscellaneous

Rule 41. Forms

Forms

16A A.R.S. Rules Crim.Proc., Form 2(b)

Form 2(b). Arrest Warrant: Limited Jurisdiction Courts

_____COURT _____County, Arizona

STATE OF ARIZONA Plaintiff	CASE NO.	ARREST WARRANT
-vs		
_____ Defendant(s) (First, MI, Last) *Address		

TO: ANY AUTHORIZED LAW ENFORCEMENT OFFICER,

YOU ARE COMMANDED to arrest and bring the defendant before this court. If this court is unavailable or if the arrest is made in another county, you shall take the defendant before the nearest or most accessible Magistrate. The defendant is accused of an offense or violation based on the following:

[List reason for issuing the warrant] [Include interstate compact statement for probation violations]

This offense or violation is briefly described as follows:

Offense Date	**Statute/Rule & Literal Description**	**Class**
_____	_____	_____

The defendant may be released if a $_____ *[secured appearance] [cash] [unsecured appearance]* bond is posted by or on behalf of the accused OR

☐ *The defendant is not eligible for release on bond. [Explain / add additional orders of the court]*

[Add fingerprint instruction if known – 01 criminal history, 04 ID print, 09 civil]

☐ Yes   ☐ No   ☐ Unknown The offense is, or is materially related to, a victims' rights applicable offense.

Date				**Judge** [Judges Name Printed]			
SEX:	**RACE:**	**DOB:**	**HGT:**	**WGT:**		**EYES:**	**HAIR:**
ADDRESS: [TYPE:____]							
COURT ORI:		WARRANT #: *			EXTRADITION: *		
DL#: *		STATE: *			PURGE DATE: *		
LE AGENCY: [Arresting Agency]		CITATION #: *			DR #: *		

[*optional information can vary by court and may include the last four digits of the defendant's SSN]

CERTIFICATE OF EXECUTION

I certify that the defendant was arrested at _____ a.m./p.m. on _____ _____, 20_____,
                                                                                                 (month)   (day)   (year)

and presented defendant before Judge _____ at _____.

_____   _____
Date   Agency

                                                                _____
                                                                Deputy Sheriff / Officer   Badge #

Credits

Added effective April 11, 2016, where available, mandatorily effective July 1, 2016.

Editors' Notes

HISTORICAL AND STATUTORY NOTES

Former Rule 2(b), relating to arrest warrant: pre-adjudication, was abrogated effective January 1, 2016.

16A A. R. S. Rules Crim. Proc., Form 2(b), AZ ST RCRP Form 2(b)

Current with amendments received through 08/15/19

Form 2(c). Abrogated

(Refs & Annos)

IX. Miscellaneous

Rule 41. Forms

Forms

16A A.R.S. Rules Crim.Proc., Form 2(c)

Form 2(c). Abrogated

Editors' Notes

HISTORICAL NOTES

Former Form 2(c), relating to arrest warrant: post-adjudication was abrogated effective January 1, 2016.

16A A. R. S. Rules Crim. Proc., Form 2(c), AZ ST RCRP Form 2(c)

Current with amendments received through 08/15/19

Form 2(d). Abrogated

(Refs & Annos)

IX. Miscellaneous

Rule 41. Forms

Forms

16A A.R.S. Rules Crim.Proc., Form 2(d)

Form 2(d). Abrogated

Editors' Notes

HISTORICAL NOTES

Former Form 2(d), relating to arrest warrant: failure to pay was abrogated effective January 1, 2016.

16A A. R. S. Rules Crim. Proc., Form 2(d), AZ ST RCRP Form 2(d)

Current with amendments received through 08/15/19

Form 2(e). Abrogated

(Refs & Annos)

IX. Miscellaneous

Rule 41. Forms

Forms

16A A.R.S. Rules Crim.Proc., Form 2(e)

Form 2(e). Abrogated

Editors' Notes

HISTORICAL NOTES

Former Form 2(e), relating to arrest warrant: probation violation was abrogated effective January 1, 2016.

16A A. R. S. Rules Crim. Proc., Form 2(e), AZ ST RCRP Form 2(e)

Current with amendments received through 08/15/19

Form 2(f). Abrogated

(Refs & Annos)

IX. Miscellaneous

Rule 41. Forms

Forms

16A A.R.S. Rules Crim.Proc., Form 2(f)

Form 2(f). Abrogated

Editors' Notes

HISTORICAL NOTES

Former Form 2(f), relating to arrest warrant: failure to appear was abrogated effective January 1, 2016.

16A A. R. S. Rules Crim. Proc., Form 2(f), AZ ST RCRP Form 2(f)

Current with amendments received through 08/15/19

Form 2(g). Abrogated

16A A.R.S. Rules Crim.Proc., Form 2(g)

Form 2(g). Abrogated

Editors' Notes
HISTORICAL NOTES
Former Form 2(g), relating to arrest warrant: long form/probable cause was abrogated effective January 1, 2016.
16A A. R. S. Rules Crim. Proc., Form 2(g), AZ ST RCRP Form 2(g)
Current with amendments received through 08/15/19

Form 2(h). Abrogated

16A A.R.S. Rules Crim.Proc., Form 2(h)

Form 2(h). Abrogated

Editors' Notes
HISTORICAL NOTES
Former Form 2(h), relating to arrest warrant: violation of promise to appear was abrogated effective January 1, 2016.
16A A. R. S. Rules Crim. Proc., Form 2(h), AZ ST RCRP Form 2(h)
Current with amendments received through 08/15/19

Form 3(a). Summons: Ten-Print Fingerprint Required

Rule 41. Forms
Forms

16A A.R.S. Rules Crim.Proc., Form 3(a)

Form 3(a). Summons: Ten-Print Fingerprint Required

_____COURT	_____County, Arizona	
STATE OF ARIZONA Plaintiff	[CASE/COMPLAINT NO.]	SUMMONS
-vs-		(Ten-print Fingerprint Required)
_____		
Defendant (FIRST, MI, LAST)		

TO:

YOU ARE ORDERED
to appear at [name of entity and address]

*(Required for all felonies, domestic violence, sexual or DUI offenses)*_____
between the hours of ___ a.m./p.m. at any time prior to your court appearance date
to be photographed and ten-print fingerprinted.
YOU ARE SUMMONED to appear before this court for the following reason:
[(List reason for summons; e.g., filing of indictment, information or complaint (list charges or other reasons)].
YOU ARE ORDERED TO REPORT on _____, 20 ___ at _____
a.m./p.m.
LOCATED AT:

IF YOU FAIL TO APPEAR AS ORDERED, A WARRANT MAY BE ISSUED FOR YOUR ARREST.
Date:

Judicial Officer

Requests for reasonable accommodation for persons with disabilities must be made to the court by parties at least 3 working days in advance of a scheduled court proceeding.

CERTIFICATE OF PERSONAL SERVICE
I swear that I personally served this summons as follows:

Date Received: Date Served: Time Served:

Person Served:

Location Where Served:

_____County.

Officer Serving Summons

CERTIFICATE OF SERVICE BY MAILING

I certify that a copy of this document was sent by Registered or Certified mail, return receipt requested, to the defendant at the above-listed address.
Dated:

CLERK

Form 3(a)

Credits

Added Sept. 5, 2007, effective Jan. 1, 2008. Amended on an emergency basis Sept. 3, 2009, effective Jan. 1, 2010. Amended on a permanent basis effective Sept. 2, 2010.

Editors' Notes

HISTORICAL NOTES

Former Form 3 was abrogated effective January 1, 2008.

16A A. R. S. Rules Crim. Proc., Form 3(a), AZ ST RCRP Form 3(a)

Current with amendments received through 08/15/19

Form 3(b). Summons: Fingerprint Not Required

(Refs & Annos)

IX. Miscellaneous

Rule 41. Forms

Forms

16A A.R.S. Rules Crim.Proc., Form 3(b)

Form 3(b). Summons: Fingerprint Not Required

_____ COURT   _____ County,
Arizona

STATE OF ARIZONA Plaintiff   [CASE/COMPLAINT
NO.]

-vs-   SUMMONS
(Fingerprint Not
Required)

Defendant (FIRST, MI, LAST)

TO:

YOU ARE SUMMONED to appear before this court for the following reason:
    *[(List reason for summons; e.g., filing of indictment, information or complaint (list
charges or other reasons)].*
YOU ARE ORDERED TO REPORT on _____, 20 ___ at ___ a.m./p.m.
LOCATED AT:

IF YOU FAIL TO APPEAR AS ORDERED, A WARRANT MAY BE ISSUED FOR
YOUR ARREST.
Date: _____

                               Judicial Officer

Requests for reasonable accommodation for persons with disabilities must be made
to the court by parties at least 3 working days in advance of a scheduled court
proceeding.

CERTIFICATE OF PERSONAL SERVICE

I swear that I personally served this summons as follows:

Date Received: Date Served: Time Served:

Person Served:

Location Where Served:

_____ County.

                          Officer Serving Summons

CERTIFICATE OF SERVICE BY MAILING

I certify that a copy of this document was sent by Registered or Certified mail,
return receipt requested, to the defendant at the above-listed address.

Dated: _____

CLERK

Credits
Added Sept. 5, 2007, effective Jan. 1, 2008.
16A A. R. S. Rules Crim. Proc., Form 3(b), AZ ST RCRP Form 3(b)
Current with amendments received through 08/15/19

Form 4(a). Release Questionnaire/Law Enforcement

(Refs & Annos)
IX. Miscellaneous
Rule 41. Forms
Forms

16A A.R.S. Rules Crim.Proc., Form 4(a)

Form 4(a). Release Questionnaire/Law Enforcement

_____ COURT [Precinct _] _____ County, Arizona

State of Arizona Plaintiff -vs- _____ Defendant (FIRST, MI, LAST)	[CASE/COMPLAINT NO.] Booking No. _____	RELEASE QUESTIONNAIRE (To be completed by Law Enforcement)

Alias(es) _____

A.   GENERAL INFORMATION

Charges: _____

Offense Date: _____ Offense Time: _____

Location: _____
_____

Arrest Date: _____ Arrest Time: _____

Arrest Location: _____

Pursuant to A.R.S. §41-1750, were ten-print fingerprints taken of the arrested Person?   [ ] Yes [ ] No

Pursuant to §13-610 does one or more of the above charges require the arresting agency to secure a DNA sample from the arrested person?   [ ] Yes [ ] No

If yes, does the defendant have a valid DNA sample on file with AZDPS?   [ ] Yes [ ] No [ ] Unknown

If no, has the arresting agency taken the required sample?
                [ ] Yes [ ] No

B.   PROBABLE CAUSE STATEMENT

1.   Summarize and include the facts which establish **probable cause for the crime(s) charged**. Certain felonies may be non-bondable and require facts which establish **proof evident or presumption great** for the crime(s) charged. These include (1) felonies involving a capital offense, sexual assault, sexual conduct with a minor who was under fifteen years of age, or molestation of a child who is under fifteen years of age, and (2) felony offenses committed when the person charged is already admitted to bail on a separate felony charge.

Explain the crime(s) in detail (e.g., arresting officer or other law enforcement officers witnessed offense, physical evidence directly connects defendant to offense, multiple eyewitnesses, defendant admissions, victim statements, nature of injuries, incriminating photographic, audio, visual, or computer evidence, defendant attempted to flee or resist arrest):

_____
_____
_____
_____
_____

_____
_____
_____
_____
_____
_____
_____

2.   The person entered or remained in the United States illegally. Explain in detail (e.g., admission of by the person, statements of co-defendants at the time of arrest, verification of illegal presence or proceeding establishes illegal presence): _____

_____
_____
_____
_____
_____
_____
_____
_____
_____
_____
_____
_____
_____
_____
_____
_____
_____
_____

3.   The crime(s) occurred while the person was admitted to bail on any separate felony. Provide information on the separate felony:

_____
_____
_____
_____
_____
_____
_____
_____
_____

Defendant's Name _____ DOB _____ Booking No. _____ Case No. _____

C.   OTHER INFORMATION (Check if applicable)

_____
_____
_____

1. [ ] Defendant is presently on probation, parole or any other form of release involving other charges or convictions.
Explain: _____
_____
_____
_____
_____

7. Reasons to oppose an unsecured release: _____
_____
_____
_____
_____

2. List any prior:
Arrests: _____
_____
_____
_____

8. [ ] Defendant speaks a language other than English
Language spoken: _____
[ ] American Sign Language
[ ] Defendant requested an interpreter

Convictions: _____
_____
_____
_____

D.   CIRCUMSTANCES OF THE OFFENSE

1. [ ] Defendant used firearm or other weapon
Type: _____

2. [ ] Defendant injured someone.
Explain: _____

Failures to Appear (FTA): _____
_____
_____
_____

3. [ ] Medical attention was necessary
Nature of injuries: _____

4. [ ] Defendant threatened someone
Nature of threats: _____

5. Did the offense involve a child victim?   [ ] Yes [ ] No
If yes, was DCS notified?   [ ] Yes [ ] No

Protective Orders: _____
_____
_____
_____

6. If property offense
a.   Value of property taken/damaged: _____
_____
b.   [ ] Property was recovered

3. There is an indication of:
[ ] Alcohol Abuse   [ ] Other Substance Abuse
[ ] Mental Health Issues   [ ] Physical Illness
[ ] Developmental Disability
Explain:_____
_____
_____
_____

7. Names of co-defendant(s), if any: _____
_____
_____
_____
_____

E.   CRIME(S) AGAINST PERSONS

4. Defendant is employed by: _____
Address: _____
_____

1. Relationship of defendant to victim: _____

2. [ ] Victim(s) and defendant reside together.

Phone: _____
How long: _____

3. Law enforcement learned of the situation by [ ] Victim
[ ] Third Party [ ] Officer observation

5. Defendant resides at: _____
_____

4. [ ] Previous incidents involving these same parties
Explain: _____

With Whom: _____
How Long: _____
Alternate address for court notification: _____
_____

5. Defendant is currently the subject of:
[ ] Order of Protection
[ ] Injunction against Harassment
[ ] Other court order: _____

6. Facts to indicate defendant will flee if released: _____
_____
_____
_____

6. [ ] Likelihood of inappropriate contact with victim(s)
Explain: _____

Defendant's Name _____ DOB _____ Booking No. _____ Case No. _____

7. [ ] Victim(s) expressed an opinion on defendant's release.
    Explain: _____
    _____

4   State whether defendant was under the influence of alcohol or drugs at the time of the offense
    [ ] Yes [ ] No [ ] Unknown
    Type of substance: _____
    _____

F.   DOMESTIC VIOLENCE DEFENDANT ISSUES

[ ] Access to or use of weapons
[ ] Children/Vulnerable adults present
[ ] Crime occurred in public
[ ] Control/ownership/jealousy issues
[ ] Depression
[ ] Frequency/intensity of Domestic Violence increasing
[ ] Kidnapping
[ ] Potential for multiple violations of court orders
[ ] Prior history of Domestic Violence
[ ] Prior Protective Order
[ ] Recent separations
[ ] Stalking behavior
[ ] Threats of homicide/suicide/bodily harm
[ ] Violence against children, vulnerable adults or animals
Explain: _____
_____
_____
_____

H.   DRUG OFFENSES

1. If the defendant is considered to be a drug dealer, state the supporting facts: _____
    _____
    _____
    _____

2   State quantities and types of illegal drugs directly involved with offense _____
    _____
    _____
    _____
    _____
    _____

[ ] Methamphetamine was involved:
[ ] Drug field test was positive
[ ] Defendant admission of drug type: _____
[ ] Approximate monetary value of drugs: _____

3. State whether money was seized
    [ ] Yes [ ] No
    Amount: _____

G.   CIRCUMSTANCES OF ARREST

1. Did defendant attempt to:
    [ ] Avoid arrest [ ] Resist arrest [ ] Self Surrender
    Explain: _____
    _____
    _____
    _____

2. [ ] Defendant was armed when arrested
    Type of weapon: _____
    _____
    _____
    _____

3. [ ] Evidence of the offense was found in defendant's possession
    Explain: _____
    _____
    _____
    _____

If this is a fugitive arrest, complete the affidavit as required by the Uniform Criminal Extradition Act (ARS 13-3841 et seq.)

I certify that the information presented is true to the best of my knowledge:

_____   _____ / _____ / _____
Date   Arresting Officer/Agency/ Serial No.
_____   Duty Phone No. _____
Departmental Report #

Credits

Amended June 17, 1999, effective Oct. 1, 1999. Amended and effective July 3, 2007. Adopted on permanent basis, effective Sept. 16, 2008. Amended on an expedited basis, effective Dec. 16, 2014, adopted on a permanent basis, effective Aug. 27, 2015. Amended Aug. 27, 2015, effective Jan. 1, 2016.

Editors' Notes

HISTORICAL NOTES

Former Form 4(a) was abrogated effective January 1, 2008.

16A A. R. S. Rules Crim. Proc., Form 4(a), AZ ST RCRP Form 4(a)

Current with amendments received through 08/15/19

Form 4(b). Release Questionnaire/Defendant

(Refs & Annos)

IX. Miscellaneous

Rule 41. Forms

Forms

16A A.R.S. Rules Crim.Proc., Form 4(b)

Form 4(b). Release Questionnaire/Defendant

_____COURT _____County, Arizona

State of Arizona Plaintiff -vs- _____ Defendant (FIRST, MI, LAST)	[CASE/COMPLAINT NO.] Booking No. _____	**RELEASE QUESTIONNAIRE** (To be completed by Defendant)

Alias(es)_____

The following information is for the purpose of determining the conditions under which you may be released at this time. You are not required to answer any question if you feel the answer might be harmful to you. The answers you give to the following questions will be used by the court for the purpose of determining the conditions of your release. However, your answers will be checked against the information supplied by the police, and with the references you yourself give on the form. Any discrepancies may result in higher bail or harsher conditions of release. **Any information you give may be used against you in this or any other matter.**

General Background

1. **Background and Residence**

   Full Name: _____

   Sex _____ Race _____Date of Birth _____

   Place of Birth [city, state, country]_____

   Have you served in the military services of the United States? [ ] Yes [ ] No

   Present Citizenship _____

   If you are not a United States of America citizen, how long have you been in this country? _____

   Do you need the court to provide an interpreter to help you communicate and to understand what is being said? [ ] Yes [ ] No

   If so, what language are you most comfortable speaking?
   [ ] Spanish [ ] American Sign Language [ ] Other language :_____

   Are you homeless? [ ] Yes [ ] No

   Present Address_____

   How long have you lived at the above address? _____

   Telephone No. (___)_____ Cell No. (___)_____

   Where else have you lived in the past year and for how long?
   _____

   _____

   Where will you go if released today? _____

2. **Family**

   Are you married/partnered If so, are you living with your spouse/partner? [ ] Yes [ ] No

   Are you living with someone? Relationship: _____

   How many other persons (including your children) are living with you? _____

   How much do you contribute to their support? _____

   Do you have regular contact with any other relatives? [ ] Yes [ ] No

   Explain _____

   _____

3. **Employment**

   Are you presently employed? [ ] Yes [ ] No If not, what is your principal means of support?

   Explain: _____

   Employer's Name _____

   Address: _____

   Telephone No. (___) _____

   What is the nature of your job? _____

   How long have you worked there?_____

4. **Criminal Record**

   Do you have any previous criminal record? [ ] Yes [ ] No

   Explain _____

   _____

5. **Record of Appearance**

   Have you ever been released on bail or other conditions pending trial? [ ] Yes [ ] No

   Did you ever fail to appear as required? [ ] Yes [ ] No

   Explain _____

   _____

6. Supervision

Is there any organization or any person who might agree to supervise you and be responsible for your return to court as required? [ ] Yes [ ] No

Organization or person to contact _____

				( )
Address	City	State Zip		Telephone

7. Other Circumstances

Are there any other matters (such as your health or illness in your family) which you feel the court should consider in making its decision? _____

8. Verification

Is there any other friend, relative, neighbor or other person who can be called as a reference to this information?

				( )
Name	Address	City	State Zip	Telephone

				( )
Name	Address	City	State Zip	Telephone

				( )
Name	Address	City	State Zip	Telephone

I certify, under penalty of perjury, that the information presented is true and correct to the best of my knowledge.

_____   _____
Date   Defendant Signature
                                                   Contact Telephone No. _____

Credits
Amended June 17, 1999, effective Oct. 1, 1999. Amended and effective July 3, 2007. Adopted on permanent basis, effective Sept. 16, 2008. Amended Aug. 27, 2015, effective Jan. 1, 2016.
Editors' Notes
HISTORICAL NOTES
Former Form 4(b) was abrogated effective January 1, 2008.
16A A. R. S. Rules Crim. Proc., Form 4(b), AZ ST RCRP Form 4(b)
Current with amendments received through 08/15/19

Form 4(c). Release Questionnaire

(Refs & Annos)
IX. Miscellaneous
Rule 41. Forms
Forms

16A A.R.S. Rules Crim.Proc., Form 4(c)

Form 4(c). Release Questionnaire

Intimate Partner Risk Assessment *

Defendant's Name _____ DOB _____ Booking No. _____
Law Enforcement Agency _____ Report No. _____
Victim's Name _____ Incident Date _____

Questions are asked on the scene; Victim participation is voluntary	Yes	No	Decline
Tier 1			
1. Has physical violence **increased in frequency or severity** over the past six months? Alternate wording: Is the pushing, grabbing, hitting, or other violence happening more often?			
2. Is he/she violently and constantly **jealous** of you?			
3. Do you believe he/she is **capable of killing** you?			
4. Has he/she ever beaten you while you were **pregnant**? (e.g. hit, kicked, shoved, pushed, thrown, or physically hurt with a weapon or object)			
5. Has he/she ever used **a weapon** or object to hurt or threaten you?			
6. Has he/she ever **tried to kill** you?			
7. Has he/she ever choked/strangled/suffocated you?			
7a. If you answered "Yes" to Question 7, has this happened more than once?			
Tier 2			
8. Does he/she **control** most or all of your daily activities?			
9. Is he/she known to carry or possess a **gun**?			
10. Has he/she ever **forced you to have sex** when you did not wish to do so?			
11. Does he/she use **illegal drugs or misuse prescription drugs**? (e.g. meth, cocaine, painkillers)			
12. Has he/she threatened to **harm people you care about**?			
13. Did you **end your relationship** with him/her within the past six months?			
13a. If you answered "No" to Question 13, does he/she know or sense you are planning on ending your relationship?			
14. Has he/she experienced **significant financial loss** in the last six months?			
15. Is he/she **unemployed**?			
16. Has he/she ever threatened or tried to commit **suicide**?			
17. Has he/she **threatened to kill** you?			
18. Has he/she threatened or abused your **pets**?			

"Yes" to 2 or 3 Tier 1 questions = "Elevated Risk" / "Yes" to 4 or more Tier 1 questions = "High Risk"
"Elevated Risk" and "High Risk" scores trigger law enforcement officers to offer follow up responses in the form of providing or connecting victims to supportive resources or resource information.

Action: ☐ Victim referred for follow up based on responses to the assessment
 ☐ Victim referred for follow up based on the officer's professional judgment
 ☐ No referral

* To be considered at Initial Appearance. *See* A.R.S. § 13-3967(B).

Credits

Added effective April 2, 2018.

16A A. R. S. Rules Crim. Proc., Form 4(c), AZ ST RCRP Form 4(c)

Current with amendments received through 08/15/19

Form 5(a). Defendant's Financial Statement

(Refs & Annos)

IX. Miscellaneous

Rule 41. Forms

Forms

16A A.R.S. Rules Crim.Proc., Form 5(a)

Form 5(a). Defendant's Financial Statement

_____ COURT   _____ County, Arizona

STATE OF ARIZONA Plaintiff	[CASE/COMPLAINT NO.]
⁻vs⁻	DEFENDANT'S FINANCIAL STATEMENT (Confidential)
Defendant (FIRST, MI, LAST)	

INSTRUCTIONS TO THE DEFENDANT: You are to answer the following questions so the Judge can decide whether to appoint an attorney to represent you and/or, if a bond is required, how much it should be, or any other matter relating to indigence. Use care in filling in your answers. If you need more space for any answer, note such and write on the back of the page. If you knowingly give false or misleading information, you may be punished for contempt of court or subjected to prosecution for fraud or perjury.

1. Full name:

2. Check the appropriate box: [ ] Single [ ] Married, living w/ spouse [ ] Married but separated [ ] Divorced [ ] Widowed [ ] Partnered

3. In addition to yourself, how many other adults do you support?

_____
How many children?

INCOME:

4. List below in Column 1 the money that you are paid or receive each month. If you are married and are living with your spouse, list below in Column 2 the money that your spouse is paid or receives each month. If you are separated, divorced, widowed, partnered or single, leave Column 2 blank.

	Column 1 Amount paid to Me Monthly	Column 2 Amount paid to Spouse Monthly
a. Wages, Salaries, Self Employment Income	$	$
b. Payroll deductions	$	$
c. Unemployment compensation	$	$
d. Welfare benefits	$	$
e. Disability benefits	$	$
f. Veteran's benefits	$	$
g. Social Security benefits	$	$
h. Worker's compensation	$	$
i. Accident benefits	$	$
j. Retirement benefits	$	$
k. Allotment checks	$	$
l. Interest	$	$
m. Dividends	$	$
n. Child support received	$	$
o. Alimony or maintenance received	$	$
p. Total of any other income received Source:	$	$
TOTAL MONTHLY INCOME:	$	$

ASSETS:

5. Cash: List below the amounts of cash held or value of:

a. Cash on you, your spouse, or in your jail property, and at home $

b. $

Cash in banks, credit unions, and elsewhere

c. $

Cash owed to you or to your spouse by others

d. $

Stocks and bonds; insurance policy cash values

e. $

Beneficial interest in a trust

6. Personal Property: List below any valuable personal property you own and have not listed above which is not needed by you or your family for day-to-day living.

a. Description

$	$	$
(value)	(owed)	(net value)

b. Description

$	$	$
(value)	(owed)	(net value)

c. Description

$	$	$
(value)	(owed)	(net value)

7. Auto: Complete the following information about any motor vehicles (e.g.: cars, trucks, trailers, boats, airplanes, motorcycles) that you are buying, that you own, or in which you claim to have an interest.

a. Make, Year and Model

$	$	$
(value)	(owed)	(net value)

b. Make, Year and Model

$	$	$
(value)	(owed)	(net value)

8. Real Estate: Complete the following information about any real property (your home, other land, or buildings) that you are buying, that you own, or in which you claim to have an interest.

a. Location

$	$	$
(value)	(owed)	(net value)

b. Location

$	$	$
(value)	(owed)	(net value)

TOTAL AVAILABLE ASSETS: $

EXPENSES:
9. List below all monthly expenses not already deducted from your pay.

   a. Rent or house payment $

   b. Total cost of utilities (water, electric, gas, telephone, $
      trash)

   c. Food $

   d. Credit card payments $

   e. Installment loan payments $

   f. Charge account payments $

   g. Motor vehicle payments $

   h. Union dues $

   i. Medical care costs (doctors, dentists, medicine) $

   j. Child support and alimony $

   k. Cost of baby-sitter $

   l. Motor vehicle insurance, maintenance and gas $

10. Do you have any expenses (monthly or otherwise) not shown above? If yes,
    please list below.

   a. $

                              (how often   (how much)
                              paid)
   b. $

                              (how often   (how much)
                              paid)
   c. $

                              (how often   (how much)
                              paid)
   TOTAL MONTHLY EXPENSES: $

11. Are any of your expenses past due? If yes, please list below.

a. _____ $ _____

                                   (how often   (how much)
                                   paid)

b. _____ $ _____

                                   (how often   (how much)
                                   paid)

c. _____ $ _____

                                   (how often   (how much)
                                   paid)

12. Do you have an attorney to help you with this case? [ ] Yes [ ] No
    If yes, what is his/her name: _____ If no, are you planning to hire your own attorney? [ ] Yes [ ] No

13. Do you want the Court to appoint an attorney (public defender) to help you with this case? [ ] Yes [ ] No
    a. How much can you pay as a down payment for $
       attorney fees?
    b. How much can you pay each month for attorney fees? $

14. Oath under penalty of perjury: I have truthfully and completely given the information in this statement. I have not knowingly concealed, or in any way misrepresented, my financial resources. I am aware that I may be held in contempt of court, or prosecuted for perjury if I have made any false statements or misrepresentation, or concealment, or if I continue to accept the services of a court appointed attorney after my financial condition has materially changed without notifying my court appointed attorney. In any such case, I understand that this application may be used against me.

I hereby make these representations under PENALTY OF PERJURY:

Date: Defendant Signature:

Witnessed by: Social Security No.:

                                                      Form 5(a)

Credits
Added Sept. 5, 2007, effective Jan. 1, 2008.
Editors' Notes
HISTORICAL NOTES
Former Form 5 was abrogated effective January 1, 2008.
16A A. R. S. Rules Crim. Proc., Form 5(a), AZ ST RCRP Form 5(a)
Current with amendments received through 08/15/19

Form 5(b). Motion for Appointment of Counsel

(Refs & Annos)
IX. Miscellaneous
Rule 41. Forms
Forms

16A A.R.S. Rules Crim.Proc., Form 5(b)

Form 5(b). Motion for Appointment of Counsel

_____COURT   [Precinct _____]   _____County, Arizona

STATE OF ARIZONA Plaintiff   [CASE/COMPLAINT NO.]
-vs-   MOTION FOR
                                                                    APPOINTMENT
                                                                    OF COUNSEL

Defendant (FIRST, MI, LAST)

MOTION FOR APPOINTMENT OF COUNSEL

Defendant moves for the appointment of Counsel and declares that Defendant's financial circumstances will not allow the hiring of a private attorney in this case.

Signature   Date   Phone No.

Address

ORDER

[ ] Motion for Court Appointed Counsel is granted.
     (Check if applicable)
     [ ] A financial assessment is ordered for a recommendation to the Court as to defendant's eligibility and any contribution amount to the cost of the court appointed attorney.
     [ ] $ _____ for financial assessment.
     [ ] $ _____ for contribution to the cost of the court appointed attorney.
     [ ] Legal Services to be provided by

     Phone No.

[ ] Motion for court appointed attorney is denied.

Judicial Officer   Date   Courtroom

Form 5(b)

Credits

Added Sept. 5, 2007, effective Jan. 1, 2008.

16A A. R. S. Rules Crim. Proc., Form 5(b), AZ ST RCRP Form 5(b)

Current with amendments received through 08/15/19

Form 6. Release Order

(Refs & Annos)

IX. Miscellaneous

Rule 41. Forms

Forms

16A A.R.S. Rules Crim.Proc., Form 6

Form 6. Release Order

_____ COURT _____ County, Arizona

STATE OF ARIZONA Plaintiff -vs-										RELEASE ORDER			
Defendant (FIRST, MI, LAST)			Booking Number				Date of Birth						
LINE #	COMPLAINT NO.	VIOLATION CODE	NF	ORR	PSR	3P	BOND	BA	UB	DB	SB	CB	NB
1							$						
2							$						
3							$						
4							$						
5							$						

(NF=Charge not filed; ORR=Own recognizance release; PSR=Pretrial supervision release; 3P=Third party custody; Bond=Amount of bond; BA=Bond applies; UB=Unsecured bond; DB=Deposit bond; SB=Secured bond; CB=Cash bond; NB=Non-bailable)

If you are released from jail, you must follow all release conditions and appear at court as indicated below:

MANDATORY AND STANDARD CONDITIONS OF YOUR RELEASE:

[X] **1.** Appear at _____ court on: _____ at _____ a.m. / p.m., Courtroom: _____
              (Court name and address)   (Date)   (Time)
    for _____ and attend all future court hearings.

[X] **2.** Violate no federal, state or local criminal laws.

[X] **3.** Not leave the state of Arizona without written permission from the court.
    [ ] Defendant may leave the state of Arizona provided defendant returns for court dates.

[X] **4.** Diligently pursue any appeal if released from custody after judgment and sentence have been imposed.

[ ] **5.** Maintain contact with your attorney.

[ ] **6.** Provide a current address and phone number to the court and to your attorney and immediately notify both of any changes.

[ ] **7.** Not threaten or initiate any type of contact with the alleged victim(s).

[ ] **8.** Not drive a motor vehicle without a valid driver's license in your possession.

[ ] **9.** Not threaten or initiate any type of contact with any person as specified here: _____.

[ ] **10.** Not possess weapons as specified here: _____.

[ ] **11.** Not consume any alcoholic beverages.

[ ] **12.** Not go to scene of the alleged crime.

[ ] **13.** Not go to locations as specified here: _____.

[ ] **14.** Comply with 3rd party custody release conditions as specified here: _____.

[ ] **15.** Contact probation or parole officer.   (See 3rd party obligations in this document.)

[ ] **16.** Electronic monitoring, if available, (mandatory if charged with a felony offense under Chapters 14 or 35.1 of Title 13)

[ ] **17.** Other: _____.

ADDITIONAL CONDITIONS FOR YOUR PRETRIAL SUPERVISION RELEASE (PSR):

[ ] **18.** Comply with the assigned pretrial supervision program as specified here: _____.

[ ] **19.** Provide a current address and phone number to Pretrial Services immediately and notify of any changes.

FINANCIAL CONDITIONS OF RELEASE: If you cannot post an appearance bond of $ _____ you will remain in custody until your next court hearing on _____.

> **IF YOU VIOLATE THIS ORDER: You have the right to be present at your trial and at all other proceedings in your case. IF YOU FAIL TO APPEAR THE COURT MAY ISSUE A WARRANT FOR YOUR ARREST AND/OR HOLD THE TRIAL OR PROCEEDING IN YOUR ABSENCE. IF CONVICTED, YOU WILL BE REQUIRED TO APPEAR FOR SENTENCING. IF YOU FAIL TO APPEAR, YOU MAY LOSE YOUR RIGHT TO A DIRECT APPEAL.**

If you violate any condition of a bond, the court may order the bond and any related security deposit forfeited to the State of Arizona. In addition, the court may issue a warrant for your arrest upon learning of any violation of the conditions of release. After a hearing, if the court finds that you have not complied with the release conditions, the court may modify the conditions or revoke the release altogether.

If you are released on a felony charge, and the court finds the proof evident or the presumption great that you committed a felony during the period of release, the court must revoke your release. You may also be subject to an additional criminal charge, and upon conviction you could be punished by imprisonment in addition to the punishment which would otherwise be imposable for the crime committed during the period of release. Upon finding that you violated conditions of release, the court may also find you in contempt of court and sentence you to a term of imprisonment, a fine, or both.

ACKNOWLEDGEMENT: I fully understand and will comply with all release conditions indicated above and further understand the consequences should I violate any part of this order.

_____

Current Address where you live   Apt. No.

_____

Address where you receive mail if different from current address

(   )_____   (   )_____
Phone No.   Phone No.

X_____   X_____
Defendant Signature   Date   Judicial Officer   Date

331

THIRD PARTY OBLIGATIONS

YOU MUST comply with the following obligations if the defendant has been placed in your custody while the case is pending in court.

    A. Supervise the defendant in accordance with all of the release conditions.

    B. Make every effort to assure that the defendant is present for all scheduled court hearings.

    C. Make every effort to assure that the defendant will contact Indigent Defense Services to determine indigency status.

    D. Notify the court immediately in the event the defendant violates any conditions of release or disappears.

As Third Party Custodian appointed by the Court, I understand and accept these obligations.

		( )_____
Third Party Custodian	Date	Phone No.

_____
Address

_____
City, State Zip

WARNING

IF YOU WILLFULLY VIOLATE ANY OF THESE OBLIGATIONS, THE COURT MAY HOLD YOU IN CONTEMPT AND IMPOSE A JAIL SENTENCE, FINE, OR BOTH, AND YOU MAY LOSE YOUR RIGHT TO APPEAL.

Credits

Adopted Dec. 14, 2016, effective April 3, 2017.

Editors' Notes

HISTORICAL NOTES

Former Form 6 was abrogated effective January 1, 2008.
Former Form 6, relating to release orders, was abrogated effective April 3, 2017.
See, now, Form 6.
16A A. R. S. Rules Crim. Proc., Form 6, AZ ST RCRP Form 6
Current with amendments received through 08/15/19

Form 7. Appearance Bond

(Refs & Annos)
IX. Miscellaneous
Rule 41. Forms
Forms

16A A.R.S. Rules Crim.Proc., Form 7

Form 7. Appearance Bond

_____ COURT _____ County, Arizona

STATE OF ARIZONA Plaintiff -vs- _____ _____ _____ Defendant (FIRST, MI, LAST)　Booking Number　Date of Birth	**APPEARANCE BOND**

WARNING TO DEFENDANT AND DEFENDANT'S SURETY (if any)

If defendant fails to appear at _____ **at** _____ **a.m./p.m. on** _____, 20_____ **and at any other hearing, or fails to follow any other court-ordered condition of release during the pendency of the case, THIS BOND MAY BE FORFEITED and the proceedings begun without defendant. If convicted, defendant will be required to appear for sentencing. If defendant fails to appear at sentencing, defendant may lose the right to a direct appeal.**

Amount of appearance bond ordered: $_____

TYPE OF APPEARANCE BOND ORDERED:

[ ] **UNSECURED APPEARANCE BOND:** Defendant and defendant's surety, _____ (if none, so state) hereby promise to pay the State of Arizona the amount of the bond ordered if defendant fails to comply with any condition of release.

[ ] **DEPOSIT BOND:** Defendant hereby deposits with the Clerk of the Court _____% of the total amount of the bond, with the remainder of $_____ as an unsecured appearance bond. Defendant and defendant's surety, _____ (if none, so state) hereby promise to pay the State of Arizona the full amount of the bond ordered if defendant fails to comply with any condition of release. The deposited amount of the bond will be returned to the defendant, if defendant complies with all conditions of release.

[ ] **SECURED APPEARANCE BOND:** Defendant hereby deposits with the Clerk of the Court cash or property having a value equal to or greater than the full amount of the bond.

Depositor or Professional Bondsman: _____

Email address: _____

Address: _____

Phone number: _____

Avowal of non-professional surety (if applicable): _____, surety for the defendant, hereby swears (or affirms) that the surety is not an attorney or person authorized to take bail, and that the surety owns property in this state (or is a resident of this state owning property) worth the amount of this bond, exclusive of property exempt from execution and above and over all liabilities, as detailed in Attachment A.

[ ] **CASH BOND:** Defendant hereby deposits cash equal to the full amount of the bond with the Clerk of the Court. The cash deposited will be returned to defendant, if defendant complies with all conditions of release.

Credits

Added by Aug. 31, 2017, effective Jan. 1, 2018.

Editors' Notes

HISTORICAL AND STATUTORY NOTES

Former Form 7, relating to appearance bond, was abrogated effective Jan. 1, 2018. See, now, this form.

Former Form 7, relating to appearance bonds, was abrogated effective April 3, 2017.

Former Form 7 was abrogated effective Jan. 1, 2008.

16A A. R. S. Rules Crim. Proc., Form 7, AZ ST RCRP Form 7

Current with amendments received through 08/15/19

Form 7. Attachment A

(Refs & Annos)

IX. Miscellaneous

Rule 41. Forms

Forms

16A A.R.S. Rules Crim.Proc., Form 7 Attachment A

Form 7. Attachment A

_____COURT [Precinct _____] _____County, Arizona

FORM 7 ATTACHMENT A

SPECIFICATION BY SURETY OF PROPERTY
CERTIFIED IN APPEARANCE BOND

_____, surety on the attached appearance bond certifies
that the surety owns the following properties, subject to the stated exemptions and liabilities, and
to the stated outstanding appearance bonds entered into by the defendant.

I. Properties, less Exemptions and Liabilities.   Value or Amount
    Items of Property
(1) _____   _____
    Less _____   _____
    Net   _____   _____
(2) _____   _____
    Less _____   _____
    Net   _____   _____
(3) _____   _____
    Less _____   _____
    Net   _____   _____
(4) _____   _____
    Less _____   _____
    Net   _____   _____

Total   _____ $_____

II. Other Outstanding Liabilities or Exemptions.
(1) _____   _____   _____
(2) _____   _____   _____
(3) _____   _____   _____
(4) _____   _____   _____

Total   _____ $_____

III. Other Outstanding Appearance Bonds.
(1) _____   _____   _____
(2) _____   _____
(3) _____   _____
(4) _____   _____

Total   _____ $_____

IV. Total Property in Excess of Liabilities, Exemptions, and Outstanding
Appearance Bonds (I less II and III). $_____

Credits
Added by Aug. 31, 2017, effective Jan. 1, 2018.
Editors' Notes
HISTORICAL AND STATUTORY NOTES
Former Form 7 Attachment A, relating to specification by surety of property certified in appearance bond, was abrogated effective Jan. 1, 2018. See, now, this form.
Former Form 7 Attachment A, relating to specification by surety of property certified in appearance bond, was abrogated effective April 3, 2017.
16A A. R. S. Rules Crim. Proc., Form 7 Attachment A, AZ ST RCRP Form 7 Attachment A
Current with amendments received through 08/15/19

Form 8. Notice of Right to Counsel and Waiver

(Refs & Annos)
IX. Miscellaneous
Rule 41. Forms
Forms

16A A.R.S. Rules Crim.Proc., Form 8

Form 8. Notice of Right to Counsel and Waiver

_____ COURT   _____ County, Arizona

STATE OF ARIZONA Plaintiff   [CASE/COMPLAINT NO.]

-vs-   NOTICE OF RIGHT TO COUNSEL AND WAIVER

Defendant (FIRST, MI, LAST)

READ THE ENTIRE FORM CAREFULLY BEFORE SIGNING IT
You have elected to proceed without an attorney either because:
[ ] you do not want an attorney,
[ ] the Court has determined that you are not entitled to a court- appointed attorney and you choose not to retain one.

The purpose of this form is to notify you of your right to an attorney, of the ways in which an attorney can be important to you in this case, and also to allow you to give up your rights if you so choose.

I understand that I am charged with the following crime(s) under the laws of Arizona:

which is a class ___ [ ] felony [ ] misdemeanor
which is a class ___ [ ] felony [ ] misdemeanor
which is a class ___ [ ] felony [ ] misdemeanor
which is a class ___ [ ] felony [ ] misdemeanor
which is a class ___ [ ] felony [ ] misdemeanor

I understand that if I am found guilty, I can be given a severe punishment, including incarceration [ ] in the Arizona State Prison, [ ] in the _____ County Jail, [ ] a fine, or other penalty.

I understand that under the Constitutions of the United States and the State of Arizona, I have the right to be represented by an attorney at all critical stages of this criminal case: before trial, at trial itself, during proceedings to determine what sentence should be imposed if I am found guilty, and for an appeal. I understand that, for certain offenses, if I am unable to obtain the services of an attorney without incurring substantial hardship to myself or to my family, one will be appointed for me at a reduced cost or at no cost to me.

I understand that the services of an attorney can be of great value, for example: in determining if the charges against me are sufficient as a matter of law; whether the procedures used in investigating the charges and obtaining evidence against me, including the lawfulness of any search, seizure or police questioning; if an act I may have committed actually amounts to the crime for which I am charged; if I have any other valid defense to the charges; if I am found guilty, whether I should be placed on probation, be required to pay a fine, or be sentenced to a term of incarceration; or if appellate review would be justified. I understand that, if I am found guilty of the offense charged, the Court may sentence me to a term of incarceration, even though I have given up my right to an attorney.

RIGHT TO AN ATTORNEY AT ANY TIME

I understand that I can change my mind about having an attorney at any time by asking the judge to appoint an attorney for me or by hiring my own attorney. I also understand that I will not be entitled to repeat any part of the case already held or to delay scheduled court proceedings based solely on changing my mind about having an attorney.

CERTIFICATION AND WAIVER

I certify that I have read and understand all of the above, and I hereby waive my right to an attorney in this case, and to have an attorney appointed at a reduced cost or at no cost to me, for eligible offenses, if I cannot afford one.

DO NOT SIGN THIS FORM UNLESS YOU HAVE READ IT COMPLETELY, OR HAD IT READ TO YOU AND UNDERSTAND IT FULLY.

DO NOT SIGN THIS FORM IF YOU WANT AN ATTORNEY.

Dated   Defendant   Interpreter

FINDING

After advising the defendant of the dangers and disadvantages of self-representation, the Court finds that the defendant's waiver of counsel is knowing, voluntary, and intelligent.

Dated   Judicial Officer's Signature

                                                                    Form 8

Credits

Added Sept. 5, 2007, effective Jan. 1, 2008.

Editors' Notes

HISTORICAL NOTES

Former Form 8 was abrogated effective January 1, 2008.

16A A. R. S. Rules Crim. Proc., Form 8, AZ ST RCRP Form 8

Current with amendments received through 08/15/19

Form 9. Notice of Appearance

(Refs & Annos)

IX. Miscellaneous

Rule 41. Forms

Forms

16A A.R.S. Rules Crim.Proc., Form 9

Form 9. Notice of Appearance

_____ COURT   _____ County, Arizona

STATE OF ARIZONA Plaintiff	[CASE/COMPLAINT NO.]	
-vs-		NOTICE OF APPEARANCE
Defendant (FIRST, MI, LAST)		

Pursuant to Rule 6.3, , I hereby enter my appearance on behalf of the above-named Defendant for all further proceedings in this case, including the filing of a Notice of Appeal, if required.

Date   Attorney's Signature

                                  Attorney's Name (please print)

Attorney's Bar Number

Firm Name

Address

City State Zip

Telephone Number

Form 9

Credits
Added Sept. 5, 2007, effective Jan. 1, 2008.

Editors' Notes
HISTORICAL NOTES
Former Form 9 was abrogated effective January 1, 2008.
16A A. R. S. Rules Crim. Proc., Form 9, AZ ST RCRP Form 9
Current with amendments received through 08/15/19

Form 10. Waiver of Preliminary Hearing

(Refs & Annos)
IX. Miscellaneous
Rule 41. Forms
Forms

16A A.R.S. Rules Crim.Proc., Form 10

Form 10. Waiver of Preliminary Hearing

_____ COURT   _____ County, Arizona

STATE OF ARIZONA Plaintiff   [CASE/COMPLAINT NO.]

-vs-   WAIVER OF PRELIMINARY HEARING

Defendant (FIRST, MI, LAST)

WAIVER OF PRELIMINARY HEARING

You are entitled to a preliminary hearing on the charge(s) against you unless charged by grand jury indictment. The purpose of this form is to notify you of your rights and of the ways in which the hearing could benefit you, and to allow you to give up your rights if you so choose. Read the entire form carefully before signing it.

RIGHT TO PRELIMINARY HEARING

I understand that I am charged with the crime(s) of

which is a felony under the law of Arizona and that if I am found guilty I can be given a severe punishment, including jail, prison, a fine, probation, or other penalties.

I understand that the Arizona Constitution provides that, if I am charged by means other than a grand jury indictment, I have a right to a preliminary hearing at which a magistrate, without making any determination of my guilt or innocence, will decide whether there is sufficient evidence against me to establish probable cause to try me on these charges. I understand that I have a right to a lawyer at the preliminary hearing and that, if I am unable to obtain the services of a lawyer without incurring substantial hardship to myself or to my family, one will be furnished for me free of charge.

I understand that the prosecutor would be required to present witnesses and evidence against me at such a hearing to demonstrate that there is probable cause to try me on the charges and that I would have the right to cross-examine such witnesses and to present evidence of my innocence. I understand that if the prosecutor failed to show probable cause to try me, the charge(s) against me would be dismissed, although the prosecutor may choose to re-file the charges.

I understand that giving up my right to a preliminary hearing gives the state the right to try me for the offense(s) charged without any determination of probable cause by a magistrate.

CERTIFICATION AND WAIVER

I certify that I have read and understand all of the above, and I hereby waive my right to a preliminary hearing in this case.

DO NOT SIGN THIS FORM UNLESS YOU HAVE READ IT COMPLETELY, OR HAD IT READ TO YOU AND UNDERSTAND IT FULLY.

DO NOT SIGN THIS FORM IF YOU WANT A PRELIMINARY HEARING.

Date   Defendant

I have explained the significance of the preliminary hearing to the defendant, and I consent to waiver of a preliminary hearing in this case.

Defense Attorney   Bar Number

I consent to waiver of a preliminary hearing in this case.

Prosecutor   Bar Number

Form 10

Credits
Added Sept. 5, 2007, effective Jan. 1, 2008.
Editors' Notes
HISTORICAL NOTES
Former Form 10 was abrogated effective January 1, 2008.
16A A. R. S. Rules Crim. Proc., Form 10, AZ ST RCRP Form 10
Current with amendments received through 08/15/19

Form 11. Bind-Over Order

(Refs & Annos)
IX. Miscellaneous
Rule 41. Forms
Forms

16A A.R.S. Rules Crim.Proc., Form 11

Form 11. Bind-Over Order

_____ COURT   _____ County,
Arizona

STATE OF ARIZONA Plaintiff   [CASE/COMPLAINT
                                        NO.]

-vs-
                                                BIND-OVER
                                                  ORDER

Defendant (FIRST, MI, LAST)

ORDER HOLDING DEFENDANT TO ANSWER BEFORE THE SUPERIOR
COURT

The Court ORDERS the defendant _____ to respond before the Superior Court in
_____ County, Arizona to the listed charges:

[ ] I find that there is probable cause to believe that the above offense(s) has/have
been committed and that the defendant committed them.
[ ] The defendant waived a preliminary hearing on the felony charge(s).
[ ] The court requests that the above misdemeanors be associated with the felony
charge(s) set forth above.

Date   Signature of Judicial Officer

                                  Printed Name and Title of Judicial
                                  Officer

Credits
Added Sept. 5, 2007, effective Jan. 1, 2008.
Editors' Notes
HISTORICAL NOTES
Source:
Pen.Code 1901, §§ 773, 774.
Pen.Code 1913, §§ 889, 890.
Rev.Code 1928, § 4956.
Code 1939, § 44-324.
1956 Rules Cr.Proc., Rule 34.
Adopted from California, see West's Ann.Pen.Code §§ 876 and 877.
Former Form 11 was abrogated effective January 1, 2008.
16A A. R. S. Rules Crim. Proc., Form 11, AZ ST RCRP Form 11
Current with amendments received through 08/15/19

Form 12. Transmittal Certification

(Refs & Annos)
IX. Miscellaneous
Rule 41. Forms
Forms

16A A.R.S. Rules Crim.Proc., Form 12

Form 12. Transmittal Certification

_____ COURT   _____ County,
                                                                     Arizona

STATE OF ARIZONA Plaintiff   [CASE/COMPLAINT
                                           NO.]

-vs-
                                                    TRANSMITTAL
                                                    CERTIFICATION

Defendant (FIRST, MI, LAST)

ORDER HOLDING DEFENDANT TO ANSWER BEFORE THE SUPERIOR
COURT
I hereby certify that the enclosed items constitute a true and complete record of the
preliminary proceedings held in the above-entitled case appearing in Docket No.
_____, at page ___.
The following items are included:

[ ] The original complaint, including amendments;
[ ] The supporting affidavits of the following witnesses:

;

[ ] The arrest warrant or summons;
[ ] The defendant's release questionnaire;
[ ] The defendant's financial statement and request for appointment of counsel;
[ ] A copy of the release order;
[ ] The defendant's appearance bond;
[ ] Security deposited with the appearance bond:

;

[ ] Defendant's waiver of counsel;
[ ] Order appointing counsel;
[ ] Waiver of preliminary hearing;
[ ] Exhibits and items of physical evidence introduced at the preliminary hearing:

;

[ ] Order holding the defendant to answer in superior court;
[ ] Audio or video record of preliminary hearing, if any;
[ ] Other:

Date   Signature of Judicial Officer

                                          Printed Name and Title of Judicial
                                          Officer

                                                              Form 12

Credits
Added Sept. 5, 2007, effective Jan. 1, 2008.
Editors' Notes
HISTORICAL NOTES
Source:
Code 1939, § 44-328.
Rules Cr.Proc. § 59.
1956 Rules Cr.Proc., Rule 35.
Former Form 12 was abrogated effective January 1, 2008.
16A A. R. S. Rules Crim. Proc., Form 12, AZ ST RCRP Form 12
Current with amendments received through 08/15/19

Form 13(a). Indictment

(Refs & Annos)
IX. Miscellaneous
Rule 41. Forms
Forms

16A A.R.S. Rules Crim.Proc., Form 13(a)

Form 13(a). Indictment

_____ COURT   _____ County, Arizona

STATE OF ARIZONA Plaintiff   [CASE/COMPLAINT NO.]

-vs-

INDICTMENT
Felony /
Misdemeanor

Defendant (FIRST, MI, LAST)

The Grand Jurors of _____ County, Arizona, accuse [name of defendant] _____ on this _____ day of _____, charging that in _____ County, Arizona:
[List and describe each charge or count]

[Foreperson writes "A True Bill"]

Date

[NAME OF PROSECUTING AGENCY]
By

Deputy County Attorney (or Other Title)

By

Foreperson of the Grand Jury

Form 13(a)

Credits
Added Sept. 5, 2007, effective Jan. 1, 2008.
Editors' Notes
HISTORICAL NOTES

Source:
Pen.Code 1901, §§ 823 to 825.
Laws 1912, Ch. 35, §§ 5, 7, 8.
Pen.Code 1913, §§ 933 to 935.
Rev.Code 1928, § 4977.
Code 1939, §§ 44-706, 44-707, 44-753.
Rules Cr.Proc. §§ 150, 186.
1956 Rules Cr.Proc., Rules 112, 113, 148.
Former Form 13 was abrogated effective January 1, 2008.
16A A. R. S. Rules Crim. Proc., Form 13(a), AZ ST RCRP Form 13(a)
Current with amendments received through 08/15/19

Form 13(b). Grand Jury Minutes

(Refs & Annos)
IX. Miscellaneous
Rule 41. Forms
Forms

16A A.R.S. Rules Crim.Proc., Form 13(b)

Form 13(b). Grand Jury Minutes

_____ COURT   _____ County, Arizona

STATE OF ARIZONA Plaintiff   [CASE/COMPLAINT NO.]

-vs-   GRAND JURY MINUTES

Defendant (FIRST, MI, LAST)

GJ No.

At a session of the Grand Jury of the County of

held this

___
day of

_____
, 20

347

___

, the above defendant being accused of the crime(s) of:

[List each charge or count]

Based upon the following witnesses:

Name	I.D. #/	Agency / Address	Date Appeared

[List each witness:]

Having appeared before the Grand Jury and having given testimony under oath before the Grand Jury, which testimony was reported by _____, Reporter of the Grand Jury, on the day(s) that such testimony was given; the Grand Jury with ___ members present, and only members of the Grand Jury present, deliberated upon evidence and with ___ jurors voting, by a vote of ___ to ___ returned a true bill, or took the following action:

_____   _____
Clerk of the Grand Jury   Date

Form 13(b)

Credits
Added Sept. 5, 2007, effective Jan. 1, 2008.
16A A. R. S. Rules Crim. Proc., Form 13(b), AZ ST RCRP Form 13(b)
Current with amendments received through 08/15/19

Form 14. Information

(Refs & Annos)
IX. Miscellaneous
Rule 41. Forms
Forms

16A A.R.S. Rules Crim.Proc., Form 14

Form 14. Information

_____ COURT   _____ County, Arizona

STATE OF ARIZONA Plaintiff   [CASE/COMPLAINT NO.]

-vs-
                                                    INFORMATION

Defendant (FIRST, MI, LAST)

The

_____
[Name / of Prosecuting Agency]

_____
, accuses

___
[Defendant]

on this

_____
[date]
_____
, charging that in

_____
County, Arizona:
[List and describe each charge or count]

                              [NAME OF PROSECUTING AGENCY]
                              By

                              [County Attorney / or Other Title]

                              Date

                                                    Form 14

Credits
Added Sept. 5, 2007, effective Jan. 1, 2008.
Editors' Notes
HISTORICAL NOTES
Source:
Pen.Code 1901, §§ 823 to 825.
Laws 1912, Ch. 35, §§ 5, 7, 8.
Pen.Code 1913, §§ 933 to 935.
Rev.Code 1928, § 4977.
Code 1939, §§ 44-705, 44-706, 44-708, 44-753.
Rules Cr.Proc. §§ 149, 151, 186.
1956 Rules Cr.Proc., Rules 111, 112, 114, 148.
Former Form 14 was abrogated effective January 1, 2008.
16A A. R. S. Rules Crim. Proc., Form 14, AZ ST RCRP Form 14
Current with amendments received through 08/15/19

Form 15(a). Notice of Appointment of Mental Health Expert (Pre-Screen)

16A A.R.S. Rules Crim.Proc., Form 15(a)

Form 15(a). Notice of Appointment of Mental Health Expert (Pre-Screen)

_____ COURT _____ County, Arizona

STATE OF ARIZONA Plaintiff	[CASE/COMPLAINT NO.]	NOTICE OF
-vs-		APPOINTMENT OF MENTAL HEALTH EXPERT (PRE-SCREEN)
Defendant (FIRST, MI, LAST)		

The Court having been presented with a motion under Rule 11.2, , for an examination to determine whether the defendant is competent, or to investigate the defendant's mental condition at the time of the offense,

IT IS HEREBY ORDERED appointing _____ as a mental expert, to prepare and send to this Court a written report of the expert's opinion and findings as to whether reasonable grounds for a mental health examination exist.

IT IS FURTHER ORDERED that if the defendant is not in custody, defense counsel is to contact the expert at [telephone number] _____ within two (2) working days of this order to schedule a time for the defendant's examination and use due diligence to secure the defendant's attendance at the examination.

IT IS FURTHER ORDERED that the prosecutor and defense counsel provide to the expert at [address] _____ the motion to have defendant's mental condition examined, copies of police reports, previous mental health reports and any other appropriate material for the screening examination.

IT IS FURTHER ORDERED that payment of the cost of the examination of the defendant is the responsibility of the _____ pursuant to A.R.S. § 13-4505.

IT IS FURTHER ORDERED that a prescreen hearing will be held in this court on the ___ day of _____ 20 ___, at _____ a.m./p.m.

IT IS FURTHER ORDERED that at least _____ days prior to the prescreen hearing date the expert will submit the written report to the Court, which will seal the original and provide a copy to defense counsel. Defense counsel shall provide a redacted copy of the report to the Court and the prosecutor's office within a reasonable time after receipt.

Signature of Judicial Officer   Date

Defense Attorney (please print name)   Prosecutor (please print name)

Telephone No.   Bar No.   Telephone No.   Bar No.

Mailing Address   Mailing Address

City State Zip   City State Zip

Form 15(a)

Credits
Added Sept. 5, 2007, effective Jan. 1, 2008.
Editors' Notes
HISTORICAL NOTES
Former Form 15 was abrogated effective January 1, 2008.
16A A. R. S. Rules Crim. Proc., Form 15(a), AZ ST RCRP Form 15(a)
Current with amendments received through 08/15/19

Form 15(b). Rule 11 Order and Stipulation

(Refs & Annos)
IX. Miscellaneous
Rule 41. Forms
Forms

16A A.R.S. Rules Crim.Proc., Form 15(b)

Form 15(b). Rule 11 Order and Stipulation

_____ COURT   _____ County,
                                                          Arizona

STATE OF ARIZONA Plaintiff   [CASE/COMPLAINT   RULE 11
                                       NO.]
-vs-
                                                         ORDER
                                                          AND
Defendant (FIRST, MI, LAST)   STIPULATION

ORDER

A Motion having been filed requesting relief under Rule 11.2, , and the Court having made a factual determination that reasonable grounds exist for an examination of the defendant pursuant to said Rule.

IT IS HEREBY ORDERED that the cause be transferred to the Superior Court of in _____ County for further proceedings pursuant to and in conformance with Rule 11, .

DONE IN OPEN COURT this ___ day of _____, 20___

Signature of Judicial Officer   Date

STIPULATION

Both counsels stipulate to the appointment of only one mental health expert.

	/			/	
Prosecutor	Bar No.		Defense Attorney	Bar No.	

Address

Telephone No.

Form 15(b)

Credits

Added Sept. 5, 2007, effective Jan. 1, 2008.

16A A. R. S. Rules Crim. Proc., Form 15(b), AZ ST RCRP Form 15(b)

Current with amendments received through 08/15/19

Form 15(c). Notice of Appointment of Mental Health Expert-Competency

(Refs & Annos)
IX. Miscellaneous
Rule 41. Forms
Forms

16A A.R.S. Rules Crim.Proc., Form 15(c)

Form 15(c). Notice of Appointment of Mental Health Expert-Competency

_____ COURT   _____ County, Arizona

STATE OF ARIZONA Plaintiff	[CASE/COMPLAINT NO.]	NOTICE OF
-vs-		APPOINTMENT OF MENTAL HEALTH

The Court, having granted the motion for competency examination pursuant to Rule 11.2, , and the defendant having been charged with:

IT IS HEREBY ORDERED
appointing

and

as mental health experts, to prepare and send to the Court a written report of the experts' opinions and findings as to the defendant's competency to stand trial (i.e. the defendant's ability to understand the nature of the proceedings and to assist counsel in the preparation of the defense.) If a mental health expert finds the Defendant is incompetent to stand trial at this time, an opinion shall also be rendered as to:

(A) The mental disease, defect or disability which is the cause of the Defendant's incompetency;
(B) Whether there is a substantial probability the Defendant will become competent within a reasonable period of time;
(C) The most appropriate form and place of treatment in this state, based on the defendant's therapeutic needs and potential threat to public safety;
(D) The defendant's prognosis; and
(E) Whether the defendant is incompetent to refuse treatment and should be subject to involuntary treatment.

IT IS FURTHER ORDERED that the report name each mental health expert who examines the defendant; that it describe the nature, content, extent and results of the examination and any test conducted; and that it include the facts on which the findings are based.

IT IS FURTHER ORDERED
that if the defendant is not in custody, defense counsel is to contact the experts at [names and phone numbers]

within two (2) working days of this order to schedule a time for the defendant's examination and use due diligence to secure the defendant's attendance at the examination.

IT IS FURTHER ORDERED
that the prosecutor and defense counsel provide to the experts at [addresses]

the motion to have defendant's mental condition examined, copies of police reports, previous mental health reports and any other appropriate material for the examination.

IT IS FURTHER ORDERED

that payment of the cost of the examination of the defendant is the responsibility of the

pursuant to ARS § 13-4505.

IT IS FURTHER ORDERED that a competency hearing will be held in _____ court on the ___ day of _____, 20 ___ at _____ a.m./p.m.

IT IS FURTHER ORDERED that the experts will submit the written reports at least 10 days prior to the competency hearing date to _____ which will seal the originals and provide copies to defense counsel. Defense counsel shall provide redacted copies of the reports to the court and the prosecutor's office within 24 hours of receipt.

Signature of Judicial Officer   Date

Form 15(c)

Credits

Added Sept. 5, 2007, effective Jan. 1, 2008.

16A A. R. S. Rules Crim. Proc., Form 15(c), AZ ST RCRP Form 15(c)

Current with amendments received through 08/15/19

Form 15(d). Notice of Appointment of Mental Health Expert --Mental Condition at Time of Offense

(Refs & Annos)

IX. Miscellaneous

Rule 41. Forms

Forms

16A A.R.S. Rules Crim.Proc., Form 15(d)

Form 15(d). Notice of Appointment of Mental Health Expert --Mental Condition at Time of Offense

_____ COURT   _____ County, Arizona

STATE OF ARIZONA Plaintiff	[CASE/COMPLAINT NO.]	NOTICE OF
-vs-		APPOINTMENT OF MENTAL HEALTH EXPERT (MENTAL CONDITION AT
Defendant (FIRST, MI, LAST)		TIME OF OFFENSE)

The Court having found a reasonable basis to support a plea of insanity pursuant to Rule 11.2, and the defendant having been charged with:

;

IT IS HEREBY ORDERED
appointing

and

as mental health experts, to prepare and send to the Court a written report of the experts' opinions as to the defendant's mental condition at the time of the offense. The report shall include:

(A) An opinion as to the mental status of the defendant at the time of the offense;

(B) If the expert determines that the defendant suffered from a mental disease, defect or disability at the time of the offense, the relationship of the disease, defect or disability to the alleged offense.

IT IS FURTHER ORDERED that if the defendant is not in custody, the defense attorney is to contact the experts at [names and phone numbers] _____ within two (2) working days of this order to schedule a time for the defendant's examination and use due diligence to secure the defendant's attendance at the examination.

IT IS FURTHER ORDERED that the prosecutor and the defense attorney provide to the experts at [addresses] _____ the motion to have defendant's mental condition examined, copies of police reports, previous mental health reports and any other appropriate material for the examination.

IT IS FURTHER ORDERED that payment of the cost of the examination of the defendant is the responsibility of the _____ pursuant to ARS § 13-4505.

IT IS FURTHER ORDERED that a hearing will be held in _____ court on the ___ day of _____, 20 ___ at _____ a.m./p.m.

IT IS FURTHER ORDERED that the experts will submit the written reports at least 10 days prior to the hearing date to _____ which will seal the originals and provide copies to the defense attorney. The defense attorney shall provide redacted copies of the reports to the court and the prosecutor's office within 24 hours of receipt.

Signature of Judicial Officer   Date

Defense Attorney (please print name)   Prosecutor (please print name)

Telephone No.   Bar No.   Telephone No.   Bar No.

Mailing Address   Mailing Address

City State Zip   City State Zip

Form 15(d)

Credits
Added Sept. 5, 2007, effective Jan. 1, 2008.
16A A. R. S. Rules Crim. Proc., Form 15(d), AZ ST RCRP Form 15(d)
Current with amendments received through 08/15/19

Form 16. Reserved

(Refs & Annos)
IX. Miscellaneous
Rule 41. Forms
Forms

16A A.R.S. Rules Crim.Proc., Form 16

Form 16. Reserved

Editors' Notes
HISTORICAL NOTES
Former Form 16 was abrogated effective January 1, 2008.
16A A. R. S. Rules Crim. Proc., Form 16, AZ ST RCRP Form 16
Current with amendments received through 08/15/19

Form 17. Waiver of Right to be Present at Deposition

(Refs & Annos)
IX. Miscellaneous
Rule 41. Forms
Forms

16A A.R.S. Rules Crim.Proc., Form 17

Form 17. Waiver of Right to be Present at Deposition

_____ COURT   _____ County,
                                                       Arizona

STATE OF ARIZONA Plaintiff   [CASE/COMPLAINT
                                        NO.]
-vs-   WAIVER OF

READ THE ENTIRE FORM CAREFULLY BEFORE SIGNING

Instructions: The purpose of this form is to advise you of your right to be present at a deposition held for the purpose of obtaining testimony which may be used at your trial, and to allow you to give up that right if you so choose. Read the entire form carefully before signing it.

RIGHT TO BE PRESENT AT DEPOSITION

I understand that I am charged with the crime of

which is a [ ] misdemeanor [ ] felony under the law of Arizona, and that if I am found guilty I can be given severe punishment, including incarceration [ ] in the Arizona State Prison, [ ] in the

_____
County Jail, [ ] a fine, or other penalty.

I understand that the allow depositions to be taken in criminal cases in certain situations, and that during a deposition a witness is asked questions under oath. I understand that testimony given by the witness at the deposition is recorded and may be used at the trial. I understand that I am entitled to be present at such proceedings in order to be able to confront the witnesses against me and to help my attorney prepare questions to ask them to test the truthfulness of their testimony.

I understand that by giving up my right to be present at a deposition I consent to the use of testimony given at the deposition later during my trial in all situations in which it would be admissible if I had been present at the deposition.

CERTIFICATION AND WAIVER

DO NOT SIGN THIS FORM UNLESS YOU HAVE READ IT COMPLETELY OR HAD IT READ TO YOU AND YOU UNDERSTAND IT FULLY. DO NOT SIGN THIS FORM IF YOU WANT TO BE PRESENT AT THE DEPOSITION.

After reading and understanding all the above, I hereby give up my right to be present at [ ] the deposition of

[ ] any deposition in this case.

_____
Date   Defendant

I have explained to the defendant the significance of a deposition and the right to be present at its taking and consent to defendant's waiver of the right to be present.

_____
Date   Defense Attorney

Form 17

Credits
Added Sept. 5, 2007, effective Jan. 1, 2008.

Editors' Notes
HISTORICAL NOTES
Former Form 17 was abrogated effective January 1, 2008.
16A A. R. S. Rules Crim. Proc., Form 17, AZ ST RCRP Form 17
Current with amendments received through 08/15/19

Form 18(a). Felony Plea Agreement--Non-Capital

(Refs & Annos)
IX. Miscellaneous
Rule 41. Forms
Forms

16A A.R.S. Rules Crim.Proc., Form 18(a)

Form 18(a). Felony Plea Agreement--Non-Capital

_____ COURT _____ County, Arizona

STATE OF ARIZONA Plaintiff   [CASE/COMPLAINT NO.]

-vs-

Defendant (FIRST, MI, LAST)

FELONY PLEA AGREEMENT (Non-Capital)

The defendant agrees to plead guilty / no contest to _____ committed on or about _____.

This crime is a [ ] dangerous [ ] non-dangerous, [ ] repetitive [ ] non-repetitive offense under the criminal code.

Terms: On the following understandings, terms and conditions:

___ 1. The crime carries a presumptive sentence of ___ years; a minimum sentence of ___ years; and a maximum sentence of ___ years. Probation is / is not available. A maximum amount of restitution for economic loss to the victim not to exceed the amount specified in paragraph 2 and waiver of extradition for probation revocation procedures may be required. The maximum fine that can be imposed is $150,000 plus a surcharge of ___ + ___. Special conditions regarding the sentence imposed by statute (if any) are:

[ ] None

[ ] If sentenced to a term of imprisonment, the defendant shall also be sentenced to a term of community supervision equal to one-seventh of the prison sentence to be served consecutively to the actual period of imprisonment. If the defendant fails to abide by the conditions of community supervision, the defendant can be required to serve the remaining term of community supervision in prison.

[ ] Other:

___

2. The parties stipulate to the following additional terms, subject to court approval at sentencing as set forth in paragraph 7:

___

3. The following charges are dismissed, or if not yet filed, shall not be brought against the defendant.

___ 4. This agreement serves to amend the complaint, indictment, or information to charge the offense to which the defendant pleads, without the filing of any additional pleading. However, if the plea is rejected by the court or withdrawn by either party, or if the conviction is subsequently reversed, the original charges and any charges that are dismissed by reason of this plea agreement are automatically reinstated.

___ 6[1]. Unless this plea is rejected by the court or withdrawn by either party, the defendant hereby gives up any and all motions, defenses, objections or requests which he or she has made or raised, or could assert hereafter, to the court's entry of judgment against him or her and imposition of a sentence upon him or her consistent with this agreement. The defendant acknowledges by entering this agreement that he or she will have no right to direct appeal (ARS 13-4033) and that the only available review is pursuant to Rule 32, .

___ 7. If after accepting this plea agreement the court concludes that any of its provisions regarding the sentence or the terms and conditions of probation are inappropriate, it can reject the plea. If the court decides to reject the plea agreement provisions regarding sentencing, it must give both the State and the defendant each an opportunity to withdraw from the plea.

___ 8. If the court decides to reject the plea agreement provisions regarding sentencing and neither the State nor the Defendant elects to withdraw the plea agreement, then any sentence either stipulated to or recommended herein in paragraph 2 is not binding upon the court, and the court is bound only by the sentencing limits set forth in paragraph 1 and the applicable statutes.

___ 9. I understand that if I am not a citizen of the United States, my decision to go to trial or enter into a plea agreement may have immigration consequences. Specifically, I understand that pleading guilty or no contest to a crime may affect my immigration status. Admitting guilt may result in deportation even if the charge is

359

later dismissed. My plea or admission of guilt could result in my deportation or removal, could prevent me from ever being able to get legal status in the United States, or could prevent me from becoming a United States citizen. I understand that I am not required to disclose my legal status in the United States to the court.

___ 10. I have read and understand the provisions of all pages of this agreement. I have discussed the case and my constitutional rights with my attorney. I understand that by pleading (guilty) (no contest) I will be giving up my right to a determination of probable cause, to a trial [ ] by jury [ ] by a judge [ ] by jury on facts used to aggravate a sentence, to confront, cross-examine, and compel the attendance of witnesses, to present witnesses on my behalf; my right to remain silent, my privilege against self-incrimination, the presumption of innocence and right to direct appeal. I agree to enter my plea as indicated above on the terms and conditions set forth herein. I fully understand that, as part of this plea agreement, if I am granted probation by the court, the terms and conditions thereof are subject to modification at any time during the period of probation in the event that I violate any written condition of my probation. I understand that if I violate any of the written conditions of my probation, my probation may be terminated and I can be sentenced to any term or terms stated above in paragraph 1.

I have personally and voluntarily placed my initials beside each of the above paragraphs and signed the signature line below to indicate that I read, or had read to me, understood and approved all of the previous paragraphs in this agreement, both individually and as a total binding agreement. My plea is voluntary and not the result of force, or threat, or promises other than those contained in the plea agreement.

DO NOT SIGN THIS FORM UNLESS YOU HAVE READ IT COMPLETELY, OR HAD IT READ TO YOU AND UNDERSTAND IT FULLY.

_____
Date   Defendant

I have discussed this case with my client in detail and advised my client of his or her constitutional rights and all possible defenses. I believe that the defendant's plea is knowing, intelligent, and voluntary and that the plea and disposition are consistent with law.

_____
Date   Defense Attorney

I have reviewed this matter and concur that the plea and disposition set forth herein are appropriate and are in the interests of justice.

_____
Date   Prosecutor

Credits

Added Sept. 5, 2007, effective Jan. 1, 2008. Amended Aug. 28, 2013, effective Jan. 1, 2014.

Editors' Notes

HISTORICAL NOTES

Former Form 18 was abrogated effective January 1, 2008.

Footnotes

1

So in original.

16A A. R. S. Rules Crim. Proc., Form 18(a), AZ ST RCRP Form 18(a)

Current with amendments received through 08/15/19

Form 18(b). Misdemeanor Plea Agreement

(Refs & Annos)

IX. Miscellaneous

Rule 41. Forms

Forms

16A A.R.S. Rules Crim.Proc., Form 18(b)

Form 18(b). Misdemeanor Plea Agreement

_____ COURT _____ County, Arizona

STATE OF ARIZONA Plaintiff   [CASE/COMPLAINT NO.]

-vs-   MISDEMEANOR
                                                        PLEA
Defendant (FIRST, MI, LAST)   AGREEMENT

The defendant agrees to plead guilty / no contest to the following offense(s):

_____ [ ] class misdemeanor [ ] petty/civil traffic offense

_____ [ ] class misdemeanor [ ] petty/civil traffic offense

_____ [ ] class misdemeanor [ ] petty/civil traffic offense

_____ [ ] class misdemeanor [ ] petty/civil traffic offense on the

following understandings, terms and conditions:

1. The Defendant agrees to a sentence of:

2. The following charges are dismissed, or if not yet filed, shall not be brought against the defendant.

3. This agreement, serves to amend the complaint, indictment, or information to charge the offense to which the defendant pleads, without the filing of any additional pleading. However, if the plea is rejected by the court or withdrawn by either party, or if the conviction is subsequently reversed, the original charges and any charges that are dismissed by reason of this plea agreement are automatically reinstated.

4. Unless this plea is rejected by the court or withdrawn by either party, the defendant hereby waives and gives up any and all motions, defenses, objections or requests which he or she has made or raised, or could assert hereafter, to the court's entry of judgment against him or her and imposition of a sentence upon him or her consistent with this agreement. The defendant acknowledges by entering this agreement he or she will have no right to direct appeal (ARS 13-4033) and the only available review is pursuant to Rule 32, .

5. If the court decides to reject the proposed sentencing in the plea agreement after accepting the defendant's plea, it must give each party an opportunity to withdraw from the plea.

6. If the court decides to reject the plea agreement provisions regarding sentencing and neither the State nor the Defendant elects to withdraw the plea agreement, then any sentence either stipulated to or recommended herein is not binding upon the court, and the court is bound only by the sentencing limits set forth in the applicable statutes.

7. I understand that if I am not a citizen of the United States, my decision to go to trial or enter into a plea agreement may have immigration consequences. Specifically, I understand that pleading guilty or no contest to a crime may affect my immigration status. Admitting guilt may result in deportation even if the charge is later dismissed. My plea or admission of guilt could result in my deportation or removal, could prevent me from ever being able to get legal status in the United States, or could prevent me from becoming a United States citizen. I understand that I am not required to disclose my legal status in the United States to the court.

8. I have read and understand the provisions of all pages of this agreement. I have discussed the case and my constitutional rights with my attorney. I understand that by pleading (guilty) (no contest) I will be giving up my right to a determination of probable cause, to a trial [ ] by jury [ ] by a judge, to confront, cross-examine, and compel the attendance of witnesses, to present witnesses on my behalf; my right to remain silent, my privilege against self-incrimination, the presumption of innocence and right to direct appeal. I agree to enter my plea as indicated above on the terms and conditions set forth herein. I fully understand that, as part of this plea agreement, if I am granted probation by the court, the terms and conditions thereof

are subject to modification at any time during the period of probation in the event that I violate any written condition of my probation. I understand that if I violate any of the written conditions of my probation, my probation may be terminated and I can be sentenced up to the maximum term.

I have personally signed the signature line below to indicate that I read, or had read to me, understood and approved all of the previous paragraphs in this agreement, both individually and as a total binding agreement. My plea is voluntary and not the result of force, or threat, or promises other than those contained in the plea agreement.

DO NOT SIGN THIS FORM UNLESS YOU HAVE READ IT COMPLETELY, OR HAD IT READ TO YOU AND UNDERSTAND IT FULLY.

_____
Date   Defendant

I have discussed this case with my client in detail and advised my client of his or her constitutional rights and all possible defenses. I believe that the defendant's plea is knowing, intelligent, and voluntary and that the plea and disposition are consistent with law.

_____
Date   Defense Attorney

I have reviewed this matter and concur that the plea and disposition set forth herein are appropriate and are in the interests of justice.

_____
Date   Prosecutor

Credits

Added Sept. 5, 2007, effective Jan. 1, 2008. Amended Aug. 28, 2013, effective Jan. 1, 2014.

16A A. R. S. Rules Crim. Proc., Form 18(b), AZ ST RCRP Form 18(b)

Current with amendments received through 08/15/19

Form 19. Guilty/No Contest Plea Proceeding

(Refs & Annos)
IX. Miscellaneous
Rule 41. Forms
Forms

16A A.R.S. Rules Crim.Proc., Form 19

Form 19. Guilty/No Contest Plea Proceeding

_____COURT   [Precinct ____]   _____County, Arizona

STATE OF ARIZONA Plaintiff   [CASE/COMPLAINT NO.]

-vs-

GUILTY/NO
CONTEST
PLEA
PROCEEDING

Defendant (FIRST, MI, LAST)

Defendant appears personally and expresses a desire to plead guilty or no contest to the charges indicated and I find the following facts:

1. Defendant understands the nature of the charges as indicated:

    .

2. Defendant appears: [ ] with counsel [ ] without counsel, (waiver of counsel with file) and understands the following:

3. Defendant has entered into a: [ ] plea agreement, and consents to its terms; [ ] plea to the court.

4. Defendant understands the range of penalties to be: (state minimum and maximum possible sanctions).

5. If arrested on a subsequent offense, defendant may be charged with a more serious offense and associated penalties.

6. The Court has advised the defendant that this guilty plea may result in a violation of probation or parole.

7. Defendant was advised of the following: If you are not a citizen of the United States, pleading guilty or no contest to a crime may affect your immigration status. Admitting guilt may result in deportation even if the charge is later dismissed. Your plea or admission of guilt could result in your deportation or removal, could prevent you from ever being able to get legal status in the United States, or could prevent you from becoming a United States citizen.

8. Defendant understands that the following constitutional rights are given up by changing the plea:

    a. Right to plead not guilty and require the State to prove guilt beyond a reasonable doubt.

    b. Right to a trial [ ] by jury [ ] by a judge [ ] by jury on facts used to aggravate a sentence.

    c. Right to assistance of an attorney at all stages of the proceeding, including appeal. In some cases, the defendant may be eligible for a court- appointed attorney at a reduced cost or at no cost, if the defendant cannot afford one.

    d. Right to confront the witnesses against the defendant and to cross- examine them as to the truthfulness of their testimony.

    e. Right to present evidence in the defendant's own behalf and to have the court compel the defendant's chosen witnesses to appear and testify free of charge.

    f. Right to remain silent, not to incriminate oneself, and to be presumed innocent unless/or until proven guilty beyond a reasonable doubt.

    g. Right to a direct appeal.
9. Defendant wishes to give up these constitutional rights after having been advised of them.
10. A basis in fact exists for believing the defendant guilty of the offenses charged.
11. The plea is voluntary and not the result of force or threat, or promises other than those contained in the plea agreement.
12. Defendant may file a Rule 32 petition for post-conviction relief and if denied may file a petition for review.

On the basis of these findings, I conclude that the defendant knowingly, voluntarily, and intelligently pleads: [ ] guilty [ ] no contest* to the above charges, and I accept this plea.

    * Rule 17.1c, states that a plea of no contest may be accepted only after due consideration of the views of the parties and the interest of the public in the effective administration of justice.

Date   Signature of Judicial Officer

I certify that the judge personally advised me of the nature of the charges, the range of penalties, and my constitutional rights as indicated above. I understand the constitutional rights which I give up by entering this plea, and I desire to plead guilty or no contest as indicated above. I desire to proceed without an attorney, or if represented, my attorney's signature appears below.

Defendant: Def. Counsel/Bar No.:   Interpreter:

                                          Form 19

Credits
Added Sept. 5, 2007, effective Jan. 1, 2008.
Editors' Notes
HISTORICAL NOTES
Source:
Pen.Code 1901, §§ 878, 879.
Laws 1912, Ch. 35, § 42.
Pen.Code 1913, §§ 989, 990.
Rev.Code 1928, § 5015.
Code 1939, § 44-1018.
Rules Cr.Proc. § 220.
1956 Rules Cr.Proc., Rule 179.
Former Form 19 was abrogated effective January 1, 2008.
Former Form 19, which provided a guilty plea checklist, was abrogated effective Jan. 20, 2005.
16A A. R. S. Rules Crim. Proc., Form 19, AZ ST RCRP Form 19
Current with amendments received through 08/15/19

Form 20. Waiver of Trial by Jury (Non-Capital)

(Refs & Annos)
IX. Miscellaneous
Rule 41. Forms
Forms

16A A.R.S. Rules Crim.Proc., Form 20

Form 20. Waiver of Trial by Jury (Non-Capital)

_____ COURT   _____ County, Arizona

STATE OF ARIZONA Plaintiff   [CASE/COMPLAINT NO.]

-vs-   WAIVER OF TRIAL BY JURY (Non Capital)

Defendant (FIRST, MI, LAST)

RIGHT TO TRIAL BY JURY

The purpose of this form is to advise you of your right to trial by jury and to allow you to give up that right if you so choose.

READ THE ENTIRE FORM CAREFULLY BEFORE SIGNING IT

I understand that I am charged with the crime of

which is a [ ] misdemeanor [ ] felony under the law of Arizona and that if I am found guilty I can be given severe punishment, including incarceration [ ] in the Arizona State Prison, [ ] in the

_____

County Jail, [ ] a fine, or other penalty.

I understand that I am entitled to a trial by jury on these charges and, if applicable, on facts used to aggravate any sentence. The right to a trial by jury means the right to have my guilt or innocence, or, if applicable, facts used to aggravate any sentence, decided by a group of citizens whose decision must be unanimous.

I understand that once I have made the decision to give up my right to a jury trial, I may change my mind only with the permission of the court, and may not change it at all once the trial has actually begun.

CERTIFICATION AND WAIVER

After reading and understanding all the above, I hereby waive my right to:

    [ ] trial by jury on guilt or innocence;

    [ ] trial by jury on facts used to aggravate any sentence.

DO NOT SIGN THIS FORM UNLESS YOU HAVE READ IT COMPLETELY, OR HAD IT READ TO YOU AND UNDERSTAND IT FULLY.

_____
Date   Defendant

I have explained to the defendant the right to trial by jury and consent to the defendant's waiver of it.

_____
Date   Defense Attorney

I consent to waiver of trial by jury in this case.

_____
Date   Prosecutor

I approve of the waiver of the trial by jury in this case.

_____
Date   Signature of Judicial Officer

Form 20

Credits

Added Sept. 5, 2007, effective Jan. 1, 2008.

Editors' Notes

HISTORICAL NOTES

Former Form 20 was abrogated effective January 1, 2008.

16A A. R. S. Rules Crim. Proc., Form 20, AZ ST RCRP Form 20

Current with amendments received through 08/15/19

Form 21. Application to Vacate Conviction Under A.R.S. § 13-907.01

(Refs & Annos)

IX. Miscellaneous

Rule 41. Forms

Forms

16A A.R.S. Rules Crim.Proc., Form 21

Formerly cited as AZ ST RCRP Form 21(a)

Form 21. Application to Vacate Conviction Under A.R.S. § 13-907.01

_____ **Court** _____ **County, Arizona**

APPLICANT	CASE NO.	APPLICATION TO VACATE CONVICTION FOR A PRIOR OFFENSE UNDER A.R.S. § 13-907.01 AND SUPPORTING DECLARATION
(Name/Address/Phone):	_____ **APPLICATION**	

APPLICANT asks the court to vacate the conviction for the crime of Prostitution, under A.R.S. § 13-3214 or a city or town ordinance that has the same or substantially similar elements as A.R.S. § 13-3214, committed before July 24, 2014. The conviction occurred on _____ in this court. This relief is sought under A.R.S. § 13-907.01. The law provides that any person so convicted may apply to the sentencing court to vacate the conviction. The applicant is entitled to relief if the applicant can establish by clear and convincing evidence that the applicant's participation in the offense was the direct result of having been a victim of sex trafficking pursuant to A.R.S. § 13-1307.

Explain how you were a victim of sex trafficking and, as a direct result, were convicted of prostitution:

_____

_____

_____

_____

_____

_____

If additional information is required, you may attach additional pages on lined paper.

I state under penalty of perjury that the information I have provided on this form is true and correct.

Date: _____   Signature _____
                                                    Applicant

CERTIFICATE OF MAILING

I CERTIFY that I delivered or mailed a copy of this application to the prosecutor's office that prosecuted the case at the following address:_____

_____

Date: _____   Signature _____
                                                    Applicant

Credits

Formerly Form 21(a), added June 4, 2015, effective on an expedited basis July 3, 2015, adopted on a permanent basis Dec. 16, 2015. Amended and effective on an emergency basis Aug. 9, 2017, adopted on a permanent basis Dec. 13, 2017. Renumbered Form 21 on an emergency basis June 15, 2018, effective Aug. 3, 2018, adopted on a permanent basis Dec. 13, 2018.

Editors' Notes

HISTORICAL AND STATUTORY NOTES

Former Form 21 was abrogated effective Jan. 1, 2008.

Former Form 21, providing application upon discharge to restore civil rights, withdraw guilty plea/vacate conviction (set aside), and restore gun rights, was abrogated on an emergency basis June 15, 2018, effective Aug. 3, 2018.

16A A. R. S. Rules Crim. Proc., Form 21, AZ ST RCRP Form 21

Current with amendments received through 08/15/19

Form 22. Transmittal of Record on Appeal to Superior Court

(Refs & Annos)

IX. Miscellaneous

Rule 41. Forms

Forms

16A A.R.S. Rules Crim.Proc., Form 22

Form 22. Transmittal of Record on Appeal to Superior Court

_____COURT   [Precinct _____] _____County, Arizona

STATE OF ARIZONA Plaintiff   [CASE/COMPLAINT
                                                 NO.]

-vs-   TRANSMITTAL
                                                              CERTIFICATION
                                                              APPEAL TO
                                                              SUPERIOR
                                                              COURT

Defendant (FIRST, MI, LAST)

TRANSMITTAL OF RECORD ON APPEAL TO SUPERIOR COURT

I hereby certify that the enclosed items constitute a true and complete record of the preliminary proceedings held in the above-entitled case appearing in Docket No. _____, at page _____.

The following items are included:

[ ] The original complaint, including amendments;
[ ] The arrest warrant, summons, or citation;
[ ] The defendant's release questionnaire;
[ ] The defendant's financial statement and request for appointment of counsel;
[ ] If the defendant is or was in custody, a copy of the release order showing the conditions under which the defendant may be, or has been, released;
[ ] The defendant's appearance bond;
[ ] Security deposited with the appearance bond:

;

[ ] Defendant's waiver of counsel;
[ ] Order appointing counsel or written appearance of counsel;
[ ] Exhibits and items of physical evidence introduced at trial:

;

[ ] A copy of all proceedings had in the case, as shown by my docket;
[ ] Audiotape or videotape of trial, if any;
[ ] Other papers or items prepared in connection with the case:

.

_____
Date   Signature of Judicial Officer

                                              Printed Name and Title of Judicial
                                              Officer

                                                            Form 22

Credits
Added Sept. 5, 2007, effective Jan. 1, 2008.
Editors' Notes
HISTORICAL NOTES
Former Form 22 was abrogated effective January 1, 2008.
16A A. R. S. Rules Crim. Proc., Form 22, AZ ST RCRP Form 22
Current with amendments received through 08/15/19

Form 23. Notice of Rights of Review after Conviction in Superior Court

(Refs & Annos)

IX. Miscellaneous
Rule 41. Forms
Forms

16A A.R.S. Rules Crim.Proc., Form 23

Form 23. Notice of Rights of Review after Conviction in Superior Court

COURT		County, Arizona
STATE OF ARIZONA, Plaintiff -vs-	[CASE/COMPLAINT NO.]	NOTICE OF RIGHTS OF REVIEW AFTER SUPERIOR COURT * (Capital & Non-Capital)
Defendant (FIRST, MI, LAST)		

*In limited jurisdiction cases, see Superior Court Rules of Appellate Procedure--Criminal Form 1

RIGHT TO APPEAL (CAPITAL)

If you are a capital defendant and sentenced to death the clerk shall file a notice of appeal at the time of entry of judgment and sentence. This notice shall be sufficient as a notice of appeal with respect to all judgments entered and sentences imposed in this case (Rule 31.2b,).

RIGHT TO APPEAL (NON-CAPITAL)

You have a right to appeal from a final judgment of conviction, from an order denying a post-trial motion, or from a sentence which is illegal or excessive. Arizona Constitution art. 2, sec. 24; A.R.S. § 13-4031. YOU DO NOT HAVE A RIGHT TO DIRECT APPEAL IF YOU HAVE PLED GUILTY OR NO CONTEST OR HAVE ADMITTED A VIOLATION OF CONDITIONS OF PROBATION OR HAVE FAILED TO APPEAR AT SENTENCING CAUSING THE SENTENCING TO OCCUR MORE THAN 90 DAYS BEYOND THE DATE OF CONVICTION. IN THAT CASE, RELIEF MAY BE SOUGHT ONLY BY PETITION FOR POST-CONVICTION RELIEF. Rules 17.1, 17.2 and 27.8, , A.R.S. § 13-4033.

IN ORDER TO EXERCISE YOUR RIGHT TO APPEAL

1. You must file a NOTICE OF APPEAL (Form 24(a)) within 20 days of the entry of judgment and sentence. If you do not file a notice of appeal within 20 days you will lose your right to appeal. The entry of judgment and sentence occurs at the time of sentencing.

2. To file a Notice of Appeal you should contact your lawyer, by letter, telephone or in person, telling him or her that you want to appeal. You can file the notice of appeal before you leave the courtroom on the day you are sentenced if you wish.

3. If you do not have a lawyer, get copies of Form 5, Defendant's Financial Statement and Request for Appointment of Counsel and Form 24 (a), Notice of Appeal, either from the clerk of the court, jail, or the prison, fill them both out and file or send them to the clerk of the superior court in the county where you were tried and sentenced. They must arrive at the clerk's office within 20 days after you were sentenced.

4. You should have a lawyer handle your appeal. If you choose to waive your right to appellate counsel, you must file a written notice no later than thirty days after filing the notice of appeal. If the notice of waiver is given before the notice of appeal is filed, or is filed with the notice of appeal, it must be filed in the trial court. If the notice of waiver is given after the notice of appeal is filed, it must be filed in the appellate court. If the trial court determines that you knowingly, intelligently, and voluntarily desire to waive the right to appellate counsel, you will be allowed to represent yourself on appeal. The court may appoint advisory counsel during any stage of the appellate proceedings.

You must file a NOTICE OF APPEAL (Form 24(a)) within 20 days of the entry of judgment and sentence. If you do not file a notice of appeal within 20 days you will lose your right to appeal. The entry of judgment and sentence occurs at the time of sentencing.

RIGHT TO POST-CONVICTION RELIEF (CAPITAL)

If you are a capital defendant and sentenced to death, the clerk of the Supreme Court shall file a notice of Post Conviction Relief with the Trial Court upon the issuance of a mandate affirming your conviction and sentence on direct appeal. If your death sentence is reduced to life on direct appeal, it is your responsibility to file your own Notice of Post Conviction Relief. (Please see Right to Post-Conviction Relief (Non-Capital) section below).

RIGHT TO POST-CONVICTION RELIEF (NON-CAPITAL)

You also have a right to petition the Superior Court for Post-Conviction Relief. Rule 32, .

In order to exercise your Post-Conviction Relief right;

1. You must file a NOTICE OF POST-CONVICTION RELIEF (Form 24(c)) within 90 days of the entry of judgment and sentence if you do not file, or you do not have the right to file, a Notice of Appeal. If you do appeal, the time you have to file a Notice of Post-Conviction Relief extends from the entry of judgment and sentence to 30 days after the issuance of the order and mandate affirming the judgment and sentence on direct appeal.

NOTE: If you do not timely file a Notice of Post-Conviction Relief, you may never have another opportunity to have any errors made in your case corrected.

2. To seek post-conviction relief, you must obtain a copy of Form 24(c) (Notice of Post-Conviction Relief), either from your attorney, the clerk of the court, or the jail or prison, fill it out and file or send it to the clerk of the Superior Court of the county where you were sentenced. The notice must arrive at the clerk's office within 90 days after you were sentenced or within 30 days after the issuance of the order and mandate affirming the judgment and sentence on direct appeal.

3. If you cannot afford to hire an attorney, you should execute the Affidavit of Indigency contained in the Notice of Post-Conviction Relief and request that an attorney be appointed to represent you.

If you want a full copy of the rules governing appeals and post- conviction relief, the clerk of the court in the county where you were convicted will send you one upon request.

RECEIPT BY DEFENDANT

I have received a copy of this notice explaining my right to appeal, my right to seek post-conviction relief and the procedures I must follow to exercise these rights.

Date   Defendant

Credits

Added Sept. 5, 2007, effective Jan. 1, 2008. Amended Aug. 27, 2015, effective Jan. 1, 2016; Dec. 16, 2015, effective Jan. 1, 2016.

Editors' Notes

HISTORICAL NOTES

Former Form 23 was abrogated effective January 1, 2008.

16A A. R. S. Rules Crim. Proc., Form 23, AZ ST RCRP Form 23

Current with amendments received through 08/15/19

Form 24(a). Notice of Appeal from Superior Court

(Refs & Annos)

IX. Miscellaneous

Rule 41. Forms

Forms

16A A.R.S. Rules Crim.Proc., Form 24(a)

Form 24(a). Notice of Appeal from Superior Court

_____ COURT   _____ County, Arizona

STATE OF ARIZONA Plaintiff   [CASE/COMPLAINT
                                    NO.]

-vs-   NOTICE OF
                                                         APPEAL
                                                    FROM SUPERIOR
                                                        COURT*

Defendant (FIRST, MI, LAST)

* In limited jurisdiction cases, see Superior Court Rules of Appellate Procedure Form
2.

NOTICE OF APPEAL FROM SUPERIOR COURT

NOTICE IS HEREBY GIVEN that _____ appeals
from the

[ ] Following judgments(s) of guilt in the following case number(s);

[ ] Following sentence(s) imposed in the following case numbers(s);

[ ] Other:

entered in the Superior Court, in _____ County, on _____, 20_____.

_____
Date   [Party filing for appeal] Defendant,
                                    Attorney for Defendant or Prosecutor

ATTACHMENT
(1) The name and address of the defendant or defendants who appeal or against
    whom the state appeals:

(2) The name and address of the attorney for the defendant or defendants:

(3) The name and address of any co-defendant at trial. (If the address is not known,
    so state):

(4) The defendant or defendants who appeal or against whom the state appeals [ ]
    were [ ] were not represented by counsel at the determination of guilt or at
    sentencing.

                                                              Form 24(a)

Credits
Added Sept. 5, 2007, effective Jan. 1, 2008.
Editors' Notes

HISTORICAL NOTES
Former Form 24(a) was abrogated effective January 1, 2008.
16A A. R. S. Rules Crim. Proc., Form 24(a), AZ ST RCRP Form 24(a)
Current with amendments received through 08/15/19
Form 24(b). Notice of Post-Conviction Relief

(Refs & Annos)
IX. Miscellaneous
Rule 41. Forms
Forms

16A A.R.S. Rules Crim.Proc., Form 24(b)

Form 24(b). Notice of Post-Conviction Relief

_____ COURT   _____ County,
                                                                  Arizona

STATE OF ARIZONA Plaintiff   [CASE/COMPLAINT
                                        NO.]
                                                        NOTICE OF
-vs-   POST-
                                                        CONVICTION
                                                          RELIEF

Defendant (FIRST, MI, LAST)

NOTICE OF POST-CONVICTION RELIEF

Instructions: When the notice is complete, file it with the clerk of the superior court of the county in which the conviction occurred.

A person unable to pay costs of this proceeding and to obtain the services of a lawyer without substantial personal or family hardship should indicate this by requesting counsel in Question 8 of this notice and execute the affidavit of indigency on page 3. In the event an attorney is not appointed, a Request for Preparation of Post-Conviction Relief Record form must be filed by the defendant if some portion of the record is needed and has not previously been obtained.

No issue which has already been raised and decided on appeal or in a previous petition for post-conviction relief may be used as a basis for a successive petition for post-conviction relief.

1. Defendant's Name:

   Defendant's prison number (if any):

2. Defendant's address:

3. (A) Defendant was convicted of the following crimes:

    (B)   Defendant was sentenced on
              _____
              , 20
              ___
              , to a term of

              , commencing on
              _____
              , 20
              ___
              , following a:
    [ ] Trial by jury
    [ ] Trial to Judge without a Jury
    [ ] Plea of Guilty
    [ ] Plea of No Contest
    [ ] Probation Revocation Admission
    [ ] Probation Revocation Violation Hearing in the Superior Court in
              _____ County with judicial officer _____ presiding.
    (C) The file number of the case was CR--_____.
4. Defendant has taken the following actions to secure relief from his convictions or
   sentences:
   (A) Direct Appeal: [ ] Yes [ ] No
   (B) Previous Rule 32 Proceedings: [ ] Yes [ ] No
5. Defendant was represented by the following lawyers at: (provide name of counsel
   and counsel's address, if known)
   Trial or change of plea:

   Sentencing hearing:

   Appeal (if any):

   Previous Rule 32 proceedings (if any):

6. Is the defendant raising a claim of ineffective assistance of counsel? [ ] Yes [ ] No
7. Defendant is presently represented by a lawyer? [ ] Yes [ ] No
   If yes, provide name and address:

8. If you are not currently represented by a lawyer, do you want the court to
   appoint a lawyer for this proceeding? [ ] Yes [ ] No
9 Respond to this section only if this is an untimely notice or the defendant has
   filed a previous Rule 32 petition in this case.

(A) Is a claim pursuant to Rule 32.1(d), (e), (f), (g) or (h) being raised in this petition? [ ] Yes [ ] No

(B) If yes, state the specific exception:

    [ ] The defendant is being held in custody after the sentence imposed has expired.

    [ ] Newly discovered material facts exist which probably would have changed the verdict or sentence.

    [ ] The defendant's failure to file a timely notice of post-conviction relief or notice of appeal was without fault on the defendant's part.

    [ ] There has been a significant change in the law that would probably overturn the conviction or sentence.

    [ ] Facts exist which establish by clear and convincing evidence that the defendant is actually innocent.

(C) State the facts that support the claim and the reasons for not raising the claim in the previous petition or in a timely manner:

I am requesting post-conviction relief. I understand that I must include in my petition every ground for relief which is known and which has not been raised and decided previously. I also understand that failure to raise any known ground for relief in my petition will prohibit me from raising it at any future date.

_____

Date   Defendant

AFFIDAVIT OF INDIGENCY

I have requested the appointment of a lawyer to represent me in post conviction proceedings. I swear under oath and penalty of perjury that I am indigent and because of my poverty I am financially unable to pay for the cost of a lawyer to represent me without incurring substantial hardship to myself or my family.

Date   Defendant

State of Arizona   )   Subscribed and sworn to or affirmed before me on:

)ss.

County of   )

                               Date

My Commission Expires

                               Notary Public

Form 24(b)

Credits

Added Sept. 5, 2007, effective Jan. 1, 2008.

Editors' Notes

HISTORICAL NOTES

Former Forms 24(b) and 24(c) were abrogated effective January 1, 2008.

16A A. R. S. Rules Crim. Proc., Form 24(b), AZ ST RCRP Form 24(b)

Current with amendments received through 08/15/19

Form 25. Petition for Post-Conviction Relief

(Refs & Annos)
IX. Miscellaneous
Rule 41. Forms
Forms

16A A.R.S. Rules Crim.Proc., Form 25

Form 25. Petition for Post-Conviction Relief

_____ COURT _____ County,
Arizona

STATE OF ARIZONA   Plaintiff [CASE/COMPLAINT
                              NO.]

-vs-   PETITION FOR
                                                    POST-CONVICTION
                                                          RELIEF

Defendant (FIRST, MI, LAST)

PETITION FOR POST-CONVICTION RELIEF

Instructions: In order for this petition to receive consideration by the court, you should first file Form 24(b).

Each applicable question in Form 25 must be answered fully but concisely in legible handwriting or by typing. When necessary, an answer to a particular question may be completed on the reverse side of the page or on an additional blank page, making clear to which question such continued answer refers.

Any false statement of fact made and sworn to under oath in this petition could serve as the basis for prosecution and conviction for perjury. Therefore, exercise care to assure that all answers are true and correct.

NO ISSUE WHICH HAS ALREADY BEEN RAISED AND DECIDED ON APPEAL OR IN A PREVIOUS PETITION MAY BE USED AS A BASIS FOR THIS PETITION.

TAKE CARE TO INCLUDE EVERY GROUND FOR RELIEF WHICH IS KNOWN AND WHICH HAS NOT BEEN RAISED AND DECIDED PREVIOUSLY, SINCE FAILURE TO RAISE ANY SUCH GROUND IN THIS PETITION WILL BAR ITS BEING RAISED LATER.

When the petition is complete, mail it to the clerk of the court in which conviction occurred.

1. Petitioner's Name:

   Petitioner's prison number (if any):

2. Petitioner is now: [ ] On Parole [ ] On Probation [ ] Confined in
3. Petitioner is eligible for relief because of:
   [ ] The introduction at trial of evidence obtained pursuant to an unlawful arrest.
   [ ] The introduction at trial of evidence obtained by an unconstitutional search and seizure.
   [ ] The introduction at trial of an identification obtained in violation of constitutional rights.
   [ ] The introduction at trial of a coerced confession.
   [ ] The introduction at trial of a statement obtained in the absence of a lawyer at a time when representation is constitutionally required.
   [ ] Any other infringement of the right against self-incrimination.
   [ ] The denial of the constitutional right to representation by a competent lawyer at every critical stage of the proceeding.
   [ ] The unconstitutional suppression of evidence by the state.
   [ ] The unconstitutional use by the state of perjured testimony.
   [ ] An unlawfully induced plea of guilty or no contest.
   [ ] Violation of the right not to be placed twice in jeopardy for the same offense.
   [ ] The abridgement of any other right guaranteed by the constitution or the laws of this state, or the constitution of the United States, including a right that was not recognized as existing at the time of the trial if retrospective application of that right is required.
   [ ] The existence of newly-discovered material which require the court to vacate the conviction or sentence.
   [Specify when petitioner learned of these facts for the first time, and show how they would have affected the trial.]

   [ ] The lack of jurisdiction of the court which entered the conviction or sentence.
   [ ] The use by the state in determining sentence of a prior conviction obtained in violation of the United States or Arizona constitutions.
   [ ] Sentence imposed other than in accordance with the sentencing procedures established by rule and statute.
   [ ] Being held beyond the term of sentence or after parole or probation has been unlawfully revoked.
   [ ] The failure of the judge at sentencing to advise petitioner of his right to appeal and the procedures for doing so.
   [ ] The failure of petitioner's attorney to file a timely notice of appeal after being instructed to do so.
   [ ] The obstruction by state officials of the right to appeal.
   [ ] Any other ground within the scope of Rule 32, (please specify):

4. The facts in support of the alleged error(s) upon which this petition is based are contained in Attachment A.

[State facts clearly and fully; citations or discussions of authorities need not be included].

5. Supporting Exhibits:
   A. The following exhibits are attached in support of the petition:
      Affidavits [Exhibit(s) # _____]
      Records [Exhibit(s) # _____]
      Other supporting evidence [Exhibit(s) # _____]
   B. No affidavits, records or other supporting evidence are attached because

6. Petitioner has taken the following actions to secure relief from his convictions or sentences:
   A. Direct Appeal: [ ] Yes [ ] No (If yes, name the courts to which appeals were taken, date, number, and result.)

   B. Previous Rule 32 Proceedings: [ ] Yes [ ] No (If yes, name the court in which such petitions were filed, dates, numbers, and results, including all appeals from decisions on such petitions.)

   C. Previous Habeas Corpus or Special Action Proceedings in the Courts of Arizona: [ ] Yes [ ] No (If yes, name the courts in which such petitions were filed, dates, numbers, and results, including all appeals from decisions on such petitions.)

   D. Habeas Corpus or Other Petitions in Federal Courts: [ ] Yes [ ] No (If yes, name the districts in which petitions were filed, dates, court numbers--civil action or miscellaneous, and results, including all appeals from decisions on such petitions.)

7. The issues which are raised in this petition have not been finally decided nor raised before because: (State facts.)

8. Because of the foregoing reasons, the relief which the petitioner desires is:
   A. [ ] Release from custody and discharge.
   B. [ ] A new trial.
   C. [ ] Correction of sentence.
   D. [ ] The right to file a delayed appeal.

E. [ ] Other relief (specify):

I declare under penalty of perjury that the information contained in this form and in any attachments is true to the best of my knowledge or belief.

Date   Defendant

Form 25

Credits
Added Sept. 5, 2007, effective Jan. 1, 2008. Amended Aug. 30, 2012, effective Jan. 1, 2013; Nov. 14, 2013, effective Jan. 1, 2014.
Editors' Notes
HISTORICAL NOTES
Former Form 25 was abrogated effective January 1, 2008.
16A A. R. S. Rules Crim. Proc., Form 25, AZ ST RCRP Form 25
Current with amendments received through 08/15/19

Form 26. Request for Preparation of Post-Conviction Relief Record

(Refs & Annos)
IX. Miscellaneous
Rule 41. Forms
Forms

16A A.R.S. Rules Crim.Proc., Form 26

Form 26. Request for Preparation of Post-Conviction Relief Record

_____ COURT   _____ County, Arizona

STATE OF ARIZONA Plaintiff   [CASE/COMPLAINT NO.]

-vs-   REQUEST FOR PREPARATION OF POST-CONVICTION

Defendant (FIRST, MI, LAST)   RELIEF RECORD

REQUEST FOR PREPARATION OF POST-CONVICTION RELIEF RECORD
The defendant has filed a Notice of Post-Conviction Relief in the above-entitled cause and requests, pursuant to Rule 32.4(d), Arizona , the preparation of the

following portions of the court record and transcripts for review. The defendant has not previously received the documents requested.

SUPERIOR COURT RECORD

[ ] Instruments
[ ] Minute Entries
[ ] Presentence Report
[ ] Criminal History
[ ] Rule 11 Reports

TRANSCRIPTS

PROBATION VIOLATION

[ ] Probation Revocation:
[ ] Admission of Violation
[ ] Violation Hearing
[ ] Predisposition Hearing, if any
[ ] Disposition Hearing

CHANGE OF PLEA

[ ] Change of Plea
[ ] Presentence Hearing, if any
[ ] Sentencing

TRIAL

[ ] All Pretrial Motions (except deletions)
[ ] Voir Dire
[ ] Opening Arguments
[ ] Closing Arguments
[ ] All Trial Proceedings (from calling of the case to the verdict)
[ ] Trial or Admission of Prior Conviction(s)
[ ] All Post-Trial Motions (except deletions)
[ ] Presentence Hearing, if any
[ ] Sentencing

DELETIONS

[ ] Motions to Continue by Defendant
[ ] Hearings Dealing with Release Conditions
[ ] Pretrial Conferences
[ ] Arraignments
[ ] Mistried Cases
[ ] Stipulated Rule 11 Hearings

Dated this _____ day of _____, 20___.

Defendant or Attorney for Defendant
Copy of the foregoing
Mailed this _____ day of
_____, 20___ to:

Credits
Added Sept. 5, 2007, effective Jan. 1, 2008.
Editors' Notes
HISTORICAL NOTES
Former Forms 26, 26(a) and 26(b) were abrogated effective January 1, 2008.
16A A. R. S. Rules Crim. Proc., Form 26, AZ ST RCRP Form 26
Current with amendments received through 08/15/19

Form 27(a). Subpoena

(Refs & Annos)
IX. Miscellaneous
Rule 41. Forms
Forms

16A A.R.S. Rules Crim.Proc., Form 27(a)

Form 27(a). Subpoena

_____COURT   [Precinct _____]   _____County, Arizona

STATE OF ARIZONA   Plaintiff [CASE/COMPLAINT NO.]
-vs-

SUBPOENA

Defendant (FIRST, MI, LAST)

SUBPOENA
TO:

YOU ARE HEREBY ORDERED to appear at ___ a.m. / p.m. on _____ ___, 20 ___,
at
_____ and to remain there until excused to give testimony
address
on behalf of
_____
and to bring with you:

.

IF YOU FAIL TO APPEAR AS ORDERED, A WARRANT MAY BE ISSUED FOR
YOUR ARREST.
Given under my hand and seal. _____ _____, 20 ___.

_____ Clerk of the Court

By

Party / Attorney for party requesting   Deputy Clerk
subpoena

Requests for reasonable accommodation for persons with disabilities must be made to the court by parties at least 3 working days in advance of a scheduled court proceeding.

CERTIFICATE OF SERVICE

The undersigned swears (or affirms) that he / she is qualified to serve this subpoena and did so by showing the original to and informing the witness of its contents and by delivering a copy thereof as follows:

Date received

_____

Date served

_____

Time served

Person served

Location served

_____ _____ County

Person Serving Subpoena

Form 27(a)

Credits

Added Sept. 5, 2007, effective Jan. 1, 2008.

Editors' Notes

HISTORICAL NOTES

Former Form 27 was repealed October 16, 2001.

16A A. R. S. Rules Crim. Proc., Form 27(a), AZ ST RCRP Form 27(a)

Current with amendments received through 08/15/19

Form 27(b). Subpoena - Alternative, Standby

(Refs & Annos)

IX. Miscellaneous

Rule 41. Forms

Forms

16A A.R.S. Rules Crim.Proc., Form 27(b)

Form 27(b). Subpoena - Alternative, Standby

_____ COURT   _____ County, Arizona

STATE OF ARIZONA Plaintiff   [CASE/COMPLAINT NO.]

-vs-   SUBPOENA
(Alternative--
Stand
by)

Defendant (FIRST, MI, LAST)

SUBPOENA
(Alternative - - Stand by)

TO:

YOU ARE HEREBY ORDERED
to stand by to appear upon 30 minutes prior notice at any time between

___
a.m. / p.m. on

_____
, 20

___
, at [Address}

_____
and to remain there until excused by the judge conducting the proceeding, to give testimony on behalf of

_____
and to bring with you:

YOU ARE FURTHER ORDERED to state on the copy of this subpoena to be returned to the issuing party, a telephone number or numbers at which you can be reached at any time between 9:00 a.m. and 5:00 p.m. between the times noted above telephone numbers: (___)_____. If you are unable to supply such numbers, YOU ARE ORDERED to appear at the time first mentioned above.
IF YOU FAIL TO APPEAR AS ORDERED, A WARRANT MAY BE ISSUED FOR YOUR ARREST.
Given under my hand and seal. _____, 20 ___.
_____ Clerk of the Court
                               By

Party / Attorney for party requesting subpoena   Deputy Clerk

Requests for reasonable accommodation for persons with disabilities must be made to the court by parties at least 3 working days in advance of a scheduled court proceeding.

CERTIFICATE OF SERVICE

The undersigned swears (or affirms) that he / she is qualified to serve this subpoena and did so by showing the original to and informing the witness of its contents and by delivering a copy thereof as follows:

Date received   Date served   Time served

Person served

Location served

_____

County

Person Serving Subpoena

Form 27(b)

Credits
Added Sept. 5, 2007, effective Jan. 1, 2008.
16A A. R. S. Rules Crim. Proc., Form 27(b), AZ ST RCRP Form 27(b)
Current with amendments received through 08/15/19

Form 28. Telephonic Guilty Plea/No Contest Plea Proceedings

(Refs & Annos)
IX. Miscellaneous
Rule 41. Forms
Forms

16A A.R.S. Rules Crim.Proc., Form 28

Form 28. Telephonic Guilty Plea/No Contest Plea Proceedings

_____ COURT   _____ County, Arizona

STATE OF ARIZONA Plaintiff   [CASE/COMPLAINT NO.]

-vs-   TELEPHONIC GUILTY/NO CONTEST

Defendant (FIRST, MI, LAST)

Defendant appears personally and expresses a desire to plead guilty or no contest to the charges indicated and I find the following facts:

1. Defendant understands the nature of the charges as indicated:
   [ ] Driving or in actual physical control of a motor vehicle while under the influence of intoxicating liquor/toxic vapor/drugs.
   [ ] Driving or in actual physical control of a motor vehicle with an alcohol concentration of .08 percent or more within 2 hours of driving or being in actual physical control.
   [ ] Driving or in actual physical control of a motor vehicle with an alcohol concentration of .15 percent or more within 2 hours of driving or being in actual physical control.
   [ ] Driving or in actual physical control of a motor vehicle with any illegal drug or its metabolite in the defendant's body.
   [ ] Driving or in actual physical control of a commercial vehicle with an alcohol concentration of .04 percent or more.
   [ ] Other:

2. Defendant appears: [ ] with counsel [ ] without counsel, (waiver of counsel with file) and understands the following:
3. Defendant has entered into a: [ ] plea agreement, and consents to its terms; [ ] plea to the court.
4. Defendant understands the range of penalties to be:
   [ ] Class 1 misdemeanor: a $2500 fine, 6 months jail, and/or 3 years probation, plus surcharges and fees.
   [ ] Class 1 misdemeanor: a $2500 fine, 6 months jail, and/or 5 years probation, plus surcharges and fees.
   [ ] Class 2 misdemeanor: a $750 fine, 4 months jail, and/or 2 years probation, plus surcharges and fees.
   [ ] Class 3 misdemeanor: a $500 fine, 30 days jail, and/or 1 year probation, plus surcharges and fees.
   [ ] Other:

5. If arrested on a subsequent offense, defendant may be charged with a more serious offense and associated penalties.
6. The Court has advised the defendant that this guilty plea may result in a violation of probation or parole.
7. Defendant was advised of the following: If you are not a citizen of the United States, pleading guilty or no contest to a crime may affect your immigration status. Admitting guilt may result in deportation even if the charge is later dismissed. Your plea or admission of guilt could result in your deportation or

removal, could prevent you from ever being able to get legal status in the United States, or could prevent you from becoming a United States citizen.

8. Defendant understands that the following constitutional rights are given up by changing the plea:
   a. Right to plead not guilty and require the State to prove guilt beyond a reasonable doubt.
   b. Right to a trial [ ] by jury [ ] by a judge.
   c. Right to assistance of an attorney at all stages of the proceeding, including appeal. In some cases, the defendant may be eligible for a court- appointed attorney at a reduced cost or at no cost, if the defendant cannot afford one.
   d. Right to confront the witnesses against the defendant and to cross- examine them as to the truthfulness of their testimony.
   e. Right to present evidence in the defendant's own behalf and to have the court compel the defendant's chosen witnesses to appear and testify free of charge.
   f. Right to remain silent, not to incriminate oneself, and to be presumed innocent unless/or until proven guilty beyond a reasonable doubt.
   g. Right to a direct appeal.
9. Defendant wishes to give up these constitutional rights after having been advised of them.
10. A basis in fact exists for believing the defendant guilty of the offenses charged.
11. The plea is voluntary and not the result of force or threat, or promises other than those contained in the plea agreement.
12. Defendant may file a Rule 32 petition for post-conviction relief and if denied may file a petition for review.

I CERTIFY that I have read and that I understand all of the matters cited above. I wish to give up my constitutional rights, including my right to a trial by jury and my right to an attorney, and to plead guilty to the charge(s) of:

.

Dated:

Defendant

Address

(

‾

)

Telephone Number

I CERTIFY that the above named defendant personally appeared before me, and acknowledge that he or she read all of the foregoing information and identified himself or herself to me

_____
(drivers license # and/or a picture ID) and that I have affixed a print of the defendant's right index finger to this document.

Dated: _____

Officer Name and Badge Number

Law Enforcement Agency

Address

(

‾‾

)

Telephone

AFFIDAVIT OF RESIDENCY

Pursuant to Rule 17.1, Arizona , I request to resolve my pending criminal misdemeanor case(s) in through a telephonic plea proceeding. I swear under oath and penalty of perjury, that:

(1) I am not a resident of the State of Arizona, that I am a resident of the County of _____ in the State of _____, or (2) I reside more than 100 miles from the Court.

Defendant (print name)

Defendant's Signature

State of

County of

I hereby certify that _____ personally appeared before me. IN WITNESS WHEREOF, I have hereunto set my hand and affixed my official seal this ___ day of _____, 20 ___.

Notary Public

Commission Expires

I CERTIFY that I have personally advised the defendant telephonically:
1. Of the nature of the charges against him or her.
2. Advised the defendant of all constitutional rights which defendant waived by pleading guilty.
3. Ascertained that the defendant wished to give up the constitutional rights of which he or she has been advised.

4. Inquired as to the defendant's probation or parole status.

The court finds a basis in fact for believing the defendant is guilty of the offenses charged and, that the defendant's plea of guilty is voluntary and not the result of force, threats or promises other than those contained in a plea agreement.

On the basis of these findings, I conclude that the defendant knowingly, voluntarily and intelligently pleads guilty to the above charges, and I accept his or her plea.

Dated:

Judge

Defendant: Def. Counsel/Bar No.:   Interpreter:

Form 28

Credits
Added Sept. 5, 2007, effective Jan. 1, 2008.
Editors' Notes
HISTORICAL NOTES
Former Form 28 was abrogated effective January 1, 2008.
16A A. R. S. Rules Crim. Proc., Form 28, AZ ST RCRP Form 28
Current with amendments received through 08/15/19

Form 28(a). Instructions for Completing the Form for Entering a "Guilty/No Contest Plea by Mail...

(Refs & Annos)
IX. Miscellaneous
Rule 41. Forms
Forms

16A A.R.S. Rules Crim.Proc., Form 28(a)

Form 28(a). Instructions for Completing the Form for Entering a "Guilty/No Contest Plea by Mail"

Warning: The submission to the court of a completed form to enter a "guilty/no contest plea by mail" will have important legal consequences. Please read the entire plea and these instructions completely and carefully.

It is your responsibility to inquire with the Arizona Motor Vehicle Department regarding any other consequences of pleading guilty to a traffic offense and what impact that has on your Driver's License, especially a Commercial Driver's License (CDL). Consult a lawyer if you have any additional questions after reading these instructions.

Note: You must have a copy of the complaint charging you with a crime to complete the form.

You must complete each step below.

(1) Enter your first name, middle name, and last name exactly as they appear on the complaint.

(2) Enter the court's case number.

(3) Check whether you are pleading guilty or no contest. Check only one box.

(4) Provide the reasons why you have an "undue hardship." An undue hardship is something that makes it difficult for you to personally appear in court, such as an illness, physical incapacity, a substantial distance to travel, or you are currently in jail. The court will decide if you are allowed to enter a plea by mail. If you do not have an "undue hardship" or the court determines your case is not appropriate to handle by mail, you must personally appear in court.

I understand that the court will not accept a plea by mail if any of the following are true:

- my case involves a victim;
- the court may impose a jail term, unless I am sentenced to time served, or unless I am currently in jail and the jail time that is imposed would not extend the length of my current jail sentence;
- the court may impose a term of probation;
- my fingerprint is required to be on the sentencing document;
- a plea by mail would not be in the interests of justice; or
- I have not described in paragraph 12 below any undue hardship that justifies my plea by mail.

(5) Provide any information you would like the judge to consider before you are sentenced. You may attach additional pages if needed and attach any other documents you'd like the judge to consider.

(6). You must sign & date the plea by mail as well as provide your current address. Your signature confirms that you have read and understand the plea by mail form as well as these instructions, or that they have been read to you and that you understand them. If you do not read or speak English, please contact the court and request the assistance of an interpreter. If you have a lawyer, they must also sign the form and provide a State Bar number. Please note that only an attorney who is licensed to practice law in Arizona may sign the form. The court will mail you a copy of the judgment and sentence.

GUILTY/NO CONTEST PLEA BY MAIL

(1) STATE OF ARIZONA, Plaintiff v. _____ Defendant (Print full legal name)	(2) Case/Complaint No. _____	GUILTY/ NO CONTEST PLEA BY MAIL & JUDGMENT OF CONVICTION

1. I have a copy of the criminal complaint in this case. I have read and I understand the charges filed against me. I hereby agree to plead (check only one): (3) ☐ Guilty or ☐ No Contest, to all of the charges in the complaint.

2. I am requesting to enter my plea by mail because my personal appearance in court would be an undue hardship for the following reasons:
(4) _____

3. I admit that if my case went to trial, the facts would support the charges.

4. I understand that the range of penalties for misdemeanor and petty offenses are as follows:

   Class 1 misdemeanor: a suspended sentence up to a $2500 fine, 6 months jail, and/or 3 years probation, plus surcharges and fees.
   Class 2 misdemeanor: a suspended sentence up to a $750 fine, 4 months jail, and/or 2 years probation, plus surcharges and fees.
   Class 3 misdemeanor: a suspended sentence up to a $500 fine, 30 days jail, and/or 1 year probation, plus surcharges and fees.
   Petty offense: a suspended sentence up to a $300 fine, plus surcharges and fees.

5. If I am convicted of a future offense, this case may be used to increase a penalty on the new offense.

6. If I was on probation or parole at the time this offense occurred, pleading guilty or no contest may result in a petition to revoke my probation or parole and could include additional incarceration.

7. I know that if I am not a citizen of the United States, pleading guilty or no contest to a crime may affect my immigration status. Admitting guilt may result in deportation even if the charge is later dismissed. My plea or admission of guilt could result in deportation or removal, could prevent me from ever being able to get legal status in the United States, or could prevent me from becoming a United States citizen.

8. I understand that by entering my plea of guilty or no contest by mail I am giving up the following constitutional rights:

   a. The right to plead not guilty and to require the State to prove guilt beyond a reasonable doubt.
   b. The right to a trial, and depending on the charge(s) against me, a right to a trial by jury.
   c. The right to assistance of an attorney at all stages of the proceeding, including appeal. If I cannot afford one, I may be eligible for a court-appointed attorney at a reduced cost or at no cost.
   d. The right to confront the witnesses against me and to cross-examine them as to the truthfulness of their testimony.
   e. The right to present evidence in my own behalf and to have the court compel my chosen witnesses to appear and to testify free of charge.
   f. The right to remain silent, not to incriminate myself, and to be presumed innocent unless/or until proven guilty beyond a reasonable doubt.
   g. The right to a direct appeal.

10. My plea is voluntary and not the result of force, threat, or promises.

11. I understand that I may file a petition for post-conviction relief in accordance with Rule 32 of the AZ Rules of Criminal Procedure, and if it is denied I may file a petition for review.

12. . I give up the right to be present at the time of sentencing. I would like the court to consider the following information in determining an appropriate sentence (attach additional pages if needed):
(5) _____
_____
_____
_____

Oath & acknowledgement. I swear or affirm that have read, truthfully answered and not misrepresented information contained in this plea under penalty of perjury. I understand that the court will determine the sentence and mail a copy of its judgment to me. I will be responsible for fulfilling the penalties and the sentence imposed by the court.

(6) Dated: _____   Defendants Signature _____

(Address) _____   (City) _____   (State) _____ (Zip Code) _____

_____ / _____
(if any) Defense Counsel Signature/AZ Bar #

ACCEPTANCE OF PLEA AND JUDGMENT OF CONVICTION

The court has reviewed the defendant's statements set forth in this Guilty/No Contest Plea by Mail form. The court finds a basis in fact for believing the defendant is guilty of the offense(s) charged, and that the defendant's plea of guilty or no contest is voluntary and intelligent. I accept the defendant's plea and find that the defendant is guilty of the following offense(s)alleged in the complaint:

Case #_____For the offenses committed on _____ 20_____

Count 1 :_____ a class 1, 2, 3 misdemeanor. or ☐ Petty offense.
        (Description of offense)

Or ☐ civil traffic offense: a violation of A.R.S. §_____

SENTENCE: The defendant is sentenced as follows:_____

Count 2 :_____ a class 1, 2, 3 misdemeanor. or ☐ Petty offense.
        (Description of offense)

Or ☐ civil traffic offense: a violation of A.R.S. §_____

SENTENCE: The defendant is sentenced as follows:_____

Count 3 :_____ a class 1, 2, 3 misdemeanor. or ☐ Petty offense.
        (Description of offense)

Or ☐ civil traffic offense: a violation of A.R.S. §_____

SENTENCE: The defendant is sentenced as follows:_____

Count 4 :_____ a class 1, 2, 3 misdemeanor. or ☐ Petty offense.
        (Description of offense)

Or ☐ civil traffic offense: a violation of A.R.S. §_____

SENTENCE: The defendant is sentenced as follows:_____

Count 5 :_____ a class 1, 2, 3 misdemeanor. or ☐ Petty offense.
        (Description of offense)

Or ☐ civil traffic offense: a violation of A.R.S. §_____

SENTENCE: The defendant is sentenced as follows:_____

Dated: _____   Judge _____

I CERTIFY that a copy of this document was mailed to defendant at the address shown above on this date: _____ by (Clerk's name or initials): _____.

Credits

Added Sept. 1, 2011, effective Jan. 1, 2012. Amended April 27, 2017, effective Oct. 1, 2017.

16A A. R. S. Rules Crim. Proc., Form 28(a), AZ ST RCRP Form 28(a)

Current with amendments received through 08/15/19

Form 29. Entry of Not Guilty Plea and Advisements

(Refs & Annos)

IX. Miscellaneous

Rule 41. Forms

Forms

16A A.R.S. Rules Crim.Proc., Form 29

Form 29. Entry of Not Guilty Plea and Advisements

COURT		County, Arizona
STATE OF ARIZONA, Plaintiff	[CASE/COMPLAINT NO.]	
-vs-		ENTRY OF NOT GUILTY PLEA AND ADVISEMENTS

Defendant (FIRST, MI, LAST)

1. A plea of not guilty is hereby entered on the defendant's behalf to the following charge(s):

2. The parties are notified that the next court appearance in this matter is for _____, on _____, 20 ___, at ___ a.m., before Judge _____, located at _____, Arizona.

3. The defendant is advised that the defendant has the right to be present at all future proceedings. If the defendant fails to appear for any proceeding other than

sentencing, that proceeding may be held regardless of the defendant's absence, the defendant may be charged with an offense for failure to appear, and a bench warrant may be issued for the defendant's arrest. If the defendant fails to appear for trial, trial may be held in the defendant's absence and the defendant may be convicted and sentenced.

4. The Defendant is advised that, if convicted, the defendant will be required to appear for sentencing. If the defendant chooses not to appear, and the defendant's absence prevents the defendant from being sentenced within ninety days from the conviction, the defendant may lose the right to a direct appeal.

5. The defendant is further advised of the right to (jury) trial in this matter.

6. The defendant is further advised that discovery is available from the Prosecutor's office, as provided in rule 15.1, .

7. The defendant is directed to contact his/her attorney within 72 hours of service of this notice.

8. The defendant has requested an interpreter: [ ] Spanish [ ] Other Language

I acknowledge that I have received a copy of this document.
Dated:

Defendant

Address

( )
Telephone Number

Dated:

Defense Attorney   Bar No.

Credits
Added Sept. 5, 2007, effective Jan. 1, 2008. Amended Aug. 27, 2015, effective Jan. 1, 2016.

Editors' Notes
HISTORICAL NOTES
Former Form 29 was abrogated effective January 1, 2008.
16A A. R. S. Rules Crim. Proc., Form 29, AZ ST RCRP Form 29
Current with amendments received through 08/15/19

Form 30. Certificate of Compliance

(Refs & Annos)

IX. Miscellaneous
Rule 41. Forms
Forms

16A A.R.S. Rules Crim.Proc., Form 30

Form 30. Certificate of Compliance

<u>Certificate of Compliance</u>

1. This certificate of compliance concerns:

A brief, and is submitted under Rule 31.12(a)(5)

A motion for reconsideration, and is submitted under Rule 31.20(e)

A petition or cross-petition for review, and is submitted under Rule 31.21(g)(3)

An amicus curiae brief, and is submitted under Rule 31.12(a)(5)

2. The undersigned certifies that the brief/motion for reconsideration/petition or cross-petition for review to which this Certificate is attached:

Uses type of at least 14 points, is double-spaced, and contains _____ words

<u>Or</u>

Contains _____ handwritten pages

3. The document to which this Certificate is attached does not, or does exceed the word or page limit that is set by Rule 31.12, Rule 31.20, or Rule 31.22, as applicable.

Signature of Attorney or Self-Represented Party

Printed Name of Attorney or Self-Represented Party
Credits
Added by Aug. 31, 2017, effective Jan. 1, 2018.
16A A. R. S. Rules Crim. Proc., Form 30, AZ ST RCRP Form 30
Current with amendments received through 08/15/19

Form 31(a). Application to Set Aside Conviction

(Refs & Annos)
IX. Miscellaneous
Rule 41. Forms
Forms

16A A.R.S. Rules Crim.Proc., Form 31(a)

Form 31(a). Application to Set Aside Conviction

[new] FORM 31(a). Application to Set Aside Conviction

_____Court_____County, Arizona

STATE OF ARIZONA, Plaintiff -vs- _____ Defendant (FIRST, MI, LAST) _____ Date of Birth Applicant is: [ ] Defendant [ ] Attorney for Defendant [ ] Probation Officer	CASE NUMBER: _____ **APPLICATION TO SET ASIDE CONVICTION** A.R.S. § 13-907 **Note:** Includes application to restore gun and firearm rights pursuant to A.R.S. § 13-907(J)

SECTION I. CONVICTION(S)

A Judgment of Guilt was entered in the _____ Court against me, the
defendant, on the _____ day of _____, _____, on the conviction of:

1. Count I: _____

2. Count II: _____

3. Count III: _____

4. Count IV: _____

[ ] Additional counts continue on a separate page.

SECTION II. SENTENCE COMPLIANCE

1. I was sentenced to: [ ] a term of probation [ ] the Department of Corrections
2. [ ] I completed the conditions of **probation**. The Probation Department's order discharging me from probation is attached to this application, if available.
3. [ ] I have complied with all required terms of the **sentence** (*including all probation, employment, classes, community service, victim restitution or other court ordered monetary obligations, drug/alcohol testing, or other requirements.*)
4. [ ] I have not complied with all terms of my sentence. Explain:

   _____

   _____

   _____

5. [ ] I received from the Arizona Department of Corrections a Certificate of Absolute Discharge from Imprisonment AND have attached a copy of that Certificate to this application, if available.

6. Have you paid victim restitution in full? [ ] Yes [ ] No
   If not, a set aside of judgment of conviction will be denied without a showing of extraordinary circumstances. If you believe you have extraordinary circumstances, explain below. *(Attach documentation you think is relevant for the court's consideration.)*

   _____

   _____

   _____

   _____

7. Have you paid all other court-ordered monetary obligations in this case (criminal fines and fees) in full?

   [ ] Yes [ ] No

   If not, please explain:

   _____

   _____

   _____

   _____

   In some circumstances, you may be eligible to apply to the court to mitigate the amount owed or convert monies owed to community restitution.

SECTION III. PRIOR SET ASIDE(S)

1. Have you previously applied to set aside any conviction? [ ] Yes [ ] No

   If so, what was the date of your last application? _____

2. Have you previously been granted a set aside? [ ] Yes [ ] No

3. Have you previously been denied a set aside? [ ] Yes [ ] No

SECTION IV. PENDING CASES AND ACTIVE WARRANTS

1. Are there any open criminal cases against you? [ ] Yes [ ] No
2. Do you have an active warrant? [ ] Yes [ ] No
   If yes to either question above, please explain:

   _____

   _____

SECTION V. OTHER INFORMATION FOR THE COURT

1. Is there anything you would like the court to consider?

_____

_____

_____

2. [ ] Attach any other information you would like the court to consider.
    List attached documents:

_____

_____

_____

3. The court may decide on this application without a hearing unless a hearing is requested by you, the
    prosecutor's office, or the victim. (*Check the box below if you are requesting a hearing.*)
    Hearing requested? [ ] Yes [ ] No

I understand that this application may be denied if information in this application is found to be inaccurate.

I understand that even if I am granted the right to possess a gun or firearm under Arizona law, it may not give me the right to possess a firearm under federal law.

I declare under penalty of perjury that the information provided in this application and any attachments is true and correct.

_____   _____
Applicant's Name Printed   Applicant's Signature

_____
Address

AUTHORIZATION TO PROCEED ON BEHALF OF DEFENDANT

I authorize _____ [ ] Attorney, or [ ] Probation Officer to

petition the Superior Court in _____ County, to take the above-indicated
action.

_____   _____
Date   Defendant's Signature

Credits

Added on an emergency basis June 15, 2018, effective Aug. 3, 2018, adopted on a permanent basis Dec. 13, 2018.

16A A. R. S. Rules Crim. Proc., Form 31(a), AZ ST RCRP Form 31(a)

Current with amendments received through 08/15/19

Form 31(b). Order Regarding Application to Set Aside Conviction and Restore Gun Rights

(Refs & Annos)

IX. Miscellaneous

Rule 41. Forms

Forms

16A A.R.S. Rules Crim.Proc., Form 31(b)

Form 31(b). Order Regarding Application to Set Aside Conviction and Restore Gun Rights

[new] Form 31(b) Order Regarding Application to Set Aside Conviction and Restore Gun Rights

_____ Court _____County, Arizona

STATE OF ARIZONA, Plaintiff -vs- _____ Defendant (FIRST, MI, LAST) _____ Date of Birth	CASE NUMBER: **ORDER REGARDING APPLICATION TO SET ASIDE CONVICTION AND RESTORATION OF GUN RIGHTS** A.R.S. § 13-907

Based upon the information presented to the Court, **THE COURT FINDS THAT:** (only those items marked)

The prosecutor has received a copy of the Application to Set Aside Conviction.

[ ]   The defendant **has met** all statutory requirements for the application; OR

[ ]   The defendant **has not met** all statutory requirements for the application.

[ ]   The defendant was convicted of a criminal offense not eligible to be set aside due to:

    [ ]   a dangerous offense.

    [ ]   an offense for which the person is required or ordered by the court to register pursuant to A.R.S. § 13-3821.

    [ ]   an offense for which there has been a finding of sexual motivation pursuant to A.R.S. § 13-118.

    [ ]   an offense in which the victim is a minor under fifteen years of age.

    [ ]   an offense in violation of section 28-3473, any local ordinance relating to stopping, standing, or operation of a vehicle, or title 28, chapter 3, except a violation of section 28-693 or any local ordinance relating to the same subject matter as section 28-693.

IT IS ORDERED:

[ ]   **GRANTING** the application setting aside the judgment of guilt, dismissing the complaint, information, or indictment, and that the applicant be released from all penalties and disabilities resulting from the conviction **except those imposed by**:

    a.   The **Department of Transportation** pursuant to A.R.S. §§ 28-3304, 28-3305, 28-3306, 28-3307, 28-3308, 28-3312, and 28-3319.

Credits

Added on an emergency basis June 15, 2018, effective Aug. 3, 2018, adopted on a permanent basis Dec. 13, 2018.

16A A. R. S. Rules Crim. Proc., Form 31(b), AZ ST RCRP Form 31(b)

Current with amendments received through 08/15/19

Form 32(a). Application to Restore Civil Rights and Gun Rights

(Refs & Annos)

IX. Miscellaneous

Rule 41. Forms

Forms

16A A.R.S. Rules Crim.Proc., Form 32(a)

Form 32(a). Application to Restore Civil Rights and Gun Rights

[new] Form 32(a). Application to Restore Civil Rights and Gun Rights

_____ Court _____ County, Arizona

STATE OF ARIZONA Plaintiff -vs- _____ Defendant (FIRST, MI, LAST) _____ Date of Birth Applicant is: [ ] Defendant [ ] Attorney for Defendant [ ] Guardian	[CASE/COMPLAINT NO.] _____ **APPLICATION UPON DISCHARGE TO:** (check all that apply) [ ] **RESTORE CIVIL RIGHTS** [ ] **RESTORE GUN RIGHTS** A.R.S. §§ 13-905, 13-906, 13-908, 13-909, 13-910, 13-911, and 13-912 [ ] **REQUEST FOR RECONSIDERATION** (for applications previously denied) [ ] Civil Rights [ ] Gun Rights

SECTION I. CONVICTION(S)

A Judgment of Guilt was entered against the me, the defendant, on the ___ day of _____, _____, on the conviction of:

1. Count I: _____
2. Count II: _____
3. Count III: _____
4. Count IV: _____

[ ] Additional counts continue on a separate page.

SECTION II. STATE CONVICTION (For federal convictions, see SECTION III.)

[ ] A Judgment of Guilt was entered against the me in the Superior Court of Arizona in _____County.

1. [ ] The above stated judgment of guilt and conviction for a felony is my first felony conviction in this or any other state and this application is for restoration of right to possess or carry a gun or firearm only.
   NOTE: If this is your first felony conviction in this or any other state, any civil rights lost or suspended by the conviction are automatically restored if you completed a term of probation or received an absolute discharge from imprisonment and paid any fine or restitution imposed; however, your right to possess or carry a gun or firearm requires an application under this rule. Refer to **Section VII** of this application.
2. [ ] I completed the conditions of probation. The Probation Department's order discharging me from probation is in the court file or attached to this form.
3. [ ] I received from the Arizona Department of Corrections a Certificate of Absolute Discharge from Imprisonment on a date two (2) or more years before today's date, AND have attached a copy of the Certificate to this petition.

4. [ ] I have complied with all required terms of probation (including all employment, classes, community restitution, victim restitution or other court ordered monetary obligations, drug/alcohol testing, or other requirements.)

5. [ ] I have not complied with all terms of my sentence. Explain:

_____

_____

SECTION III. FEDERAL CONVICTION (for state convictions, see SECTION II.)

[ ] A Judgment of Guilt was entered against the me in United States District Court for the District of _____. On the _____ day of_____, _____:

1. [ ] The above stated judgment of guilt and conviction for a felony is my first felony conviction in this or any other state and this application is for restoration of right to possess or carry a gun or firearm only.

    NOTE: If this is your first felony conviction in this or any other state, any civil rights lost or suspended by the conviction are automatically restored if you completed a term of probation or received an absolute discharge from imprisonment and paid any fine or restitution imposed; however, your right to possess or carry a gun or firearm requires an application under this rule. Refer to **Section VII** of this application.

2. [ ] I was sentenced to and successfully served a term of federal probation, received an Affidavit of Discharge from the judge who discharged me from probation, **AND** have attached a copy to this petition and have completed the conditions of probation.

3. [ ] I was sentenced to and successfully served a federal prison term and received from the Federal Bureau of Prisons a Certificate of Absolute Discharge, or other official documentation provided by the Bureau of Prisons that indicates successful discharge from Imprisonment on a date two (2) or more years before today's date, **AND** I have attached a copy of the Certificate.

4. [ ] I have complied with all required terms of probation (including all employment, classes, community restitution, victim restitution or other court ordered monetary obligations, drug/alcohol testing, or other requirements.)

5. [ ] I have not complied with all terms of probation. Explain:

_____

_____

_____

_____

SECTION IV. VICTIM RESTITUTION AND COURT ORDERED MONETARY OBLIGATIONS

1. Have you paid victim restitution in full? [ ] Yes [ ] No

    If no, a restoration of rights will be denied without a showing of extraordinary circumstances. If you believe you have extraordinary circumstances explain below. *(Attach documentation you think is relevant for the court's consideration.)*

    _____

    _____

    _____

    _____

2. Have you paid all other court-ordered monetary obligations in this case (criminal fines and fees) in full? [ ] Yes [ ] No
    If no, please explain:

    _____

    _____

    _____

    _____

    In some circumstances you may be eligible to apply to the court to mitigate the amount owed or convert monies owed to community restitution (State offenses only, not for Federal convictions).

SECTION V. PRIOR RESTORATION OF RIGHTS

1. Have you previously applied to have your rights restored? [ ] Yes [ ] No

    If so, what was the date of your last application? _____

2. Have you been granted the restoration of your rights previously? [ ] Yes [ ] No

3. Have you been denied the restoration of your rights previously? [ ] Yes [ ] No

SECTION VI. PENDING CASES AND ACTIVE WARRANTS

1. Are there any open criminal cases against you? [ ] Yes [ ] No

2. Do you have an active warrant? [ ] Yes [ ] No

    If yes to either question above, please explain:

    _____

    _____

    _____

    _____

SECTION VII. RESTORATION OF FIREARM RIGHTS

NOTE: Arizona Revised Statutes require: If the person was convicted of an offense which would be a dangerous offense under section 13-704, the person may not file for the restoration of the right to possess or carry a gun or firearm. If the person was convicted of an offense which would be a serious offense as defined in section 13-706, the person may not file for the restoration of the right to possess or carry a gun or firearm for **ten years** from the date of the person's absolute discharge from imprisonment or discharge from probation. If the person was convicted of any other felony offense, the person may not file for the restoration of the right to possess or carry a gun or firearm for **two years** from the date of the person's absolute discharge from imprisonment or discharge from probation.

1. [ ] I was convicted of a felony offense **not** listed in A.R.S. §§ 13-704 or 13-706 and it has been **two** years since absolute discharge from imprisonment or probation.
2. [ ] I was convicted of a serious offense as defined in A.R.S. § 13-706 and it has been **ten** years since absolute discharge from imprisonment or probation.
3. [ ] I was convicted of a dangerous offense as defined in A.R.S. § 13-704. (If yes, you are not eligible to file for restoration of the right to possess or carry a gun or firearm.)

If you are requesting that your civil right to possess a gun or firearm be restored, please write your reasons for the request below:

_____

_____

_____

_____

I understand that even if I am granted the right to possess a gun or firearm under Arizona law, it may not give me the right to possess a gun or firearm under federal law.

SECTION VIII. OTHER INFORMATION FOR THE COURT

Is there anything you would like the court to take into consideration?

_____

_____

_____

_____

[ ] Attached is other pertinent documentation. List attached documents:

_____

_____

_____

_____

I understand that this application may be denied if information in this application is found to be inaccurate.

Under Oath I swear or affirm, under penalty of perjury, the information provided in this application is to the best of my knowledge true and correct.

_____   _____

Defendant's Name Printed   Defendant's Signature

_____

Address

OR

To the best of my knowledge, the information provided in this application is true and correct.

_____   _____

Attorney's Name Printed   Attorney's Signature

_____

Attorney's Address

AUTHORIZATION TO PROCEED ON BEHALF OF DEFENDANT

I authorize my Attorney, _____ to petition the Superior

Court in _____ County, to take the above-indicated action.

_____   _____

Date   Defendant's Signature

I understand that this application may be denied if information in this application is found to be inaccurate.

Under Oath I swear or affirm, under penalty of perjury, the information provided in this application is to the best of my knowledge true and correct.

_____   _____
Defendant's Name Printed   Defendant's Signature

_____
Address

OR

To the best of my knowledge, the information provided in this application is true and correct.

_____   _____
Attorney's Name Printed   Attorney's Signature

_____
Attorney's Address

AUTHORIZATION TO PROCEED ON BEHALF OF DEFENDANT

I authorize my Attorney, _____ to petition the Superior

Court in _____ County, to take the above-indicated action.

_____   _____
Date   Defendant's Signature

Credits
Added on an emergency basis June 15, 2018, effective Aug. 3, 2018, adopted on a permanent basis Dec. 13, 2018.
16A A. R. S. Rules Crim. Proc., Form 32(a), AZ ST RCRP Form 32(a)
Current with amendments received through 08/15/19

Form 32(b). Order Regarding Application to Restore Civil Rights and Gun Rights

(Refs & Annos)
IX. Miscellaneous
Rule 41. Forms
Forms

16A A.R.S. Rules Crim.Proc., Form 32(b)

Form 32(b). Order Regarding Application to Restore Civil Rights and Gun Rights

[new] Form 32(b). Order Regarding Application to Restore Civil Rights and Gun Rights

_____Court _____County, Arizona

STATE OF ARIZONA, Plaintiff -vs- _____ Defendant (FIRST, MI, LAST) _____ Date of Birth	CASE NUMBER: _____ **ORDER REGARDING APPLICATION TO RESTORE** **CIVIL RIGHTS AND/OR RIGHT TO POSSESS OR OWN A GUN OR FIREARM**

Based on the information presented to the Court, **THE COURT FINDS:** (only those items marked)
The prosecutor has received a copy of the Application to Restore Civil Rights and/or Right to Possess or Own A Gun or Firearm.

[ ] The Defendant **has met** all of the statutory requirements for the application to restore civil rights and to possess or own a gun or firearm.

[ ] The Defendant **has not met** all of the statutory requirements for the application to possess or own a gun or firearm including:

    [ ] The Defendant was convicted of a **dangerous** offense as defined in A.R.S. § 13-704.

    [ ] The Defendant was convicted of a **serious** offense as defined in A.R.S. § 13-706 and **less than ten years** have passed from the date of discharge from probation or prison.

    [ ] The Defendant was convicted of any other felony offense and **less than two years** have passed from the date of discharge from probation or prison.

IT IS ORDERED:

[ ] GRANTING the application to restore civil rights **and** right to possess or own a gun or firearm.

[ ] GRANTING the application to restore civil rights **excluding** the right to possess or own a gun or firearm.

[ ] GRANTING the application to restore the right to possess or own a gun or firearm.

[ ] DENYING the application to restore civil rights and right to possess or own a gun or firearm for the following reasons:

    [ ] The applicant **has not met** all statutory requirements for the application (as noted above):

    [ ] Other reasons:_____.

DATED this _____ day of _____, _____.

_____
Judicial Officer

Credits

Added on an emergency basis June 15, 2018, effective Aug. 3, 2018, adopted on a permanent basis Dec. 13, 2018.

16A A. R. S. Rules Crim. Proc., Form 32(b), AZ ST RCRP Form 32(b)

Current with amendments received through 08/15/19

CPSIA information can be obtained
at www.ICGtesting.com
Printed in the USA
LVHW011809230720
661378LV00011B/567